014018058

D1380958

WITHDRAWN FROM STOCK

Social Welfare and EU Law

The assumption that Member States of the European Union enjoyed exclusive competence over social provision has been shaken by the realisation that they are now 'semi-sovereign welfare states' whose policy choices are subject to increasing scrutiny under Community law. This book seeks to take stock of how Community membership is reshaping the legal environment of welfare provision across Europe. Topics covered include: the evolving economic and governance debates about Community intervention in social rights; the relationship between public services and Community competition and state aids law; the crucial developments that have taken place in the sphere of health care; and recent judgments on free movement and equal treatment for Union citizens as regards national education and social assistance policies. *Social Welfare and EU Law* provides a valuable collection of essays that explores the emergence of new models of social solidarity within the European Union.

Social Welfare and EU Law

Edited by

ELEANOR SPAVENTA
University of Birmingham

and

MICHAEL DOUGAN
University of Liverpool

·HART·
PUBLISHING

OXFORD AND PORTLAND, OREGON
2005

Hart Publishing
Oxford and Portland, Oregon

Published in North America (US and Canada) by
Hart Publishing
c/o International Specialized Book Services
5804 NE Hassalo Street
Portland, Oregon
97213-3644
USA

© The Editors and Contributors severally, 2005

The Editors and Contributors have asserted their right under the Copyright,
Designs and Patents Act 1988, to be identified as the authors of this work.

Hart Publishing is a specialist legal publisher based in Oxford, England.
To order further copies of this book or to request a list of other
publications please write to:

Hart Publishing, Salters Boatyard, Folly Bridge,
Abingdon Rd, Oxford, OX1 4LB
Telephone: +44 (0)1865 245533 Fax: +44 (0)1865 794882
email: mail@hartpub.co.uk
WEBSITE: http//:www.hartpub.co.uk

British Library Cataloguing in Publication Data
Data Available

ISBN 1-84113-490-2 (hardback)

Typeset by Datamatics Technologies Ltd, Mumbai
Printed and bound in Great Britain by
TJ International, Padstow, Cornwall

Foreword

The present book has its origin in a conference on social welfare and EU law held in Cambridge on 13–14 June 2003. It is thanks to Michael Dougan and Eleanor Spaventa who took the effort to organise it that this subject, of great importance for the Member States of the European Union and the overwhelming majority of its citizens, was discussed in all its facets by eminent speakers and a very competent audience. I am glad to see that the essence of that fruitful event will now be accessible to a larger public by means of this collection.

Cases related to social welfare present the European Court of Justice with a vast range of difficult and delicate questions. For instance, where lie the limits of obligations based on equality and transnational solidarity? Where lie the limits of the basic freedoms of European Community law, and where lie those of the rules on competition? The Court approaches such questions in a cautious manner, proceeding case by case. An example is the Court's judgment in Case C–385/99 *Müller-Fauré and van Riet*, which concerns the Netherlands sickness insurance scheme and is confined in its operative part to 'legislation of a Member State, such as that at issue in the main proceedings'. This style of judging with its low level of abstraction may create difficulties for those who want to draw consequences from the Court's rulings beyond the individual case in question. At the Cambridge conference, I appreciated the way in which some speakers developed careful generalisations from the Court's caselaw. The inherent tendencies thus became more visible.

Dougan and Spaventa rightly state that new models of social solidarity within the European Union are emerging. Already now the citizens of the European Union live—as they put it—in a system of 'multi-level social welfare'. If the potential of that system is fully used, the social component of united Europe would be strengthened.

Judge Ninon Colneric
Court of Justice of the European Communities

Contents

List of Contributors

Catherine Barnard is a Fellow of Trinity College and a Senior Lecturer at the Faculty of Law, University of Cambridge.

Nick Bernard is a Reader in European Law at Queen Mary, University of London.

Andrea Biondi is a Senior Lecturer in European Law at King's College London, and Co-Director of the Centre of European Law.

Simon Deakin is a Fellow at Peterhouse and Robert Monks Professor of Corporate Governance at the Judge Institute of Management Studies, University of Cambridge.

Michael Dougan is Professor of European Law at the University of Liverpool.

Panos Koutrakos is Professor of European Law at the University of Durham. He is the author of *Trade, Foreign Policy and Defence in EU Constitutional Law* (Oxford, Hart Publishing, 2001). He writes in the areas of trade law and external relations of the European Union.

Jonathan Montgomery is Professor of Health Care Law at the University of Southampton.

Mića Panić, FRSA, is Fellow of Selwyn College, University of Cambridge and Visiting Professor of International Economics at the Catholic University, Milan, and Vice Chairman of the United Nations Committee on Development Policy. His previous posts include senior positions in the United Kingdom Government Economic Service and the Bank of England. He has also served on a number of international committees and groups of experts. He is the author of many books and articles on international economics (theory, history and policy), economic policy under different conditions and stages of development, and industrial economics.

Frans Pennings is Professor of International Social Security at Tilburg University and Utrecht University, the Netherlands.

Luca Rubini is a Doctoral Student at King's College London.

Eleanor Spaventa is a Lecturer in European Law at the University of Birmingham.

John Temple Lang is in the Brussels office of Cleary, Gottlieb, Steen & Hamilton. His practice focuses primarily on competition law. He has published over 200 articles on a variety of legal subjects, including EC competition law. He frequently lectures in the United States, Canada, and Europe. Dr Temple Lang served as Director of the Directorate General for Competition of the European Commission from 1988 to 2000. Previously, he served as a legal adviser in the Legal Service of the European Commission, focusing on competition law and international trade issues, and before that was in private practice in Dublin. Dr Temple Lang is a member of the Bar in Brussels.

Anne Pieter van der Mei is a Lecturer in European Law at the University of Maastricht.

Derrick Wyatt is a Fellow of St Edmund's Hall and Professor of Law at the University of Oxford. He is also a Queen's Counsel.

Introduction

This collection of essays is the outcome of a conference organised in Cambridge in June 2003, under the auspices of the Centre for European Legal Studies (Faculty of Law, University of Cambridge). We are grateful to all those who contributed to making a success of the conference, especially the speakers: Simon Deakin, Mića Panić, Barbara Helfferich, Nick Bernard, Ann Pieter van der Mei, Catherine Barnard, Frans Pennings, John Temple Lang, Andrea Biondi, Panos Koutrakos, Derrick Wyatt, Jonathan Montgomery; and also those who kindly chaired each session: Alan Dashwood, Robertus Cornelissen, John Bell and Ninon Colneric. The conference could not have happened without the generous support and unfailing encouragement of John Bell (Director of the Centre for European Legal Studies). Special thanks are also due to Catherine Bedford (Secretary to the Centre) for her invaluable help and dedication, and her uplifting good humour. Matthew Dyson, Massimo Marelli and Oeyvind Boe provided valuable support over the two days of the conference, and deserve our warm appreciation. We gratefully acknowledge the financial support of the Centre for European Legal Studies, the Yorke Fund and the Faculty of Law at the University of Cambridge, as well the generous sponsorship of Baker & McKenzie. Last but not least, we are very grateful to Richard Hart and his team at Hart Publishing for all their patience and help.

This collection brings together contributors from different areas of European integration studies to take stock of how Community membership is reshaping the legal environment of welfare provision across Europe. The book opens with an historical analysis of the development of the welfare state, reflecting also upon the theoretical relationship between economic and social rights (Deakin). Subsequent chapters address the impact of primarily economic Treaty rules upon the national welfare societies, in particular, competition law (Temple Lang), state aids (Biondi and Rubini) and Economic and Monetary Union (Panić). Another set of essays explores the recent expansion of individual rights to social support under Community law, together with the often difficult implications of this process for the traditional organisation of the Member States' welfare systems, having particular regard to cross-border healthcare (Koutrakos, Wyatt, Montgomery), Union citizenship (Barnard, van der Mei, Dougan and Spaventa) and social security co-ordination (Pennings). The book then closes with an assessment of the shift from hard to soft law as a vehicle for the Community's influence over the evolution of domestic welfare policies (Bernard).

This collection is by no means intended to provide an exhaustive statement of the law. Our aim is rather to convey something of the complexities, the opportunities and the controversies that result from the haphazard development of a system of multi-level social solidarity in the European Union.

Michael Dougan and Eleanor Spaventa

1

The 'Capability' Concept and the Evolution of European Social Policy

SIMON DEAKIN*

I INTRODUCTION

The concept of 'capability', developed by Amartya Sen in a series of economic and philosophical texts,[1] could play a major role in the reshaping of the European Union's social and employment policies. The prominence of the capability concept in contemporary European debates owes much to the use made of it in the report on the *Transformation of Work and the Future of Labour Law in Europe* which was prepared for the European Commission by a group led by Alain Supiot.[2] The Supiot Report argued that a capability-based approach would help to overcome the opposition between 'security' and 'flexibility' which had been established in neoliberal critiques of labour law and the welfare state, and provide a basis for 'real freedom of choice' in relation to labour market participation. This analysis was further developed in a paper published in *Droit Social* by the economist Robert Salais, one of the members of the Supiot group.[3] A research programme was subsequently initiated, designed among other things to explore the potential role of a new 'politics of capabilities' within the wider project of European integration.[4]

The present chapter aims to contribute to that programme of research by exploring some of the legal aspects of the capability concept. There is no precise juridical equivalent to Sen's notion of 'capability'. However, certain

---

[1] See in particular A Sen, *Commodities and Capabilities* (Amsterdam, North Holland, 1985) and *Development as Freedom* (Oxford University Pess, 1999).
[2] A Supiot (ed), *Au delà de l'emploi: transformations du travail et l'avenir du droit du travail en Europe* (Paris, Flammarion, 1999).
[3] R Salais, 'Libertés du travail et capacités: pour une construction Européenne?' [1999] *Droit Social* 467.
[4] For the homepage of the 'Eurocap' network, see: <http://www.idhe.ens-cachan.fr/Eurocap/index.html>.

legal concepts undoubtedly bear a certain resemblance to it. This is particularly true of notions of contractual *capacity* which are recognised in both common law and civilian systems of private law. The task of exploring the links between 'capability' and legal 'capacity' has begun.[5] My aim here is to focus on a different strand of legal thought, namely the set of ideas associated with the *duty to work* in labour and social security law. The content of the duty to work has shifted over time according to different notions of the capacity or ability of individuals to make themselves available for employment. These in turn have been shaped by particular conceptions of the employment relationship and of the family. To see how this process has occurred is to gain some insight into how the capability concept might operate if, as its proponents intend, it comes to serve as a new conceptual cornerstone for social law.

To this end, section II below explores Sen's definition of 'capability' and the use made of the notion in the Supiot report. Section III then looks at the historical development of legal analogues of capability in the English poor law and law of social insurance. Section IV returns the debate to a European level by considering some ways in which the capability concept is being (or could be) operationalised within the current employment and social policy of the EU. Section V concludes.

II SEN'S NOTION OF CAPABILITY
AND ITS ADAPTATION IN THE SUPIOT REPORT

Sen's account of capabilities describes individual well being in terms of a person's ability to achieve a given set of functionings. In this context,

> the 'concept of functionings'... reflects the various things a person may value doing or being. The valued functionings may vary from elementary ones, such as being adequately nourished and being free from avoidable disease, to very complex activities or personal states, such as being able to take part in the life of the community and having self-respect... A capability [is] a kind of freedom: the substantive freedom to achieve alternative functioning combinations.[6]

An individual's feasible set of utilisation functions is constrained by the limits upon their own resources. This is not simply a question of choice. Non-choice factors affect functioning; for example, an individual's metabolic rate which is a consequence of their physical state. The state of an individual's knowledge may also be a non-choice factor, although this can be improved by education. Here the element of choice may lie elsewhere, at the

---

[5] This was the subject of seminars held under the chairmanship of Alain Supiot and the author at the Maison des Sciences de l'Homme Ange Guépin, Nantes, in March 2003 and at Cambridge University in March 2005.

[6] See n 1 p 75.

collective or societal level, that is to say, with policy makers, government officials, and judges. Apart from the resources available to an individual, their capability to make use of a commodity may depend upon access to a legal system which recognises and guarantees protection of contract and property rights, but also upon access to healthcare, education and other resources which equip them to enter into relations of exchange with others. Thus an individual's capability is to some degree a consequence of their entitlements, that is, their ability to possess, control and extract benefits from a particular economic commodity or resource.

Thus pivotal within Sen's 'capability approach' is the idea of *conversion factors*. These are the characteristics of an individual's *person*, their *society* and their *environment* which together determine their capability to achieve a given range of functionings. *Personal characteristics*, in this sense could include an individual's metabolism, or their biological sex, and *environmental characteristics* could refer to climate, physical surroundings, or technological infrastructure. But in addition, *institutional* or *societal characteristics* would include social norms, legal rules and public policies. These can act to entrench inequality of capability, as is the case with social norms which result in institutionalised racial discrimination or gender stereotyping, or, conversely, to offset inequality through legal interventions of various kinds, including anti-discrimination law.

Sen has not sought to develop a juridical theory which might give some institutional shape to the capability concept, beyond insisting that his 'capability approach' does not prescribe any particular set of outcomes for a given society or group of societies. The high level of generality and theoretical abstraction of the capability approach lends itself to adaptations which may be far from Sen's initial formulation; the Supiot report is perhaps best thought of in this way. In the Supiot report, the capability concept appears in the context of a discussion of the meaning of labour flexibility.[7] The report notes that 'flexibility' is frequently associated with greater variability in the application of social protection and labour standards, and thereby appears to be opposed to 'security'. However, this view, it is argued, overlooks the degree to which the capabilities of an individual depend on them having access to the means they need to realise their life goals. These include guarantees of a certain minimum standard of living and the resources needed to maintain an 'active security' in the face of economic and social risks, such as those arising from technological change and uncertainty in labour and product markets. Thus 'real freedom of action' for entrepreneurs, in the form of protection of property rights and recognition of managerial prerogative, has its equivalent in guarantees for the development of human resources for workers. However, these, the report suggests, would not necessarily take the same form as the 'passive

---

[7]   See n 2 ch 7, pp 267–91: 'Flexibilité du travail et capacités des personnes'.

protections' traditionally provided, in twentieth century welfare states, against unemployment and other interruptions to earnings. 'Protection against' social risks is not the same as mechanisms aimed to maintain 'security in the face of' risks:

> We can understand the fundamental difference between protection, on the one hand, and security in the face of risks, on the other, by seeing that the latter includes but goes beyond the former. The capacity to work flexibly is conditional upon being able to deal with the consequences of risks. Protective regulations, because of the essentially negative way in which they are formulated, go against this kind of learning process. Security in the face of risk, on the other hand, is about providing the individual with the means to anticipate, at any given moment, long-term needs ... Thus guarantees of minimum living standards (for example, that each person should have an effective right to housing, and not just to a minimum income), far from being undermined by the need for flexibility, should be reinforced by virtue of this need, and, if anything, more clearly and concretely defined as a result.[8]

Phrased in this way, the capability concept can be understood as an answer, of sorts, to the neoliberal critique of labour and social security law. That holds, among other things, that regulation which interferes with freedom of contract upsets the process of mutual learning and adjustment which is implicit in market relations. As Hayek put it, private law is the precondition of the market order in the sense that without it, individuals are not free to use their own information and knowledge for their own purposes. Private law is certainly a product of governmental action: 'in most circumstances the organisation which we call government becomes indispensable to assure that those rules are obeyed'.[9] However, legal coercion to enforce contract and property rights is justified 'where this is necessary to secure the private domain of the individual against interference by others'.[10] By contrast, public or regulatory law, which Hayek regarded as consisting of specific commands and directions aimed at the substantive redistribution of resources, introduces an illegitimate form of interference *by the state*. Where this occurs, the 'spontaneous order' of the market is upset, and a certain part of the advantages to individuals and society alike of a market order, in terms of a higher degree of specialisation and a more extensive division of labour, are lost.

The capability approach offers a response, based on the *market-creating* function of the rules of social law. In order to participate effectively in a market order, individuals require more than formal access to the institutions of property and contract. They need to be provided with the economic means to

---

[8]   *Ibid*, p 278.
[9]   F A Hayek, *Rules and Order* (Routledge and Kegan Paul, 1973) p 47.
[10]   *Ibid*, p 57.

realise their potential: these include social guarantees of housing, education and training, as well as legal institutions which prescribe institutionalised discrimination. Mechanisms of this kind, by extending labour market participation on the part of otherwise excluded or disadvantaged groups, may enhance the aggregate value of production.[11]

If the capability approach attempts to answer, at a certain theoretical level, some aspects of the neoliberal critique, it also moves beyond the conceptualisation of social rights in the post-1945 welfare state. TH Marshall, perhaps the most articulate exponent of this tradition, saw social rights as operating in tension with market relations. Civil and political rights had 'harmonized with the individualistic phase of capitalism' in the nineteenth century.[12] By contrast, social rights, which Marshall defined as ranging 'from the right to a modicum of economic welfare and security to the right to share to the full in the social heritage and to live the life of a civilised being according to the standards prevailing in society' created entitlements which were 'not proportionate to the market value of the claimant'.[13] Marshall, it is true, made something of an exception in this respect for collective bargaining, which he thought was 'a normal peaceful market operation' which also gave expression to 'the right of the citizen to a minimum standard of civilized living'.[14] But for the most part, social rights were in 'basic conflict' with the market.[15]

The capability approach, by contrast, sees one of the principal purposes of social legislation and social rights as encouraging the participation of individuals in the labour market. It is only by putting in place effective mechanisms for dealing with the effects upon individuals of economic uncertainty that the legitimacy and effectiveness of the market order can be maintained. This is not necessarily a call for the individualization of labour law; the 'conversion factors' by which individual capabilities are enhanced are likely to be collective in nature.[16] But in the passage from 'passive protection' to 'active security',[17] it is likely that many features of existing welfare state and labour law systems would not survive unscathed.

---

[11] See generally S Deakin and F Wilkinson, 'Capabilities' ordineo spontaneo del mercato e diritti sociali' (1999) 2 *Il diritto del mercato del lavoro* 317 (also published in English as CBR Working Paper No 174, September 2000 <http://www.cbr.cam.ac.uk/pdf/wp174.pdf>; S Deakin and J Browne, 'Social rights and market order: adapting the capability approach' in T Hervey and J Kenner (eds), *Economic and Social Rights under the EU Charter of Fundamental Rights. A Legal Perspective* (Hart, 2003); J Browne, S Deakin and F Wilkinson, 'Capabilities, social rights and European market integration', in R Salais and R Villeneuve (eds), *Europe and the Politics of Capabilities* (Cambridge University Press, 2004). See also S Deakin and F Wilkinson, *The Law of the Labour Market: Industrialisation, Employment and Legal Evolution* (OUP, 1995) ch 5.

[12] TH Marshall, *Citizenship and Social Class* (Cambridge University Press, 1949, reprinted Pluto, 1992) p 26 (all references are to the 1992 edition).

[13] *Ibid*, p 8.

[14] *Ibid*, p 42.

[15] *Ibid*.

[16] See n 2 p 268.

[17] *Ibid*, p 269.

The capability approach to labour and social security law appears particularly novel when set against the post-1945 paradigm of protection based around 'stable employment for an adult male able to provide, by these means, for the needs of a nuclear family'.[18] That model makes certain assumptions about employment and family relations which no longer command general assent, and perhaps never did. However, the 'standard employment contract' was itself a reaction to a quite different view of the conditions under which individuals should make themselves available for waged work.

III THE PREHISTORY OF THE CAPABILITY CONCEPT: NOTIONS OF ABILITY TO WORK IN THE ENGLISH POOR LAW AND SOCIAL INSURANCE

The English 'poor law' was the precursor not just of the welfare state but of modern employment policy. In the sixteenth and seventeenth centuries, the 'poor' were not simply those with a low income, but all who were dependent on wages from employment as their principal means of subsistence: 'those who labour to live, and such as are old and decrepit, unable to work, poor widows, and fatherless children, and tenants driven to poverty; not by riot, expense and carelessness, but by mischance'.[19] The poor law was, in one sense, a survivor of feudalism; as TH Marshall put it, 'as the pattern of the old order dissolved under the blows of a competitive economy . . . the Poor Law was left high and dry as an isolated survival from which the idea of social rights was gradually drained away'.[20] However, there was another sense in which the poor law was a response to the emergence of a labour market. The enactment of legislation dealing with wage rates, poor relief and labour mobility (or, as it was put, 'vagrancy') from the fourteenth century onwards is evidence of how far traditional feudal ties based on obligatory service (villeinage or serfdom) had already declined by that point.

Under the poor law, relief was delivered locally, through parishes (small administrative units covering only a few square miles), but organised nationally, in the sense that within the framework set by the Elizabethan legislation, every parish was required to set a local tax to be paid by householders (a 'poor rate'), to suppress indiscriminate giving, and to organise in its place a regular system of welfare support.[21] Legislation called for the unemployed to be set to work, but the cost of implementing this provision was found to be excessive, and only a minority of parishes constructed workhouses for the purpose; for the most part, those suffering destitution

---

[18] *Ibid*, p 267.

[19] M Dalton, *The Country Justice: Containing the Practice, Duty and Power of the Justices of the Peace, as well In as Out of Their Sessions* (Lintot, 1746) p 164.

[20] See n 12 p 14.

[21] Poor Relief Act 1601 (43 Elizabeth I c 2) s 1.

for lack of work received cash doles ('outdoor relief') in the same way as the sick and the aged. Local poor law officers were required to provide relief to all those with a *settlement* in the parish in question. Thus relief became, in a customary sense, if not necessarily in the modern legal sense of a justiciable entitlement, the 'peculiar privilege' of the rural poor.[22]

One of the principal means of acquiring a settlement, from the late seventeenth century, was through a yearly hiring, which was the normal form of employment for young, unmarried workers in agriculture. The young thereby had an incentive to leave their home parish to search for employment elsewhere, acquiring a settlement in return for annual service as they moved from one employer to another, thereby ensuring that they would not be subject to removal to their parish of origin. In this way, the poor law, along with the emerging notion of the contract of service, encouraged and supported labour mobility.[23]

The second half of the eighteenth century saw falling real wages in agriculture at the same time as access to the land was restricted by enclosure.[24] The social upheaval which accompanied the depopulation of rural areas was matched by a similarly far-reaching process of transformation in the poor law and labour legislation. The response of those charged with the administration of the poor law to falling real incomes in agriculture in the 1790s was the institution of a practice of wage supplementation, known as the Speenhamland system after the rural district in which it was first adopted. It began as an ad hoc addition of poor relief to wages, designed to bring incomes up to subsistence level. At the same time, attempts to deal with the problem through the implementation of a minimum wage (through the revival of the wage fixing powers of the Elizabethan Statute of Artificers) were rejected both locally and in the national parliament.[25] The combined effect was to relieve employers of the obligation to pay the customary level of wages; during the same period, yearly hirings were becoming increasingly uncommon,[26] and changes to the law of settlement made it more difficult for wage earners and their dependants to acquire the right to relief.[27] As employment grew less stable and access to relief by the traditional route of the settlement by hiring, under which the employer absorbed the costs of short-term interruptions to earnings, became increasingly

---

[22] KDM Snell, *Annals of the Labouring Poor: Social Change and Agrarian England 1660–1900* (Cambridge University Press, 1985) p 73.

[23] P Slack, *The English Poor Law 1531–1782* (Macmillan, 1990) pp 37–8.

[24] *Ibid*, p 66.

[25] The classic account of Speenhamland remains JL and B Hammond, *The Village Labourer 1760–1832* (Longmans, Green and Co, 1920).

[26] E Hobsbawm and G Rudé, *Captain Swing* (Penguin, 1973) ch 2; KDM Snell, *Annals of the Labouring Poor Social Change and Agrarian England* 1660–1900 (Cambridge University Press, 1985) ch 2.

[27] S Deakin, 'The Contract of Employment: A Study in Legal Evolution' (2001) 11 *Historical Studies in Industrial Relations* 1, pp 12–17.

restricted, expenditure on poor relief grew to the point that a national debate was launched on the feasibility of maintaining the poor law system. This continued, at intervals, over several decades in the early nineteenth century, during which time the administration of poor relief became steadily more restrictive and punitive. This process culminated in the 1834 Poor Law Report[28] and the Poor Law (Amendment) Act[29] of the same year.

The new poor law which was put in place after 1834 was founded on the principle of 'less eligibility', meaning that relief should not provide a standard of living superior to that enjoyed by the least-well off 'independent' household. The assumption was that once the 'distortion' of wage supplementation was removed, wages would rise to the point where the subsistence needs could be met. On this basis, the unwillingness of individuals to accept wages set by the market could only be evidence of poor 'character', which it was the role of the law to address by disciplinary means. Thus a wilful refusal to accept an offer of employment at the going rate of wages became a criminal offence punishable by imprisonment.[30] At this point, in the absence of a minimum wage and before the development of collective bargaining, the relevant wage was whatever an employer was willing to offer, and not the customary rate for that trade. In addition, the simple fact of destitution as a result of unemployment or sickness would normally lead to the confinement in the workhouse of the wage earner and other family members.[31] Beginning in the 1840s, a series of regulatory orders spelled out the implications of this policy for the administration of poor relief: outdoor relief was to be limited as far as possible to the aged and infirm, denied to the adult 'able bodied', and under no circumstances combined with wages; if it were to be paid, exceptionally, to those who were able to work, it had to be combined with a 'labour test' designed to deter the work shy; and in order to ensure that conditions inside the workhouse were, as far as possible, below those of the worst-off household outside, a consciously degrading and punitive regime for workhouse inmates was put in place.[32]

In this context, being *able* to work was defined as having the physical capacity to labour, and the labour test functioned to distinguish the work-shy

---

[28] Reproduced in SG and EOA Checkland (eds), *The Poor Law Report of 1834* (Penguin, 1973).

[29] 4 & 5 George IV c 76.

[30] Under the Vagrancy Act 1824 (5 George IV c 83) it was an offence punishable by one month's hard labour to become chargeable to poor relief in the case of 'every person being able wholly or in part to maintain himself, or his or her family, by work or other means, and wilfully refusing or neglecting to do so'. In earlier vagrancy legislation, dating from 1744, a crime was committed only where there was 'a refusal to work for the usual and common Wages given to other Labourers in the like Work'. In the 1824 Act, the reference to 'usual and common wages' was removed.

[31] Workhouses existed in certain parishes prior to 1834, but after that point their use increased substantially thanks to the restriction of outdoor relief.

[32] The principal orders were the Outdoor Relief Prohibitory Order of 21 December 1844, the Outdoor Relief Regulation Order of 14 December 1852, and General Consolidated Order of 24 July 1847 (dealing with workhouse conditions). They are reproduced, with amendments and consolidations, in HR Jenner-Fust, *Poor Law Orders* (PS King, 1907).

from those genuinely incapable of working. But of course physical ability to work was only one aspect of being 'able bodied'. A further, implicit assumption was that claimants for relief had no means of their own; that they were *propertyless*. Capability, then, was a function of the duty to work which was imposed on those with no means of subsistence but their own capacity to labour. The independently wealthy were not subject to the duty to work.

Bentham recognised, and implicitly endorsed, the dual standard at work here. The old poor law, he complained, had ceased to draw an appropriate distinction between 'natural' poverty, which the law could not hope to relieve, and the 'evil' of indigence. By enabling 'the condition of persons maintained without property by the labour of others [to be] rendered more eligible than that of persons maintained by their own labour' the old poor law removed the incentive to work upon which the market depended for its effectiveness:

> Individuals destitute of property would be continually withdrawing themselves from the class of persons maintained by their own labour, to the class of persons maintained by the labour of others; and the sort of idleness, *which at present is more or less confined to persons of independent fortune*, would thus extend itself sooner or later to every individual . . . till at last there would be nobody left to labour at all for anybody (emphasis added).[33]

It was because the numbers of the propertyless greatly outweighed those of the idle (or 'independent') rich that the law had to coerce the former into employment, while leaving the latter to enjoy their 'fortune' undisturbed.

Just as the new poor law was a response to the perceived failings of Speenhamland, so the welfare state of the twentieth century was constructed by way of reaction against what were seen as the shortcomings of the system put in place after 1834. By the end of the nineteenth century, there was a growing consensus that the new poor law had failed in its own terms. Wages had risen following the restriction of outdoor relief, but not to the extent which had been anticipated. Destitution was an ever-present phenomenon in Britain's major urban areas and in many rural districts. When numbers of the unemployed increased, as they did in particular during the long recession which lasted from the 1870s to the 1890s, the response of the poor law administrators was to tighten the disciplinary operation of the system; outdoor relief was made more selective, the labour test more severe, and workhouse conditions made more demeaning. Thus throughout the 1880s and 1890s, a number of urban poor law unions were constructing special 'test workhouses' with the aim of subjecting the adult able-bodied to a particularly stringent regime of discipline.[34]

---

[33] Cited in JR Poynter, *Society and Pauperism: English Ideas on Poor Relief 1795–1834* (Routledge and Kegan Paul, 1969) pp 125–26.

[34] S and B Webb, *The Public Organisation of the Labour Market: Being Part Two of the Minority Report of the Poor Law Commission* (Longmans, Green and Co, 1909) chs 1 and 2.

The sheer expense of this effort was one factor which helped to turn the tide of opinion; also important was the work of the 'social science' movement which set out to measure the extent of destitution outside the poor law system. 'Independent' households could not subsist on the wages offered for low-paid work, and were reliant in practice on ad hoc charitable giving; the casualisation of urban occupations undermined efforts to establish a living wage and imposed unnecessary search costs on employers and workers alike.[35]

A key text in laying bare the deficiencies of the new poor law was the Minority Report of the Poor Law Commission of 1909, which was drafted by Sidney and Beatrice Webb. For the Webbs, the new poor law was constructed on a false premise, namely that destitution was always and everywhere the result of personal irresponsibility. This, in turn, was the result of the undue attention placed in 1834 on 'one plague spot—the demoralization of character and waste of wealth produced in the agricultural districts by an hypertrophied Poor Law'.[36] The Webbs did not believe that the 'personal character' of those in poverty was completely irrelevant; it was 'of vital importance to the method of treatment to be adopted with regard to the individuals in distress'. However, it was not 'of significance with regard to the existence of or the amount of Unemployment'.[37]

As Beveridge had put it, unemployment was 'a problem of industry', that is, a feature of economic organisation, rather than the result of personal irresponsibility. His research on casualisation[38] was called in aid to show that 'chronic over supply of casual labour in relation to the local demand was produced and continued, irrespective of any excess of population or depression of trade, *by the method by which employers engaged their casual workers*' (emphasis in original). This 'inevitably creates and perpetuates what have been called "stagnant pools" of labour in which there is nearly always some reserve of labour left, however great may be the employer's demand'.[39] It was continued exposure to the effects of underemployment which precipitated decline into the permanently unemployed, a body which, leaving aside 'the rare figure of the ruined baronet or clergyman' consisted of 'those Unemployables who represent the wastage from the manual, wage earning class'.[40]

To this, the Webbs added an important rider: the effects of casualisation were exacerbated by the poor law itself. The outdoor labour test, by

---

[35] On the significance of the surveys of urban poverty carried out by Booth and Rowntree, see the account of Rowntree's work in A Briggs, *Social Thought and Social Action: A Study of the Work of Seebohm Rowntree* (Longmans, 1961); on Beveridge, see J Harris, *William Beveridge: A Biography* 2nd edn (Clarendon Press, 1997).
[36] See above n 34 p 4.
[37] See above n 34 233.
[38] WH Beveridge, *Unemployment: A Problem of Industry* (Longmans, Green and Co, 1909).
[39] See above n 34 p 200.
[40] *Ibid.*

providing intermittent work for the unemployed, 'facilitates and encourages the worst kind of Under-employment, namely, the unorganized, intermittent jobs of the casual labourer'. Likewise, the workhouse test for the able-bodied, by 'establishing a worse state of things for its inmates than is provided by the least eligible employment outside', not only engendered 'deliberate cruelty and degradation, thereby manufacturing and hardening the very class it seeks to exterminate'; it also 'protects and, so to speak, standardizes the worst conditions of commercial employment'.[41] Thus the 'fatal ambiguity'[42] of 'less eligibility' was that standards inside and outside the workhouse, since they were mutually reinforcing, would drive each other down, until 'the premises, the sleeping accommodation, the food and the amount of work exacted, taken together, constitute a treatment more penal and more brutalizing than that of any gaol in England'.[43]

The solutions advanced by the Minority Report reflected its diagnosis of the problem. Their principal aim was to remove the 'able-bodied' from the reach of the poor law. The key mechanisms for achieving this end were labour exchanges which, in addition to reducing search costs, would break the power which employers had to maintain 'pools of labour' in reserve, waiting for work:

> What a National Labour Exchange could remedy would be the habit of each employer of keeping around him his own reserve of labour. By substituting one common reservoir, at any rate for the unspecialised labourers, we could drain the Stagnant Pools of Labour which this habit produces and perpetuates.[44]

The Minority Report also addressed the issue of unemployment compensation as an alternative to poor law relief. It argued in favour of a hybrid public-private system, under which government would have the power to subsidise the private insurance schemes already run, at that point, by certain trade unions. In the event, Part II of the National Insurance Act 1911 went further by instituting a fully state-administered system. However, the form of unemployment compensation which initially emerged was similar to that discussed by the Minority Report, namely a system of compulsory insurance 'applied only to particular sections of workers or to certain specified industries, under carefully considered conditions'.[45] This was gradually extended during the inter-war period to cover the vast majority of the workforce; a key feature of the system, and a significant departure from the poor law, was that workers were entitled for the most part to refuse work at wages below those which they had received in their previous employment,

---

[41] See above n 34 p 67.
[42] See above n 34 p 72.
[43] See above n 34 p 79.
[44] See above n 34 p 261.
[45] See above n 34 p 291.

or which were out of line with standards set by collective agreements between employers' associations and trade unions in the relevant district.

In this respect, social insurance dovetailed with state support for labour standards. The case for general legislative standards in the labour market was put by the Webbs in *Industrial Democracy*, the first edition of which appeared in 1896. Their 'National Minimum' of living and working conditions would 'extend the conception of the Common Rule from the trade to whole community'. Low-paying and casualised trades were 'parasitic' as by paying wages below subsistence they received a subsidy from the rest of the community; thus 'the enforcement of a common minimum standard throughout the trade not only stops the degradation, but in every way conduces to efficiency'. In this respect, the deficiencies of the selective model of regulation contained in nineteenth century factory legislation were clearly recognised:

> this policy of prescribing minimum conditions, below which no employer is allowed to drive even his most necessitous operatives, has yet been only imperfectly carried out. Factory legislation applies, usually, only to sanitary conditions and, as regards particular classes, to the hours of labour. Even within this limited sphere it is everywhere unsystematic and lop-sided. When any European statesman makes up his mind to grapple seriously with the problem of the 'sweated trades' he will have to expand the Factory Acts of his country into a systematic and comprehensive Labour Code, prescribing the minimum conditions under which the community can afford to allow industry to be carried on; and including not merely definite precautions of sanitation and safety, and maximum hours of toil, but also a minimum of weekly earnings.[46]

A third component in the re-regulation of the labour market was provided by full employment policy. In Beveridge's view, an effective social insurance scheme could not work unless 'employment is maintained, and mass unemployment prevented'.[47] The responsibility for providing the conditions for full employment lay with the state:

> It must be function of the State to defend the citizens against mass unemployment, as definitely as it is now the function of the State to defend the citizens against attack from abroad and against robbery and violence at home.[48]

Full employment, in turn, had a specific sense. It did not just refer to the absence of unemployment, but to the availability of employment of a particular kind:

---

[46] S and B Webb, *Industrial Democracy* (Longmans, Green and Co, 1920) (originally published 1896) p 767.

[47] WH Beveridge, *Full Employment in a Free Society* (Allen and Unwin, 1967) (originally published 1944) p 17.

[48] *Ibid*, p 29.

at fair wages, of such a kind, and so located that the unemployed men can reasonably be expected to take them; it means, by consequence, that the normal lag between losing one job and finding another will be very short.[49]

Beveridge's combined scheme for social security and full employment therefore sought to complete the work of the Minority Report of 1909 in reversing the effect of the poor law. As he put it, 'the labour market should always be a seller's market rather than a buyer's market'.[50]

The welfare state of the mid twentieth century therefore gave rise to a specific conception of social rights: a model of social citizenship based on employment. The duty to work was not completely neutralised. On the contrary, access to economic security depended on labour market participation. However, this was conditional upon the capacity of the state, through a combination of regulation and macroeconomic management, to guarantee access to stable and well remunerated employment, and to provide for collective provision against the principal hazards for wage earners in a market economy, in particular unemployment, illness and old age. Encoded in the complex mass of detail of national insurance legislation was a commitment to social integration and solidarity across different occupational groups:

> Workers of every grade in every town and village in the country are now banded together in mutual State-aided insurance They are harnessed together to carry the industrial population through every vicissitude.[51]

There were qualifications to this idea, the most important of which was the differential treatment of male and female workers. Beveridge's social insurance scheme treated married women as dependent on a male breadwinner, and allowed them to opt out of most aspects of the scheme; in return they were able to claim the long-term benefits of retirement and widows' pension on the basis of their husbands' contributions. As a result of decisions taken in the 1940s, a high proportion of married women either stayed outside the national insurance scheme altogether or opted to pay a lower rate, up to the late 1970s.[52]

The roots of the differential treatment of men and women in social insurance systems are to be found in contemporary assumptions about the family and the employment relationship. This is most clearly seen in the extensive discussion by the Webbs in the 1909 Minority Report of the question, 'are women able-bodied?'

The new category of 'unemployment' differed from the concept of 'able-bodiedness' in the way it carefully defined the status of the applicant for

---

[49] *Ibid*, p 18.
[50] *Ibid*.
[51] P Cohen, *Unemployment Insurance and Assistance in Britain* (Harrap, 1938) p 10.
[52] D W Williams, *Social Security Taxation* (Sweet and Maxwell, 1982) para 10.04.

relief by reference to the employment which had been lost and to which the applicant was expected to return: as the Minority Report recognised in referring to the intentions of the Unemployed Workmen Act 1905, the 'bona fide Unemployed' were 'the men and women who, having been in *full work at full wages*, find themselves without employment through no fault of their own' (emphasis added).[53] This category, in the view of the authors of the Report, necessarily excluded women whose domestic responsibilities prevented them from becoming 'regular and efficient recruits of the industrial army'.[54] Thus in response to the questions 'are women able-bodied?', posed at the beginning of the Report, and 'are women unemployed?', posed at the end, the same answer was supplied: only if they were 'unencumbered independent wage earners, both supporting themselves entirely from their own earnings and having no one but themselves to support'.[55]

The logical conclusion was the male breadwinner wage:

> we have chosen so to organise our industry that it is to the man that is paid the income necessary for the support of the family, on the assumption that the work of the woman is to care for the home and the children. The result is that mothers of young children, if they seek industrial employment, do so under the double disadvantage that the woman's wage is fixed to maintain herself alone, and that even this can be earned only by giving up to work the time that is needed by the care of the children. When the bread-winner is withdrawn by death or desertion, or is, from illness or Unemployment, unable to earn the family maintenance, the bargain which the community made with the woman on her marriage–that the maintenance of the home should come through the man–is broken. It seems to us clear that, if only for the sake of the interest which the community has in the children, there should be adequate provision made from public funds for the maintenance of the home, conditional on the mother's abstaining from industrial work, and devoting herself to the care of the children.[56]

In this way, the welfare state was constructed on a notion of ability to work which presupposed a particular family structure.

IV CONTEMPORARY EUROPEAN SOCIAL AND EMPLOYMENT POLICY FROM A CAPABILITY PERSPECTIVE

In the post-war welfare state, the duty to work was qualified by state guarantees of full employment and by access to a breadwinner wage, under-

---

[53] See n 34 p 1.
[54] See n 34 p 209.
[55] See n 34 p 208. For further discussion of the Webbs' analysis of the issue of female 'able-bodiedness', see A Picchio del Mercado, *Social Reproduction: the Political Economy of the Labour Market* (Cambridge University Press, 1992) pp 86–94.
[56] See n 34 p 211.

pinned by collective bargaining. The decline of the breadwinner wage, which has accelerated since the 1970s, is a complex phenomenon.[57] On the one hand, increasing female participation in paid employment, coupled with the growing importance of sex discrimination and equal pay legislation, has eroded the assumption that well-paid, secure and stable jobs should be reserved for male earners. On the other, the notion of a breadwinner wage is of declining relevance for the increasing proportion of households with children which contain a single parent, normally the mother (up from 7 per cent of all such households in 1971 to 21 per cent by 1994).[58] Both trends are particularly visible in the UK, but also illustrate the range of forces involved.

Thus overall participation rates for married women have increased markedly, from 10 per cent in 1931 (this low figure influenced Beveridge to believe that married women should be a special class of contributors to national insurance) to 22 per cent in 1951, 42 per cent in 1971 and 53 per cent in 1971. However, this growth has increasingly taken the form of part-time work: in 1971 this accounted for one third of all female employment, but by 2001 had reached almost half of the total.[59] An unduly large proportion of female part-timers are employed on very low weekly wages, in part because of an artificial fiscal subsidy which until recently applied to employment below the level of national insurance contributions.[60]

In general, and notwithstanding attempts to legislate for equality of treatment,[61] part-time work still confers relatively lower incomes and proportionately fewer employment-related benefits than is the case with full-time work. There has been a narrowing of the gender pay gap and average job tenure rates for women have been lengthening at the same time as those of men have been falling. Equal pay legislation, beginning in the

---

[57] See generally C Creighton, 'The Rise and Decline of the "Male Breadwinner Family" in Britain' (1999) 23 *Cambridge Journal of Economics* 519.

[58] *Ibid*, p 527, citing figures of the Office of National Statistics and official Census data which also show that during roughly the same period, the divorce rate in the UK rose from 2.0 per 1,000 members of the married population (in 1960) to 13.6 (in 1995) and the number of births outside marriage from 5.4% of all live births (in 1961) to 37% (in 1994).

[59] Overall participation rates are drawn from the official Census of Population (published by the *Office of Population Censuses and Surveys*) and those on part-time work from the Labour Force Survey (published monthly in the Department of Trade and Industry's *Labour Market Trends*).

[60] See S Deakin and F Wilkinson, 'Labour Law, Social Security and Economic Inequality' (1991) 15 *Cambridge Journal of Economics* 125. Changes made to the law of national insurance in the late 1990s removed much of the subsidy effect (see Social Security Act 1998, s 51, and Social Security Benefits and Contributions Act 1992, s 6A, as inserted by the Welfare Reform and Pensions Act 1999).

[61] Principally in the form of the Protection of Part-Time Workers (Prevention of Less Favourable Treatment) Regulations, SI 2000/1551, implementing Directive 97/81 Concerning the Framework Agreement on Part-Time Work concluded by ETUC, UNICE and CEEP, OJ 1998 L14/9. On the important limitations in the 2000 Regulations, see A McColgan, 'Missing the Point? The Part-Time Workers (Prevention of Less Favourable Treatment) Regulations 2000' (2000) 29 *Industrial Law Journal* 260.

1970s, contributed significantly to the substantial reduction in wage inequality between men and women, and the longer job tenure of women was the result in part of the passage of maternity protection legislation, mandating a period of maternity leave and providing for the right to return to employment. However, these gains are largely concentrated on the situation of full-time working women; in the 1990s, while the gender pay gap was falling in overall terms, it remained constant for part-time work. Thus notwithstanding the elimination of discrimination against part-time workers in relation to terms and conditions of employment and access to occupational pension schemes, part-time work remains poorly paid in relation to full-time employment.[62]

Conversely, the rise in single-parent households, while undermining the idea that it is necessarily a male earner's duty to provide for the other family members, has been accompanied by a growing polarisation of income and opportunities: while dual-earner households have been growing in number, an increasing proportion of households are without employment altogether. In 2002, of those households with married or cohabiting couples between the ages of 25 and 49, around one third had two full-time earners and a further third had a full-time male earner and a part-time female earner. Less than 20 per cent had a sole male breadwinner, around 4 per cent had a sole female breadwinner, and around 6 per cent of this age group had neither partner in work. At the same time, the division of household tasks between men and women remains unequal. This is so across all households, including those with two full-time earners and even those with sole female breadwinners, but it is particularly marked for households with part-time female earners and for those solely dependent on a male breadwinner.[63]

The overall effect is that 'the erosion of the [male breadwinner family wage] has been only partial and has been accompanied by a number of interrelated problems, including increasing polarisation between households, greater poverty, an uneven distribution of opportunities between households and difficulties in combining paid work with childcare'.[64] The principle of family subsistence no longer guarantees access to a living wage; instead, low pay is topped up with fiscal subsidies (tax credits), avoiding the 'burden' of regulation of employment.[65] In turn, the absence of a living

---

[62] See H Robinson, 'Gender and Labour Market Performance in the Recovery', in R Dickens, P Gregg and J Wadsworth (eds), *The Labour Market under New Labour: the State of Working Britain 2003* (Palgrave, 2003).

[63] S Harkness, 'The Household Division of Labour: Changes in Families' Allocation of Paid and Unpaid Work, 1992–2002', in R Dickens, P Gregg and J Wadsworth (eds), *The Labour Market under New Labour: the State of Working Britain 2003* (Palgrave, 2003).

[64] See n 57.

[65] The tax credit scheme is governed by the Tax Credit Acts 1999 and 2000. See generally N Wikeley, *Wikeley, Ogus and Barendt's Law of Social Security* 5th edn (Butterworths, 2002) ch 10. Although a statutory minimum wage was put into place in the late 1990s by virtue of the National Minimum Wage Act 1998, it operates at a low level and is intended to be topped up by tax credits in order to provide a sustainable income for households.

wage is no longer, as it was at various points in the evolution of social insurance system, a good ground for refusing an offer of employment.[66] The withdrawal of benefits from the unemployed, now termed 'jobseekers', who refuse work on the grounds of its unsuitability or low level of remuneration is a policy which successive governments, Conservative and Labour, have followed during the 1990s.[67] Nor are lone parents completely exempt from the duty to work; although they cannot be deprived of benefit for refusing to take up paid work, they are obliged to attend periodic interviews with an employment adviser, on pain of losing part of their social security entitlements.[68]

This is the background, at least in the UK, against which the capability debate is currently being played out: a neoliberal-inspired *activation policy*, which is in many respects the polar opposite of the policy of full employment which it has replaced. Full employment, in its classic, Beveridgian sense, implied a set of measures to control and stabilise the labour supply.[69] The policy of 'a high employment rate', by contrast, aims to increase numbers in employment even if this is carried out at the cost of creating categories of low paid and 'flexible' work which do not provide access to a living wage. Deregulation of terms and conditions of employment goes hand in hand with the restriction of the conditions under which social security benefits are made available. For the time being, contemporary policy is closer to the old, pre-1834 poor law, in the use being made of tax credits and other forms of wage subsidisation which echo Speenhamland, than it is to the late Victorian institutionalisation of the workhouse and labour yard. Yet it was precisely the same combination of rising expenditure and the use of poor relief to subsidise low wages which prompted the 1834 reforms, the last vestiges of which were swept away as recently as the 1940s.[70]

---

[66] The National Insurance Act 1911, s 86(3) made disqualification from unemployment benefit under this heading conditional upon it being shown that the work in question was outside the claimant's normal occupation and/or, in certain instances, was remunerated below the going rates set by collective agreement or custom and practice in the industrial sector or district in question. Despite some weakening of the test during the 1920s, it remained more or less in place up to the 1980s, when it was diluted in various ways (on which, see S Deakin and F Wilkinson, n 60.

[67] The Jobseekers Act 1995, passed by a Conservative government, confirmed the trend begun in the 1980s towards the tightening of benefit conditions and expansion of the grounds for disqualification from benefit on the basis of non-availability for work (see previous footnote). The Labour administration, elected in 1997, has maintained the same approach to the definition of benefit entitlements for those out of work.

[68] By virtue of the Welfare Reform and Pensions Act 1999, inserting ss 2A–2C into the Social Security Administration Act 1992.

[69] See Section III of this chapter.

[70] The last workhouses were converted into hospitals with the creation of the National Health Service in 1946 and poor relief for the sick and aged was replaced by national assistance in 1948.

The UK is, from one point of view, something of a special case within the European Union. Other systems, in particular the Nordic countries, appear to have been more successful in replacing the male breadwinner model with alternatives based on an equitable household division of labour, regulation of working time aimed at achieving a more effective balance between working time and family time, and the use of active labour market policy measures to support transitions into paid employment.[71] However, while this model exists within certain Member States, it is striking that, to date, the European Union has done little to propagate it.

This is the consequence, first of all, of the restricted scope for harmonisation of social security law at European level. In lieu of harmonisation, the Treaty of Rome provided for the limited alternative of the coordination of social security systems. In the traditional meaning of this term (prior to its use as part of the 'open method of coordination' or OMC), coordination referred to measures designed to ensure that in moving between different social insurance regimes, migrant workers were not unduly penalised by comparison to those whose employment remained within a single Member State.[72] Far from seeking to set a common standard for social security across different national regimes, it presupposed difference between them. Notwithstanding the far-reaching changes made since the 1950s in other areas of competence, social security remains an area in which the organs of the Community have very little capacity to act, as opposed to reacting to the effects of national diversity.

The inability of the European Union to take the initiative in this area also results from the approach which has been adopted to the implementation of the employment strategy. A full assessment of the use of the OMC in the context of employment is beyond the scope of the present paper. However, notwithstanding the attention justifiably devoted to the OMC as a novel technique of regulatory learning, it is looking less likely over time that it can serve as a viable means for implementing a progressive policy agenda, in particular one of the kind set out by the Supiot report. This is because the employment strategy bears the traces of its origin in the early and mid-1990s, at a series of European summits which set out the goals of counter-inflation policy and macroeconomic stability which accompanied the adoption of the single currency.[73] This accounts for the emphasis within the employment strategy upon the promotion of labour flexibility and the reduction of social security expenditure, themes which have led the Commission

---

[71] See n 2, ch 3 'Travail et temps'.

[72] For an overview of this highly complex and, within European legal studies, relatively neglected topic, see N Wikeley, *Wikeley, Ogus and Barendt's Law of Social Security* 5th edn (Butterworths, 2002) ch 3.

[73] See S Deakin and H Reed, 'The Contested Meaning of Labour Market Flexibility: Economic Theory and the Discourse of European Integration' in J Shaw (ed) *The Evolution of EC Social Policy* (Hart, 2000).

to give negative evaluations of the employment record of the Nordic systems while leaving the UK's neoliberal approach relatively free of criticism.[74] The 'learning process' encouraged by the employment strategy is, at least for the time being, skewed towards neoliberal policy objectives; as such it is a potential force for the kind of deregulatory competition between European welfare states which has been long debated but, until now, has been limited in its impact.[75]

Against this rather unpromising background, what are the prospects for the capability approach as the foundation of a new conceptual framework in labour and social security law? The 'prehistory' of the concept of capability suggests the need for care here. For most of the period of the poor law, notions of 'able-bodiedness' were derived from the existence of a duty to work which the law imposed on the propertyless. Social insurance carved out a limited series of exceptions to this principle, based on a model of the breadwinner wage which now lacks legitimacy. Is it possible to see in the concept of capability a basis for reversing the logic of the poor law and reinventing the welfare state, so that the duty to work is *only* imposed under circumstances where the state has provided the conditions under which individuals are equipped for *effective* labour market participation? Simply to state this proposition in such terms is to see how far removed today's mainstream debate is from any such conception of capability.

The capability approach may nevertheless be helpful in providing a particular way of thinking about social rights with respect to market processes. The purpose of the capability approach is not to provide a blueprint for social reform; as Sen has put it, '[i]t is not clear that there is any royal road to evaluation of economic or social policies.'[76] This insistence that there is no universally-applicable, prescriptive list of functionings and capabilities means that attention is focused instead on social choice procedures by which the content of capability sets can be collectively determined in particular contexts.

In the context of social welfare, the capability approach suggests a particular way of thinking about social rights: either as claims to resources, such as social security payments, or as rights to take part in forms of procedural or institutionalised interactions, such as those arising out of collective bargaining. When social rights take the form of claims on resources,

---

[74] See G Raveau, 'The European Employment Strategy: From Ends to Means?' in R Salais and R Villeneuve (eds), *Europe and the Politics of Capabilities* (Cambridge University Press, 2004).

[75] On regulatory competition in EU welfare state and labour law policy, see generally KH Paque, 'Does Europe's Common Market Need a Social Dimension?' in J Addison and WS Siebert (eds), *Labour Markets in Europe: Issues of Harmonisation and Regulation* (Dryden, 1997); and S Deakin, 'Labour Law as Market Regulation' in P Davies, A Lyon-Caen, S Sciarra and S Simitis (eds), *European Community Labour Law: Principles and Perspectives, Liber Amicorum Lord Wedderburn* (Clarendon Press, 1996).

[76] A Sen, *Development as Freedom* (Oxford University Press, 1999) p 84.

they are the equivalent of commodities which individuals can convert into potential or actual functionings. When they take the form of proceduralised rights, they come close to what Sen calls 'social conversion factors', that is, social or institutional settings which shape the set of possibilities open to individuals in terms of achieving their goals. Social rights shape the institutional environment in such a way as to enable all (or more) individuals to convert endowments in the form of human and physical assets into positive outcomes.

Juridical support for the idea is beginning to appear in the interstices of European Union social welfare law. One illustration of this is the parity accorded to social and economic rights in the Charter of Fundamental Rights of the European Union, adopted in 2000.[77] Whatever the limitations of particular provisions of the Charter (and there is evidence that they diluted in the drafting process), the equivalence accorded to the rights contained in the 'Equality' and 'Solidarity' chapters on the one hand, and those dealing with economic and political rights on the other, marks an important departure from the practice of subordinating social rights to economic considerations, which is to be found, for example, in the relationship between the European Convention on Human Rights and Freedoms and the European Social Charter, and arguably in the Treaty of Rome and its various successors. The significance of this move is reflected in the determined (but so far unsuccessful) effort made to restore the traditional priority of market considerations in the 2003 draft of the European Constitution.[78]

A second source of institutional support for the capability approach may be found in the developing caselaw of the European Court of Justice on the concept of solidarity. As Catherine Barnard explains, this idea is underpinned by

> the notion that the ties which exist between the individuals of a relevant group justify decision-makers taking steps—both negative and positive—to ensure that the individual is integrated into the community where they have the chance to participate and contribute fully. The negative steps include removing obstacles to integration and participation; positive steps include active programmes to encourage participation of those otherwise excluded. If this reading is correct then the use of solidarity as a guiding principle can help liberate decision-makers and decision-takers from the straitjacket of formal equal treatment.[79]

---

[77] See generally T Hervey and J Kenner (eds), *Economic and Social Rights under the EU Charter of Fundamental Rights* (Hart, 2003).

[78] On this see B Bercusson, 'Episodes on the path towards the European social model: the EU Charter of Fundamental Rights and the European Convention on the Future of Europe' in C Barnard, S Deakin and G Morris (eds), *The Future of Labour Law. Liber Amicorum for Bob Hepple* (Hart, 2004).

[79] C Barnard, 'The future of equality law: equality and beyond' in C Barnard, S Deakin and G Morris (eds), *The Future of Labour Law. Liber Amicorum for Bob Hepple* (Hart, 2004) and her contribution in this collection.

The claim that participation in a market presupposes active measures of integration, and not simply the removal of formal obstacles, is very much in the vein of recent writing on capability theory. The appearance of this idea in the context of the caselaw of persons[80] indicates its potential, but also its limits. It goes beyond the requirements of formal equality in insisting on the need for state action to remove the conditions which inhibit effective market participation. At the same time, it is only within a relatively narrow and established legal framework that the idea, to date, has much purchase. The Court's approach is suggestive of the kind of reasoning which might be put to good effect, if the legislative structure of European social law were to be developed further.

V CONCLUSION

This chapter has examined the concept of capability from an historical perspective in order to try to gain some traction on the issue of its usefulness for contemporary EU social law. The idea has potential as a way of breaking out of the impasse established by neoliberal policies, which increasingly view social rights as a fetter on the growth and integration of markets. Capability theory, in contrast, insists on paying regard to the institutional preconditions for the effective participation of individuals in market activities. Contrary to neoliberalism, these are not limited to the provision, by private law, of contractual capacity or the right to hold property, but extend to collective mechanisms for the sharing and distribution of social risks arising from the operation of markets. However, the example of the male breadwinner model offers an example of the urgent need to review and renew these mechanisms. The EU, which already recognises that social rights have a place within an integrated market order, is ideally placed to play a central role in this process. It is disappointing, therefore, that the 'learning process' associated with the employment strategy has done more to endanger than to encourage institutional innovations of the kind needed to move this debate forward. This should perhaps serve as a reminder that notions of capacity or capability represent contested terrain, in which many different conceptions of the market order struggle for acceptance.

---

[80] The most important decisions are those in Case C–184/99 *Grzelczyk* [2001] ECR I–6193 and Case C–413/99 *Baumbast* [2002] ECR I–7091.

2

The Euro and the Welfare State

MIĆA PANIĆ*

I INTRODUCTION

The most distinctive feature of the European Monetary Union (EMU), recognition of which is essential to an understanding of its problems and prospects, is its uniqueness. It is impossible to find a single case since the beginning of the Industrial Revolution in which a number of independent, sovereign states have created a *complete* monetary union with a common currency, central bank, monetary and exchange rate policies without first establishing a *political* union!

There is, of course, a very good reason for this: significant national differences and the difficulty of reaching a consensus on how to deal with them. If all countries forming a complete monetary union had similar efficiency and income levels, rates of economic growth to maintain this similarity in the long term, similar socio-economic problems and objectives, similar institutions, and identical business cycles—such a monetary union could operate successfully without the need for a political union. The problem is that these conditions are not satisfied even in the different regions of one country. A political union becomes essential, therefore, if the constituent countries / regions are to be able: (i) to share similar values and goals; and (ii) to mobilise their resources for the provision of socially optimal public goods that benefit the whole union. It is also needed for creating the common institutions without which it is virtually impossible to pursue with consistency the objectives and policies that, by keeping regional and personal inequalities within socially acceptable limits, make it possible for the whole union to work towards the same goals without coercion.

It is difficult to overstate the importance of this. The history of international monetary unions, all of which have operated under much less restrictive conditions than the EMU, shows that sovereign states will participate in

* Selwyn College, Cambridge.

such unions only so long as they are satisfied that it is in their national interests to do so.[1] In other words, independent countries will participate in a monetary union so long as there is a consensus between them that they are better off inside such an international grouping than they would be outside it.

The greatest danger confronting the EMU in its present form is that economic stagnation in member countries, and the restrictions imposed on the ability of national governments to reverse it, are raising serious doubts about its long-term viability. Inflation apart, the European Central Bank shows little sensitivity to the economic problems of member countries. Deteriorating economic conditions in Germany and France have made it politically impossible since 2002 for these two key members of the eurozone to keep central government budget deficits below the 3 per cent ceiling, as required by one of the union's most important rules. In 2003 the Swedes voted by a clear majority in a national referendum against adopting the euro. It is extremely unlikely that British and Danish referenda on the subject would produce a different outcome in the absence of significant changes, of the kind suggested later in this chapter, in the way that the EMU operates.

Economic and social inequalities within the eurozone are greater than in any of its Member States. What is more, they are increasing. The European Commission has neither the power nor the resources to reduce them and, in this way, give greater economic and political legitimacy to the European Union. To make matters worse, the Treaty of Maastricht and the Stability and Growth Pact have made it virtually impossible for national governments to deal effectively with economic and social problems within their own countries. This has wide-ranging implications for the welfare state, the very institution around which the founding fathers and their successors have built the European Union.

This chapter will consider briefly two important issues: the sequence of events that made the welfare state a European creation of global significance; and why, by weakening the welfare state, the Treaty of Maastricht and the Stability and Growth Pact pose a threat to the whole project of European unity.

II THE QUEST FOR 'ETERNAL' UNITY AND PEACE IN EUROPE

Although it seems to come as a surprise to many Europeans, not least the British, the centuries old dream of 'eternal' unity and peace in Europe has always envisaged some form of a political union of European states. The King of Bohemia, who in the fifteenth century called for the creation of a

---

[1] See M Panić, *European Monetary Union: Lessons from the Classical Gold Standard* (Macmillan and St Martin's Press, 1992); M Panić, *Globalization and National Economic Welfare* (Palgrave/Macmillan, 2003).

European Federation to repel the threat of a common enemy (the Ottoman Empire), was the first in a long line of politicians, philosophers and writers who have advocated a political union as the only way to secure permanent peace and stability on the continent.[2] Jean Monnet and other 'founding fathers' of the European Community, who shared this view, did no more, therefore, than attempt to realise at last, following the unprecedented bloodshed and destruction of the Second World War, a project that has been around for a very long time.

The problem with political unions, like international alliances, is that there is no guarantee that they will continue once the crisis or threat that led to their creation passes. Coercive measures may prevent their dissolution for a time, but as the history of great empires shows, this is not a permanent solution. More recently, in the 1990s, three European states disintegrated: the Soviet Union, Yugoslavia and Czechoslovakia. Clearly, something else is needed to bind together the constituent parts of a political union: a general feeling that it is in the best interest of the majority of those who live in the countries and regions concerned to be part of it.

In the nineteenth century, the Industrial Revolution appeared to create exactly the kind of conditions needed to hold together a large political union. Industrial progress depends on the continuous division of labour and specialisation. This progressively increases the economic interdependence of individuals, groups and nations as it becomes impossible for any of them to satisfy their needs and aspirations without the active cooperation of those with whom they have close economic ties. The higher the level of economic development the more is this the case. As a result, under these conditions war becomes extremely costly as a means of resolving national conflicts of interest.

John Stuart Mill, who saw Britain transform in his lifetime into the 'workshop of the world', made this point in the middle of the nineteenth century. As he put it,

> commerce first taught nations to see with goodwill the wealth and prosperity of one another. Before, the patriot, unless sufficiently advanced in culture to feel the world his country, wished all countries weak, poor, and ill governed, but his own: he now sees in their wealth and progress a direct source of wealth and progress to his own country. It is commerce which is rapidly rendering war obsolete, by strengthening and multiplying the personal interests which are in natural opposition to it.[3]

At the beginning of the twentieth century Norman Angell, a well-known international economist, argued the economic case against war even more forcefully in a book translated and acclaimed around the world. According

---

[2] F Machlup, *A History of Thought on Economic Integration* (Macmillan, 1977).
[3] J S Mill, *Principles of Political Economy* (Routledge, [1848] 1965) p 594.

to Angell, the extent of international economic integration and interdependence had become so great that war between industrial states would be 'futile—useless even when completely victorious' because of the huge costs that it would inflict on all the combatants.[4]

In fact, the link between economic performance and war is even more important and complex than the case made by Mill and Angell suggests. International economic interdependence and 'commerce' are not in themselves sufficient to prevent wars because trade liberalisation and greater international specialisation and exchange do not necessarily bring prosperity to all those who participate in the process. This is equally true of individuals, groups and countries.[5] In fact, 'there are large potential costs if [international economic] integration is not carefully managed'.[6] As this is bound to have political consequences sooner or later, political matters—including war and peace—become inseparable from those of economic and social policy.

The founders of the European Community were acutely aware of this from personal experience, having lived through two world wars and the costly economic and social failures of unregulated capitalism that contributed to them. And that experience was to play a major role in the approach to European unification that they adopted after the Second World War. Their long-term goal was still a *political* union of European states. However, they realised that, given the strength of national feeling in Europe, successful economic and social policies within these countries—achieved in conditions of close economic cooperation between them—were essential to achieve this goal in the long term.[7]

Such economic cooperation required far-reaching institutional changes that would give central governments the power to expand the scope of the welfare state—particularly its economic role—in order to ensure that national social needs and aspirations were met. Macroeconomic policy took on a critical role in achieving these goals for the simple reason that, as the architect of the German Social Market Economy, Dr Erhard, pointed out, 'the best social policy is an effective economic policy'.[8]

An effective economic policy ensures low unemployment, rising incomes, a narrowing of income inequality and, for all these reasons, a reduction in poverty. Hence, by eliminating one of the most serious economic and social

---

[4]   N Angell, *The Great Illusion* (Heinemann, 1912) pp v–vi.

[5]   See n 1.

[6]   World Bank, *Private Capital Flows to Developing Countries: The Road to Financial Integration* (Oxford University Press, 1997) p 3.

[7]   See A Milward, *The European Rescue of the Nation State* (Routledge, 1992); M Panić, 'The UK and the Euro: Some Key Economic Issues' (2002–03) 5 *Cambridge Yearbook of European Legal Studies*.

[8]   Quoted in S Mangen, 'Social Policy, the Radical Right and the German Welfare State' in H Glennerster and J Midgley (eds), *The Radical Right and the Welfare State* (Harvester Wheatsheaf, 1991) p 108.

problems, it lowers government expenditure. At the same time, high levels of economic activity increase government receipts from taxation. The result is a rise in state revenue, making it possible for the government to pursue successfully policies that achieve the most important goal of the welfare state: equality of opportunity through a more equitable distribution of income and wealth. The view that governments had to follow an active macroeconomic policy enjoyed strong international support after 1945, as there was a general consensus that 'the invisible hand' of unregulated 'market forces' was incapable of achieving the improvements in economic and social welfare demanded by a modern industrial society.

The other widely shared view, based on the interwar experience of autarky and beggar-my-neighbour policies, was that trade liberalisation and active economic cooperation between European states were essential if they were to achieve their national objectives of full employment and rising living standards. Their economies were integrated and interdependent to such an extent that it would be impossible for any one of them in isolation to achieve widely desired levels of welfare. In other words, close economic cooperation between European countries formed an integral part of the quest for greater unity and peace in Europe.

The change in West European inter-state relations since the 1950s, a direct consequence of the success of national welfare states and the contribution that European economic cooperation has made to this, has been extraordinary by any criterion and would, no doubt, have astonished Monnet and his contemporaries. Fifty years after the creation of the European Coal and Steel Community, it is inconceivable now that two European countries, especially two major countries, would go to war to settle a dispute. This is historically unique. And, as the founding fathers hoped, these improvements have ensured that all the states in Western Europe have a stake in preserving unity and peace on the continent.

Equally important, as they anticipated, the widely shared improvements in national well being have restored legitimacy to the existing economic, social and political systems within the individual states—all of which were on trial after the Second World War following disastrous failures of national policies in the first half of the twentieth century. They have also given legitimacy to the European Union, thanks to its role in demonstrating the importance of close cooperation between the states for improvements in their individual economic and social welfare.

III INDUSTRIALISATION AND THE WELFARE STATE

As a result of the revival of neo-liberalism, it is now frequently forgotten that the *raison d'être* of the modern welfare state was never paternalism, even less altruism. Its main purpose since the beginning has been to promote social solidarity and political stability—a goal that took on, as already mentioned, special significance after the Second World War. To that end, the state has assumed collective responsibility for achieving, by a combination of economic and social policies, three important, closely related objectives—none of which can be realised in the long term without success in attaining the other two. These objectives are: equality of opportunity so that the stock of human ability and skills can be developed and employed optimally from an individual and social point of view; reduction in the inequality of income and wealth; and public responsibility for those individuals and households that are unable to achieve a certain ('minimum') standard of living through their own efforts.

The modern welfare state is, therefore, essentially 'an answer to basic and long-term developmental processes and the problems created by them'. It is a response 'to increasing demands for socio-economic equity ... [and] ... the growing needs and demands for socio-economic security'.[9]

Hence, contrary to the claims frequently made by entrenched vested interests, the modern welfare state owes its existence primarily to the need to make the existing socio-political order acceptable to most of the population and in this way to protect it from revolutions and wars that would overturn the *status quo*.

For instance, even in the most advanced forms of the welfare state, in the Scandinavian countries and the Netherlands, the basic features of the capitalist economic system remain intact. Private ownership of the means of production predominates, individuals are responsible for their own wellbeing, property incomes (rent, interest and profit) retain their importance in resource allocation, and the distribution of pre-tax income and wealth is determined by the market. The main difference from the liberal (*laissez-faire*) version of capitalism is that in the welfare state the government plays an active role in ensuring that the economic dynamism of the system serves to improve both private *and* social welfare.[10]

To enable the government to discharge these responsibilities, political institutions have to be adapted continuously to cope with changes brought about by the dynamics of the economic system. Needs, values, aspirations and power relations keep altering over time. They also vary from country to country. It is impossible, therefore, to produce a universally applicable model of the welfare state.[11] To state the obvious, there is no such thing as a precise definition of the minimum standard of living below which nobody

[9] P Flora and AJ Heindenheimer, *The Development of Welfare States in Europe and America* (Transaction Books, 1981) p 8.
[10] See N Barr, *The Economics of the Welfare State* 3rd edn (Oxford University Press,1998) and M Panić, *Globalization and National Economic Welfare* (Palgrave/Macmillan, 2003) for the economic and institutional reasons why the state has to play this role.
[11] See M Kleinman, *A European Welfare State? European Union Social Policy in Context* (Palgrave, 2002).

should fall in a single country, let alone internationally. The same applies also, of course, to the resources available to national governments to help those who need its assistance.

Moreover, some fundamental, lasting changes can occur over a relatively short period. For example, since the early 1970s the industrialised world, in particular, has increasingly experienced a number of new problems. These have been the result of demographic changes (an ageing population), changes in family structure (a significant increase in single parent families), changes in the pattern of employment (strongly in favour of professional and highly skilled labour) and globalisation (which makes it increasingly difficult for governments to deal effectively with national needs and priorities).

Given the far-reaching economic, social and political transformation that the world has experienced over the last two centuries, it is only natural that this should have been accompanied by important changes in the general perception of the state's social responsibility. In *The Wealth of Nations*, published in 1776, Adam Smith expressed the prevalent view at the time, as did John Locke a century earlier, that the state had two important responsibilities: to provide internal order and external security. Its duty was to protect the freedom of individuals to act as they chose—provided that this did not infringe on the freedom of others. Aid for the needy was not the state's business. It was to be left to religious and philanthropic institutions.

However, in the nineteenth and, especially, in the twentieth century there was a radical change in what people expected from the state—with an increasing acceptance of the need for collective responsibility for social welfare. Although demand for this change originated with communists and socialists, it was gradually accepted and implemented even by governments that were strongly opposed to socialist and communist ideas.

Four major developments, which transformed beyond recognition the world of Locke and Adam Smith, were responsible for this. First, there was the formation of national states bringing together in many cases for the first time a diversity of ethnic and interest groups. Their formation and survival required the support of powerful socio-economic groups. However, as unrest and revolutions in the nineteenth and twentieth centuries demonstrated, this was not enough to safeguard the existing order if an important proportion of the population felt that they would be significantly better off if they joined or created a different kind of state. The justification for this was as old as the nation state. Influential philosophers like Hobbes, Locke and Rousseau argued that citizens of a state which broke 'the social contract' with them by failing to protect their rights or to act in their interest were morally right to rebel and/or leave it.[12]

---

[12] See JW Gough, *The Social Contract* (Clarendon Press, 1936).

Second, the Industrial Revolution, together with the scientific and technical progress that accompanied it, transformed permanently the relationship between individuals and the groups of which they are a part. One of its consequences is a continuous specialisation and division of labour that inevitably reduces the degree of self reliance enjoyed by individuals and basic social units such as the nuclear family. The higher the level of industrialisation the greater their dependence on other individuals and groups and, ultimately, on the society within which they live and work. As a result, industrialisation increases their vulnerability to economic instability and the risks associated with industrial activity such as accidents, illnesses and the loss of employment and income. This vulnerability is exacerbated by the geographic and occupational mobility of labour—an integral part of the process of industrialisation—as in due course it breaks labour links with the land and, at the same time, weakens family and community ties. With nothing to fall back on in case of adversity, individuals depend increasingly for their survival and well being on the provision of public goods by the state.

Third, the process of industrialisation and wealth creation over the last two centuries has been driven predominantly by capitalism, the most dynamic of all economic systems so far. The problem is that the same is also true of its capacity—if left entirely to 'market forces'—to destroy wealth and give rise to major economic and social crises. Individualism, economic instability, the constant creation of new wants, coupled with inequality of the means with which to satisfy them, are all part of the competitive process that gives the system its extraordinary capacity for change. However, it is this very competitive spirit and energy, the continuous search for innovation and change that is also an ever-present threat to the system's survival. The competitive struggle inevitably produces winners and losers and, consequently, if nothing is done to redress the imbalance, the potential for social friction and political instability.

Finally, these far-reaching economic and social changes have coincided with the rise of mass democracy, following the French Revolution and a series of revolutions across Europe in the 1840s. The rise of democracy was, of course, no accident. Industrialisation requires an educated labour force. It also, as already pointed out, increases interdependence. Interdependence means teamwork and that demands consensus. The higher the level of industrialisation the greater the importance of these factors—all of which increase the competitive power of labour, especially skilled labour. An educated labour force, conscious of its strategic role in the competitive struggle, is unlikely to accept meekly the maltreatment and exploitation rife in pre-industrial societies. It becomes too dangerous, therefore, for those whose interests depend on the preservation of the established order to ignore the general will of the masses, their needs and wishes.

The sheer scale, novelty and speed of these changes and the welfare problems that they created were too great to be left to the care of religious and philanthropic institutions. Only the state had the power to mobilise the resources needed to reward wage earners' loyalty to the established order and, thus, discourage them from supporting revolutionary changes that would bring about its downfall.[13]

Nothing illustrates this better than the fact that the foundations of the modern welfare state were formulated and laid down in nineteenth-century Germany, a country that was at the time neither liberal nor democratic and which actively persecuted the social democrats who demanded some of these changes.

For example, it was Adolph Wagner, the country's most distinguished economist at the time and a staunch conservative, who outlined in the 1870s and 1880s (a century after Adam Smith) the basic principles of the welfare state. It was to be achieved by gradual transformation of liberal capitalism through the growth of public and state activities.[14] In the 1880s he therefore predicted a steadily rising proportion of public expenditure in GDP (which became known as 'Wagner's Law'), something that did happen in the twentieth century. Wagner's motive, which he shared with other German social conservatives at the time, for advocating welfare reforms was his realisation that they were needed to save the existing order from the growing influence of social democrats. And the only way to do this was to integrate the working class into the German Reich—giving the newly founded state its legitimacy.

It is exactly these considerations that also prompted the government led by Otto von Bismarck, a deeply conservative landowner, to take the first steps towards introducing a modern welfare state. Although generally recognised as one of the greatest political leaders of his time, Bismarck was not a moderniser, and certainly not a revolutionary. He disliked liberal capitalism, had no time for democracy and regarded socialism in any form as a grave threat to the established order and the German State.[15]

Yet it was under his leadership that the Germans introduced compulsory sickness insurance in 1883, compulsory industrial insurance in 1884 and compulsory pension insurance in 1889—all before any other industrial country, with the UK lagging several decades behind and the United States even more so.[16]

German welfare reforms are sometimes attributed to feudal paternalism. In fact, as Bismarck's personal reminiscences show, they are the result of

[13] G Esping-Andersen and W Korpi, 'Social Policy as Class Politics in Postwar Capitalism' in J Goldthorpe (ed), *Order and Conflict in Contemporary Capitalism* (Oxford University Press, 1984).

[14] A Wagner, 'Three Extracts on Public Finance' in RA Musgrave and AT Peacock (eds), *Classics in the Theory of Public Finance* (Macmillan, 1967).

[15] See S Whitman, *Personal Reminiscences of Prince Bismarck* (John Murray, 1902) and E Eyck, *Bismarck and the German Empire,* 2nd edn (Allen and Unwin, 1958).

[16] See P Flora and AJ Heindenheimer, *The Development of Welfare States in Europe and America* (Transaction Books, 1981) p 59.

something much more modern: pragmatism—for reasons that should strike a very familiar cord in contemporary Europe.[17] Bismarck had achieved for Germany something that Monnet, Schuman and others were hoping to create in Western Europe after 1945. He had presided over the transformation of an economic union (the Zollverein) into a full political and monetary union of German States—with a single currency, uniform rules and regulations across the whole country and, above all, with a central authority and military power to prevent military conflicts between them.

The revolutions of 1848, a direct result of economic failure and widespread poverty, together with long standing grievances and the inability of outdated institutions to deal with them,[18] had convinced Bismarck that the various insurance laws that he was introducing were essential to preserve the existing order. In his view, they would prevent socialists from gaining widespread support that would lead to:

> a revolution of possibly more far-reaching consequences than that of 1789. It might bring about the advent of a new era in the history of civilisation such as was the Reformation, and, probably, as in that case, the running of rivers of German blood.[19]

The lessons of the French Revolution and the upheavals in the first half of the nineteenth century were, it seems, forgotten in the decades of peace and industrial progress that followed until another and even more serious economic crisis. The Great Depression of the 1930s caused large-scale unemployment, inequality, poverty and social deprivation in the industrialised world and beyond. The established socio-economic and political order felt even more threatened than in the nineteenth century, especially as all this was happening only a little over a decade after the Russian revolution of 1917. Social unrest and the breakdown of internal order took different forms in different countries, from the rise of organised crime in the United States to the rise of Nazism in Germany, with the latter leading to the Second World War. When the war started people in some countries, including France,[20] refused to defend the state that had done so little in the past to protect them from the misery and hopelessness inflicted by unemployment and poverty.

In other words, the interwar experience had demonstrated yet again that the state was unable to perform even the two basic responsibilities that justify its existence—internal order and external security—if its economic performance fell persistently below the level desired by the society.

---

[17] See n 15.
[18] EJ Hobsbawm, *The Age of Revolution* (Weidenfeld & Nicholson, 1962).
[19] See n 15 p 95.
[20] A Milward, *The European Rescue of the Nation State* (Routledge, 1992).

Beveridge articulated succinctly the dangers inherent in such a failure:

> The greatest evil of unemployment is not the loss of additional material wealth which we might have with full employment: there are two greater evils. First, that unemployment makes men seem useless, not wanted, without a country; second, that unemployment makes men live in fear, and that from fear springs hate.[21]

He quotes with approval from President Roosevelt's address to the US Congress in 1938:

> 'The liberty of a democracy is not safe if its business system does not provide employment and produce and distribute goods in such a way as to sustain an acceptable standard of living'.[22]

The view was widely shared. A national committee of US business firms declared that: 'Never again will doles and subsistence levels be tolerated'.[23]

The Beveridge Report reflected the new consensus on both sides of the Atlantic by broadening the state's responsibility for national well being. It did this by redefining the basic necessities of life to include decent education, health and housing. In other words, the state was charged with the task of providing equal opportunities for people to acquire the ability and resources ('positive freedom') without which the vast majority of them would be unable to enjoy the individual liberty ('negative freedom') to which Locke and Adam Smith attached so much importance.[24]

At the same time, as mentioned earlier, it was widely recognised in the 1940s that all these plans depended on a successful economic policy. Full employment, price stability and an equitable distribution of income became, therefore, key economic objectives of national governments to be achieved by an active pursuit of macroeconomic policies. This was a complete reversal of the approach to economic 'management' adopted by governments in the 1920s and 1930s. According to the liberal ideology dominant at the time, governments had a single economic responsibility (the maintenance of price stability) to be achieved by a combination of tight monetary policies and balanced budgets—irrespective of their economic and social costs. The result was the Great Depression with all its consequences, something that the founding fathers of the European Union wanted to ensure would never happen again.

---

[21] WH Beveridge, *Full Employment in a Free Society* (Allen and Unwin, [1944] 1967) p 248.
[22] *Ibid* p 249.
[23] See n 21 p 249.
[24] See I Berlin, *Four Essays on Liberty* (Oxford University Press, 1969) for a discussion of the two freedoms.

The main problem with the EMU in its present form is that, whatever the original intention, it has turned out in practice to be nothing less than an attempt, in the macroeconomic management at least, to put the clock back to the 1930s!

IV EUROPEAN MONETARY UNION: THE BANK AND THE PACT

The main reason for creating a monetary union is to remove the exchange rate risks and uncertainties that may act as a barrier to international trade. The problem stems directly from the existence of competing currencies issued and managed by the monetary authorities of individual countries in response to their national problems, objectives and priorities. The expectation is that, by imposing a common monetary and exchange rate policy, a complete monetary union in particular will improve economic welfare both in the short run (thanks to greater monetary stability) and in the long run (by accelerating the rate of economic growth through greater specialisation and trade).

In fact, such an outcome depends on much more than a reduction in transaction costs by eliminating exchange rate risks and uncertainties. It can be expected with confidence *only* provided that greater financial certainty is not achieved at the cost of an increase in economic stagnation and political instability of the kind that welfare states have been created to avoid. That, in turn, requires either that differences in welfare levels between the countries are small or that a complete monetary union has the supranational institutions whose responsibility is to narrow down these differences through resource transfers so that the union is demonstrably of benefit to all its members.[25] Historical experience shows clearly that in the absence of such an outcome no international monetary union is sustainable in the long term. This is especially true of monetary unions that not only lack the necessary supranational institutions but also impose uniform policy requirements to which all their members have to adhere rigidly irrespective of the nature of their economic and social problems.

The EMU, as presently constituted, has major, potentially fatal, flaws in both these respects. For instance, the Treaty of Maastricht pays hardly any attention either to the welfare costs that some countries are bound to incur by adopting the euro or to the effect of these costs on the viability and survival of the EMU. It carefully sets financial criteria that a country must satisfy in order to join the monetary union. These give specific, numerical targets for the rate of inflation, interest rates (short and long), public debt and budget deficits. That is all. There are no criteria for the convergence of the levels of

---

[25] See Commission, *Report of the Study Group on the Role of the Public Finance in European Integration* (1977) (the 'MacDougall Report') for the importance of resource transfers for the creation and viability of a European monetary union.

per capita incomes, sustainable rates of economic growth, unemployment levels, or even of the members' business cycles. Yet it is the growing disparities in economic welfare, the result of rigid adherence to the rules of a monetary union, that have invariably been the Achilles heel of all international monetary unions, including the Classical Gold Standard and the Bretton Woods System.[26] And unlike in the case of these unions, there are no provisions that allow a country to leave the EMU if it finds the welfare costs of the membership too high.

One of the major problems has always been the difficulty of creating supranational institutions that could smooth out differences in national economic welfare in the short run and assist in achieving their convergence in the long run. This is made worse in the EMU, as the scope for discretionary policies is much more limited in a complete monetary union. It has one supranational institution, the European Central Bank (ECB). But there is no common fiscal authority, as the responsibility for fiscal policy remains, for political reasons, with national governments.[27] The eurozone is left, therefore, with the very difficult task of trying to reconcile a common monetary policy with a number of potentially conflicting fiscal policies.

In fact, the task is even more difficult than the institutional division of responsibilities suggests. To achieve the best possible mix of macroeconomic policies it is essential for the overall fiscal authority and the central bank to work in tandem. That requires the responsibilities and policy objectives of each to be clearly defined, avoiding policy biases that might prevent the other institution from discharging its responsibilities. Such a degree of consensus and cooperation is virtually impossible in the EMU. As the ECB is not accountable to the national parliaments of member countries, there is a complete separation of monetary and fiscal policies in the eurozone. The potential for conflict is increased by the rigidities and the policy bias imposed by the Treaty of Maastricht and the Stability and Growth Pact on both the ECB and national governments.

A The European Central Bank

According to the Treaty of Maastricht, the ECB's 'primary objective' is price stability.[28] There is a provision that it 'shall support the general economic policies in the Community' such as 'a high level of employment and of social protection'.[29] However, the ECB is instructed to provide this kind of 'support' only if it is not prejudicial to its primary objective.[30]

[26] See n 1.
[27] See M Panić, 'The UK and the Euro: Some Key Economic Issues' (2002–03) 5 *Cambridge Yearbook of European Legal Studies.*
[28] Art 105(1) EC.
[29] Arts 105(1) and (2) EC.
[30] See n 28.

Not surprisingly, the Bank has interpreted this to mean that it has a single responsibility: to maintain price stability.[31] The Bank might justify such a narrow interpretation of its remit by pointing out that, like any other central bank, it has at its disposal only one macroeconomic policy instrument, monetary policy, and that consequently it cannot be responsible for more than one policy target.[32] However, the same policy constraint applies also to other major, politically independent, central banks such as the US Federal Reserve and the Bank of England. Nevertheless, both of them take account of the state and prospects of their national economies in deciding what monetary policy stance to adopt. In fact, as Bloomfield shows, many national central banks were careful not to ignore the state of their economies even under the Classical Gold Standard (1880–1914).[33]

Equally important has been the failure of EU governments to specify clearly in the Treaty (a) what they meant by price stability and (b) how far and for how long inflation rates could deviate from the target rate before the ECB had to alter its policy stance. As a result, it was left to unelected officials of the ECB to define price stability as an increase in consumer prices of less than 2 per cent to be achieved in the 'medium term'.[34] The ECB's definition of its primary responsibility may be more specific than the Treaty's in the sense that it quantifies the inflation target. But how long is 'the medium term'? Not surprisingly, to be on the safe side the, ECB has interpreted this in practice to mean that the target rate of inflation of 0–2 per cent has to be maintained in the short term.

For a number of reasons, the ECB's interpretation of its main responsibility is even more restrictive than it appears. For instance, it ignores the effect of quality improvements on prices, something that is important in all dynamic economies. These are estimated to be responsible for price increases of about 1.5 per cent per annum.[35] A target of 0–2 per cent means therefore that, once the effect of improvements in quality is excluded, the maximum permissible rate of inflation is no more than 0.5 per cent!

As an average for a group of countries as diverse as those comprising the EMU this is very low. It imposes a strong deflationary bias on monetary policy that affects all member countries—especially those with low inflation rates!

There are two reasons for the latter. First, if the average rate of inflation in EMU is, for example, 2 per cent this means that in some of the countries the actual rate will be negative. The danger, as the recent Japanese experience

---

[31] See ECB, *Monetary Policy Strategy Monthly Report* (January 1999), Ch 8.

[32] See J Tinbergen, *On the Theory of Economic Policy* (North-Holland, 1952) for an analysis of this problem.

[33] A I Bloomfield, *Monetary Policy under the International Gold Standard: 1880–1914* (Federal Reserve Bank of New York, 1959).

[34] See n 31.

[35] Advisory Commission to Study the Consumer Price Index (Boskin Report), *Towards a More Accurate Measure of the Cost of Living: Final Report* (Washington DC, 1996).

demonstrates, is that falling prices may set in motion economic stagnation that is difficult to reverse.[36]

Second, suppose that the ECB sets the interest rate for the eurozone at 4 per cent, and that the rate of inflation is 2.5 per cent in Italy and 1.0 per cent in Germany. The result would be real rates of interest in the two countries of 1.5 and 3.0 per cent respectively. To the extent that real rates of interest discourage borrowing for consumption and investment purposes, thus reducing aggregate demand, the deflationary effect will be greater in Germany than in Italy. This inequality—which penalises countries with low rates of inflation (!)—creates another serious problem for the conduct of macroeconomic policy in the eurozone, as it is Germany and France, the two largest economies in the EMU, that since the mid-1990s have had the lowest rates of inflation. In both cases, the rates have been well within the target range of 0–2 per cent, often below 1.0 per cent (without 'the quality' adjustment). Given their size, the adverse impact on the two economies of the deflationary bias built into EMU monetary policy by the Treaty will be felt in all EU countries.

These are serious shortcomings, as the ECB is the only supranational economic institution in EMU with the authority and power to influence the socio-economic well being of countries within the eurozone. Yet it is not accountable either to the peoples of these countries or to their democratically elected representatives! In other words, the ECB, which is run by representatives of the financial sector only, is empowered to override the needs and wishes of the millions who bear the brunt of the welfare costs imposed by its policies.

To change this would require a revision of the Treaty, which is far from easy. According to the agreement reached when the Treaty was ratified, the revision requires a unanimous support of *all* EU countries. The enlargement of the Community to 25 countries is bound to make necessary changes even more difficult. Built into the Treaty of Maastricht, therefore, is the potential for a serious conflict of national interests that poses a major long-term threat to EMU.

B The Stability and Growth Pact

The deflationary bias and the potential for national conflicts of interest in the eurozone are compounded by the Stability and Growth Pact adopted by the European Council in 1997.

The Treaty left responsibility for fiscal and social policy to national governments for the simple reason that it was the only course of action open

---

[36] See HW Sinn and M Reutter, 'The Minimum Inflation Rate for Euroland', *NBER Working Paper No 8085* (NBER, 2001); P De Grauwe, *Economics of Monetary Union*, 5th edn (Oxford University Press, 2003) Ch 4.

to the EU countries determined to create a complete monetary union. Europe is still not ready for a political union; and without such a union a supranational fiscal authority would have neither the legitimacy nor the resources to perform the role of a national ministry of finance. Hence, if the countries in favour of the single currency insisted on a fiscal union, to balance the monetary policy stance adopted by the ECB, they would have never been able to secure agreement for the creation of a European Monetary Union.

However, in order to reconcile monetary and fiscal policies within the union, the Treaty and the Pact have imposed important constraints on the conduct of fiscal policy in countries that comprise the eurozone as well as those which wish to join it at some future date. The Maastricht compromise has left EMU, therefore, without an institutional framework to pursue consistent, effective macroeconomic policies at either the national or the European level.

National governments are required to keep their budgets 'close to balance or in surplus' in 'the medium term'. However, as in the case of the inflation target, this has been interpreted to mean that they are not permitted to borrow more than 3 per cent of GDP in the short run (a year), even during economic recessions. If they fail to do so they are liable to fines of up to 0.5 per cent of their GDP. The fines will be waived in 'exceptional circumstances', ie when GDP falls by more than 2 per cent per annum. The same applies also, if the Ministers of Finance of EU countries agree, when the GDP of a country declines by 0.75–2.0 per cent.[37]

Several explanations have been offered for such a rigid enforcement of the 3 per cent rule.[38] First, a country whose government borrowing exceeds the 3 per cent ceiling will experience an increase in the public debt/GDP ratio. This, so the argument goes, is inflationary and will make it difficult for the country to maintain price stability. The problem with the argument is that there is no evidence to support this particular assertion. Even a cursory comparison of public debt/GDP ratios and inflation rates, regularly published by the European Commission (*European Economy*) and the OECD (*Economic Outlook*), will show this.

Second, countries in which the debt/GDP ratio is increasing have to borrow frequently on capital markets. As European capital markets are highly integrated, their borrowing will raise the general level of interest rates and,

---

[37] See, in particular: Art 104 EC; European Council, *Resolution on the Stability and Growth Pact*, 1997 OJ C236/1; and Reg 1467/97 on speeding up and clarifying the implementation of the excessive deficit procedure, 1997 OJ L209/6. On the implementation and enforcement of the excessive budget deficit procedure, consider the judgment in Case C–27/04 *Commission v Council* (Judgment of 13 July 2004).

[38] See M Artis and F Nixson (eds), *The Economics of the European Union,* 3rd edn (Oxford University Press, 2001) and P De Grauwe, *Economics of Monetary Union,* 5th edn (Oxford University Press, 2003) for a more detailed discussion of these issues.

in this way, increase the burden of government debt in other EU countries—including those in which budget deficits are below the 3 per cent ceiling. The snag is that this scenario, although plausible, cannot be easily elevated to a general principle. As global (not just European) capital markets are highly integrated now, the effect of national borrowing on the level of international interest rates will depend on the relative size of the economy and its government debt.

Third, countries in which the burden of servicing public debt is rising may put pressure on the ECB to relax its monetary policy. This could encourage their governments to borrow even more as interest rates fall and, according to this view, the rate of inflation would then accelerate reducing the real value of government debt. Again, the argument overlooks two important facts. It ignores the political independence of the ECB, which makes it effectively accountable to no one.[39] How exactly would national governments, not all of which are likely to be in favour of a more relaxed monetary policy, force the Bank to change its policy stance in these circumstances? Moreover, even if they succeeded, there is no empirical evidence to support the assertion that lower interest rates and economic expansion would automatically lead to higher prices.

Fourth, bonds issued by one government will be bought widely within the eurozone. Hence, if that government defaults there will be strong pressure on other governments to bail it out from those individuals and institutions in their country who hold these bonds. Although there is a possibility of this happening, Eichengreen and von Hagen provide a counter argument and empirical evidence to show that the risk is small in the eurozone.[40] According to them, the reason for this is that all EU countries have a large domestic tax base and extensive taxing powers. They can use these powers to reduce government deficits and avoid the risk of default. The authors conclude therefore that the need to impose tight budgetary rules on these countries has been exaggerated.

Prudence demands that governments be responsible in the management of their finances. There is always the risk with a growing public debt that, over time, it may (a) become unsustainable and (b) make it difficult to implement counter cyclical policies when the country needs them most. The important question is 'whether the stability and growth pact may not have gone too far in stressing rigid rules on the conduct of fiscal policies'.[41]

---

[39] On the proper scope of the independence of the ECB, consider Case C–11/00 *Commission v European Central Bank* [2003] ECR I–7147. Cf the parallel proceedings in Case C–15/00 *Commission v European Investment Bank* [2003] ECR I–7281.

[40] B Eichengreen and J von Hagen, 'Fiscal Policy and Monetary Union: Federalism, Fiscal Restrictions and the No-Bailout Rule', *CEPR Discussion Paper No 1247* (London, 1995).

[41] P De Grauwe, *Economics of Monetary Union,* 5th edn (Oxford University Press, 2003) p 211.

An important reason for answering the question in the affirmative is that the ceiling on government borrowing makes no distinction between borrowing (i) for investment and current expenditure and (ii) by countries with large and small public debts. Borrowing to invest in education, health, infrastructure, housing and other public goods will benefit future generations. It is right, therefore, that the cost should be spread over time with future generations bearing some of them. Equally important, the assumption that an increase in budget deficit carries exactly the same risk of default in countries where the public debt is small as in those where it is large is also difficult to justify by rational economic analysis. Hence, in judging whether a country's budget deficit is 'excessive' it is essential to take into account both the nature of government borrowing and the country's debt level.

The other serious shortcoming of the Pact concerns the 'exceptional circumstances' under which the government of a country is allowed to borrow more than 3 per cent of GDP. As it stands, the definition of 'exceptional circumstances' overlooks completely the relationship between changes in potential (roughly, average annual growth of the labour force and labour productivity) and actual output. The welfare consequences of this can be illustrated with a simple example. Suppose that a country's labour force is increasing annually at a rate of 0.5 per cent and its labour productivity at 2.5 per cent. The annual rate of growth of its productive potential is, therefore, 3 per cent. This means, assuming that there is no change in the growth of productivity, that there will be a rise in unemployment even if actual output increases by 2 per cent. Nevertheless, that country would have to pay the fine if its government borrowed in excess of 3 per cent of GDP in an attempt to stem the rise in unemployment. Sanctions could be applied against the country, in fact, even if its output fell by 1.5 per cent, causing a large increase in unemployment. Yet, as happened in the UK in the early 1980s, economic stagnation on this scale, unless rapidly reversed, is certain to increase income inequality, poverty and social-political problems such as crime, deterioration in health standards and political discontent.[42]

Finally, the Pact fails to take into account fluctuations in government income and expenditure over the business cycle—despite their welfare consequences. Expenditure rises relative to income in recession and vice versa when levels of economic activity are high.

---

[42] See JK Galbraith and M Berner (eds), *Inequality and Industrial Change: A Global View* (Cambridge University Press, 2001); S Field, *Trends in Crime and their Interpretation* (HMSO, 1990); DL Patrick and G Scambler, *Sociology as Applied Medicine*, 2nd edn (London Tindal, 1986); C R Taylor, *Growth, Inequality and the Politics of Discontent in the Industrialised Countries* (Group of Thirty, 1992).

The main components of government budget in a country that belongs to a complete monetary union like EMU can be summarised as:

$$G + D - T - F = b \, [+ \, m - e]$$

where
G = public sector expenditure
D = interest payment on outstanding government debt
T = taxes
F = intergovernmental equalisation grants
b = borrowing from the public
m = changes in money supply
e = changes in foreign exchange reserves.

If the country is in recession, with underutilised productive capacity and high and rising unemployment, its government needs to raise G to stimulate aggregate demand, output and employment—to stabilise the economy. In the EMU it cannot increase m or e, both of which are controlled by the ECB. It cannot raise T because that would offset increases in G and aggregate demand. F could help finance G if the EU intergovernmental resource transfers were not too small to play a significant role in stabilising national economies. Hence, the only way to finance higher G is through public borrowing (b)—which is capped by the Pact! National governments are, therefore, in no position to resort to the Keynesian stabilisation policies that have played such a critical role in protecting the world economy from plunging into another Great Depression.

V CONCLUSION

There is a strong case in theory for countries whose economies are highly integrated to form a complete monetary union. However, for the socio-economic benefits of such a union to outweigh the costs, it is imperative for the countries to create an institutional framework that ensures long-term improvement, rather than deterioration, in the economic welfare of *all* of them. It is clear from the analysis in this chapter that the governments that participated in the drafting and ratification of the Treaty of Maastricht and the Stability and Growth Pact failed demonstrably to provide such a framework. Even more seriously, by rejecting Keynesian economics and the use of fiscal policy to stimulate output and employment, they have exposed EU countries to the kind of risks associated with the economic stagnation and political instability of the 1930s that had such disastrous consequences. It should be of concern to European governments that most of the economies that have adopted the euro are stagnating relative to those (the UK, Sweden and Denmark) that have refused to do so.

The danger is that by undermining the welfare state, the foundation on which the European Community was built, the Treaty and the Pact will reverse the unprecedented progress in unity, cooperation, prosperity and political stability that Western Europe has achieved since the Second World War. There is no evidence that this has yet happened.[43] However, as the proposed welfare 'reforms' in some of the key EU countries and the popular resentment that they have provoked show, it is highly unlikely that the welfare state can be protected for long in conditions of economic stagnation.

This may be serious. But it is far from being irreversible. Institutions, rules and regulations exist to achieve particular objectives. If the underlying problems, needs and priorities of a society change, institutions have to be adapted to achieve new objectives that reflect these changes. This chapter has identified a number of major flaws in the management of the common monetary policy and national fiscal policies within the eurozone. All these can be revised to reflect national needs and objectives, the goal that led to the creation of the European Community and the difficulties in meeting them experienced since the establishment of EMU. The Pact should be relatively easy to change. It was approved by the European Council, which has the power to revise it. Altering the Treaty may be more complex, but it is not impossible.

Whatever the changes which European governments decide to make they are unlikely to be effective if they fail to confront and solve the most important institutional problem that a complete monetary union of independent, sovereign states raises and which was brushed under the carpet with the Maastricht compromise. If Europe is not ready for a political union with a common fiscal authority and policy—which it clearly is not—the critical question is whether it is possible to reconcile *effective* national responsibilities for macroeconomic stability and welfare with the existence of a complete monetary union.

In other words, members of the EU will either need to take back the means (policies) that enable their governments to discharge their economic and social responsibilities to the satisfaction of those they represent *or* they will have to delegate these responsibilities and accountability to joint Community institutions. The Maastricht compromise is not a sustainable, long-term solution. If what they really want is the former it would, of course, require a different form of a European monetary union, one much closer to the Classical Gold Standard than to EMU.[44]

---

[43] M Kleinman, *A European Welfare State? European Union Social Policy in Context* (Palgrave, 2002); D Swank, *Global Capital, Political Institutions, and Political Change in Developed Welfare States* (Cambridge University Press, 2002).

[44] See further: M Panié, *European Monetary Union: Lessons from the Classical Gold Standard* (Macmillan and St Martin's Press, 1992).

3

Privatisation of Social Welfare: European Union Competition Law Rules

JOHN TEMPLE LANG[*]

This chapter looks at the EU competition principles applying before privatisation of social welfare services, at the rules affecting the privatisation process, and finally at the rules applying after privatisation.

These rules apply to both payment of social welfare benefits and provision of social welfare services. This chapter does not deal with State aid issues, although they are likely to arise, as they are considered in another paper.[1] The chapter deals with the subject in a practical, pragmatic way:

Part I   Principles of EC law on State measures
Part II   After privatisation
Part III   The privatisation process
Part IV   Conclusion

I PRINCIPLES OF EC LAW ON STATE MEASURES

A Why the Law on State Measures is Untidy

It may be useful to explain why the law on State measures restricting competition is untidy.

One reason is that Article 86 EC, which is the only Treaty provision on State measures restricting competition, is not very clearly drafted. It means,

---

[*] Cleary Gottlieb Steen and Hamilton, Brussels and London; Professor, Trinity College, Dublin; Senior Visiting Research Fellow, Oxford.
[1] See the contribution of A Biondi and L Rubini in this collection.

in effect, '[even] in the case of State enterprises and enterprises to which the State has given monopoly or special rights, States may not adopt or maintain measures contrary to the Treaty'. But it does not say 'even', so it suggests, wrongly, that it imposes a special stricter rule in connection with State-owned or privileged enterprises. In fact, essentially the same substantive rule applies in connection with all other enterprises, but as a result of Article 10 (ex-5) EC, a provision the importance of which has been very much under-estimated.

Article 86(2) EC allowed Member States to exempt enterprises responsible for services of general economic interest from Treaty rules. For this reason, and because Article 86 EC was potentially applicable to a diverse range of politically sensitive situations in different Member States, the Commission made very little use of Article 86 EC until the late 1980s, and the questions which arose were referred to the Court of Justice from national courts. These questions were answered without the Court or the Commission finding it necessary to formulate general principles. The result was to develop several legal rules on a case-by-case basis, which have not been explicitly related to one another, which overlap, and which have not clearly answered several entirely foreseeable questions which, due to accidents of litigation or to the prudence or tactics of plaintiffs, have not so far been raised.

The nearest that the Commission has come to stating any comprehensive view was in the 1990s when, under French pressure, it produced several rather cautious Notices limited to 'services of general economic interest' under Article 86(2) EC, which did little to clarify the overall legal position.

The legal principles which have emerged have therefore never been authoritatively stated as a single set of rules in a clear conceptual framework. That does not prevent them from being sufficient to deal with most cases which are likely to arise. However, they have not been developed in relation to social welfare, and they do not apply specially to the social welfare area. In fact they could not have done so, because until recently in most Member States social welfare has been provided almost entirely by State bodies which were not 'enterprises', which were not subject to competition rules, and the monopolies of which could not have been questioned because they were not in general providing services for payment. Necessarily the competition law cases which have come before the Court of Justice have concerned markets on which there were non-State companies. However if and insofar as provision of social welfare is privatised or, for instance, pensions come to be increasingly provided by private companies, the rules on State measures restricting competition will become increasingly important, and the rules of competition applicable to enterprises will become applicable.

B Member States May Choose Public or Private Ownership and Decide Their Social Welfare Systems

The EU Treaty is clear: it does not limit the freedom of Member States to choose public or private ownership. Article 295 (ex-222) EC reads:

> This Treaty shall in no way prejudice the rules in Member States governing the system of property ownership.

Similarly, Community law does not limit the powers of Member States to organise their social welfare systems.[2]

However, when a Member State owns or controls wholly or in part any 'enterprise' (essentially, any body or company providing goods or services as an economic or commercial activity), the body in question is subject to the EU rules on competition which apply to enterprises, as well as to the special EU rules applicable to State measures concerning State-owned enterprises. If a publicly owned or controlled entity has both economic activities and official regulatory powers, it is subject to the rules on competition insofar as its economic activities are concerned, and to the rules on State authorities insofar as its regulatory powers are concerned.

Member States may not for example use State owned companies for protectionist purposes, or give them more favourable treatment than would be permitted for private companies under for instance State aid rules. The only exceptions to the EU Treaty rules are for services of general economic interest under Article 86(2) EC, and these apply whether the company involved is State owned or not.

---

[2] Case 238/82 *Duphar v Netherlands* [1984] ECR 523 para 16; Joined Cases C–159/91 and C–160/91 *Poucet and Pistre* [1993] ECR I–637 para 6; Case C–70/95 *Sodemare v Regione Lombardia* [1997] ECR I–3395 para 27; Case C–157/99 *Geraets-Smits and Peerbooms* [2001] ECR I–5473. See generally Edward and Hoskins, 'Article 90: Deregulation and EC laws: Reflections arising from the XVI FIDE Conference' (1995) 32 Common Market Law Review 157; M Siragusa, 'Privatization and EU competition law' in BE Hawk (ed), *Annual Proceedings of the Fordham Corporate Law Institute 1995* (1996) 375; F Blum and A Prior-Logue, *State Monopolies under EC Law* (Wiley, 1998); J L Buendia Sierra, *Exclusive Rights and State Monopolies under EC Law* (Oxford University Press, 1999); D Geradin (ed), *The Liberalization of State Monopolies in the European Union and Beyond* (Kluwer, 2000); C M von Quitzow, *State Measures Distorting Free Competition in the EC* (Kluwer, 2002); J Temple Lang, 'Community antitrust law and government measures relating to public and privileged enterprises: Article 90 EEC Treaty' in BE Hawk (ed), *Annual Proceedings of the Fordham Corporate Law Institute 1984* (1985) 543; P Slot, 'Applying the competition rules in the healthcare sector' (2003) 11 *European Competition Law Review* 580. Member States retain sole competence to decide the level and duration of social welfare benefits: Case C–471/99 *Martinez Domingo, Urbano v Bundesanstalt für Arbeit* (Judgment of 24 Sept 2002); Case C–113/96 *Gomez Rodríguez* [1998] ECR I–2461.

C Limits on State Measures Restricting Competition

The legal constraints imposed by Community law on the powers of Member States to take national legislative, executive or administrative measures restricting competition are based on two overlapping principles:

1. The general duty of national authorities not to adopt or maintain any measure which would deprive Community competition law of its effectiveness.[3]

2. The duty not to adopt or maintain any measure restricting freedoms granted or guaranteed by the EC Treaty except for a legitimate (*i.e.*, non-protectionist) purpose in the public interest and using means which are no more restrictive than is necessary to achieve that purpose.[4]

---

[3] Case 13/77 *INNO v ATAB* [1977] ECR 2115, para 31; Case 229/83 *Leclerc* [1985] ECR 1; Case C–260/89 ERT [1991] ECR I–2925, para 35; Case 267/86 *Van Eycke v ASPA* [1988] ECR 4769, para 16; the cases reviewed by AG Van Gerven in joined cases C–48/90 and C–66/90 *PTT Netherlands v Commission* [1992] ECR I–565 at pp 615 ff; Case C–320/91 *Corbeau* [1993] ECR I–2533; Case C–41/90 *Höfner and Elsner* [1991] ECR I–1979; Case C–60/91 *Batista Morais* [1992] ECR I–2085; Case C–2/91 *Meng* [1993] ECR I–5751, para 14; Case C–185/91 *Reiff* [1993] ECR I–5801, para 14; Case C–245/91 *Ohra* [1993] ECR I–5851, para 10; Case C–153/93 *Delta* [1994] ECR I–2517, para 12; Case C–55/93 *van Schaik* [1994] ECR I–4837, para 25; Case C–379/92 *Peralta* [1994] ECR I–3453, para 21; Joined Cases C–401/92 and C–402/92 *Heukske and Boermans* [1994] ECR I– 2199, para 16; Case C–96/94 *Centro Servizi Spediporto* [1995] ECR I–2883, para 20; Case C–134/94 *Esso Española* [1995] ECR I–4223; Joined Cases C–140/94 *DIP v Comune di Bassano* [1995] ECR I–3257, para 14; see also Case C–250/95 *Futura Participations* [1997] ECR I–2471. In almost all these cases the Court said Member States may not 'take measures which may render ineffective the competition rules applicable to undertakings'; Case C–38/97 *Librandi v Cuttica* [1998] ECR I–5955. See also Case C–67/96 *Albany International* [1999] ECR I–5751; Joined Cases C–115/97 to C–117/97 *Brentjens'* [1999] ECR I–6025, and Case C–219/97 *Drijvende Bokken* [1999] ECR I–5751, 6025 and 6121; Joined Cases 46/87 and 227/88 *Hoechst* [1989] ECR 2859, para 33 ('Member States are required to ensure that the Commission's action is effective'); Case T–228/97 *Irish Sugar* [1999] ECR II–2629, para 130. In Case C–387/93 *Banchero* [1995] ECR I–4663, the Court said (at p 4697) 'the obligations which Member States must perform in good faith under Article 5 include the obligation, set out in Article 90(1), whereby they must not let public undertakings and undertakings to which they grant special or exclusive rights enact or maintain in force any measure contrary to the rules contained in the Treaty.' Joined Cases C–147/97 and C–148/97 *Deutsche Post v GZS and Citicorp* [2000] ECR I–825, para 39; cf. Joined Cases C–153/94 and 204/94 *R v Commissioners of Customs and Excise, ex p Faroe Seafood* [1996] ECR I–2465 (national measures for collecting Community revenues must not make it excessively difficult to implement Community legislation). See also Case C–271/91 *Marshall v Southampton Area Health Authority ('Marshall II')* [1993] ECR I–4367. See J Temple Lang, 'Community antitrust law and national regulatory procedures' in BE Hawk (ed), *Annual Proceedings of the Fordham Corporate Law Institute 1997* (1998) 297; J Temple Lang, 'State measures restricting competition' (2001) 2 *Europarättlig Tidskrift* 206.

[4] In relation to the freedom of establishment, the freedom of services and the freedom to compete, see the following judgments: Case 33/74 *van Binsbergen* [1974] ECR 1299; Case 352/85 *Bond von Adverteerders* [1988] ECR 2055; Case C–353/89 *Commission v*

The two principles are the basis for several rules:[5]

— Member States may not adopt measures which lead enterprises to
  do anything which, if done directly by the State itself, would be
  contrary to the EC law rules binding on States. For example, a
  national measure may not require enterprises to give preference to
  goods or services produced in the Member State concerned, or to
  indulge in any other form of protectionism.
— The rule that States may not make competition law ineffective
  means that Member States may not adopt measures which lead to
  enterprises acting contrary to EC law rules on enterprises, even if
  the enterprises in question are State enterprises or enterprises
  which have been granted special or exclusive rights.
— The rule against restrictions on freedom of establishment and services means that there are limits on how far Member States may
  adopt measures which create or strengthen a dominant position.

To these rules there is one exception, in Article 86(2) (ex-90(2)) EC Treaty,
which is discussed below.

Netherlands [1991] ECR I–4069; Case C–288/89 *Antenne de Gouda* [1991] ECR I–4007;
Case C–76/90 *Säger v Dennemeyer* [1991] ECR I–4221; Case C–320/91 *Corbeau* [1993]
ECR I–2533; Case C–275/92 *Schindler* [1994] ECR I–1039; Case C–323/93 *Crespelle*
[1994] ECR I–5077; Case C–384/93 *Alpine Investments* [1995] ECR I–1141; Case
C–189/95 *Franzén* [1997] ECR I–1509, at 5976–5977; Case C–264/96 *ICI v Colmer* [1998]
ECR I–4695, paras 28–9; Case C–222/95 *Parodi v Banque Bary* [1997] ECR I–3899; Case
C–167/97 *Seymour Smith* [1999] ECR I–623; Case C-212/97 *Centros* [1999] ECR I–1459;
Case T–266/97 *Vlaamse Televisie* [1999] ECR II–2329; Opinion of AG La Pergola, in Case
C–124/97 *Läärä* [1999] ECR I–6067; Case C–67/98 *Zenatti* [1999] ECR I–7289; Case
C–58/99 *Commission v Italy* [2000] ECR I–3811; Case C–205/99 *Empresas Navieras* [2001]
ECR I–1271; Case C–108/96 *MacQuen* [2001] ECR I–837; Case C–390/99 *Canal Satellite*
[2002] ECR I–607; Case C–439/99 *Commission v Italy* [2002] ECR I–305; Joined Cases
C–430/99 and C–431/99 *Sea-land Service* [2002] ECR I–5235. All such measures must pass
three tests: the objective must be important enough to justify restricting the freedom guaranteed by the Treaty (the balancing test); the measure must be appropriate to the objective
(the appropriateness test); there must be no less restrictive way of achieving the objective (the
necessity test); see N Emiliou, *The Principle of Proportionality—a Comparative Study*
(Kluwer, 1996); Case T–266/97 *VTM* [1999] ECR II–2329.

[5] There is also the rule that Member States must not interfere with the operation of a
  Community institution (the Community Courts or the Commission) in the competition law
  sphere. They must not interfere with the ability of the Commission to obtain evidence, or
  adopt decisions likely to conflict with decisions of the Commission or judgments of the
  Community Courts. Case 14/68 *Walt Wilhelm* [1969] ECR I; Case 234/89 *Delimitis* [1991]
  ECR I–935; Case C 9/99 *Echirolles Distribution* [2000] ECR I–8207; Case C–344/98
  Masterfoods [2000] ECR I–11369; J Temple Lang, 'General report, the duties of cooperation of national authorities and courts and the Community institutions under Article 10 EC'
  in *XIX FIDE Congress* (Helsinki, 2000) Vol I 373 and Vol IV 65; JTemple Lang, 'The duties
  of cooperation of national authorities and courts under Article 10 EC: two more reflections'
  (2001) 26 *European Law Review* 84.

D The General Principle that National Measures must Not Make Community Competition Law Ineffective

This is a general duty based on Article 3 and Article 10 EC combined: Member States must not defeat the purpose of Community rules. This means that national measures must not lead to infringements of Articles 81 and 82 EC by enterprises. There would be little point in preventing companies from restricting competition if national authorities were free to restrict it (or to order companies to restrict it) with similar effects. Article 86 EC, which is among the Treaty rules on competition although it refers to all the Treaty rules and not only to competition rules, makes it clear that the Articles on State aids are not the only Treaty competition rules binding on Member States.

The Court of Justice has frequently repeated this principle in general terms. There are many ways in which national authorities could use their legislative, executive and administrative powers so as to create situations in which the Community competition rules would be made ineffective to achieve the economic results which they are designed to achieve.

This rule is relevant to national measures specifically restricting competition for instance, by controlling prices, and to measures giving selected enterprises privileged positions protected from competition, whether or not infringements of Articles 81–82 EC by the enterprises are likely to result directly.

E The General Principle that Freedoms Given by the Treaty may Be Restricted Only for Legitimate Purposes and by Proportional Measures

Any measure that restricts competition significantly is also likely to restrict freedom to supply services or freedom of establishment, or both. Since Article 86 EC is a specific example of the general duties of Member States under Article 10 EC,[6] and since Article 86 EC refers specifically to the rules on competition, the principle that freedoms may be restricted only for legitimate reasons applies to national measures regulating or restricting freedom to compete. This is so even though competition is not usually thought of as one of the 'freedoms' guaranteed by the Treaty, and even though competition law is subject to the effectiveness principle already mentioned.

A non-discriminatory measure which restricts the freedom in question (whether freedom to provide services, freedom of establishment, or freedom to compete) of all companies equally, is almost always adopted for a good reason, and so is relatively easy to justify under Article 10 EC. A discriminatory measure which gives a protected or privileged position to one or some limited number of companies, is much more difficult to justify on public interest grounds under Article 86 EC. Both the legitimate purpose test and the proportional means test are harder to fulfil in the case of a measure giving a special position to a monopoly or to a limited number of companies.

---

[6] Case C–18/88 *GB–Inno* 1991 ECR I–5941.

F The Rule that Member States must not Adopt Measures which Lead to Breaches of Articles 81 or 82 EC by Enterprises

This rule has a series of consequences, according to the case law:

— National authorities cannot order a company to infringe Article 81 or 82 EC.
— National authorities may not encourage, reinforce, or contribute to a violation of Article 81 or 82 EC. This rule prohibits measures allowing companies to agree minimum prices for automatic 'rubber-stamp' approval by public authorities. It prohibits measures requiring companies to join a restrictive agreement, or making the terms of such an agreement binding on non-parties. There is also a duty not to approve any practice which is contrary to Community competition law, and therefore not to extend the effects of any practice contrary to Community competition law, or making violations of Community law inevitable.[7]
— A regulatory or price control authority (or any other national authority) may not approve or authorise, even for non-competition objectives and under national law, any price fixing arrangements between companies or any price fixed by an agreement between competitors which is contrary to Article 81 EC,[8] or a price which is contrary to Article 82 EC. National authorities must not promote or encourage price fixing between competitors, and must not authorise competitors to fix prices, even by way of settlement of disputes. Any committees of competitors set up to advise State authorities must be purely advisory.
— There is a duty not to adopt any measure which leads to a breach of Article 82 EC by the enterprise in question. Any company in a dominant position acts unlawfully if it abuses its dominant position (unless Article 86(2) EC applies), whether or not it is a State enterprise or an enterprise having special or exclusive rights, and whether or not the abuse was prompted by a State measure. A Member State cannot authorise an abuse of a dominant position, except in the special situations to which Article 86(2) EC applies. If the abusive conduct is *required* by national legislation, or if the legislation creates a situation in which there is no possibility of competition, Articles 81 and 82 EC apparently do not apply,[9] but the measure is a violation of the duties of the State. If a State measure obliges the companies to which it applies to do something which infringes Article 81 or 82

---

[7] Case C–163/96 *Silvano Raso* [1998] ECR I–533, p 579; Case C–258/98 *Carra* [2000] ECR I–4217.

[8] Case 66/86 *Ahmed Saeed* [1989] ECR 803; Case 209/84 *Asjes* [1986] ECR 1425; Case C–18/93 *Corsica Ferries* [1994] ECR I–1783.

[9] Case T–228/97 *Irish Sugar* [1999] ECR II–2969, para 130.

EC, the measure is illegal, but since the companies have no choice, they are acting legally,[10] until the measure is declared unlawful by a national authority or by the Commission.[11]

If a State measure is sufficiently likely to lead to a violation of Article 82 EC without requiring it, both the measure and the behaviour are unlawful. On the question when a State measure is so likely to lead to an abuse that the measure itself is contrary to Community law, the Court has made a number of rulings, saying almost the same thing in different words. A Member State must not give exclusive rights which are 'liable to create a situation in which that undertaking is led to infringe' Article 82 EC.[12] A State must not adopt or maintain a measure which creates a situation in which a dominant enterprise 'cannot avoid infringing' Article 82 EC[13] or a situation in which the enterprise is 'induced to commit' an infringement of Article 86 EC.[14] A State may not create 'a situation in which the provision of a service is limited', contrary to Article 82 EC, if the statutory monopolist is obviously unable to satisfy the demand for these services.[15] A State may not require an enterprise to infringe Community competition law as a condition of obtaining an official licence or concession.[16] A State which 'facilitates' an abuse will normally be acting contrary to the Articles on free movement of goods[17] or to the Articles on freedom to supply services. Most recently, and strikingly, the

---

[10] Case C–379/97 *Ladbroke Racing* [1997] ECR I–6265, paras 20, 33; Case T–513/93 *Consiglio Nazionale* [2000] ECR II–1807, para 58.

[11] Case C–198/01 *Fiammiferi* [2003] ECR I–000.

[12] Case C–260/89 *ERT* [1991] ECR I–2925, para 38; Case C–462/99 *Connect Austria v Telekom-Control-Kommission* [2003] ECR I–5197, para 80.

[13] Case C–41/90 *Höfner* [1991] ECR 1979, para 27; Case C–55/96 *Job Centre* [1997] ECR I–7119, paras 29, 31, 35, 38; Case C–179/90 *Port of Genoa* [1991] ECR I–5889, para 17; Case C–323/93 *Crespelle* [1994] ECR I–5077, p 5104. In Case C–387/93 *Banchero* [1995] ECR I–4663, p 4699, the Court also referred to violation by the State if 'in merely exercising the exclusive right granted to it, the undertaking in question cannot avoid abusing its dominant position'. In Case C–163/96 *Raso* [1998] ECR I–533, p 579–80, the Court pointed out that if one company had an exclusive right to provide temporary workers to its competitors, it has a conflict of interest, because merely exercising its monopoly will enable it to distort conditions of competition in its favour. It is therefore 'led to abuse' its monopoly. The exclusive right is therefore unlawful even if no specific case of abuse is found. See however Case C–203/96 *Dusseldorp* [1998] ECR I–4075, paras 61, 63 ('enables an undertaking on which it has conferred exclusive rights to abuse its dominant position') and AG Jacobs at p 4106, and Case C–340/99 *TNT Traco v Poste Italiane* [2001] ECR I–4109, paras 44–48 and 54–58.

[14] Case C–170/90 *Port of Genoa* [1991] ECR I–5889, at p 5928, citing Case C–260/89 *ERT* [1991] 2925, para 37, both use the concept of 'inducing' an abuse: see also AG La Pergola in Joined Cases C–147/97 and C–148/97 *Deutsche Post v GZA* and *Citibank Kartenservice* [2000] ECR I–825, at para 18.

[15] Case C–55/96 *Job Centre* [1997] ECR I–7119, paras 31–36 (this refers to Article 82(b) EC which prohibits actions limiting production of the competitors of the dominant enterprise).

[16] Case 30/87 *Bodson v Pompes Funèbres* [1988] ECR 2479, paras 34 and 35.

[17] Case 13/77 *GB-Inno v Atab* [1977] ECR 2115, para 35; Case C–170/90 *Port of Genoa* [1991] ECR I–5889, p 5929.

Court said that competition rules would be 'less effective' if a national competition authority was not able to declare a national measure contrary to Article 10 EC.[18]

A dominant company may not be authorised to regulate its competitors.[19] That would involve a conflict of interest. This means, among other things, that a dominant company may never be the ultimate judge of the lawfulness of its own or its competitors' behaviour. A supposedly impartial regulator may not delegate its powers to companies which have a conflict of interest. Advocate General Fennelly in *Silvano Raso*[20] distinguished between the situation in which a State measure compels or encourages the dominant enterprise to commit an abuse and the situation in which the measure merely enables the enterprise to commit an abuse, but does not directly compel or encourage it. The Court in *Silvano Raso*[21] confirmed his view that it is unlawful encouragement of an abuse, if the dominant company has a conflict of interest as a result of the State measure. Merely exercising its powers in the *Raso* case would have enabled the dominant company to distort conditions of competition in its own favour, by charging its competitors too much or supplying them with a less satisfactory service than it gave itself. So if the State measure creates a situation in which the enterprise has both a power and an incentive to do something which would be contrary to Article 82 EC, the measure is contrary to EU law. It is the probable consequence of the measure that a violation of Article 82 EC will be committed. Enterprises can be expected to act in their own interests. There is no need to prove that any particular example of abuse has occurred.

When a measure which strengthens or extends an already existing dominant position is unlawful,[22] there is no need to see whether it is likely to lead to any other abuse. The test of likelihood of abuse is needed only where the measure does not extend dominance, and therefore the *only* objection to the State measure is that it is likely to lead to behaviour contrary to Article 82 EC. Some of the State measures in the case law of the Court, because they granted special or exclusive rights, could have been challenged on the grounds that they created a dominant position or constituted an unjustified restriction on freedom of establishment or freedom to provide services. The latter argument accepted by the Court in *VTM*, the Flemish advertising case.[23] If

---

[18] Case C–198/01 *Fiammiferi* [2003] ECR I–0000, para 50.

[19] Case 267/86 *van Eycke v Aspa* [1988] ECR 4769; Case C–202/88 *France v Commission (Telecommunications Equipment)* [1991] ECR I–1223, para 51; Case C–18/88 *RTT v GB-Inno* [1991] ECR I–5941; Case C–48/90 *Netherlands v Commission* [1992] ECR I–565, AG Van Gerven at p 616; Case C–163/96 *Silvano Raso* [1998] ECR I–533.

[20] Case C–163/96 *Silvano Raso* [1998] ECR I–533.

[21] *Ibid*, p 579. See also AG La Pergola, in Joined Cases C–147/97 and C–148/97 *Deutsche Post v GZS and Citicorp* [2000] ECR I–825, para 21: the Court came to a different result, but on the grounds that there had been no unlawful conduct.

[22] See Case C–18/88 *GB-Inno BM* [1991] ECR I–5941, discussed below.

[23] Case T–266/97 *Vlaamse Televisie* [1999] ECR II–2329.

a measure is unlawful because an exclusive or special right unjustifiably creates a dominant position or restricts freedoms protected by Community law, this might be the real objection to it, rather than an argument, even if it was justified, that it led to infringements of Article 82 EC.

Logically, the first question therefore is whether a State measure creating exclusive or special rights is legitimate. The second question is whether it is unjustifiably extending or strengthening existing dominance. It has been realised only slowly that measures granting exclusive rights, and measures extending or strengthening dominance, can be challenged. Companies often have more interest in attacking behaviour than in attacking a measure conferring dominance. But national courts are required to raise questions of Community law, if they arise on the facts before them, on their own initiative.[24] Article 82(b) EC prohibits a dominant enterprise from limiting the production of its competitors, as well as its own production,[25] so that Article 82(b) EC prohibits all forms of foreclosure by the dominant company, and therefore also indirectly prohibits State measures foreclosing competition unless they are specifically justified under Article 86 EC.

So a State measure is contrary to EU law:

— Where the measure unjustifiably extends an existing dominant position.
— Where the measure directly orders or encourages the unlawful conduct.
— Where the measure creates a dominant position for the supply of a specified service, and the dominant enterprise is unable to meet the demand (so that the monopoly cannot be justified), the *Höfner* rule.
— Where the measure creates a situation of conflict of interest (the *Silvano Raso* rule). This arises if the dominant enterprise has both regulatory and economic activities, or where it has two commercial activities, and it is likely to discriminate in one of its activities in favour of its operations in the other. The rule means that the enterprise should not be allowed to have regulatory powers over its competitors. But this rule does not prevent the enterprise being consulted, if the regulatory powers are exercised by another body. The rule also means that the enterprise should not be given a monopoly in the supply of an input needed by its own and its competitors' downstream operations.

---

[24] Case C–312/93 *Peterbroeck* [1995] ECR I–4599; Joined Cases C–340/93 and C–431/93 *von Schijndel* [1995] ECR I–4705; Case C–72/95 *Kraaijveld* [1996] ECR I–5403, paras 54–62.

[25] Joined Cases 40–48/73 and others *Suiker Unie* [1975] ECR 1663, paras 399, 482–83, and in particular 523–27; Case 41/83 *Italy v Commission (British Telecommunications)* [1985] ECR 873; Case 311/84 *Télémarketing CBEM* [1985] ECR 3261, para 26; Case 53/87 *CICR and Maxicar v Renault* [1988] ECR 6039; Case 238/87 *Volvo v Veng* [1988] ECR 6211; Joined Cases C–241/91P *RTE and ITP ('Magill')* [1995] ECR I–743, para 54; Case C–41/90 *Höfner and Elsner* [1991] ECR I–1979, pp 2017–18, in particular para 30; C–55/96 *Job Centre* [1997] ECR I–7119, pp 7149–50, paras 31–36; Case C–258/98 *Carra* [2000] ECR I–4217.

G The Rule that a Member State Must Not Create or Strengthen a Dominant Position without Sufficient Justification

It seems that there are two principles:

— A Member State may not adopt a measure which unjustifiably extends an existing dominant position without sufficient justification. A measure which extends an existing dominant position is likely to be discriminatory, and can probably be justified only under Article 86(2) EC.
— A Member State may not adopt a measure which restricts freedom of establishment or freedom to provide services which *creates* a dominant position without a sufficient justification. A measure which creates a dominant position is inherently discriminatory (because it gives one enterprise a privileged position), and can probably be justified only under Article 86(2) EC.

It is not clear whether these two principles really are separate, or whether the first of these two principles is based on Article 82 EC combined with Article 86 EC (on the basis that if the dominant enterprise itself extended its dominant position it would infringe Article 82 EC), or under Article 86 EC combined with the rules on freedom of establishment and services. In most cases this distinction has no practical significance, but in theory it might affect the analysis and the justification. There is no *economic* reason for distinguishing between an extension of a dominant position in another market and creating a new separate dominant position.

The first principle was stated by the Court of Justice in *GB-Inno*. A Member State

must not by laws, regulations or administrative measures put public undertakings and undertakings to which they grant special or exclusive rights in a position which the said undertakings could not themselves attain by their own conduct without infringing Article 86. Accordingly where the extension of the dominant position of a public undertaking or undertaking to which a State has granted special or exclusive rights results from a State measure, such a measure constitutes an infringement of Article 90 in conjunction with Article 86.[26]

The second principle was stated by the Court of First Instance in a Flemish advertising case.[27]

---

[26] Case C–18/88 *GB-Inno BM* [1991] ECR I–5941, pp 5980–81; see also AG Van Gerven in Joined Cases C–48/90 *Netherlands v Commission* [1992] ECR I–565, pp 619–22; Joined Cases C–271/90 *Spain v Commission (Telecommunications Services)* [1992] ECR I–5833, para 36; Case C–320/91 *Corbeau* [1993] ECR I–2533; Case T–266/97 *Vlaamse Televisie* [1999] ECR II–2329.
[27] Case T–266/97 *Vlaamse Televisie* [1999] ECR II–2329.

The Court in *GB-Inno* specifically rejected the argument that the State measure was unlawful *only* if the dominant enterprise had committed or would be led by the measure to commit an abuse.

> It is sufficient to point out in this regard that it is the extension of the monopoly in the establishment and operation of the telephone network to the market in telephone equipment, without any objective justification, which is prohibited as such by Article 86, or by Article 90(1) in conjunction with Article 86 where that extension results from a measure adopted by a State. As competition may not be eliminated in that manner, it may not be distorted either.[28]

This judgment shows that a State measure strengthening or extending a dominant position is prohibited even if it does not cause the dominant enterprise *itself* to do anything which would constitute an abuse. All that is needed for the measure to be illegal (unless Article 86(2) EC applies) is that it extends or strengthens a dominant position.

The Court's statements[29] that a State measure creating a dominant position is contrary to EC law *only* if it is likely to lead to a violation of Article 82 EC by the company concerned have been made in cases in which the issue was whether the State measure was contrary to EU rules *only* because it was likely to lead to an abuse of the dominant position. In such cases the principle is that the measure is illegal if, but only if, the measure is sufficiently likely to lead to the abuse. The cases in which this is the essential issue are distinct from the (so far) relatively few cases in which the issue was whether the creation or extension of the dominant position was unjustified.

In *Crespelle*,[30] for example, the Court considered whether a State measure was likely to lead to an abuse of a dominant position without considering the question whether there was a justification for the measure creating the dominant position. Implicitly the Court assumed that there was sufficient justification, but it seems odd that the Court did not say why, as the second question should logically precede the first. The answer presumably is simply that in Article 234 EC cases the Court answers only the questions which have been asked by the national court.

In effect, the Court said in *GB-Inno* that a Member State must not, without justification, extend a monopoly. If the dominant enterprise did it, it would be contrary to Article 82 EC; if the State does it, the State measure is contrary to Article 86 EC because it eliminates or distorts competition, not because it leads to behaviour by the dominant enterprise which is contrary to Article 82 EC (although of course it may do so). Several comments are appropriate:

---

[28] At para 24.
[29] In, eg, Case C–209/98 *Sydhavnens Sten & Grus* [2000] ECR I–3743, para 66; Case C–67/96 *Albany* [1999] ECR I–5751, para 93; Joined Cases C–115/97 to C–117/97 *Brentjens* [1999] ECR I–6025, para 93.
[30] C–323/93 *Crespelle* [1994] ECR I–5077.

— The judgment in *GB-Inno* could be deduced from either or both of the two general principles stated at the beginning of this article. Any exclusive right involves a restriction on freedom of establishment and freedom to supply goods and services.

— The rule is a strict one, because even a dominant enterprise can extend a dominant position and obtain a de facto monopoly if it does so only by legitimate competition—essentially by offering better bargains. What the Court is saying is that a dominant position may not be extended by the State except when the State has 'objective justification'.

— If a Member State needs a justification to extend a dominant position into a new, second market, it needs a justification to create a dominant position. There is no rational basis for stricter rules on extending dominant positions than for creating them.[31]

— The *GB-Inno* case shows that the rule prohibits distortions of competition, resulting from giving a dominant company power to regulate its competitors, as well as prohibiting measures eliminating competition.

— The judgment makes sense. It would be odd and irrational if the Member States, *without* special justification, could bring about by a State measure a situation which the dominant enterprise itself would not be allowed to create.

— *GB-Inno* is consistent with the principle that national measures hindering the exercise of fundamental freedoms guaranteed by the Treaty must be justified by important requirements in the general interest, proportionate, and non-discriminatory,[32] and suggests that it is a principle which applies to freedom of competition as well as to free movement of goods, persons, services and freedom of establishment.[33]

— The judgment means that the Member States are obliged to respect the underlying aim of the Treaty provisions, to maintain a competitive market. They are, in other words, obliged to avoid interfering with the Community objective of competition stated in Article 3 EC.[34] This obligation, in so far as State enterprises are

---

[31] AG Tesauro Case C–320/91 *Corbeau* [1993] ECR I–2533, at p 2555: 'Provisions extending the scope of an exclusive right are not by their nature different from provisions establishing an exclusive right. They both eliminate, in a given sector, the possibility of the free exercise of economic activity and hence of competition. They may therefore be examined in the light of Articles 90 and 86. And in both cases what is essential to check is whether or not the provisions in question are objectively justified' (emphasis in original). See also p 2556, and AG Jacobs, Case C–271/90 *Spain v Commission (Telecommunications Terminals)* [1992] ECR I–5833, p 5855.

[32] See the cases cited in n 4.

[33] Case C–323/93 *Crespelle* [1994] ECR I–5077; Case C–320/91 *Corbeau* [1993] ECR I–2533; Case T–266/97 *Vlaamse Televisie* [1999] ECR II–2329.

[34] In Case C–202/88 *France v Commission (Telecommunications Terminals)* [1991] ECR I–1223 (a judgment given nine months before *RTT v GB-Inno-BM*), the Court said '... Articles 2 and 3 of the Treaty set out to establish a market characterized by the free movement

concerned, now results from Article 86 (2) EC. This can also be deduced from the duty not to deprive the Community competition rules of their effectiveness.[35] The competition rules are intended to protect competition, so Member States should not, without sufficient reason, restrict competition in a way which a dominant enterprise would not be allowed to bring about, whatever the legal nature of the means by which they restrict it.

— In respect of enterprises which are *not* State-owned or privileged, Member States have the same obligation, but it results from Article 10 (ex 5) EC. Article 86 (1) EC is merely a specific example of the general principle set out in Article 10 EC.[36] If there is a duty not to extend or create a new dominant position in a market in which one does not already exist, there is no reason why that duty should be confined to situations in which there is a State owned company. The principles referred to in Article 86 (1) EC apply equally to enterprises without State ownership or special privileges.

— The Court has confirmed the *GB-Inno* judgment, without elaborating or explaining it, in *Dusseldorp*,[37] *Glöckner*,[38] and *Connect Austria*,[39] and it is consistent with *Telecommunication Terminals*.[40]

The Advocate General in *Sydhavnens Sten & Grus*[41] called attention to the two approaches which can be seen in the case-law of the Court: the view that '*the mere finding that exclusive rights were conferred automatically made it possible to establish the existence of abuse*' within the meaning of Article 82 EC, and the view that EU law is infringed only if the enterprise '*merely by exercising the exclusive rights granted to it, is led to abuse its dominant position*'. These two approaches both refer to 'abuse', and they have not yet been fully and clearly reconciled, but clearly an exclusive right which is said to be in the public interest cannot be justified if it leads to a breach of Article 82 EC or if the privileged enterprise is unable to satisfy the demand which it was intended to meet.[42]

---

of goods where the terms of competition are not distorted thin... Article 30 *et seq.* must therefore be interpreted in the light of that principle, which means that the competition aspect of Article 3 (f) of the Treaty has to be taken into account' (para 41).

[35] See n 3. On the duties of Member States to make Community law work effectively in the way it was intended to work, see J Temple Lang, 'The duties of cooperation of national authorities and courts and the Community Institutions under Article 10 EC Treaty' in Sundström (ed), *FIDE Congress* (Helsinki, 2000).

[36] Case 13/77 *INNO v ATAB* [1977] ECR 2115, paras 30–31; Case C–323/93 *Crespelle* [1994] ECR I–5077, para 15.

[37] Case C–203/96 *Dusseldorp* [1998] ECR I–4075, para 61.

[38] Case C–475/99 *Ambulanz Glöckner* [2001] ECR I–8089.

[39] Case C–462/99 *Connect Austria v Telekom-Control-Kommission* [2003] ECR I–5197, paras 81–82.

[40] Case C–202/88 *France v Commission* [1991] ECR I–1223; see also Case C–209/98 *Sydhavnens Sten & Grus* [2000] ECR I–3743.

[41] Case C–209/98 *Sydhavnens Sten & Grus* [2000] ECR I–3743, pp 3763–66.

[42] Case C–258/98 *Carra* [2000] ECR I–4217.

Granting of an exclusive licence, or of one of a very limited number of licences, is only one of the ways in which a Member State may create or strengthen a dominant position. The Treaty would apply similarly to any other measure with the same economic effects for example, a government instruction that civil servants should travel only on the State owned airline[43] or that public property should be insured only with the State owned insurance company,[44] or that medical expenses should be refunded only for services provided by certain hospitals.

In *Vlaamse Televisie*[45] the Court of First Instance said that a State measure was illegal because it established a monopoly contrary to the rules on freedom of establishment and services, although it was not alleged to lead to an abuse of a dominant position, or to involve extension of a dominant position. This case is therefore clearly an example of the principle about restriction of freedoms, and not an example of the rule on Article 82 EC. However, the *Vlaamse Televisie* principle would equally apply to a State measure *extending* a dominant position without justification. This would be a more natural approach than the rather artificial argument in *GB-Inno*, that the State measure extending the dominant position was illegal because the dominant company could not have extended its position in the same way.

In *Connect Austria*[46] the Court held that a State measure is illegal if it causes a new entrant into a market to pay the State for a licence when a dominant State-owned enterprise gets the same rights without payment, as this reinforces the dominant position. The Court said that the State measure was contrary to Article 82 EC, together with Article 86 EC, because it did not guarantee 'equality of chances'.

To summarise, there are several categories of State measures:

— Measures which restrict freedom of establishment or services on a non-discriminatory basis, without creating any privileged position, on the basis of 'imperative requirements in the general interest', which are relatively easy to justify.
— Measures which are likely to lead to a dominant enterprise committing an abuse contrary to Article 82 EC.
— Measures which restrict freedom of establishment or services on a discriminatory basis, creating a monopoly or a privileged position, without a justification under Article 86(2) EC. In addition, measures which without justification extend an existing dominant position are clearly illegal, but the principle involved may not be separate from that concerning creation of dominant positions.

---

[43] See J Temple Lang, 'Community anti-trust law and government measures relating to public and privileged enterprises: Article 90 EEC Treaty' in BE Hawk (ed), *Annual Proceedings of the Fordham Corporate Law Institute 1984* (1985) 543, at 556–60.

[44] See Commission decision on Greek insurance law, 1985 OJ L152/25.

[45] Case T–266/97 *Vlaamse Televisie v Commission* [1999] ECR II–2329.

[46] Case C–462/99 *Connect Austria v Telekom-Control-Kommission* [2003] ECR I–5197, paras 80–87.

H Article 86(2) EC: The Kinds of Tasks which may be Exempted from the Treaty Rules

Article 86(2) EC is a remarkable provision. It says that enterprises entrusted with the operation of services of general economic interest may be relieved from the rules contained in the Treaty, in particular the rules on competition, insofar as the application of these rules would obstruct the performance, in law and in fact, of the particular tasks given to them.

This is such a potentially far-reaching provision that it is natural that it has been interpreted strictly. Most of the cases in which is has been found to be applicable are very different from social welfare matters. However, an enterprise which has public service obligations imposed on it may be relieved of some of the consequences of Treaty rules, for instance, on State aids, insofar as that is necessary to enable it to finance its public service obligations and to break even.[47] The Article applies only if the tasks have been entrusted by an act of a public authority, and the tasks must be clearly identified and defined in order to justify any exemption from Treaty rules.

Article 86(2) EC allows undertakings entrusted with the operation of services of general economic interest to be relieved from the duties imposed by Community competition law only 'in so far as the application of such rules would obstruct the performance, in law or in fact, of the particular tasks assigned to them'. As already mentioned, Article 86 EC would be clearer if it had been written 'Even in the case of public undertakings ... (and *a fortiori* in the case of all other enterprises) Member States shall not enact or maintain ...' Article 86 EC creates the exception in Article 86(2) EC, but it does not create any other special substantive rule. That is why the Court has said that it is only an example of the general principle stated in Article 10 EC.[48] A legitimate purpose must be in the general interest, that is, it must not be for the benefit of any private persons or a limited group of persons. Any restriction on competition must be necessary to enable the enterprise to do the job it has been given, or to enable it to do its job on a financially acceptable basis, that is, not incurring substantial losses as a result of being required to carry on some unprofitable activities.

In *Commission v Spain*[49] ('golden shares') the Court of Justice said that if Article 86(2) EC is said to apply 'the Member State must set out in detail the reasons for which, in the event of the elimination of the contested measures, the performance under economically acceptable conditions of the tasks of general economic interest which it has entrusted to an undertaking would in its view be jeopardised.'

---

[47] Case C–280/00 *Altmark Trans* [2003] ECR I–7747.
[48] Case 13/77 *Inno v Atab* [1977] ECR 2115, paras 30–31.
[49] Case C–463/00 *Commission v Spain* [2003] ECR I–4581 para 82; see Case C–157/94 *Commission v Netherlands* [1997] ECR I–5699, para 39.

The tasks recognised as falling under Article 86(2) EC have included controlling navigation on an important waterway,[50] a universal and continuous mooring service at ports,[51] operating the public telephone network,[52] broadcasting television,[53] operating the national public electricity supply,[54] the basic postal service,[55] supplementary pension schemes,[56] operating an unprofitable air route for reasons of the general interest,[57] and management of environmentally undesirable waste.[58] However, private interests are not providing services of general economic interest for the purposes of Article 86(2) EC unless some specific tasks have been assigned to them by the State.[59]

The specific purposes and factual situations on which such exclusive rights are justified, insofar as relevant to social welfare, are considered below.

I The Justification for Monopolies and Special Rights for Services of General Economic Interest under Article 86(2) EC

Exclusive rights (ie, monopolies) and special rights (ie, rights granted to a strictly limited number of companies) have often been accepted, in most cases without serious analysis, in EU law cases. In most of these cases the justification for the exclusive or special rights was clear and uncontested. However, in a number of other cases the monopoly was challenged, and in some of these it was not justified.

---

[50] Case 10/71 *Müller* [1971] ECR 725.

[51] Case C–266/96 *Corsica Ferries* [1998] ECR I–3949.

[52] See Case 41/83 *(British Telecommunications)* [1985] ECR 873; Case C–18/88 *GB-Inno BM* [1991] ECR I–5941.

[53] Case 155/73 *Sacchi* [1974] ECR 409, paras 15–17; Case C–260/89 *ERT* [1991] ECR I–2925; Case T–69/89 *Radio Telefis Eirann v Commission* [1991] ECR II–485, para 82. But see *Television Advertising in Flanders*, 1997 OJ L244/18, Case T–266/97 *Vlaamse Televisie Maatschappij v Commission* [1999] ECR II–2329. The BBC fell within what is now Art 86(2) EC *BBC/Valley Printing*, Sixth Report on Competition Policy (1976), point 163.

[54] Case C–393/92 *Almelo* [1994] ECR I–1477; Case C–157/94 *Commission v Netherlands* [1997] ECR I–5699; Case C–158/94 *Commission v Italy* [1997] ECR I–5789 and Case C–159/94 *Commission v France* [1997] ECR I–5815. Similarly for water authorities, see Case 96/82 *IAZ* [1983] ECR 3369 and the Commission's decision in *NAVEWA-ANSEAU*, 1982 OJ L167/39.

[55] Case C–320/91 *Corbeau* [1993] ECR I–2533; Case T–106/95 *FFSA* [1997] ECR II–229; Joined Cases C–147/97 and C–148/97 *Deutsche Post v GZS and Citicorp* [2000] ECR I–825.

[56] The *Dutch Pension Funds* cases: Case C–67/96 *Albany* [1999] ECR I–5751; Cases C–115 to 117/97 *Brentjens* [1999] ECR I–6025; Case C–219/97 *Drijvende Bokken* [1999] ECR I–6121.

[57] Case 66/86 *Ahmed Saeed* [1989] ECR 803; Case T–260/94 *Air Inter v Commission* [1997] ECR II–997.

[58] Case C–209/98 *Sydhavnens Sten & Grus* [2000] ECR I–3743, paras 75–76; Case C–203/96 *Dusseldorp* [1998] ECR I–4075, paras 53–68.

[59] Case 127/73 *BRT v SABAM* [1974] ECR 313; Case 7/82 *GVL* [1983] ECR 483; Case C–179/90 *Porto di Genova* [1991] ECR I–5889; Case C–242/95 *GT-Link* [1997] ECR I–4449; Cf Case C–266/96 *Corsica Ferries* [1998] ECR I–3949.

Of these cases, the judgment most likely to be relevant to health services is *Corbeau*,[60] although it dealt with a postal monopoly. The justification claimed for the monopoly was that some postal services are inevitably unprofitable, and that a post office with a universal service obligation and postal rates which are the same for everyone must be able to cross-subsidise if it is to break even overall. It therefore needs to be protected against competitors which would 'cherry pick' the profitable services and leave it with the unprofitable ones, which would force it to raise postal rates unacceptably. The Court accepted this, but held that the justification did not apply to an express postal service, recently introduced, which was not essential for financial balance. The judgment therefore confirms that any statutory monopoly needs a justification, and that the justification must be looked at carefully to see how far it validly extends. The judgment has little relevance in cases where different kinds of justification are suggested.

The *Corbeau* judgment is important because it shows that there must be a precise reason for saying that the restriction on competition is needed to enable the monopoly to carry out its task, or to do so on a break-even basis. It would not be enough to say that a monopoly would enable the enterprise to make more money, and that it would then be better able to invest and improve its services. The monopoly must be a necessary element in its financial stability.

The *Corbeau* judgment is important in any case in which a monopoly is said to be justified to allow an enterprise to break even, in spite of a public service obligation which obliges it to provide some services on an unprofitable basis (in other words, where the justification for the monopoly is economic or financial). This could arise in connection with for instance an ambulance service, which may be obliged to be available at all times to provide services, some of which will be performed at a loss. In this context, it does not seem to make a difference who pays for each service, if the officially authorised payment is a standard one which sometimes does not cover the cost of providing the service.

In *Dusseldorp*[61] the Court said that rules giving an undertaking an exclusive right to process dangerous waste are illegal 'if, without any objective justification and without being necessary for the performance of a task in the general interest, those rules have the effect of favouring the national undertaking and increasing its dominant position.'

---

[60] Case C–320/91 *Corbeau* [1993] ECR I–2533. The cases in which a monopoly is needed for simple practical or physical reasons (one cannot have more than one authority controlling traffic, it may not make sense to have more than one national electricity grid) do not seem relevant to social welfare cases. See also Case C–340/99 *TNT Traco v Poste Italiane* [2001] ECR I–4109, paras 54–58 (contributions paid by competitors to the cost of providing a universal service); LM Soriano, 'How proportionate should anti-competitive State measures be?' (2003) 28 *Europeon Law Review* 112.

[61] Case C–203/96 *Dusseldorp* [1998] ECR I–4075, para 68; Cf Case C–159/94 *Commission v France* [1997] ECR I–5815, para 49 (exclusive right to import and export electricity, may be justified under Article 86(2) EC).

On ambulance services, the principal case is *Glöckner*,[62] in which the issue was the lawfulness of a measure extending a monopoly for the provision of non-emergency ambulance services over a defined geographical area. The Court confirmed that a medical aid organisation which provides services for payment by users is an enterprise, and that as only a limited number of organisations had been licensed, they held 'special' rights under Article 86 EC. The Court, rather surprisingly, said that the national court was asking 'essentially' whether the measure created a situation in which medical aid organisations are led to infringe Article 82 EC. Having thus altered the question, the Court repeated that 'the mere creation of a dominant position through the grant of special or exclusive rights is not in itself illegal', and went on:

> A Member State will be in breach of [Articles 82 and 86 EC] only if the undertaking in question, merely by exercising the special or exclusive rights conferred upon it, is led to abuse its dominant position, or where such rights are liable to create a situation in which that undertaking is led to commit such abuses.

The Court then went on to rule that the grant of an exclusive right to provide non-emergency services to companies which already had exclusive rights to provide emergency services (ie, the extension of a dominant position) limited markets, contrary to Article 82(b) EC. The Court decided that this was justified under Article 86(2) EC, because the revenue from non-emergency transport helps to cover the cost of emergency services. Unlike *Corbeau*, in this case emergency and non-emergency services were closely linked, and the non-emergency revenue enabled the services to break even. However, if they had been unable to meet the demand, the monopoly would be unjustifiable (the *Höfner* principle).

It will be seen that:

— The Court was not asked by the national court to consider whether the *original* monopoly for emergency services was justified.
— The *extension* of the monopoly by the official measure was contrary to Articles 82 and 86 EC: *GB-Inno BM* was cited specifically for this statement, as was *Dusseldorp*.
— The statement that an official measure is illegal *only* if it leads to abuse committed by the dominant enterprise appears inconsistent with the statement that the extension, though an official measure and not through any act of the dominant company, and without evidence that any abuse is likely, is incompatible with Articles 82 and 86 EC. In both *Glöckner* and *Dusseldorp*, the Court considered that the measure limited production, contrary to these Articles,

---

[62] Case C–475/99 *Ambulanz Glöckner* [2001] ECR I–8089.

even without any act of the enterprise. There are two possible explanations. First, the limitation of production could be attributed to the enterprise (on the assumption that it will assert exclusive rights, if it has any, or on the basis that the extension of dominance is not something which the enterprise could lawfully do). Second, more convincingly, the statement that a measure is illegal *only* if it leads to an abuse by the dominant enterprise is applicable when the only objection to the grant of a monopoly is that it is likely to lead to an abuse, but irrelevant if the extension of dominance through a State measure is illegal in itself unless there is justification.

In other words, in *Glöckner* the Court has confirmed the ruling in *GB-Inno BM* and *Dusseldorp* that an official measure extending a dominant position can be illegal, but without explicitly reconciling that view with the statement about abuse, (and without considering how far it is unlawful to create a dominant position, as distinct from extending one).[63]

The Court has not had to consider the situation in which changing circumstances in the sector in question would make it no longer necessary to protect an enterprise with public service obligations, or subject to price control, from competition. However, exclusive or special rights, if they are to be legal, must be justifiable at all times. Also, it might become justifiable to confer exclusive rights, for instance if the area of an ambulance service was enlarged and due to for example, universal service obligations it was not allowed to charge more for services carried out over longer distances.

In *Sydhavnens Sten & Grus*[64] the Court accepted the argument that an exclusive right was necessary to make a high-capacity waste management plant profitable—in effect, to ensure the maximum obtainable economies of scale. The exclusive right was 'limited in time to the period over which the investments could foreseeably be written off and in space to the land within the boundaries' of Copenhagen. In other words, an exclusive right which is not needed for physical or practical purposes is justified to avoid net losses (otherwise the service would not be provided), but is not justified merely to increase profits.

---

[63] When a judgment contains two apparently inconsistent statements without reconciling them explicitly, it is sometimes a sign of an unresolved disagreement within the Court: see the Opinion of the Advocate General in Case C–209/98 *Sydhavnens Sten & Grus* [2000] ECR I–3743, pp 3763–66.

[64] Case C–209/98 *Sydhavnens Sten & Grus* [2000] ECR I–3743, paras 77–81; Cf Joined Cases C–147/97 and C–148/97 *Deutsche Post v GZS and Citicorp* [2000] ECR I–825, paras 49–54 (the right of a statutory postal monopoly to charge for delivering incoming international mail, in order to operate under 'economically acceptable conditions'); Joined Cases C–115/97 and others *Brentjens* [1999] ECR I–6025, para 107; Case C–157/99 *Geraets-Smits and Peerbooms* [2001] ECR I–5473.

L Services of General Economic Interest

Some steps have been taken to define the range of services that Member States may declare to be of general economic interest and therefore capable of being exempted from Treaty rules.[65] Whether to designate any particular service is a matter for each Member State. Article 16 EC says that 'services of general economic interest' should operate on the basis of principles and conditions which enable them to fulfil their missions. This seems to add nothing to Article 86(2) EC. EU law governs the procedures for selecting enterprises to be made responsible for these services, as well as the privileges which may be conferred on them to ensure that they break even or can make a limited profit.

II AFTER PRIVATISATION

A 'Enterprises'

In general hospitals, clinics, ambulance services and self-employed doctors are all 'enterprises' for the purpose of competition rules. However, public hospitals which provide all their services free and which are financed by the State are not.

A health insurance fund is not an enterprise if it is based on 'solidarity', that is, if it receives standard contributions, offers standard services, is non-profit making, and membership is compulsory. It is an enterprise if members have a choice as to the level of their contributions and benefits, and if the body decides its own contribution rates and benefits—in short, if it is run as a business, is intended to be self-financing, and does not simply redistribute whatever funds it receives.[66] An economic activity which competes with life

---

[65] The Commission has adopted two Communications on services of general economic interest: 1996 OJ C281/3 and 2001 OJ C17/4; see also the Report to the Laeken European Council, Services of General Interest, COM(2001) 598 final.

[66] Case C–41/90 *Höfner and Elser* [1991] ECR I–1979, para 21; Joined Cases C–159 and 160/91 *Poucet* and *Pistre* [1993] ECR I–637; Case C–244/94 *Fédération Française des Sociétés d'Assurance* [1995] ECR I–4013; Case C–67/96 *Albany* [1999] ECR I–5751; Cases C–155 to 157/97 *Brentjens* [1999] ECR I–6025; C–219/97 *Drijvende Bokken* [1999] ECR I–6121 (the Dutch social fund cases). Joined Cases C–180 to C–184/98 *Pavlov* [2000] ECR I–6451 (self-employed medical specialists who provide medical services, who are paid by their patients and who bear the financial risks resulting from that activity are 'enterprises' even though the practice of their profession is regulated); AG Fennely's Opinion in Case C–222/98 *Van der Woude* [2000] ECR I–7111, pp 7120–21 and 7123 (a 'collective agreement with social policy objectives of a kind which justify the exclusion of the competition rules'); Case C–368/98 *Van Graekel* [2001] ECR I–5363; Case C–157/99 *Peerbooms* [2001] ECR I–5473; Case C–475/99 *Ambulanz Glöckner* [2001] ECR I–8089; Case C–218/01 *Cisal di Battistello*, 22 January 2002; Case C–309/99 *Wouters* [2002] ECR I–1577 (lawyers are enterprises); Case C–35/99 *Arduino* [2002] ECR I–1529. See generally V Hatzopoulos, 'Killing the national health systems but healing patients?' (2002) 39 *Common Market Law Review* 683. On the status of the professions under EU competition law, see also: Case C–221/99 *Conte v Rossi*; Case C–309/99 *Wouters* [2002] ECR I–1577; Case T–144/99 *EPI v Commission* [2001] ECR I–1087.

assurance companies is clearly an enterprise. But a social welfare body is not an enterprise merely because it is a large *buyer* of products or services.[67]

The production in a hospital of a substance used for medical services is an economic activity, even if it is paid for from public funds and not by the patients.[68]

B Consultative Bodies

The case law distinguishes between companies being represented on consultative bodies, which is legal as long as official powers are exercised by an official authority, and situations in which a dominant enterprise or a group of companies are themselves allowed to take the operative decisions or to exercise official regulatory powers, which is illegal.[69] It is lawful for prices to be proposed by committees including representatives of enterprises, provided that the legislation granting the power to propose prices requires the public interest to be taken into account (so that judicial review would be possible on this ground) and the public authority has power to alter or override the committee's proposal.[70]

C The Right to Join Together to Lobby for Regulatory Measures

EU law recognises, implicitly and rather imprecisely, the right of enterprises to join together to request legislative or other governmental policy changes.[71]

---

[67] Case T–319/99 *Federación Nacional de Empresas de Instrumentación* [2003] ECR II–357, para 37.

[68] Case C–203/99 *Henning Veedfald* [2001] ECR I–3569; Case C–157/99 *BSM Smits/Stichting Ziekenfonds* [2001] ECR I–5473; Case C–368/98 *Abdon Vanbraekel* [2001] ECR I–5363.

[69] See eg, Case C–96/94 *Centro Servizi Spediporto* [1995] ECR I–2883; Case C–140/94 *DIP v Comune di Bassano* [1995] ECR I–3257; Case C–70/95 *Sodemare v Regione Lombardia* [1997] ECR I–3395 (social welfare healthcare services: a Member State may decide to allow only non-profit making operators to provide social welfare, under contracts refunding their expenses to them); Case C–38/97 *Librandi* [1998] ECR I–5955; Case C–266/96 *Corsica Ferries* [1998] ECR I–3949; Case C–35/96 *Commission v Italy* [1998] ECR I–3851 (legislation allowing a price set by a national committee of customs agents, to be charged by all customs agents, is illegal: the national legislation 'wholly relinquished to private economic operators the powers of the public authorities as regards the setting of tariffs'); Case T–513/93 *CNSD v Commission* [2000] ECR II–1807.

[70] Cf Case C–38/97 *Librandi* [1998] ECR I–5955, para 29 and Case C–35/96 *Commission v Italy* [1998] ECR I–3851.

[71] J Temple Lang, 'EEC competition action in Member States' courts—claims for damages, declarations and injunctions for breach of Community antitrust law' in BE Hawk (ed), *Annual Proceedings of the Fordham Corporate Law Institute 1983* (1984) 219, 260–62; J Temple Lang, 'Trade associations and self-regulation under EEC antitrust law' in BE Hawk (ed), *Annual Proceedings of the Fordham Corporate Law Institute 1984* (1985) 605, 649–50; J Temple Lang, 'Reconciling European Community antitrust and antidumping, transport and trade safeguard policies—practical problems' in BE Hawk (ed), *Annual Proceedings of the Fordham Corporate Law Institute 1988* (1989) Ch 7. In joined Cases

This right exists even if the changes desired would restrict competition in a way which it would be illegal for the enterprises themselves to attempt. Legally, this principle allows companies to ask for legislation to restrict competition, but does not allow them to behave as if the legislation had already been enacted. It is this principle which allows, among other things, trade associations to make antidumping complaints, the aim and effect of which is to raise prices. A broadly similar principle in US antitrust law, Noerr-Pennington immunity, has been the subject of substantial case law, and much criticism. Nevertheless, some such principle is necessary in a democracy. The principle in EU law is potentially relevant to for instance, joint submissions to public authorities by the medical profession and by hospitals and insurance companies.

In EU law, the principle is in substance that it is lawful for competitors to join together solely for the purpose of urging or influencing official action. However, the principle would probably not apply if the State action requested would itself infringe EU law. In any case, a campaign to propose a measure could not legitimise anticompetitive behaviour by the lobbyists, and if there is no anticompetitive behaviour, no defence is needed. Certainly it would not apply if the campaign was merely a disguise for a concerted exchange of price information or other conduct influencing competitors' behaviour directly.[72] Probably it would not make lawful any discussion of a specific price level to be recommended for official adoption, and it would certainly be illegal to exchange price information which was not strictly necessary to reach agreement on the submission to the authorities. On the other hand, the principle should *not* be limited to situations in which the governmental authorities have set up consultation mechanisms or have taken the initiative in some other way. There are special rules applicable to the development of officially recognised standards.[73] The principle applies to both lobbying for Member State action and lobbying for action by the EU institutions.

The right to associate in order to lobby for official action is protected by Article 10 of the European Convention on Human Rights (freedom of expression) and Article 11 (freedom of association), but these

---

C–180/98 to C–184/98 *Pavlov* [2000] ECR I–6451, paras 98–99, the Court said that it was not contrary to Article 81 for an organisation representing members of a profession to request public authorities to make membership of an occupational pension scheme which it had set up compulsory, because similar regimes are designed to promote the creation of secondary pensions, and include safeguards. Clearly this is not a blank cheque. See also Case C–67/96 *Albany International* [1999] ECR I–5751, paras 52–70 (agreement not contrary to Article 81 EC, so it cannot be unlawful to ask for it to be made compulsory).

[72] AG Capotorti's Opinion Case 82/77 *Van Tiggele* [1978] ECR 25, p 48.
[73] J Temple Lang, 'European Community antitrust law: innovation markets and high technology industries' in BE Hawk (ed), *Annual Proceedings of the Fordham Corporate Law Institute 1996* (1997) 519, 567–70; M Dolmans, 'Standards for Standards' (2002) 26 *Fordham International Law Journal* 163.

Articles do not significantly clarify the scope of the exemption from EU competition law.

It is important to note that under EU law a national competition or regulatory authority is bound by the same rules of EU law as any other national authority, and so a regulatory authority has no power to approve or authorise a breach of EU competition law, except to the extent permitted by Article 86(2) EC.[74] This means that a national authority cannot legitimise a breach of Article 81 EC by inviting enterprises for example to agree on a price to be charged for a given service. Companies and individuals need to be careful when offering advice to public authorities even when they have been asked to do so.

D Exchanges of Information between Competitors

Agreements between competitors to exchange information which would otherwise normally be confidential are likely to be illegal, in particular if the sector is oligopolistic and if price information is exchanged. Aggregated statistical information, not identifying any individual enterprise, on the total production, capacity, and sales of an industry may be compiled. Even information identifying individual enterprises may be exchanged if it is out of date and no longer relevant to their future behaviour.[75] The exchange of information on costs, in particular on total costs or on the cost of the most significant inputs, would normally be illegal.

E Influence Resulting from Minority Interests: Article 81

Although the rule has rarely been applied, under EU law a minority shareholding resulting from an agreement between the two companies involved is subject to Article 81 EC if the result is to give the shareholder company influence over a competitor.[76] However, Article 81 EC (as distinct from the EU Merger Regulation) does not apply to acquisition of shares on the stock exchange, or in other circumstances involving no agreement between the new shareholder and the company in which the shares are held.

---

[74] Case 66/86 *Ahmed Saeed* [1989] ECR 803; Case C–35/96 *Commission v Italy* [1998] ECR I–3851; Case T–513/93 *CNSD v Commission* [2000] ECR II–1807; Case C–198/01 *Fiammiferi* [2003] ECR I–0000.

[75] Case T–34/92 *Fiatagri* [1994] ECR II–905 and Case T–35/92 *John Deere* [1994] ECR II–957; on appeal, Case C–7/95P *John Deere* [1998] ECR I–3111 and Case C–8/95 *New Holland Ford* [1998] ECR I–3175; Case T–16/98 *Wirtschaftsvereinigung Stahl* [2001] ECR II–1217; Commission, *XXIX Report on Competition Policy* (1999) pp 156–58.

[76] Joined Cases 142 and 156/84 *British American Tobacco and Reynolds* ('the Philip Morris case') [1987] ECR 4487; *Gillette*, 1993 OJ L116/21; *Microsoft-Liberty Media-Telewest*, European Commission, *XXX Competition Policy Report* (2000) pp 186–87; JTemple Lang, 'International joint ventures under Community law' in BE Hawk (ed), *Annual Proceedings of the Fordham Corporate Law Institute 1999* (2000) 381, 423–27.

F Cross-subsidies

Cross-subsidies (using profits from one kind of activity to compensate for losses incurred on another kind of activity carried on by the same enterprise) may be relevant in EU competition law in three ways.

First, if the loss-making activity is deliberately carried on by a dominant enterprise at a price below the relevant average variable costs (so that every transaction results in a loss which would not otherwise be incurred), that is predatory (unfairly low) pricing, which is illegal under Article 82 EC.[77]

Second, if a dominant enterprise carries on an activity at a selective price below its average total costs of that activity, and if there is sufficient other evidence (whether of its intentions or from other anticompetitive conduct)[78] that this is being done deliberately to force a competitor out of the market, the conduct (including the selective price) can be illegal under Article 82.

Third, the need for cross-subsidies may be inevitable in providing a service on the basis of a standard charge, if the cost of providing the service varies greatly in individual cases. In these circumstances a State measure protecting the enterprise from 'cherry picking' competition (in practice, to ensure that it can carry out a general public service obligation without incurring losses overall) can be justified, as explained below in this paper.

G Price Fixing to Counteract Monopsony Power

In various industries the argument is sometimes heard that suppliers of goods or services should be allowed to fix prices in order to counteract the power of buyers. This argument might be suggested in defence of price-fixing agreements between doctors or hospitals which are designed to improve their position in negotiations with insurance companies.

Such an argument has always been rejected in competition law, because the result would be either to increase the ultimate price to the consumer (whoever pays it) or to alter the division of profits between the two parts of

---

[77] Case C–62/86 *Akzo* [1991] ECR I-3359; see the Commission decision in *Deutsche Post*, 2001 OJ L125/27. The Court of Justice has indicated that cross-subsidies can be illegal, but the circumstances envisaged were not defined and probably predatory prices were envisaged; Case C–179/90 *Merci Convenzionali Porto di Genova* [1991] ECR I–5889, para 19; *Guidelines on the Application of the EEC Competition Rules in the Telecommunications Sector*, 1991 OJ C233/2, para 86 (on predatory prices due to cross-subsidies); Cf *Napp Pharmaceutical Holdings v Director General of Fair Trading*, UK Competition Appeal Tribunal (15 January 2002) [2002] ECC 13.

[78] J Temple Lang and RO'Donoghue, 'Defining legitimate competition: how to clarify pricing abuses under Article 82 EC' (2002) 26 *Fordham International Law Journal* 83; J Temple Lang, 'Some current problems of applying Article 82 EC' in C Baudenbacher (ed), *Neueste Entwicklungen im europäischen und internationalen Kartellrecht* (Helbing & Lichtenhahn, 2000) 57, 63–73 and 89–96.

the industry, which (whatever its other merits) would provide no benefit for consumers. Even if the insurance industry itself was fixing prices, that would not justify hospitals or doctors in doing so (although it would entitle them to complain to competition authorities). Collective price fixing between suppliers is unlawful even if the buyers of the services are also involved in the price fixing, so that collective negotiations between doctors, hospitals and insurance companies would also be illegal.

H The Need to Protect the National Health Service as a Buyer

The National Health Service is, and any equivalent body will presumably continue to be, a major buyer of healthcare services. It is therefore likely that competition law will be used whenever appropriate to reduce or stabilise the prices of goods or services provided to the NHS,[79] or the prices of important inputs into those services. This vigilance would be especially likely during the first years after privatisation.

I The Implications of the Merger Control Regulation

The Merger Regulation, Regulation 4064/89,[80] applies to mergers and to the establishment of 'full-function' (ie, self-sufficient) joint ventures if the turnover of the companies involved exceeds certain thresholds. Below these levels, national merger laws apply. Privatisation is subject to the Merger Regulation when it involves, as it almost always does, a lasting change of control. A change of control is illegal if it creates or strengthens a dominant position.

Privatisation may be in stages, or all at once. It may result in acquisition of sole control or acquisition of joint control or ownership by a number of unrelated shareholders. In the case of joint control, one of the two or more controlling entities may be the State, if the State acting as a shareholder must agree to strategic decisions of the enterprise in question, and has a real possibility of vetoing decisions of the other parent. The fact that the State might also have regulatory or legislative powers over the enterprise is irrelevant for this purpose, if its powers are exercisable only in limited circumstances and to protect the general interest.[81] Joint control may also result from a shareholders' agreement.

---

[79] See eg Monopolies and Mergers Commission (UK), *IMS Health Inc and Pharmaceutical Marketing Services Inc: A report on the merger situation (1999)* <http://www.competition-commission.org.uk/rep_pub/reports/1999/fulltext/425c1.pdf>.

[80] Regulation 4064/98 on the control of concentrations between undertakings, 1990 OJ L257/13.

[81] Case C–503/99 *Commission v Belgium* [2002] ECR I–4809.

Where social welfare or other State activities are privatised in such a way that more than one new enterprise is created, so that there is scope for competition between them which did not exist before, that would not necessarily be a defence if one of them was acquired by a third enterprise which already had, or would thereby obtain, a dominant position.

If privatisation leads to the creation of more than one new enterprise, the possibility that they may be jointly dominant may need to be considered.[82]

III THE PRIVATISATION PROCESS

Privatisation can be done on a large scale or a small scale.[83] However, it always involves converting existing public bodies into companies, if they are not already companies, and then putting the companies into private ownership, on some appropriate financial basis. This second step is subject to certain constraints under competition law.

The fact that there will be more competition after privatisation than there was before is not sufficient to justify whatever restrictions on competition may remain, or to justify imposing new ones. Restrictions on competition are not justified by mere administrative convenience, or to increase the value of the businesses being privatised so as to increase the price to be paid for it. Whatever restrictions on competition may be in force at any given time must be justified in the circumstances at that time.

As soon as each hospital, fund or other service has become an enterprise and therefore is subject to the competition rules, it is treated for competition law purposes like any other new business. It is not free, for example, to make price fixing agreements with other newly-privatised enterprises merely to stabilise or strengthen its financial position. Similarly, the government authority responsible for the privatisation must not authorise or encourage anticompetitive arrangements between the entities being privatised.

It follows that if a medical service or an ambulance is privatised on a basis which protects it from competition and gives it a dominant position in for instance, a region, the monopoly or other privileged position must be justified by some objective in the general interest, and there must be no less restrictive way of achieving the objective identified.

The most frequently suggested justification is that the service in question is self-supporting financially (if indeed it can be self-supporting) only through cross-subsidies, because some of its services will necessarily be provided at a loss and others will be more than paid for by the payments made (from whatever source) for them. This is discussed below.

---

[82] J Temple Lang, 'Oligopolies and joint dominance in Community antitrust law' in BE Hawk (ed), *Annual Proceedings of the Fordham Corporate Law Institute 2001* (2002) 269–359.
[83] See Commission, *XXIII Report on Competition Policy* (1993) pp 30–34.

The privatisation should not be structured in such a way that competition will be unnecessarily or unjustifiably restricted after privatisation, for instance, by privatising vertically integrated operations having a dominant position at one level which could be used to restrict competition at another level. For example, a medical fund having a dominant position in a given region should not be privatised in common ownership with a hospital, since it would have both an opportunity and an incentive to discriminate in favour of its associated hospital.[84] In other words, the privatisation process must be carried out in such a way as to allow normal competition after it is completed, except insofar as restrictions on competition at that stage may be necessary.

A Member State is not free, without sufficient justification, to adopt a measure restricting competition so much that the measure creates or reinforces a dominant position. However, in other respects a State is not obliged to divide up the operations to be privatised in such a way that none of them will have a dominant position after privatisation, provided that the dominance so created is not protected by any regulatory or other official measure. So a State is not obliged to divide the operations being privatised into small pieces merely to ensure that no one of them is dominant. Dominance may result from privatising a large entity, a large block of operations, or all the former publicly-run activities in a large region. As long as the privatised entity is not protected from competition by any official measures, the fact that it may initially be dominant is legal.

However, when privatisation is decided upon, the policy normally is based on the idea that competition is desirable. There would be no point merely in converting a State monopoly into a private monopoly. So the privatised entities in practice are designed so that they can become efficient competitors of one another. This may mean that although an enterprise is dominant at the time it is privatised, its dominance may be short-lived. If the apparent dominance is certain to end soon, it may not be regarded as dominance for EU competition law purposes—but the enterprise may be tempted to use its declining market power to restrict competition, for instance by making contracts 'tying' the services for which it is exposed to competition with the services for which it is still dominant or nearly dominant.

The change from public to private ownership of an already dominant enterprise does not, in itself, create or extend a dominant position. However, if an already dominant enterprise is acquired by a competitor, the effect may be to extend or consolidate the existing dominant position. The fact that the enterprise being privatised is the acquired rather than the acquirer is not necessarily a defence, as the economic consequences are essentially similar. However, the Commission's policy is to apply Article 86

---

[84] Cf Case C–163/96 *Silvano Raso* [1998] ECR I–533.

EC (as distinct from the Merger Regulation) only when the acquirer is dominant.

Privatisation in several parts of what had previously been a single entity may make it necessary to formalise relationships between the parts, and the resulting agreements may have to be looked at under Article 81 EC.[85]

When a Member State decides to sell the shares in a previously State-owned enterprise, it must offer the shares to potential buyers in a non-discriminatory manner, without discriminating on the basis of nationality. The State must not limit the freedom of investors to acquire controlling interests in the company being privatised or to exercise control when acquired.[86] However, a State may retain the means of exercising control insofar as this might be necessary to protect a public interest in for example, energy supply networks.

IV CONCLUSIONS

A Regulation may Still be Needed after Privatisation

Until the market is fully competitive, regulation may still be needed after privatisation to correct or avoid the effects of market imperfections, and of course it may be needed on a permanent basis to ensure for instance that doctors are properly trained, or that unapproved drugs are not prescribed. Regulation may be needed to determine how much hospitals may charge for services, or to specify what services will be paid for out of public funds. Regulation may be needed to prevent for example cross-subsidies within a newly privatised entity, to prevent it from competing unfairly against privately owned competitors.

Regulation may also be useful to make clear obligations that would in any case arise under competition law. For example, an enterprise operating partly in a competitive market and partly in a market in which it was dominant may be tempted to 'tie' its services, by providing the services for which it is dominant only on condition that the buyer also takes the services for which it is exposed to competition. That can, depending on the circumstances, be contrary to Article 82 EC, but it might also be useful to prohibit it explicitly by regulatory measures, or to say in what circumstances it might be permissible.

---

[85] M Siragusa, 'Privatisation and EU Competition Law' in BE Hawk (ed), *Annual Proceedings of the Fordham Corporate Law Institute 1995* (1996) 375, 426–31.

[86] The 'golden share' cases: Case C–483/99 *Commission v France* [2002] ECR I–4781; Case C–367/98 *Commission v Portugal* [2002] ECR I–4732; Case C–503/99 *Commission v Belgium* [2002] ECR I–4809; Case C–463/00 *Commission v Spain* [2003] ECR I–4581; Case C–98/01 *Commission v UK* [2003] ECR I–4641.

If some regulation is under consideration, doctors, hospitals or other interests may be consulted, or may consider lobbying, and in those circumstances the extent of their freedom to do so under EU competition law, discussed above, would be relevant.

Regulation may limit the freedom of the regulated enterprises to compete. Competition authorities may rely on regulatory authorities to enforce obligations, such as duties not to discriminate, which might otherwise have to be imposed and enforced under competition law. Price control, if it is necessary, should be done under regulatory powers rather than competition law.

A company has a right under EU law to insist that its competitors comply with at least some kinds of regulatory requirements.[87]

Regulatory measures of these kinds must comply with Article 86 EC or, if no enterprise subject to Article 86 EC is involved, with Article 10 EC.

B Social Welfare Payments, Health Funds and Payments for Medical Services

Social welfare involves both provision of services and provision of money. Social welfare payments can be made, to whoever is entitled to receive them, through banks or post offices. Payments for medical services provided to someone else is a form of insurance, and can be privatised and regulated accordingly, as far as thought necessary.

This means that a privatised health fund or system for paying social welfare benefits will be operating in a wholly different market and will have a wholly different group of competitors from a hospital.

It would be illegal under EU law for a government to confer on for instance the post office the task of making social welfare payments, without going through the normal procedure for public contracts. This would be illegal whether the task conferred is a public contract (a service for which the State pays the contractor) or a concession (a service for which the public pays the contractor). It would also be illegal whether or not the arrangement involved State aid to the enterprise to which the tasks were given.

Health funds, at least those which administer national insurance schemes, and other groups and organisations which exercise some power over individuals and which are in a position to impose conditions which adversely affect the exercise of the fundamental freedoms guaranteed by the Treaty, may not discriminate on the grounds of nationality.[88] Such bodies are in a quasi-regulatory position which makes their actions similar to those of a State.[89]

---

[87] Case C–253/00 *Muñoz and Superior Fruiticola* [2002] ECR I–7289; cf Case C–453/99 *Courage v Crehan* [2001] ECR I–6297.

[88] Case C–411/98 *Ferlini* [2000] ECR I–8082, para 50; Case 36/74 *Walrave v Koch* [1974] ECR 1405; Case 43/75 *Defrenne v Sabena* [1976] ECR 455; Case C–415/93 *Bosman* [1995] ECR I–4921.

[89] AG Cosmas' Opinion; in Case C–411/98 *Ferlini* [2000] ECR I–8081, pp 8106–8.

C Contributions from One Competitor to Another

In network industries such as telecommunications, new entrants are given a right to interconnect. It has been considered reasonable to allow Member States, when necessary, to require new entrants and other competitors to contribute to the cost of the universal service by making payments to the company providing it. Another situation, said to be analogous, arises where a long-established health insurance company, a former monopoly, has a much higher proportion of elderly (and therefore expensive) insured patients than the new entrants have. However, if there is no network relationship from which new entrants benefit and no universal service obligation, it is doubtful if any duty on competitors to contribute to the older company would be compatible with EU law.

D EU Law Aspects of Public-Private Partnerships

Public-Private Partnerships are a new and very varied type of contractual arrangement by which private finance and management join with governmental measures to provide an infrastructure or a capital asset which can be operated profitably, but which involves a large investment which the public authorities are unable or unwilling to finance fully or at all. Legally such partnerships involve, or may involve:

— Agreements for the supply of goods or services *to* the public authorities.
— A concession enabling the private interests to provide goods or services to the public on a privileged basis (a 'special or exclusive right' under Article 86 EC).
— State aid to the private interests involved.
— Sometimes, some protection against competition.
— Agreements between the members of any consortium which is involved.

The choice of the private partner for the first two purposes must be made in accordance with the normal procedures governing public contracts and granting of concessions.[90] State aids are outside the scope of this paper, but it is worth noting that if the partnership involves a joint venture from which the private partner makes a profit and the public partner a loss, this involves a State aid. Restrictions on competition, or on freedom of establishment and freedom to provide services, must comply with the principle

---

[90] See Commission interpretative communication on concessions under Community law, 2000 OJ C121/2; P Asbo Baistrocchi, 'Can the award of a public contract be deemed to constitute State aid?' (2003) 10 *European Competition Law Review* 510.

summarised above, that restrictions on freedoms granted or guaranteed by the Treaty must be imposed for a legitimate purpose in the public interest, and then only if no less restrictive measures would achieve the purpose.

In this context, the important point is that any restriction must be imposed in the public or general interest. A restriction, the principal aim or result of which is to increase the profits or reduce the losses of the private interests, is *not* justified, even if it is said that some such measure is needed to persuade them to invest. In other words, the justifications for restrictions of competition in favour of public-private partnerships are essentially the same as the justifications for any other restrictions on competition.

Public-private partnerships are only likely to be used or needed where there is very large capital expenditure involved. They are not likely to be needed for the operation of a service, even one of general economic interest.

It is important for public authorities involved in negotiation of public-private partnerships, which are often complicated, to avoid giving any unjustified protection against competition, and to avoid improving the terms given to the private interests to an extent which constitutes a State aid. It is also important to remember that the choice or approval for a consortium, given by the public authority partner for negotiating purposes, does not (and indeed could not) constitute authorisation or approval under competition law. A public authority partner would be wise to satisfy itself that a consortium with which it is negotiating is permissible under competition rules.

E Implications for Purchasers of Shares

Many of these rules have implications for potential purchasers of shares in privatised companies. It may be essential to know whether any protection against competition which a company has been given is valid or is open to challenge under EU law. Lawyers doing 'due diligence' investigations of companies being acquired need to understand clearly the possible consequences of all the rules discussed here.[91] Since there are no formal procedures for getting Commission approval for many kinds of national measures restricting competition (except for technical barriers[92] and State aids), lawyers advising investors need to be able to take the responsibility of assessing the risks. Since the Commission is not the ultimate judge of whether a national measure is permitted under EU law or not, the Commission cannot give a conclusive guarantee that a national measure is

[91] J Temple Lang, 'Precautions programmes, compliance programmes and strategies' (1999) 24 *European Law Review* 305.
[92] Directive 83/189 laying down a procedure for the provision of information in the field of technical standards and regulations 1983 OJ L109/8, as amended by Directive 88/182 1988 OJ L81/75.

lawful: that can be done only by the Court of Justice.[93] At most, the Commission can tie its own hands under the principle of legitimate expectations (similar to estoppel).[94]

F Conclusion

The basic EU law principles affecting privatisation of social welfare services may seem complex, but this is because they apply, or may apply, to a wide variety of situations. They give Member States a good deal of freedom, whether the State chooses a public-sector or a private-sector approach. What the rules mean, in brief, is that whichever approach is chosen, the State must respect the EU law rules applicable to that approach, unless the State has an objective in the general interest which genuinely can be achieved only by exemption from EU rules. If this exception applies, it does not matter whether the company providing the service of general interest is privately or publicly owned. The Court has applied these principles prudently, and it is understandable that neither the Commission nor any Advocate General has so far tried to summarise and synthesise all of the consequences of these principles, since they could hardly all arise in any one case.

In the USA, a series of Hearings are being held by the Department of Justice and the Federal Trade Commission on healthcare competition law and policy, and both authorities have brought antitrust proceedings against doctors, hospitals, and medical insurance funds. As the costs of medical care rise, public authorities in Europe are likely to make increasing use of competition law to bring them down, and the rules summarised here will become increasingly important in practice.

---

[93] Case C–415/93 *Bosman* [1995] ECR I–4921; Case C–393/98 *Valente* [2001] ECR I–1327.
[94] J Temple Lang, 'Legal certainty and legitimate expectations as general principles of law' in U Bernitz & J Nergelius (eds), *General Principles of European Community Law* (Kluwer, 2000) 163–84.

4

Aims, Effects and Justifications: EC State Aid Law and Its Impact on National Social Policies

ANDREA BIONDI & LUCA RUBINI*

I INTRODUCTION

The model adopted by the European Community Treaty as far as public financial intervention in the market is concerned, is based on the interplay of two main notions: 'that state aid distorts competition and must, therefore, be regulated and that the market does not function perfectly and some state aid may, therefore, be necessary'.[1] Thus, the framework of State aid regulation has been clearly designed to reconcile on the one side the prohibition on State intervention that may result in distortion within the market with the authorisation to fulfil, through financial assistance, certain objectives on the other.

The substantive and procedural regime sketched by the Treaty performs such a dual function. Article 87(1) EC, in laying down the necessary criteria for the definition of aid (advantage, selectivity, State imputability, use of State resources, distortion of competition, effect on trade), is based on the assumption that if a measure of financial assistance satisfies those requirements it should be deemed 'incompatible with the common market'. However, under Articles 87(2) and (3) EC, the alleged socio-economic objectives of the measure may be considered with the result that an otherwise incompatible aid becomes 'compatible with the common market'. Such an approach is reinforced by Article 86(2) EC, which provides that undertakings entrusted with the operation of public services should not be subjected to the EC rules on competition if these can affect the performance of the particular tasks assigned to these undertakings. The operation

---

King's College London.

[1] P Nicolaides, 'The New Frontier of State Aid Control—An Economic Assessment of Measures that Compensate Enterprises' (2002) 37 *Intereconomics* 190, 194.

of these provisions is different from that of Article 87(1) EC. While the latter involves an objective appraisal strictly based on an economic analysis of the negative effects on competition of the measure, the broad exceptions provided for require instead complex economic and social assessments of its redeeming impact and necessarily involve political and value (read: discretionary) judgements by the European Commission.[2] The Treaty itself thus acknowledges that a certain leeway is desirable in addressing market failures and in the pursuit of social or even economic objectives that the Community considers desirable but that cannot be achieved through market forces alone.[3] National governments may, for instance, grant aid to bridge the gap with regard to disadvantaged regions and to favour the creation of employment, to facilitate the adoption of higher environmental standards or to sustain investment in small and medium sized enterprises or in research and development.

However a clear separation between economic assessment and the presence of certain public objectives may prove difficult to achieve. This contribution will therefore examine the relationship between State aid and social welfare at two different levels. We first attempt to assess in general the relevance (if any) of national social policies for the operation of State aid rules. It is argued that, in particular, the European Court of Justice (ECJ) has been faced with the arduous task of trying to reconcile different needs. Secondly, the impact of State aid rules on the financing of public services is considered as a specific example of a possible tension between EC regulation of the market and State intervention.

II STATE AID AND SOCIAL OBJECTIVES: SCOPE, AIM AND JUSTIFICATIONS

It should be emphasised that not every form of State intervention in the market will be considered as State aid. As is well known, the ECJ has

---

[2] Such an operational difference has a significant impact on the procedural regime as well. Whereas it is only for the Commission to review plans of new aid and assess whether they are compatible with the common market, national courts enjoy more limited powers, being only allowed to order the recovery of any aid that is granted in contravention of the duties of prior notification and non-implementation embodied in Art 88(3) EC; see Case C–354/90 *FNCE* [1991] ECR I–5505, paras 8–14. On decentralisation of State aid control, see further M Ross, 'Decentralization, Effectiveness, and Modernization: Contradictions in Terms?' in A Biondi, P Eeckhout and J Flynn (eds), *The Law of State Aid in the European Union* (Oxford University Press, 2004) 85.

[3] In this sense, State aids are an important instrument of welfare or normative economics which is the study of how economic activities ought to be organised, as distinguished from positive economics which studies how economies actually work.

developed a very broad notion of 'state aid'. As early as 1961 it held in the *Steenkolenmijnen* case[4] that

> the concept of aid is ... wider than that of a subsidy because it embraces not only positive benefits, such as subsidies themselves, but also interventions which, in various forms, mitigate the charges which are normally included in the budget of an undertaking and which, without, therefore, being subsidies in the strict meaning of the word, are similar in character and have the same effect.[5]

Consistent case law of the Court has therefore clarified that 'aid' is to be defined in relation to its effects,[6] thus allowing the Court itself to subject many forms of governmental financial assistance to the Treaty provisions.[7]

However broad it may be, the definition of State aid—and consequently the scope of the State aid rules—does nevertheless find boundaries. The first obvious limits derive from the fact that the measure under scrutiny must satisfy all the requirements of Article 87(1) (advantage, selectivity, State imputability, transfer of State resources, distortion of competition, effect on intra-Community trade). More significantly, however, the Court of Justice has demonstrated in another respect that it does not yield to the temptation of over-expanding the notion of State aid, in particular, by transplanting from the internal market acquis the notion of a measure having equivalent effect to an aid. That was first evident in the *Poor Farmers* case,[8] and has more recently been confirmed in the *PreussenElektra* judgment.[9] In the latter case, the Court held that an obligation imposed on private electricity suppliers to purchase electricity produced from renewable energy sources at fixed minimum prices did not involve any direct or indirect transfer of State resources to undertakings which produced that type of electricity. More significantly with regard to our analysis, the Court also roundly rejected an argument presented by the Commission that, in order to preserve the effectiveness of State

---

4 The case concerned the interpretation of the concept of 'subsidy or aid' under Art 4(c) ECSC: 'The following are recognised as incompatible with the common market for coal and steel and shall accordingly be abolished or prohibited within the Community, as provided in this Treaty: ...(c) subsidies or aids granted by States, or special charges imposed by States, in any form whatsoever'.
5 Case 30/59 *Steenkolenmijnen v High Authority* [1961] ECR 1, 19.
6 See, for instance, Case C–387/92 *Banco Exterior de España* [1994] ECR I–877, para 13; Case C–241/94 *France v Commission (Kimberly Clark)* [1996] ECR I–4551, para 34; Case C–256/97 *DMT* [1999] ECR I–3913, para 19; Case C–251/97 *France v Commission* [1999] ECR I–6639, para 35.
7 For example, direct subsidies, loans, guarantees, exemption from the ordinary rules concerning taxes and social contributions, under-price sales, capital injections, provision of market research and advertising activities or logistical and commercial assistance, payment of outstanding wages or redundancy costs, or exemption from the normal application of insolvency rules.
8 Case 290/83 *Commission v France (Poor Farmers)* [1985] ECR 439, para 19.
9 Case C–379/98 *PreussenElektra v Schleswag* [2001] I–2099, paras 64 and 65.

aid supervision, the duty of loyal co-operation under Article 10 EC required that the concept of State aid be interpreted in such a way as to include support measures which are mandated by the State but financed by private undertakings. The Court firmly responded that such provision cannot be used to extend the scope of Article 87 EC to State conduct that does not fall within it. This is arguably the right approach. As the findings of *Steenkolenmijnen* and their stress on effects identify, the concept of aid is already a functional expansion of the concept of subsidy with the result that the former can already be regarded as if it were a 'measure of equivalent effect' to the latter. Any further extension would simply be contrary to the aim of Article 87 EC itself.

However, the main question to be tackled is whether the 'effect-based' definition of aid implies that the reasons or aims underlying the granting of a subsidy, and in particular its social objectives, are irrelevant in determining whether or not the measure is in contravention of EC law. As the Court itself once recognised, the decision regarding whether or not to grant a financial advantage to certain undertakings 'refers to the decisions of the Member States, in pursuit of their own economic and social objectives' and is inextricably linked with 'the attainment of certain economic and social objectives sought'.[10] Is it therefore right that such a vital consideration does not play any part at all in deciding whether a certain aid is to be considered incompatible with Community law?

The consistent caselaw of the Court provides an apparently unequivocal answer: the aim, even if social, of a certain measure is irrelevant when it comes to classifying it as a State aid.[11] The *locus classicus* can be found in the early *Italy v Commission* judgment.[12] Italy argued, inter alia, that the reduction in social charges pertaining to family allowances did not constitute a State aid within the context of Article 87 EC because it was a measure of internal taxation, which is reserved to the sovereignty of Member States, and a measure of social nature, which falls outside the scope of Article 87 EC. The Court rejected this view. It made it clear that

> the aim of Article (87) is to prevent trade between Member States from being affected by benefits granted by public authorities which, in various forms, distort or threaten to distort competition by favouring certain undertakings or the production of certain goods. Accordingly, Article (87) does not distinguish between the measures of State intervention concerned by reference to their causes or aims but define them in relation to their effects. Consequently, the

---

[10] Case 61/79 *Amministrazione delle Finanze dello Stato v Denkavit* [1980] ECR 1205, para 31.

[11] Compare with the *chapeau* of Art 140 EC, which states that the social policy provisions of the Treaty are to be applied 'without prejudice to the other provisions of this Treaty' which certainly include the rules on State aid. See Case 342/96 *Spain v Commission* [1999] ECR I–2459, para 22.

[12] Case 173/73 *Italy v Commission* [1974] ECR 709.

alleged fiscal nature or social aim of the measure in issue cannot suffice to shield it from the application of Article (87).[13]

These findings, which importantly refer to the purpose of State aid rules (ie the protection of competition), are in line with the *Steenkolenmijnen* case and admittedly build upon it.[14]

The principle whereby State aid rules do not make a distinction according to the reasons or aims of the State measures concerned but define them according to their effects has been consistently reiterated in the following case law.[15] The Court has thus repeatedly found that the social character of the measure is not sufficient to exclude it outright from classification as aid for the purposes of Article 87 EC.[16] In *Kimberly Clark*,[17] for instance, French law provided that, in the event of redundancies on economic grounds, undertakings with fifty or more employees which were envisaging ten or more redundancies within a 30-day period had to draw up and implement a social plan. The aim was to avoid redundancies or, at least, to limit their number and facilitate the employees' redeployment. The social plan could include certain measures which, with agreement between the undertaking concerned and the Fonds National de l'Emploi (FNE), a State body, could be financed by the State within defined limits. The Commission had found that, although justifiable under Article 87(3)(c) EC, the contributions by the FNE constituted State aid because they were determined on a case-by-case basis depending on the undertaking's financial situation and own efforts. After underlining that the social character of the measure was not sufficient to shield it from the application of State aid rules, the Court agreed with the Commission's finding that the scheme was only formally applicable to all undertakings as the FNE adjusted its financial assistance on a case-by-case basis. The Court also rejected the argument whereby the measures at issue were aimed at limiting the social repercussions of redundancy for the employees affected and were thus for the direct benefit of the

---

[13] Case 173/73 *Italy v Commission* [1974] ECR 709, para 13.

[14] See also Case 310/85 *Deufil* [1987] ECR 901, para 8. It is along this line that the Court of First Instance has observed that the concept of State aid is an objective one, the test being whether a State measure confers an advantage on one or more particular undertakings: Case T–67/94 *Ladbroke Racing v Commission* [1998] ECR II–1, para 52.

[15] See, for instance, Case 56/93 *Belgium v Commission (Gasunie)* [1996] ECR I–723, para 79; Case C–241/94 *France v Commission (Kimberly Clark)* [1996] ECR I–4551, para 20; Case C–75/97 *Belgium v Commission (Maribel bis/ter)* [1999] ECR I–3671, para 25; Case C–480/98 *Spain v Commission (Magefesa)* [2000] ECR I–8717, para 16; Case T–46/97 *SIC v Commission* [2000] ECR II–2125, para 83; Case C–5/01 *Belgium v Commission (Cockerill)* [2002] ECR I–11991, para 45; Case C–409/00 *Spain v Commission* [2003] ECR I–1487, para 46; Case T–109/01 *Fleuren Compost v Commission* (Judgment of 14 January 2004), para 54.

[16] See, for instance, Case C–241/94 *France v Commission (Kimberly Clark)* (1996) ECR I–4551, para 21; Case 342/96 *Spain v Commission* [1999] ECR I–2459, para 23; Case C–75/97 *Belgium v Commission (Maribel bis/ter)* [1999] ECR I–3671, para 25; Case C–5/01 *Belgium v Commission (Cockerill)* [2002] ECR I–11991, para 46.

[17] Case C–241/94 *France v Commission (Kimberly Clark)* [1996] ECR I–4551.

employees only. According to the Court, the system was liable to place Kimberly Clark in a more favourable situation than others, by relieving it of certain legal obligations *vis-à-vis* its employees, and thus met the conditions for classification as aid within the meaning of Article 87(1) EC.[18]

Various measures concerning social contributions have also been consistently considered as State aid, irrespective of the alleged social character of the assistance. In the *Maribel bis/ter* case, for instance, the Court found that the increased reduction in social contributions for manual workers in certain industrial sectors which were allegedly most affected by redundancies and restructuring did constitute State aid.[19] The arguments of the Belgian government which maintained that the scheme was a general measure reflecting a choice of economic policy consisting in the decision to promote the creation of jobs in industrial sectors which employ mostly manual workers who earn low wages owing to their minimal qualifications was rejected. Quite similarly, in *France v Commission*, the Court did not accept the applicant's argument that relief on social security contributions was not State aid because it was merely intended to offset the costs arising for undertakings from collective agreements concerning the reorganisation and reduction of working time, and that was to the exclusive benefit of employees.[20] In *Cockering Sambre*, the Court concluded that Article 4(c) ECSC prohibited financial assistance (involving a reduction in the employer's social security contributions) intended to offset a decrease in the pay of the salaried employees of a Belgium steel company resulting from a reduction in their working hours.[21] The supplement paid to the employees was held to be an incidental element of the salary and consequently came under the labour costs which that undertaking should have normally met. Significantly, it was irrelevant that, according to the Belgian Government, the measures were intended to create jobs and to attenuate, in the interest of the employees, the financial consequences of the reduction in working hours.

It should also be noted that, even in the application of the so-called 'private investor principle', which is used to determine whether the State intervention at issue is comparable to that of a private investor and, therefore, does not confer any unlawful advantage, the relevance of social objectives has been firmly rejected by the Court. In *Meura*, for instance, the Court made it clear that

> the test is ... whether in similar circumstances a private shareholder, having regard to the foreseeability of obtaining a return *and leaving aside all social, regional-policy and sectoral considerations*, would have subscribed the capital in question.[22]

---

[18] *Ibid*, paras 24 and 40.
[19] Case C–75/97 *Belgium v Commission (Maribel bis/ter)* [1999] ECR I–3671.
[20] Case C–251/97 *France v Commission* [1999] ECR I–6639.
[21] Case C–5/01 *Belgium v Commission (Cockerill)* [2002] ECR I–11991.
[22] Case 234/84 *Belgium v Commission (Meura)* [1986] ECR 2263, para 14 (emphasis added).

In a similar tone, Advocate General Jacobs underlined in *Spain v Commission* that

> State aid is granted whenever a Member State makes available to an undertaking funds which in the normal course of events would not be provided by a private investor applying ordinary commercial criteria and *disregarding considerations of a social, political or philanthropic nature.*[23]

Thus, according to what can be considered as settled case law, a measure, which has the effect of conferring a selective advantage on an undertaking or a sector, is not relieved of its quality as an aid merely because it was adopted for social purposes. Quite interestingly, the irrelevance of social or other aims implies that the opposite also holds true. If a practice is objectively justified on commercial grounds, and hence does not confer any advantage, the fact that it also furthers a political (and, admittedly, even a social) aim does not mean that it constitutes State aid for the purposes of Article 87 EC.[24]

A Some Problematic Areas: Selectivity and Labour Law Provisions

If the field of State aid law is considered as a whole, the picture is a little more unclear than it would at first appear. If specific strands of the caselaw are examined, it seems that the aim of the measure can be taken into account under certain circumstances. As an English judge candidly phrased it, although the Court of Justice's case law establishes that that the social aim of a measure cannot shield it from the application of Article 87 EC, it does not 'go so far as to say that the aim or purpose of the measure is irrelevant'.[25]

In particular, the ECJ has indicated that reference should be made to the purpose of the measure when it is necessary to determine whether it is a general or a selective measure.[26] It may be recalled that State aid rules only apply to measures that have a selective impact, that is measures that confer an advantage on certain undertakings or sectors only. Measures that are generally available across the board (ie to all undertakings or sectors) fall outside the scope of Article 87(1) EC.

In *Italy v Commission* the Court specifically referred to the relevance of the aim of a given measure in assessing whether the selectivity requirement

---

[23] Cf also AG Jacobs in Joined Cases C–278/92, C–279/92 and C–280/92 *Spain v Commission* [1994] ECR I–4103, para 28 (emphasis added).

[24] See Case 56/93 *Belgium v Commission (Gasunie)* [1996] ECR I–723, para 79.

[25] Per Clarke LJ in *R v Customs and Excise Commissioners, ex parte Lunn Poly and Bishopsgate* [1999] CMLR 1357, para 61.

[26] For a comprehensive analysis of the various issues surrounding the distinction between State aids and general measures, see K Bacon, 'State Aids and General Measures' (1997) 17 *Yearbook of European Law* 97.

was fulfilled. It noted that a measure designed to give the undertakings of a particular industrial sector a partial reduction of the financial charges arising from the normal application of the general social security system, without there being any justification for this exemption on the basis of the nature or general scheme of this system, must be regarded as aid.[27] A differential treatment between undertakings is therefore only an indicator of the existence of a State aid. If such differential impact is justified on the basis of the nature or general scheme of the system, the generality of the measure is not defeated and there is not State aid. This assessment clearly requires the consideration of the aim of the measure as, only by doing so is it possible to decide whether it is in line with the logic of the system. An example of the application of this analysis in the field of social contributions can be found in the *Maribel bis/ter* case. The Court found that the increased reductions in the social contributions of the Maribel schemes could not be justified in terms of the logic of the Belgian general system of social protection, and its underlying objectives of employment policy, but had rather the 'sole direct effect of according an economic advantage to the recipient undertakings alone, relieving them from part of the social costs which they would normally have to bear'.[28]

Two observations seem necessary. First, the *Italy v Commission* case is paradigmatic of the ambivalent role played by aims in the context of State aid law. On the one side, the Court says that a State aid is defined in relation to its effects and not to its aims.[29] On the other, it acknowledges that those aims may indeed become relevant to determine whether the differential impact previously detected may in fact be justified on the basis of the nature or general scheme of the system.[30] Secondly, the exact definition of the 'logic of the system' test is proving to be elusive as the Court seems in fact to conflate in one step the separate issues of scope and possible justifications. It is not by chance that the case law on selectivity has been construed as introducing specific extra derogations that Member States can rely on.[31] It could therefore be questionable whether that 'inherent in the logic test' is consistent with the 'effect-based' approach that the Court has traditionally

---

[27] Case 173/73 *Italy v Commission* [1974] ECR 709, para 15.

[28] Case C–75/97 *Belgium v Commission (Maribel bis/ter)* [1999] ECR I–3671, para 38. Quite interestingly, at para 57, while discussing the different issue of the possibility of applying the justification under Art 87(3)(c) EC, the Court underlined that 'the aid system introduced by the Maribel bis/ter scheme does not in any way guarantee attainment of the objective of creating jobs'.

[29] Case 173/73 *Italy v Commission* [1974] ECR 709, para 13.

[30] *Ibid*, para 15.

[31] On the application of the 'logic of the system' analysis in English Courts, see K Bacon, 'State Aids in the English Courts: Definition and Other Problems' in A Biondi, P Eeckhout and J Flynn (eds), *The Law of State Aid in the European Union* (Oxford University Press, 2004) 337, 348 et seq. The author interestingly notes that 'too often the buzzwords "general system" and "general measures" have been used as a cloak for judicial reticence in areas of fiscal and social policy'.

adopted with respect to the definition of State aid.[32] The tentative suggestion is therefore that, quite often, the proper place for considering arguments as to the 'logic of the system' would not be Article 87(1) EC (when it is necessary to establish whether the measure in question is a State aid), but rather Article 87(3) EC (when the possible justifications of the measure are assessed).

Another interesting line of case law where the Court seems to have taken into account the aim of the national measure is that in which labour law related provisions were at stake. In *Sloman Neptun,* the Court held that the partial non-application of German employment legislation to foreign crews of vessels flying the German flag did not constitute a grant of aid to the ship owners.[33] This is because

> the system at issue does not seek, through its object and general structure, to create an advantage which would constitute an additional burden for the State or the above-mentioned bodies, but only to alter in favour of shipping undertakings the framework within which contractual relations are formed between those undertakings and their employees.[34]

Similarly, in *Kirshammer-Hack,* the Court concluded that the exclusion of small businesses from a legal regime requiring payment of compensation in the event of unfair dismissals did not amount to the grant of an aid to the businesses concerned, reasoning that it

> does not entail any direct or indirect transfer of State resources to those businesses but derives solely from the legislature's intention to provide a specific legislative framework for working relationships between employers and employees and to avoid imposing on those businesses financial constraints which might hinder their development.[35]

A similar conclusion was reached in the *Viscido* case where the measure at issue allowed only one undertaking, Ente Poste Italiane, to derogate from the general rule under Italian law that employment contracts should be of indeterminate duration, and permitted the recruitment of staff under fixed-term

---

[32] It should, however, be noted that in some recent cases, the ECJ has been particularly rigid in dismissing Member State arguments relying on such a test. See, most notably, Case C–143/99 *Adria-Wien Pipeline and Wietersdorfer & Peggauer Zementwerke* [2001] ECR I–8365 and C–409/00 *Commission v Spain* [2001] ECR I–8365. According to Ross, the *Adria-Wien* judgment can be seen as the Court reacting to the vagueness of the specificity test by giving more specific reasons to reject Member States arguments: see M Ross, 'Decentralization, Effectiveness, and Modernization: Contradictions in Terms?' in A Biondi, P Eeckhout and J Flynn (eds), *The Law of State Aid in the European Union* (Oxford University Press, 2004) 90.

[33] Joined Cases C–72/91 and C–73/91 *Sloman Neptun* [1993] ECR I–887.

[34] *Ibid*, para 21.

[35] Case C–189/91 *Petra Kirsammer Hack* [1993] ECR I–6185, para 17.

contracts.[36] Contrary to the previous two cases, the Court did not refer to the regulatory aim of the legislation but merely concluded that

> the non-application of generally applicable legislation concerning fixed-term employment contracts to a single undertaking does not involve any direct or indirect transfer of State resources to that undertaking.[37]

The response to this case law has been controversial. Some have welcomed it as a correct recognition that State aid law should not interfere with labour law provisions.[38] Others have reached the same conclusion as the Court (the measures in issue should escape the prohibition of Article 87(1) EC) by using a different reasoning which, in reference to the aim of the measures, considers it a justifiable derogation from the system for the special characteristics of the cases.[39] Others, finally, have simply considered it bad case law.[40]

It is obviously necessary to define the boundaries of application of the State aid rules. What is doubtful, however, is whether the Court has drawn the line correctly.[40a] The Court places heavy emphasis on the use of State resources in its reasoning. Such an emphasis may be misleading however as it does not capture the rationale of state aid regulation which is to ensure fairness of competition rather than to control how public money is spent.[41] More fundamentally, however, it seems that there are no reasons (based either on their regulatory nature,[42] or on their objectives) to carve out an exception for these

---

[36] Joined Cases C–52/97, C–53/97 and C–54/97 *Vscido* [1998] ECR I–2629.

[37] *Ibid*, para 13.

[38] P Davies, 'Market Integration and Social Policy in the Court of Justice' (1995) 24 *Industrial Law Journal* 49, 58.

[39] K Bacon, 'State Aids in the English Courts: Definition and Other Problems' in A Biondi, P Eeckhout and J Flynn (eds), *The Law of State Aid in the European Union* (Oxford University Press, 2004) 313.

[40] See, for example, M Slotboom, 'State Aid in Community Law: A Broad or Narrow Definitions?' (1995) 20 *European Law Review* 289; BJ Rodger, 'State Aid—A Fully Level Playing Field?' [1999] *European Competition Law Review* 251; M Ross, 'State Aids and National Courts: Definitions and Other Problems—A Case of Premature Emancipation?' (2000) 37 *Common Market Law Review* 401.

[40a] It must be asked, for example, how it is possible to distinguish between cases such as *Sloman Neptun* and cases such as Case C–310/99 *Italy v Commission* [2002] ECR I–2289. Why did the non-application of German employment legislation intended to reduce labour costs of certain undertakings (*Sloman Neptun*) not amount to State aid, whereas the introduction of special legislation (training and work expirience contracts) which provided for a reduction of social contributions (*Italy v Commission*) *did* amount to State aid?

[41] See K Bacon, 'State Aids in the English Courts: Definition and Other Problems' in A Biondi, P Eeckhout and J Flynn (eds), *The Law of State Aid in the European Union* (Oxford University Press, 2004) 282 et seq; M Ross, 'State Aids and National Courts: Definitions and Other Problems—A Case of Premature Emancipation?' (2000) 37 *Common Market Law Review* 401, 413 et seq. The Court has, however, recently confirmed that the notion of State aid requires a use of State resources: see Case C–379/98 *PreussenElektra v Schleswag* (2001) I–2099.

[42] We refer to an alleged distinction between State aid measures and regulatory measures (cf the OECD's document 'Competition Policy in Subsidies and State Aid' (12 November 2001) DAFFE/CLP(2001)24, which can be found in the OECD's website <www.oecd.org>, last visit on 31 March 2004). According to this categorisation, only financial transfers to firms would constitute State aid and be regulated by State aid rules. Mere regulatory measures, such as

measures and exclude them outright from the application of State aid rules. If laudable objectives are pursued by Member States, these might find a justification under the admittedly wide provisions of the third paragraph of Article 87 EC. The *Sloman Neptun* case law instead runs the risk once again of conflating scope and justification in the context of an Article 87(1) EC analysis, thus creating an imbalance in the application of State aid rules and in the institutional arrangement, based on a clear division of roles between national courts and Commission, envisaged in the EC Treaty.[43]

III THE FINANCING OF SERVICES OF GENERAL ECONOMIC INTEREST AND STATE AID RULES

A Public Services and State Aid

The same kinds of questions and, in particular, the necessity to distinguish between economic effects and public objectives have arisen as far as the financing of public services is concerned.

The provision and access to certain public services that is provided for all citizens is one of the main features of the Welfare State. EU law and policy attributes a crucial role to what are known as 'services of general economic interest' (SGEI). This has been reaffirmed by the Amsterdam Treaty by inserting a specific provision on the role of SGEI among the Principles of the EC Treaty. Article 16 EC expressly recognises that they belong to the 'shared values of the Union' and fulfil an important role in 'promoting social and territorial cohesion', with the result that 'the Community and the Member States, each within their respective powers and within the scope of application of this Treaty, shall take care that such services operate on the basis of principles and

---

price-fixing or labour law and environmental regulation, which does not involve any transfer of government resources, would not amount to State aid and would be subject (if at all) to other sets of provisions. This distinction seems to underlie the caselaw of the Court which has held that price-fixing public measures do not constitute State aid. Cf Case 82/77 *Van Tiggele* [1978] ECR 25; Case C–379/98 *PreussenElektra v Schleswag* [2001] I–2099.

[43] See also Case C–59/03 *Cigliola v Ferrovie dello Stato* (pending), where the Court is called to decide on facts remarkably similar to the *Sloman Neptun* strand of caselaw. The Tribunale di Genova referred a question as to whether Italian legislation which 'allows an undertaking, Ferrovie dello Stato, to dismiss its older employees—thereby creating a situation in which the undertaking can save on labour costs (salaries and insurance obligations), with an immediate resulting burden to the State in the form of reduced contribution revenue and the payment of pensions to dismissed workers—fall within the concept of aid that is incompatible with the common market within the meaning of Article 87 of the Treaty' (2003 OJ C83/12, 5 April 2003). It remains to be seen whether the Court intends to adhere to its previous caselaw and conclude that this measure falls outside the scope of Art 87(1) EC, or is rather prepared to review its *acquis*, by accepting that this measure may constitute a State aid. From an enquiry at the Registry of the Court on 8 March 2004, it seems that the application of Art 104(3) Rules of Procedure has been proposed. This provision allows the Court to decide a case with reasoned order (and without an Advocate General's Opinion) 'where a question referred to the Court for a preliminary ruling is identical to a question on which the Court has already ruled, where the answer to such a question may be clearly deduced from existing case-law or

conditions which enable them to fulfil their missions'.[44] This special status is confirmed by the recent draft Constitution approved by the European Convention in summer 2003.[45] Although there is therefore a general agreement that public services are essential, it is more difficult to find the right balance between their preservation and market integration. Without wanting to reiterate the whole debate on the definition of what constitutes a service of general economic interest,[46] the argument will be developed only as far as the issue of their financing is concerned.

It has indeed been observed that the economic problem of SGEI is 'about ensuring that providers of SGEI generate enough revenue to cover their costs.... Indeed, the heart of the problem is the inability of providers to cover their costs because of the conditions imposed on them by the member states'.[47] It should also be observed that the liberalisation process affects the mechanisms adopted by Member States in operating such services. Member States do not usually grant exclusive rights within a specific sector of activity but provide instead for some form of financial support to the undertakings entrusted with the operation of SGEI.[48] Although it has been argued that direct subsidies are not necessarily the first-best solution for financing public services,[49] as a matter of fact State subsidies are a very common means of financing SGEI in Europe.[50]

---

where the answer to the question admits of no reasonable doubt'. If the proposal to dispose of the case with order were accepted, this would mean that the Court has decided to abide by its previous caselaw. It has finally to be reminded that orders adopted pursuant to Art 104(3) Rules of Procedure are not necessarily published in the European Court Reports.

[44] See further M Ross, 'Article 16 EC and Services of General Interest: From Derogation to Obligation?' (2000) 25 *European Law Review* 22.

[45] See Convention on the Future of Europe, *Draft Treaty Establishing a Constitution for Europe*, 2003 OJ C169/1: Art II–36 (access to services of general economic interest); Art III–6 (legislative competence); Art III–17 (possibility of direct initiation of infringement proceedings). See now the final text of the Constitutional Treaty agreed by the Intergovernmental Conference meeting in Brussels (17–18 June 2004).

[46] See in general E Szyszczak, 'Public Service Provision in Competitive Markets' (2001) 20 *Yearbook of European Law* 35; C Quigley and A M Collins, *EC State Aid Law and Policy* (Hart Publishing, 2003) pp 45–48 and 118–20; A Alexis, 'Services publics et aides d'État: Évolution récente de la jurisprudence' 1/2002 *Revue de Droit de l'Union Européenne* 63; P Nicolaides, 'Competition and Services of General Economic Interest in the EU: Reconciling Economics and Law' (2003) 1 *European State Aid Law Quarterly* 183. Cf also Commission, *Green Paper on Services of General Interest*, COM(2003) 270 Final.

[47] P Nicolaides, 'Competition and Services of General Economic Interest in the EU: Reconciling Economics and Law' (2003) 1 *European State Aid Law Quarterly* 183, 188.

[48] See further L Hancher and J Buendia Sierra, 'Cross Subsidization in the European Community' (1998) 35 *Common Market Law Review* 901.

[49] P Nicolaides, 'Competition and Services of General Economic Interest in the EU: Reconciling Economics and Law' (2003) 1 *European State Aid Law Quarterly* 183, 190, suggests that they are the 'third-best if not the fourth-best' option.

[50] There are indeed various methods of financing public services (conferral of special or exclusive rights, direct financing such as subsidies or provision of coupons to users, tariff-fixing, contributions by market participants, solidarity-based financing etc) which may be chosen by governments on the basis of the different economic impact, in particular in terms of incentives, they want to produce.

Having said that, if we now turn to the specific theme of this section—the impact of State aid rules on the financing of SGEI—a lively debate has recently sparked off on whether support given by the State to enable undertakings entrusted with SGEIs to discharge their public service obligations (PSOs) should be considered as a State aid. This depends on the risk that, far from merely compensating the costs of PSOs, the recipient undertakings may redirect the resources intended to finance the SGEI to support other activities open to competition. An ancillary issue concerns the role played by the justification provided for under Article 86(2) EC. These questions have produced a jurisprudential clash between the Community Courts and also between Advocates General, and are also currently subject to a wide political discussion.[51]

B The Caselaw on the Financing of SGEIs under State Aid Rules: The *Ferring* and *Altmark* Decisions

Two main approaches have traditionally been adopted when analysing the classification of financial compensation of SGEIs under State aid law. The first approach (the 'compensation approach') considers that financial assistance that merely compensates a PSO does not constitute a State aid. The underlying concept is that such financial compensation is a mere *contropartie* for the public service rendered to the extent that it matches the extra costs incurred by the operation of the SGEI. In State aid jargon, this translates as saying that this compensation does not qualify as State aid within the meaning of Article 87(1) EC because it does not confer any advantage to the undertaking operating the SGEI. This approach was first upheld in the *ADBHU* judgment of 1985. This case concerned the compensation of the extra costs generated by the obligation that French law (implementing Directive 75/439 on the disposal of waste oils)[52] imposed on certain undertakings to dispose of waste oils. The Court found that those 'indemnities do not constitute aid within the meaning of Article 87 of the Treaty, but rather *consideration for the services performed* by the collection or disposal undertakings'.[53] Subsequent Commission practice followed this line, considering that mere financial compensation of public service duties did not constitute State aid.

---

[51] See, for instance, *Communication on Services of General Interest in Europe*, 2001 OJ C17/4; Report to the Laeken European Council on *Services of General Interest*, COM(2001) 598 Final; Report to the Seville European Council on *The Status of Work on the Guidelines for State Aid and Services of General Economic Interest*, COM(2002) 280 Final; Commission, *Non-Paper on Services of General Economic Interest and State Aid* (12 November 2002); Report to the Copenhagen European Council on *The State of Play in the Work on the Guidelines for State Aid and Services of General Economic Interest*, COM(2002) 636 Final; Commission, *Green Paper on Services of General Interest*, COM(2003) 270 Final.

[52] 1975 OJ L194/23.

[53] Case 240/83 *ADBHU* [1985] ECR 531, para 18 (emphasis added).

This approach has been contradicted by the Court of First Instance in the *FFSA* and *SIC* decisions. The *FFSA* case dealt with a tax concession granted by the French Government to *La Poste* to offset its SGEI.[54] The Commission had found that the tax concession was inferior to the cost that it had to bear for its additional public service and that it therefore did not constitute State aid. Although upholding in substance the decision taken by the Commission, the Court of First Instance chose a different route in considering the tax concession to be a State aid. The provision of a service of general interest was not believed to be relevant at this stage. Instead, the fact that La Poste had a specific duty to serve the entire national territory, including even the most remote rural areas, became relevant at the stage of the possible justification of the measure. In particular, Article 86(2) EC was then held to be applicable as the effect of competition law in the area of postal services could have obstructed the development of such a task. This position (dubbed the 'State aid approach') was reaffirmed in the *SIC* case, concerning public broadcasting. The Court of First Instance concluded that 'the fact that a financial advantage is granted to an undertaking by the public authorities in order to offset the cost of public service obligations which that undertaking is claimed to have assumed has no bearing on the classification of that measure as aid within the meaning of Article 87(1) of the Treaty, although that aspect may be taken into account when considering whether the aid in question is compatible with the common market under Article 86(2) of the Treaty'.[55]

The Court of Justice was again called upon to decide on the issue in the *Ferring* case.[56] This case dealt with tax concessions granted to wholesale distributors of medicines. These tax exemptions were made because of the specific public obligations that distributors had to bear (stocking at all times a quantity of medicines sufficient to satisfy the needs of regular customers and to deliver within a 24 hour period any medicines required to any location in their distribution area). The Court maintained that this exemption could be regarded as compensation for the services provided and not as State aid within the context of Article 87 EC. As Advocate General Tizzano argued,

> the fact that such measures do not confer any real advantage on an undertaking entrusted with a service of general interest and therefore are not likely to alter the conditions of competition appears a decisive argument to me....
>
> In other words, the imposition of the obligation and the provision of compensation cannot be considered as separate matters as they are two sides of the same public measure which is intended, as a whole, to guarantee that public interests of primary importance are satisfied'.[57]

---

[54] Cases T–106/95 *FFSA and Others v Commission* [1997] ECR II–229.
[55] Case T–46/97 *SIC v Commission* [2000] ECR II–2125, para 84.
[56] Case C–53/00 *Ferring* [2001] ECR I–9067.
[57] *Ibid*, paras 60–61 Opinion.

Thus, since one element of the definition of State aid under Article 87(1) EC was lacking—namely the advantage—the compensation intended to offset the additional costs of the SGEI could not be qualified as State aid. Quite importantly for the operation of the system, the Court also deemed it necessary to add that if the compensation were to exceed the additional costs incurred by the provision of the SGEI, then this compensation would qualify as State aid. In this case, Article 86(2) EC could not apply to the compensation which exceeds the additional costs of the operation of the SGEI as the extra compensation cannot, in any event, be regarded as necessary to enable the undertakings entrusted with the operation of SGEI to carry out their specific tasks.

The *Ferring* decision has been subject to some criticism. The official critique came from the Advocate General in *Altmark*, a case that concerned the granting of licences to operate regular bus services through public subsidies. In his two Opinions, Advocate General Léger strongly criticised *Ferring*, arguing that it was liable to undermine the structure and logic of the Treaty provisions in respect of State aid, and reaffirmed that the preferred approach is the State aid one.[58] He put forward various arguments. He first argued that State aid must not be defined on the basis of its aims but of its effects. It is an objective concept which focuses on a notion of 'net' (in contrast to 'gross') aid. In other words, what matters under Article 87(1) EC is whether the measure at issue is capable of conferring a selective advantage that distorts competition and affects intra-Community trade. In his view, the compensation approach confuses two distinct legal issues, the classification of the measure as State aid and its possible justification. Secondly, he noted that Article 86(2) EC would be deprived of any meaningful role in the field of State aid. If mere compensation would not constitute aid under *Ferring*, over-compensation, as was expressly recognised by the Court, could not be justified under Article 86(2) EC because it would not be necessary and proportionate. He finally observed that, as a result of the compensation approach, the surveillance role of the Commission in controlling measures financing public services would be diminished.

Advocate General Jacobs expressed his view in this debate in *GEMO*.[59] In his Opinion in this case, on the issue of whether the public financing of animal carcass disposal undertakings constituted aid, he presented what has been dubbed as the '*quid pro quo* approach' but which could more properly be referred to as a 'differentiated compensation approach'.[60] He suggested

---

[58] Opinion delivered by AG Léger on 19 March 2002 in Case C–280/00 *Altmark Trans* [2003] ECR I–7747. Cf also the second Opinion delivered on 14 January 2003 as a consequence of the *Ferring* decision and the Opinion of Advocate General Jacobs in Case C–126/01 *Ministere de l'Economie v GEMO* [2003] ECR I–0000.

[59] See Opinion delivered on 30 April 2002 in Case C–126/01 *Ministere de l'Economie v GEMO* [2003] ECR I–0000.

[60] Cf P Nicolaides, 'Competition and Services of General Economic Interest in the EU: Reconciling Economics and Law' (2003) 1 *European State Aid Law Quarterly* 183, 196.

that the Court should distinguish between two types of situations. Where there is a direct and manifest link between the State financing and clearly defined public service obligations, the sums paid by the State would not constitute State aid within the context of Article 87(1) EC. On the other hand, where there is no such link or the public service obligations are not clearly defined, the sums paid by the public authorities would constitute aid within the context of that provision. In *GEMO*, such an indubitable and direct link *did* exist as the services were awarded through a specific public tender procedure. The position of Advocate General Jacobs has been followed by Advocate General Stix-Hackl in *Enirisorse*.[61]

The reply of the ECJ came in its *Altmark* judgment of 24 July 2003.[62] The question referred to the Court was whether subsidies granted by Germany to an undertaking in order to operate a regular bus service in a specific region had to be considered aid or merely a compensation for the services offered. The Court held that such compensation did not confer an advantage for the undertaking concerned and therefore could not be considered to be State aid within the context of the EC Treaty. The Court clarified that no advantage could be established where a State financial measure must be regarded as compensation for the services provided by the recipient undertakings in order to discharge public service obligations. However, so that such compensation is not seen to provide the undertaking with an unfair advantage, it should satisfy four conditions. Firstly, the recipient company must have actual public service obligations to discharge and those obligations must be clearly defined. Secondly, the parameters on the basis of which the compensation is calculated must be established in advance in an objective and transparent manner. Thirdly, the compensation cannot exceed what is necessary to cover all or part of the costs incurred in the discharge of the public service obligations, taking into account the relevant revenue and a reasonable profit. Fourthly, when the company is not chosen through a public procurement procedure, the level of compensation must be determined in relation to an analysis of the costs that a typical company in the sector would incur (taking into account its revenues and a reasonable profit for the discharging of the obligations).

C An Appraisal of *Altmark* and Its Conditions

The first comments have generally welcomed *Altmark*.[63] This decision can be regarded as a desirable 'fine-tuning' of *Ferring* on the basis of some of

---

[61] Opinion of 7 November 2002 in Joined Cases C–34/01 to C–38/01 *Enirisorse v Ministero delle Finanze* [2003] ECR I–0000.

[62] Case C–280/00 *Altmark Trans* [2003] ECR I–7747.

[63] A Biondi, *'Justifying State Aid: The Financing of Services of General Economic Interest' in* T Tridimas and P Nebbia (eds), *European Union Law for the Twenty-First Century* (Volume II)

the arguments that emerged in the debate that followed the latter decision. It seems that the Court, in adhering to the compensation approach, has been particularly receptive of the Opinion of Advocate General Jacobs in *GEMO* and its differentiated compensation approach based on the dividing criterion of the direct and manifest link between financing and clearly defined public service obligations. More fundamentally, however, it seems that the four conditions of *Altmark* represent a rather successful transplant, after the necessary adjustments, of the main requirements of Article 86(2) EC.[64] That is evident with respect to the entrustment of particular tasks of public service obligation, but is also true with regard to the concepts of necessity and proportionality, and the underlying idea that distortions are to be kept to the minimum possible. The *Altmark* criteria clarify *Ferring* i) by ensuring the adoption of a transparent process and ii) by compensating only those costs that are necessary to execute the SGEI. In this regard, apart from the requirement that compensation be linked to an explicit PSO and does not exceed the latter's cost,[65] two new important conditions have been introduced. First, the parameters on which the compensation is calculated must be established 'beforehand in an objective and transparent manner'.[66] Quite significantly, the determination of the compensation *ex ante* should prevent operators from passing all of their commercial risk to the State and avoid *ex post* rescue of inefficient undertakings. Secondly, in any event, compensation is not supposed to cover any cost claimed to be 'extra' or 'additional' but only those costs that satisfy objective, market-based benchmarks and are determined after certain procedures.[67] This is an important recognition that the costs of SGEI cannot be determined if the costs of other potential providers are not considered.[68]

(Hart Publishing, 2004); P Nicolaides, 'Compensation for Public Service Obligations: the Floodgates of State Aid' (2003) *European Competition Law Review 561;* JM Thouvenin and MP Lorieux, 'L'arrêt de la CJCE du 24 Juillet 2003 Altmark' (2003) *Revue du Marché commun et de l'Union européenne 633.* See also the Commission Staff Working Paper, *Report on the Public Consultation on the Green Paper on Services of General Interest,* SEC (2004) 326 (15 March 2004) para 4.8. Available at http://europa.eu.int/comm/secretariat_ general/services_general_interest (last visit on 31 March 2004).

[64] This tendency is not new. See, for instance, Case C–387/92 *Banco Exterior de España* [1994] ECR I–877, para 21 where the Court refers to the possibility that an aid is 'capable of falling outside the scope of application of Article (87) by virtue of Article 86(2) of the Treaty'. See also Cases T–106/95 *FFSA and Others v Commission* [1997] ECR II–229, para 16.

[65] Case C–280/00 *Altmark Trans* [2003] ECR I–7747, paras 89 and 92.

[66] *Ibid,* paras 90 and 91.

[67] See n 65, para 93.

[68] P Nicolaides, 'Competition and Services of General Economic Interest in the EU: Reconciling Economics and Law' (2003) 1 *European State Aid Law Quarterly* 183, 189.

1 *The Measurement of Costs*

However, there are some specific questions that need to be addressed.

In primis: the problem of the measurement of the costs of PSOs. The *Ferring* decision has been criticised with various arguments. Among the most interesting are those based on economic grounds.[69] According to economic analysis, the main finding of *Ferring*, whereby mere compensation of the 'additional costs actually incurred' by undertakings entrusted with SGEIs is not State aid, far from restoring a level playing field ends up strengthening anti-competitive advantages. Two problems in particular can be highlighted. First, *Ferring* does not seek to establish whether compensation is necessary. Indeed, it may well be that public compensation is not necessary because the undertaking would have *willingly* offered the service. Further, although public policies impose several obligations on companies, the relevant extra costs are not necessarily compensated. Why, and how, then to distinguish between SGEIs (which may be compensated) and other obligations (which would not)? The suggestion is that financial assistance would be needed only when, in its absence, the supply of the relevant service would not be guaranteed.

The second problem concerns the difficulty in determining the amount of the subsidy that is in any event necessary to compensate the costs for discharging the PSO. This depends on the inherent difficulty of measuring costs and allocating them (particularly fixed costs) between various operations.[70] But, more importantly, *Ferring* does not seem to ensure that the costs are kept at the lowest possible level, quite the contrary in fact. As Nicolaides explains,

> The problem with [*Ferring's*] approach is that it weakens the incentives to firms to keep costs low. It weakens the discipline imposed by the market on

---

[69] These have mainly been raised by P Nicolaides: see 'Distortive Effects of Compensatory Aid Measures: A Note on the Economics of the *Ferring* Judgement' (2002) *European Competition Law Review* 313; 'The New Frontier of State Aid Control—An Economic Assessment of Measures that Compensate Enterprises' (2002) 37 *Intereconomics* 190; 'Competition and Services of General Economic Interest in the EU: Reconciling Economics and Law' (2003) 1 *European State Aid Law Quarterly* 183; 'Compensation for Public Service Obligations: the Floodgates of State Aid' (2003) *European Competition Law Review* 561.

[70] It may be recalled that Commission Dir 2000/52 amending Commission Dir 80/723 on the transparency of financial relations between Member States and public undertakings, 2000 OJ L193/75 imposes on undertakings entrusted with the operation of a SGEI pursuant to Art 86(2) EC, which receive State aid in any form whatsoever and which carry on at the same time other activities separate from the operation of the SGEI, an obligation to maintain separate internal accounts reflecting the costs and revenues associated with different activities and full details of the methods by which costs and revenues are assigned or allocated to different activities. Dir 2000/52, however, excludes the obligation to keep separate accounts when the State aid received is fixed for an appropriate period following an open, transparent and non-discriminatory procedure. The draft proposal for a directive, recently presented by the Commission after *Altmark* (available at <http://europa.eu.int/comm/competition/state_aid/others>), would remove this derogation requiring undertakings receiving public service compensation to keep separate accounts irrespective of the legal classification of such compensation in the light of Art 87(1) EC.

firms to keep their costs at least as low as those of their competitors. Even worse, this kind of state aid may enable firms to expand into adjacent markets without being caught by any of competition rules.[71]

The proposed solution to these two problems is to auction the obligation to provide the relevant services.[72] By creating a market to obtain the services in question, the public authorities would succeed in not favouring any firm (to the detriment of others) and in keeping the subsidy to the minimum necessary.[73] The use of public procurement procedures was discussed before the delivery of *Altmark*.[74] It was underlined that the award of a

---

[71] P Nicolaides, 'Competition and Services of General Economic Interest in the EU: Reconciling Economics and Law' (2003) 1 *European State Aid Law Quarterly* 205–6. There may be cases where over-compensation might not distort the functioning of adjacent competitive markets. For instance, where the extra costs depend on the inefficiency of the undertaking entrusted with the SGEI (because it recruits for social reasons more personnel than necessary for the performance of the service) but do not cause any significant anti-competitive effect (because the undertaking does not use the extra personnel for the performance of other services open to competition). An outright prohibition of any over-compensation is, however, very attractive in its simplicity.

[72] The problem of the cost measurement, and the 'auction' solution, is described by P Nicolaides, 'The New Frontier of State Aid Control—An Economic Assessment of Measures that Compensate Enterprises' (2002) 37 *Intereconomics* 190, 195 as follows: 'If public authorities could know what companies would do without aid and if they could measure their costs, then it would be relatively easy to calculate the minimum necessary amount of aid that would lead to the desired increase in supply. Unfortunately public authorities do not have that kind of knowledge. Under conditions of imperfect or incomplete information, the only feasible way for public authorities to grant aid without over-compensating is to auction the obligation to provide the relevant service; the purpose of the auction is to identify the firm or firms which would be willing to offer that service with the lowest possible subsidy. These are the firms that have lower operating costs in comparison to their competitors. This means that competition among bidders would bring the required subsidy to the lowest possible level. If some firms would have voluntarily offered the service in a free market without any subsidy because the revenue they earn would exceed any extra costs, then bidding would bring the amount of the required subsidy close to zero. That is how public authorities get to discover whether a subsidy is needed or not'. On the advantages of transparent and competitive tendering procedures, cf also Commission, *Non-Paper on Services of General Economic Interest and State Aid* (12 November 2002), paras 84–89.

[73] P Nicolaides, 'The New Frontier of State Aid Control—An Economic Assessment of Measures that Compensate Enterprises' (2002) 37 *Intereconomics* 190, 196. The creation of competitive pressure is not new in the caselaw. To remain in the context of Art 86 and undertakings entrusted with exclusive rights, reference can be made to Case C–41/90 *Höfner* [1991] ECR I–1979. An even more interesting parallel can be made with the recent 'healthcare services cases' in the area of free movement of services (see n 89 below). These decisions, which indirectly concern the issue of the financing of public services from the perspective of the user, arguably increase the pressure on Member States to run more efficient national health systems and to guarantee a higher standard of service.

[74] Cf AG Jacobs in Case C–126/01 *Ministere de l'Economie v GEMO* [2003] ECR I–0000, paras 119 and 129 Opinion; AG Stix-Hackl in Joined Cases C–34/01 to C–38/01 *Enirisorse v Ministero delle Finanze* [2003] ECR I–0000, para 157; second Opinion of Advocate General LÇger in Case C–280/00 *Altmark Trans* [2003] ECR I–7747, note 97. The idea that an open and fair tendering procedure excludes the existence of aid can be found in other cases. Cf for instance, C Quigley and A M Collins, *EC State Aid Law and Policy* (Hart Publishing, 2003) pp 37–39; R D'Sa, 'When Aid is not an Aid? The Implications of the English Partnerships Decision for European Competition Law and Policy' (2000) 25 *European Law Review* 139.

public service contract after a public procurement procedure would constitute the clearest example of the existence of a direct and manifest link between State financing and clearly defined PSOs.[75] It was nonetheless suggested that, although Member States may have an incentive in using unequivocal and transparent arrangements such as public procurement procedures,[76] it would be disproportionate to always require it.[77]

The Court has clearly taken account of these arguments. The most significant advancement in *Altmark* is that only the compensation of those costs that are *necessary* to discharge the SGEI does not constitute State aid. To determine the right amount of financing, the Court indicated its preference for public procurement procedures. It stopped short, however, of imposing them and put forward an alternative benchmark, ie the analysis of the costs of a 'typical undertaking' which is 'well run and adequately provided' with the necessary means to meet the public service requirements. However, besides its inherent interpretative difficulties, this benchmark is not as economically sound as the use of auctions or other open selection procedures.[78] As underlined by Advocate General Jacobs, it is predictable that, to dispel any doubts, Member States will have an incentive to grant compensation through public procurement procedures.[79]

2 Separating Scope and Justification?

One of the main critiques of Advocate General Léger towards *Ferring* was that it did not distinguish between the characterisation of a measure as State aid and its justification. It is submitted, however, that these cases very much resemble purchases where the compensation is a mere *contropartie* of the PSOs. It is as if the government is *paying* for the public service. As Advocate General Jacobs observed, a parallel should be drawn to the situation where a State buys something and pays the price. It seems indeed immaterial that

---

[75] AG Jacobs in Case C–126/01 *Ministere de l'Economie v GEMO* [2003] ECR I–0000, para 125 Opinion. Cf also the second Opinion of AG Léger in Case C–280/00 *Altmark Trans* [2003] ECR I–7747, para 83.

[76] AG Jacobs in Case C–126/01 *Ministere de l'Economie v GEMO* [2003] ECR I–0000, para 129.

[77] Cf AG Stix-Hackl in Joined Cases C–34/01 to C–38/01 *Enirisorse v Ministero delle Finanze* [2003] ECR I–0000, para 157; and second Opinion of AG Léger in Case C–280/00 *Altmark Trans* [2003] ECR I–7747, para 97.

[78] P Nicolaides, 'Compensation for Public Service Obligations: the Floodgates of State Aid' (2003) *European Competition Law Review* 561, 573 observes that public procurement procedures are 'based on firmer economic foundations because what matters are expected future costs of delivering services'.

[79] AG Jacobs in Case C–126/01 *Ministere de l'Economie v GEMO* [2003] ECR I–0000, para 129 Opinion. See, however, A Bartosch, 'Much Ado about Nothing?' (2004) 2 *European State Aid Law Quarterly* 1.

the service is not provided to the State but to the collectivity. According to Advocate General Jacobs,

> the same global analysis must prevail where the link between State funding and the clearly defined general interest obligations imposed is so direct and manifest that financing and obligation must be regarded as a single measure.[80]

Consequently, there will be aid only if, and only as far as, the price paid exceeds the market price.

The compensation of public services should thus be distinguished from other measures that are aimed at compensating market failures and disadvantages. Whereas the former seems to largely rest on a purely technical assessment, where there is no discussion about the public nature or aim of the measure, the latter cases involve socio-economic assessments which should be properly addressed by the Commission that bears legal and political responsibility for its decisions. *Altmark*, therefore, cannot be said to conflate scope and justification but is in line with the findings in *Italy v Commission*, whereby a disputed measure is mainly defined on the basis of its effects and not its causes or aims.

Quite similarly, cases involving the compensation of the costs borne by undertakings entrusted with PSOs should be distinguished from those other cases where normal regulations of business introduced to meet various, even social or public, objectives (such as consumer safety, health or environmental protection) impose extra-costs on undertakings. It seems indeed that, should governments decide to compensate these undertakings for these costs, the financial assistance would undoubtedly constitute a State aid, irrespective of its proportionality with the costs. The distinguishing element seems to lie in the consideration that, whereas these costs are normally borne by the undertakings operating in the relevant market, costs for discharging PSOs, which are specifically entrusted by Member States to certain undertakings, do not present the same characteristics of normality.[81]

3 The Institutional Issue and the Role for Article 86(2) EC

It is now necessary to examine the two other critiques that have been raised by Advocate General Léger against *Ferring*.

The first concerns the alleged institutional problem of the compensation approach. To consider these measures as not constituting State aid would mean subtracting them from the control of the Commission. But the most

---

[80] AG Jacobs in Case C–126/01 *Ministere de l'Economie v GEMO* [2003] ECR I–0000, para 122 Opinion.

[81] Cf C Quigley and A Collins, *EC State Aid Law and Policy* (Hart Publishing, 2003) pp 42 et seq.

striking counter-objection to this critique is that, if there is no aid, there are no reasons why it should be notified to the Commission.[82] Moreover, the conditions now imposed by the Court in *Altmark* seem to limit the room for manoeuvre for Member States and to reasonably ensure that there is no over-compensation and hence no State aid.[83]

The second, more important criticism concentrates on the role of the justification under Article 86(2) EC in those cases where State support in favour of an undertaking entrusted with public service would not benefit from the *Altmark* test.[84] It seems indeed that, after *Altmark*, this provision will not have any substantial role to play in the justification of the financing of public services. As has been amply underlined in the debate preceding the decision of the Court, if there is no over-compensation the measure is not a State aid and falls outside the scope of Article 87(1) EC. If, by contrast, there is over-compensation, the measure does constitute a State aid under Article 87(1) EC but does not qualify under Article 86(2) EC as the proportionality requirement would not be satisfied.[85] In its recent proposals on the application of Article 86(2) EC to aid in the form of public service compensation,[86] however, the Commission seems to suggest that the latter provision is applicable even when the conditions of *Altmark* (in particular the fourth) are not fulfilled. It is particularly interesting to underline that, although reaffirming that only public compensation that does not exceed

---

[82] As P Nicolaides, 'The New Frontier of State Aid Control—An Economic Assessment of Measures that Compensate Enterprises' (2002) 37 *Intereconomics* 190, 193 rightly observes: 'there are many public measures which are not assessed by the Commission for the simple reason that they are not state aids'.

[83] It has to be noted that the *Altmark* decision does not seem to have caused a loophole in the EC system of State aid control as, after it, many measures have not passed its test. The *Altmark* conditions have been recently applied in Joined Cases C–34/01 to C–38/01 *Enirisorse v Ministero delle Finanze* [2003] ECR I–0000. This preliminary reference from Italy concerned legislation that entrusted the management of stevedoring equipment, warehouses, depots and other port property to certain undertakings in Italian ports. The allocation to these undertakings of two thirds of port charges levied on goods passing through those ports contributed to the financing of these statutory tasks. The Court concluded that the criteria laid down in *Altmark* were not fulfilled in the case in issue. Cf also Case T–157/01 *Danske Busvognmænd v Commission* (Judgment of 16 March 2004), para 98. On the first decisions of the Commission (on public broadcasting financing) that have been adopted after *Altmark* and have invariably found no measure to satisfy its conditions: see A Bartosch, 'Much Ado about Nothing?' (2004) 2 *European State Aid Law Quarterly* 1.

[84] We do not concentrate on the important procedural issue of the direct effect of this provision in the context of the application of State aid rules and on its impact on the procedural obligations under Art 88(3) EC. For an account, see C Rizza, 'The Financial Assistance Granted by Member States to Undertakings Entrusted with the Operation of a Service of General Economic Interest' in A Biondi, P Eeckhout and J Flynn (eds), *The Law of State Aid in the European Union* (Oxford University Press, 2004) 41.

[85] Cf Case C–53/00 *Ferring* [2001] ECR I–9067.

[86] Cf the proposals for a Community Framework for State aid in the form of public service compensation, DG D(2004), and for a Decision on the application of Article 86 of the Treaty to State aid in the form of public service compensation granted to certain undertakings entrusted with the operation of services of general economic interest, both available at <http://europa.eu.int/comm/competition/state_aid> (last visit on 31 March 2004).

the costs for performing a SGEI may be compatible, both documents make reference to costs 'incurred' without indicating any objective benchmark ensuring that they are really necessary to perform the PSOs and thus probably highlighting a lighter scrutiny on the part of the Commission. That said, however, a full appraisal of the impact of these measures should not be carried out until they become fully operational.[87] Besides the case of public service compensation, it could ultimately be suggested that when a certain advantage is to be considered as distinguishable from mere compensation, the Article 86(2) EC justification should have a role to play.[88]

IV SOME TENTATIVE CONCLUSIONS

It is doubtless that, in order to pursue certain social objectives, State intervention is necessary and actually desirable. It is here suggested that the constitutional settlement proposed by the original Treaty in Article 87 EC is still a valid one. The analysis of the case law on the relevance of the aims in State aid rules and of the financing of public services has shown that a proper construction of State aid law (ie one which is consistent with its substantive and procedural system) requires that scope and justification are kept separate. Whilst the definition of the former should rest on a mere effect-based analysis largely based on economic findings of the distortions produced by the measure, consideration of the objectives pursued by the latter should take place at a second stage, during which the existence of justifications is assessed by the Commission under Articles 87(3) EC and 86(2) EC. Under these provisions, it should be recalled that the Commission enjoys a wide discretion and may take account of social and other (economic and non-economic) considerations.[89] Quite crucially, in exercising its discretion in that context, 'the Commission has to ensure that the aims of

---

[87] It may, however, be interesting to sketch the main features of the system as it is currently envisaged by the Commission. Under the Decision pursuant to Art 86(3) EC, three categories of aid (small amounts of aid to undertakings with a limited turnover, aid to hospitals and social housing undertakings, aid to maritime transport undertakings for links to islands with an annual traffic of no more than 100,000 passengers per year) would be exempted from the duty of notification and would be considered as compatible with the common market provided that there is no over-compensation. The Framework would apply when the conditions for applying the Decision are not present. Prior notification of the planned aid is required but should be assessed against criteria substantially similar to those of the Decision.

[88] Consider, for instance, the case where it is necessary to rescue the only provider of a fundamental public service which is undergoing serious financial difficulties that may threaten the performance of its PSOs.

[89] The distinction between scope and justification seems to find support also in the recent caselaw, especially concerning public services, focusing on the issue of whether certain bodies or activities should be subject to the rules of free movement of services and competition. See, for services: C–157/99 *Smits and Peerbooms* (2001) ECR I–547; Case C–368/98 *Vanbraekel* (2001) ECR I-5363; C–385/99 *Müller-Fauré* (2003) ECR I–4509. See, for competition rules (and Art 82 EC in particular): Case C–475/99 *Ambulanz Glôckner* (2001) ECR I–8089. Admittedly, however, other decisions seem to show a different trend with the Court deciding that certain bodies or activities that share a social, or in any event a public,

free competition and Community solidarity are reconciled, whilst complying with the principle of proportionality'.[90]

In this delicate area, although the role of the ECJ and that of litigation has been proven necessary, in our view, Community institutions and more generally the political process should remain central. For this reason, we should welcome the firm and rather innovative approach adopted by the European Commission on State aid control and on the financing of services of general economic interest.[91] On the one side, the Commission proposes to grant a greater degree of flexibility for Member States to adopt certain aid measures. In particular, the Commission identified two categories of aid measures which deserve a simplified approach to the assessment of their compatibility with the common market: measures involving lesser amounts of State aid ('LASA' measures) may be regarded as too modest in size to present a significant threat to competition at Community level and trade between Member States; and measures which, because of their nature, can be expected to produce only limited effects on intra-Community trade ('LET' measures). The underlying ethos is that these forms of aid should be handled by Member States, provided that the aid is granted in a manner which facilitates the achievement of Community objectives of common interest and does not unduly distort competition.

The same ethos is apparent in the proposals in the area of public services, notably the Framework and the Decision on the application of Article 86 EC to the forms of public service compensation that do not fulfil the *Altmark* conditions and hence amount to State aid.[92] The Commission fully acknowledges the vital function of public services and recognises that Member States retain full power in organising them. The role of the

---

element do not fall within the scope of competition rules in the first place. Cf for instance, Cases C–264/01, C–306/01, C–354/01 and C–355/01 *AOK* (Judgment of 16 March 2004) (where the Court does not subject certain sickness funds to competition rules). Also: Case C–67/97 *Albany* (1999) ECR I–5751, para 60 Cases C–115 to 117/97 *Brentjens* (1999); ECR I–6029, para 157; Case C–291/97 *Maatschappij* (1999) ECR I–6125, para 47 (where the Court found that collective labour agreements fall outside the scope of Art 81(1) EC); Case C–390/99 *Wouters* (2002) ECR I–1577 (where the Court blurred the traditional distinction between prohibition and exemption in the context of Art 81 EC by introducing a new justification under Art 81(1) EC).

[90] Case T–380/94 *AIUFASS and AKT v Commission* (1996) ECR II–2169, para 54.
[91] See Draft Communications from the Commission: *A new framework for the assessment of lesser amounts of State aid*; *A new framework for the assessment of State aid which has limited effects on intra-Community trade*; *Community framework for state aid in the form of public service compensation*, all available at <http://europa.eu.int/comm/competition/state_aid/> (last visit on 31 March 2004).
[92] Proposals for a Community Framework for State aid in the form of public service compensation, DG D(2004), and for a Decision on the application of Article 86 of the Treaty to State aid in the form of public service compensation granted to certain undertakings entrusted with the operation of services of general economic interest, both available at <http://europa.eu.int/comm/competition/state_aid> (last visit on 31 March 2004).

Commission is limited to controlling that the State is really pursuing a public service obligation, and to impeding cases of over-compensation that effectively distort competition and trade in the Community.

Although it remains to be seen whether these proposals manage to address the call for clarification and simplification of State aid rules that have recently emerged,[93] they represent an important effort in a crucial moment for the modernisation of State aid law. The link between all these proposals is the acknowledgement that the preservation of certain values and objectives is common to both the European Union and its Member States. More fundamentally, they demonstrate the continuing quest for the 'European model of society'[94] which seems to rest on a well-balanced and flexible approach aimed at ensuring that social and economic policies are simultaneously and harmoniously pursued.[95]

---

[93] With respect to the financing of SGEIs, see Commission, *Green Paper on Services of General Interest*, COM(2003) 270 Final, para 4.8.

[94] Commission, *Green Paper on Services of General Interest*, COM(2003) 270 Final, para 2.

[95] See further G Amato, 'When the Economy is affected with a Public Interest' in F Snyder (ed), *The Europeanisation of Law* (Hart Publishing, 2000).

5

Healthcare as an Economic Service under EC Law

PANOS KOUTRAKOS*

I INTRODUCTION

In the not too distant past, the regulation of healthcare was viewed as an area over which EC law would have very limited effect, if any. This perception appeared to be borne out by the EC Treaty which stresses the complementary role of EC policies.[1] It was in the light of Article 152(4)(c) EC that Germany challenged Directive 98/43 on the advertising and sponsoring of tobacco products before the European Court of Justice.[2] In other words, the drafters of the Treaty were viewed as seeking to delineate the extent to which the Community institutions would act in the area of public health by means of positive action.

However, the implications of negative harmonisation produced by the Court's interpretation of the free movement provisions were more difficult to confine. It is the genesis and development of the Court's caselaw on the application of the fundamental provision of Article 49 EC[3] to healthcare that this chapter will examine. The material scope of Article 49 has been interpreted on the basis of an objective factor: a service should be 'normally provided for remuneration'.[4] This definition has been construed widely by the Court. The tone for this was set by Article 50 EC which provides a

---

[*] Professor of Law, University of Durham.

[1] See Arts 152(1) subparas 2 and 3, 152(2) and (4)(c) EC.

[2] Case C–376/98 *Germany v European Parliament and Council* [2001] ECR I–2247.

[3] Case 279/80 *Webb* [1981] ECR 3305, para 17.

[4] Art 50 subpara 1 EC. In addition, Art 50 makes it clear that its application is of a residual nature, that is, it should apply where neither the provision on free movement of goods nor that on capital or establishment apply: see V Hatzopoulos, 'Recent Developments of the Case Law of the ECJ in the Field of Services' (2000) 37 *Common Market Law Review* 43, 45–52. Furthermore, 'the person providing a service may, in order to do so, temporarily pursue his activity in the State where the service is provided, under the same conditions as are imposed by that State on its own nationals'.

non-exhaustive enumeration in the context of which the provision of healthcare services was deemed to fall within the scope of Article 49 EC quite early on. In particular, medical treatment was deemed to be a service within the meaning of Article 49 back in 1982, hence affording EU citizens travelling to other Member States in order to receive medical treatment EC law protection.[5] The same conclusion was reached in the early 1990s regarding termination of pregnancy in the (in)famous *Grogan* judgment.[6] However, the general principles underlying the extent to which the free movement provisions applied to healthcare were set out in the early 1990s. It was also then that the relationship between Article 49 EC and secondary law was determined by the Court. It is recalled that under Regulation 1408/71 individuals were entitled to receive medical care in another Member State, provided that certain conditions were met.[7]

This chapter will be structured as follows. The first part will place the principles set out in earlier caselaw within the Court's general jurisprudence. The second part will argue that the more recent caselaw, whilst relying upon a broad application of the free movement provision, was focused on the economic dimension of medical care and sought to strike the balance between compliance with Article 49 EC and national regulatory autonomy. The third part will analyse the recent judgment in *Müller-Fauré* and argue that, its consolidating and reforming function notwithstanding, it strengthens the legal position of individuals in a manner which is neither complete nor unconditional.[8]

II THE FIRST PHASE: SETTING OUT THE PRINCIPLE

In *Decker*[9] and *Kohll*[10] the Court examined the legal status of the provision of healthcare services in relation to the principles of free movement of goods and services. As both judgments have been analysed often and at

---

[5] Joined Cases 286/82 and 26/83 *Luisi and Carbone* [1984] ECR 377.

[6] Case C–159/90 *SPUC v Grogan* [1991] ECR I–4685.

[7] Reg 1408/71 on the application of social security schemes to employed persons, to self-employed persons and to members of their families moving within the Community (last consolidated version published at 1997) OJ L28/1. Under this set of rules, cross-border healthcare could be provided in cases of frontier workers, emergency care and non-emergency care pursuant to prior authorisation. For an exhaustive analysis of the EC provisions pursuant to which EC citizens may receive medical care across the border, see A P van der Mei, *Free Movement of Persons within the European Community: Cross-Border Access to Public Benefits* (Hart Publishing, 2003) pp 221–78. For the implementation of Reg 1408/71, see Y Jorens and B Schulte, 'The Implementation of Regulation 1408/71 in the Member States of the European Union' (2001) 3 *European Journal of Social Security* 237. See now: Reg 883/2004 on the coordination of social security systems, 2004 OJ L200/1 (partially repealing and replacing Reg 1408/71); discussed by F Pennings in his contribution to this collection.

[8] Case C–385/99 *Müller-Fauré* [2003] ECR I–4509.

[9] Case C–120/95 *Decker* [1998] ECR I–1831.

[10] Case C–158/96 *Kohll* [1998] ECR I–1931.

length,[11] this chapter will merely highlight their main tenets. In summary, the Court introduced the principle that the national regulation of social security system should be consistent with EC law. As the national rules in question rendered reimbursement of costs for medical treatment received in another Member State subject to prior authorisation whilst that was not the case regarding medical services received in the State of insurance, the Court had no difficulty in concluding that they were contrary to Article 49 EC. Finally, it was accepted that the authorisation requirement was justifiable on three grounds, namely control of health expenditure, protection of public health and the need to maintain a balanced medical and hospital service available to all its insured. However, it was concluded that the national requirement was in fact unjustified: whilst 'it cannot be excluded that the risk of seriously undermining the financial balance of the social security system may constitute an overriding reason in the general interest capable of justifying a barrier of that kind',[12] that was not the case because reimbursement would have incurred in accordance with the tariff of the State of insurance; the protection of public health did not have the effect of excluding the public health sector 'as a sector of economic activity and from the point of view of freedom to provide services, from the application of the fundamental principle of freedom of movement';[13] finally, it had not been proved that the authorisation requirement was 'necessary' to provide a balanced medical and hospital service accessible to all or that it was 'indispensable for the maintenance of an essential treatment facility or medical service on national territory'.[14]

In its judgments, the Court seeks to strike the balance between national regulatory autonomy and compliance with EC law. Indeed, the premise upon which the application of the principle of free movement is based is that the special nature of social security does not render it beyond the scope of the Community legal order. The Court supports this proposition on two interrelated pronouncements: on the one hand, it is for the Member States to regulate their social security policies and, hence, the conditions concerning

---

[11] A Baeyens, 'Free movement of goods and services in health care: a comment on the Court cases *Decker* and *Kohll* from a Belgian point of view' (1999) 6 *European Journal of Health Law* 373; P Cabal, 'Cross-border medical care in the European Union—bringing down a first wall' (1999) 24 *European Law Review* 387; R Giesen, Annotation of Case C–120/95 *Decker* and Case C–158/96 *Kohll* (1999) 36 *Common Market Law Review* 841; H E G M Hermans, 'Cross-border health care in the European Union: recent legal implications of *Decker* and *Kohll*' (2000) 6 *Journal of Evaluation in Clinical Practice* 431; A P Van der Mei, 'Cross-Border Access to Medical Care within the European Union—Some Reflections on the Judgments in *Decker* and *Kohll*' (1998) 5 *Legal Issues of Economic Integration* 277; Y Jorens, 'The Right to Health Care across Borders' in M McKee, E Mossialos and R Baeten (eds), *The Impact of EU Law on Health Care Systems* (PIE-Peter Lang, 2002) 83.

[12] Para 41 of the judgment in *Kohll*.

[13] *Ibid*, para 46.

[14] *Ibid*, para 52. The Court opined that a deviation from Art 49 EC could be justified 'in so far as the maintenance of a treatment facility or medical service on national territory is essential for the public health and even the survival of the population' (para 51).

insurance with a social security scheme and the conditions for entitlement to benefits; on the other hand, in doing so they should comply with EC law. The Court hardly breaks new ground, as this principle has underpinned its approach to a number of areas the typology of which indicates considerable diversity. Whilst some of them might appear to be of a technical nature, such as the determination of conditions for the registration of vessels,[15] certain others are associated with the core of national sovereignty. These include the exercise of monetary powers,[16] direct taxation,[17] criminal legislation,[18] and the protection of public security and the conduct of foreign policy. As regards the latter, it is recalled that, whilst acknowledging the fact that Member States have retained the power to conduct their foreign policy, they should do so 'in a manner consistent with Community law'.[19] In a similar vein, it was held that the foreign and security objective of a national measure whose effect is to prevent or restrict the export of certain products could not render it beyond the scope of the EC Treaty.[20] Another area where the application of EC law was upheld, the special nature of the national measure notwithstanding, is the organisation of the armed forces: the Court has held that national measures in that area were not excluded from the application of EC law merely because they aimed at the protection of public security or national defence.[21] Finally, it was held that 'although in principle criminal legislation and the rules of criminal procedure are matters for which the Member States are responsible, it does not follow that this branch of the law cannot be affected by Community law'.[22]

In light of the above, the Court's approach in *Decker* and *Kohll* does not take us into uncharted territory. In seeking to strike the balance between national regulatory autonomy and compliance with EC law, it provides yet another illustration of the considerable extent to which negative harmonisation enables the fundamental principles of EC law to penetrate the

[15] Case C–221/89 *Factortame* [1991] ECR I–3905. See also the determination of rules of civil procedure in Case C–122/96 *Saldanha* [1997] ECR I–5325, para 19 (with reference to Case 186/87 *Cowan* [1989] ECR 195).

[16] Joined Cases 6/69 and 11/69 *Commission v France* [1969] ECR 523; Case 57/86 *Greece v Commission* [1988] ECR 2855; Case 127/87 *Commission v Greece* [1988] ECR 3333.

[17] See Case C–80/94 *Wielockx* [1995] ECR I–2493, para 16; Case C–107/94 *Asscher* [1996] ECR I–3089, para 36; Case C–311/97 *Royal Bank of Scotland* [1999] ECR I–2651, para 17; Joined Cases C–397/98 and C–410/98 *Metallgesellschaft* [2001] ECR I–1727, para 37; Case C–324/00 *Lankhorst-Hohorst* [2002] ECR I–11779, para 26.

[18] Case 299/86 *Drexl* [1988] ECR 1213, para 17.

[19] Case C–124/95 *Centro-Com* [1997] ECR I–81, para 25.

[20] Case C–70/94 *Werner* [1995] ECR I–3189, para 10.

[21] See Case C–273/97 *Sirdar* [1999] ECR I–7403; C–285/98 *Kreil* [2000] ECR I–69; Case C–186/01 *Dory* [2003] ECR I–2479. For a comment, see I Canor, 'Harmonizing the European Community's Standard of Judicial Review?' (2002) 8 *European Public Law* 135; P Koutrakos, 'EC law and equal treatment in the armed forces' (2000) 25 *European Law Review* 433; P Koutrakos, 'How far is far enough? EC law and the organisation of the armed forces after *Dory*' (2003) 66 *Modern Law Review* 759; J Langer, Annotation of Cases C–273/97 *Sirdar* and C–285/98 *Kreil* (2000) 37 *Common Market Law Review* 1433.

[22] Case C–226/97 *Lemmens* [1998] ECR I–3711, para 19.

national legal orders. The legal principle underlying this approach has a solid constitutional foundation. Indeed, the duty of Member States 'to take all appropriate measures, whether general or particular, to ensure fulfilment of the obligations arising out of th[e EC] Treaty', as enshrined in Article 10 EC attests to this. The absence of a reference to that provision in both *Decker* and *Kohll* is as curious as it is revealing. Instead of putting forward an elaborate line of reasoning, the Court appears to view the application of the freedom to provide services to healthcare as a 'common sense' case. This is further illustrated by the absence of any reference to the *effet utile* argument, which has underpinned the introduction of the main constitutional principles of the EC legal order. It was only in relation to the organisation of the armed forces, an area associated with national sovereignty *par excellence*, that the Court was later to engage in a more detailed analysis of both the exceptional[23] and 'wholly exceptional'[24] EC Treaty provisions in order to reach the conclusion that no general exception might be inferred.[25]

III THE SECOND PHASE: PRINCIPLE *VERSUS* PRAGMATISM

Approximately four years ago, the full Court delivered its judgment in *Peerbooms*.[26] The importance of that case is illustrated by the fact that the Governments of ten Member States intervened along with Iceland and Norway and the European Commission. The reference from a Netherlands district court was about certain aspects of the sickness insurance scheme in the Netherlands. The central aspect of that scheme was the establishment of a system of benefits in kind according to which free treatment was provided for all insured persons pursuant to a number of agreements between sickness funds and providers of healthcare. It was reimbursement of the cost of medical services provided outside the Netherlands that was at stake in *Geraets-Smits and Peerbooms*: in the former case for Parkinson's disease in Germany and in the latter for special intensive therapy in Austria. Under the Netherlands law, the cost for the cross-border treatment could be reimbursed subject to prior authorisation from the sickness insurance fund. However, for the treatment in question to be regarded as a benefit within the context of the scheme and, hence, to be authorised prior to its provision, two conditions ought to be met: on the one hand, it should be regarded as normal in the professional circles concerned; on the other hand, it should be necessary for the medical treatment of the insured person.

---

[23] Namely Arts 30, 39, 46, 55, 58 and 64 EC.
[24] Namely Arts 296 and 297 EC.
[25] See C–285/98 *Kreil* [2000] ECR I–69, paras 16–18.
[26] Case C–157/99 *Geraets-Smits and Peerbooms* [2001] ECR I–5473. For a comprehensive analysis of the judgment, see V G Hatzopoulos, 'Killing national health and insurance systems but healing patients?' (2002) 39 *Common Market Law Review* 683.

A Medical Treatment in Hospitals as an Economic Service

The Court first deals with the application of Article 49 EC to medical care provided in hospitals. Having reaffirmed the position of medical services as within the scope of free movement, the Court opined that there was 'no need to distinguish between care provided in a hospital environment and care provided outside such an environment',[27] as the special nature of the former could not remove it from the ambit of the fundamental principle of free movement. This was the case notwithstanding the specific features of the Netherlands national insurance scheme. Furthermore, the element of remuneration was deemed present, and the applicability of Article 49 EC was not affected by the fact that remuneration is determined pursuant to various agreements between the sickness insurance fund and hospitals on the basis of pre-set scales of fees.

B The Legality of the Requirement of Prior Authorisation

The Court then assessed the legality of the national rule of prior authorisation under Article 49 EC. Its first condition, namely that treatment be classified as 'normal in the professional circles concerned', was deemed 'by its very essence … liable to lead to refusals of authorisations'.[28] As to the requirement that hospital treatment be a medical necessity, the Court held that 'by its very nature it will severely limit the circumstances in which such authorisation can be obtained'.[29] As the prior authorisation requirement does not actually apply for the majority of hospitals in the Netherlands,[30] the Court concluded that the national rules 'deter, or even prevent, insured persons from applying to providers of medical services established in another Member State and constitute, both for insured persons and service providers, a barrier to freedom to provide services'.[31]

C The Issue of Justification

In assessing whether the national rules were justifiable in the light of the overriding reasons already mentioned in *Decker* and *Kohll*, the Court

---

[27] Para 53.
[28] Para 63.
[29] Para 64.
[30] The Court pointed out that only hospitals situated near the Netherlands' borders were likely to enter into an agreement with sickness funds and, in any case, the greater part of hospital treatment provided in the Netherlands is by contracted hospitals.
[31] Para 69.

opined that the requirement for prior authorisation was both necessary and reasonable. The reason for that was the 'very distinct characteristics [of the] infrastructure' within which medical services were provided, that is in a hospital.[32] These were held to include

the number of hospitals, their geographical distribution, the mode of their organisation and the equipment with which they are provided, and even the nature of the medical services which they are able to offer, for all of which 'planning [should] be possible'.[33]

The central role of planning for hospital treatment was deemed to be vital in order to meet two objectives: on the one hand, to ensure the existence of sufficient and permanent access to a balanced range of high-quality hospital treatment; on the other hand, to control costs and prevent any wastage of financial, technical and human resources.[34]

However, the Court opined that the prior authorisation requirement would be necessary and reasonable in so far as the conditions attached to it were themselves justified and proportionate. This assessment involved an extraordinarily lengthy and detailed analysis. The requirement that the relevant medical treatment be normal in the professional circles was sanctioned in principle, as it was applicable to all hospitals, irrespective of whether they were contracted or not. In the light of the expressly recognised power of the Member States to organise their social security system, the Court had no difficulty accepting the right of the Member States to exclude medical and hospital treatment from reimbursement.[35] However, this right should be exercised in compliance with EC law, that being so only where the list of reimbursable benefits is drawn up in accordance with objective criteria, without reference to the origin of the products. Following a detailed description of such criteria, it was held that the notion of 'normal' hospital treatment should be construed in the light of 'what is sufficiently tried and tested by international medical science'.[36] The Court went on to give specific guidance on the grounds upon which the sickness insurance fund should determine whether treatment is normal.

---

[32] Para 76.

[33] *Ibid.*

[34] See paras 78–81. The Court mentions the severe consequences that the organisation of an accessible and stable supply of hospital services would suffer were insured persons free to receive hospital treatment in hospitals with no contractual links to their sickness insurance fund.

[35] This had already been held to be the case regarding medical products: Case 238/82 *Duphar* [1984] ECR 523.

[36] Para 94. The reason for this is that '[t]o allow only treatment habitually carried out on national territory and scientific views prevailing in national medical circles to determine what is or is not normal will not offer [objective] guarantees and will make it likely that Netherlands providers of treatment will always be preferred in practice' (para 96).

As for the second criterion, that is for the hospital treatment to be considered 'necessary' for its cost to be reimbursed, it was deemed justified by the Court in so far as

> it is construed to the effect that authorisation to receive treatment in another Member State may be refused on that ground only if the same or equally effective treatment can be obtained without undue delay from an establishment with which the insured person's sickness insurance fund has contractual arrangements.[37]

In an interesting coda, the day when the judgment in *Peerbooms* was delivered, the Court decided another relevant case. In *Vaenbraekel*,[38] the Court ruled that the State of insurance should provide additional reimbursement to patients who receive medical services in another Member State where the cost of the services in question is lower than that in the State of insurance.[39]

IV THE ECONOMIC DIMENSION OF MEDICAL CARE

The central tenet of the Court's approach is the economic nature of medical services. It is for this reason that they are held to be within the scope of Article 49 EC, as payment made by the sickness funds 'unquestionably' constitutes remuneration for the hospital.[40] It is recalled that not only does Article 49 EC apply to economic activities[41] but also the element of remuneration has been central to the exercise of the freedom to provide services since the establishment of the Community. It is that notion of remuneration which renders medical care within the scope of the freedom to provide services. Remuneration has been interpreted quite widely by the Court. It is not necessary, for instance, to be paid by the person for whom the service is provided. In the case of television broadcasting, for instance, it was irrelevant whether remuneration was provided by means of a licence fee or advertising.[42] In its standard definition in *Humbel*, it was defined in terms of 'the fact that it constitutes consideration for the service in question, and is normally agreed upon between the provider and the recipient of the service'.[43]

---

[37] Para 103.
[38] Case C–368/98 *Vanbraekel* [2001] ECR I–5363.
[39] See A P van der Mei, *Free Movement of Persons within the European Community: Cross-Border Access to Public Benefits* (Hart Publishing, 2003) pp 306–11.
[40] Para 58 of the judgment.
[41] Case C–369/89 *Roux* [1991] ECR I–273, para 9.
[42] Case 352/88 *Bond van Adverteerders* [1988] ECR 2085, para 16.
[43] Case 263/86 *Belgium v Humbel* [1988] ECR 5365, para 17, the logic of which was subsequently applied in Case C–109/92 *Wirth* [1993] ECR I–6447, paras 16 and 18. On the rights conferred upon students by EC law, see A P van der Mei, 'Freedom of Movement and Financial Aid for Students: Some Reflections on *Grzelczyk* and *Fahmi* and *Esmoris-Gerdeiro Pinedo Amoris*' (2001) 3 *European Journal of Social Security* 181.

What is noteworthy about the construction of remuneration in *Peerbooms* is its foundation upon clearly objective criteria. In order to determine its presence and, hence, the applicability of Article 49 EC, neither the identity of the person or institution paying for the service, nor their intention for paying, nor the procedure pursuant to which payment is ascertained is relevant. Instead, it is the very fact that remuneration is actually provided as consideration for the service rendered. It was thus objectively construed that remuneration was 'unquestionably' present in *Peerbooms*.

The objective construction of remuneration makes sense on the following grounds. First, it is consistent with the wide construction of the material scope of Article 49 EC by the Court. It is recalled that the illegal nature of an activity in one Member State may not prevent its classification as a service within the meaning of Article 49 EC.[44] As for the widely contested moral character of an activity in one Member State, it was held to be irrelevant to the applicability of Article 49 EC.[45] The same applies to the special nature of an activity, for instance the supply of manpower.[46]

Second, to ascertain the applicability of Article 49 EC on the basis of subjective criteria would be a retrograde step in the free movement jurisprudence. It is recalled that the intention underpinning the adoption of a national measure has always been irrelevant to the classification of that measure as *prima facie* contrary to the EC Treaty provisions on free movement. In the area of free movement of goods, for instance, this has always been the case regarding the prohibition on measures of an equivalent effect to customs duties.[47] Most importantly, it was also the central tenet of the *Dassonville* formula[48] as exemplified with great clarity in striking down German legislation on beer purity based on rules adopted in 1516.[49] The absence of subjective, intent-based criteria in the application of the free movement provisions is not negated even in the light of the post-*Keck* debate about the logic of removing 'certain selling arrangements' from the ambit of Article 28 EC because their application

> is not such as to hinder directly or indirectly, actually or potentially, trade between Member States ... provided that [they] apply to all affected traders operating within the national territory and provided that they affect in the

---

[44] See Case 15/78 *Koestler* [1978] ECR 1971 and Case C–275/92 *Schindler* [1994] ECR I–1039.

[45] Case C–159/90 *SPUC v Grogan* [1991] ECR I–4685.

[46] Case 279/80 *Webb* [1981] ECR 3305, para 10. In that case, it was the relevance of social policy rules which was put forward by the French Government as an argument against the application of Art 49 EC.

[47] See Case 24/68 *Commission v Italy* [1969] ECR 193. Also: J H H Weiler, 'The Constitution of the Common Market Place: The Free Movement of Goods' in P Craig and G de Búrca (eds), *The Evolution of EU Law* (OUP, 1999) 349.

[48] Case 8/74 *Dassonville* [1974] ECR 837, para 5.

[49] Case 178/84 *Commission v Germany* [1987] ECR 1227.

same manner, in law and fact, the marketing of domestic products of those from other Member States.[50]

It is recalled that this formulation was accused of introducing an intent-based discrimination criterion in the application of Article 28 EC approximately twenty years after such a criterion had been deemed unsuitable.[51] Close attention to the wording of the *Keck* formula, its applicability to *certain* selling arrangements and its focus on the *fact* that imported national products should not be affected more heavily than domestic products suggested that such concerns were exaggerated. This conclusion was borne out by the post-*Keck* caselaw which illustrated the Court's emphasis on a flexible application of Article 28 EC on the basis of an analysis of the factual context within which national restrictions were imposed.[52] Viewed from this angle, the objective construction of remuneration in the medical care caselaw constitutes a unifying factor in the interpretation of Articles 28 and 49 EC by the Court.

It is interesting that, in adopting this objective approach to the definition of remuneration, the Court ignored the advice given by two of its Advocates General.[53] The most interesting argument was put forward by Advocate General Colomer who stressed the manner in which payment was provided in the Netherlands by the sickness insurance funds. He pointed out that not only was a number of factors only indirectly related to the treatment taken into account, but also that, in some cases, payment was provided in the absence of actual treatment. In essence, by focusing on the method pursuant to which remuneration is determined and the service actually provided, the Advocate General questioned the economic nature of the service itself.

This position raises a legitimate concern: is an excessively wide definition of remuneration not likely to lead to the elimination, in essence, of the economic nature of the service? Would that not construe the scope of Article 49 EC too widely, hence undermining its wording? Legitimate though they may be in theory, these concerns are not justified on the basis of the Court's construction of remuneration in *Peerbooms*. This is so because the very central element of remuneration, namely its role as consideration for a service rendered, was undoubtedly present. The question is not whether the service was provided as part of the function of a State

---

[50] Joined Cases C–267–68/91 *Keck and Mithouard* [1993] ECR I–6097, para 16.

[51] See the criticism by AG Jacobs in Case C–412/93 *Leclerc-Siplec* [1995] ECR I–179 and S Weatherill, 'After *Keck*: Some Thoughts on how to Clarify the Clarification' (1996) 33 *Common Market Law Review* 885.

[52] See, for instance, Case C–254/98 *Heimdienst* [2000] ECR I–151; Joined Cases C–34–6/95 *De Agostini* [1997] ECR I–3843; and most famously Case C–405/98 *Gourmet* [2001] ECR I–1795. For an analysis of this position, see P Koutrakos, 'On groceries, alcohol and olive oil: more on free movement of goods after *Keck*' (2001) 26 *European Law Review* 391.

[53] Namely AG Saggio in Case C–368/98 *Vanbraekel* [2001] ECR I–5363 and AG Colomer in Case C–157/99 *Geraets-Smits and Peerbooms* [2001] ECR I–5473.

paternalistically construed. Instead, it was whether the medical professional providing the service received payment for the relevant service. At a more general level, whilst the distinction drawn in *Humbel* between remunerated economic activities and the performance of State duties towards its citizens may appear 'anomalous',[54] it should not be interpreted as introducing a fully commercial element.[55] The reference to the gainful character of the activity in *Humbel* itself was merely one illustration of the nature of education as beyond the scope of Article 49 EC. Instead, the Court's *dictum* should be interpreted within an economic context more generally construed. In his Opinion, for instance, Advocate General Slynn, as he then was, referred to remuneration as 'related to the economic cost of providing the services'.[56] In essence, what is central to the definition of remuneration is its very *raison d'être* as identified early on by the then Advocate General Warner:

> [T]he purpose of the definition of 'services' .... is to identify the kinds of services to which the Treaty applies and in particular to exclude those that are normally provided gratuitously.[57]

That purpose was clearly met in *Peerbooms*.

Fourth, the objective construction of remuneration and, hence, the applicability of Article 49 EC offers a viable alternative for a Court not keen in dwelling in what has been defined as 'post-welfare state'.[58] This term connotes the current phenomenon according to which the state delegates its role as the primary provider of services to (semi) private actors.[59]

V PARALLEL DISPLAY OF LEGAL PRINCIPLE AND PRAGMATISM

The most significant aspect of the judgment in *Peerbooms* is the assertion that medical care provided within hospitals falls entirely within the scope of Article 49 EC. This approach has two distinctive features. The first one is that, in construing hospital care under the free movement provision, the Court displays a flexible and pragmatic approach. This is apparent in its acknowledgement of both the central role of hospitals within the national

---

54 S O'Leary, 'The Free Movement of Persons and Services' in P Craig and G de Búrca (eds), *The Evolution of EU Law* (OUP, 1999) p 398.

55 See G Davies, 'Welfare as a Service' (2002) 29 *Legal Issues of Economic Integration* 27, 34–39 for an analysis of the distinction between the education cases and those on healthcare.

56 See n 43, p 5379, followed closely by 'otherwise fixed by commercial criteria'.

57 Opinion in Case 52/79 *Debauve* [1980] ECR 833 and Case 62/79 *Coditel* [1980] ECR 881, 876.

58 M Freedland, 'Law, Public Services, and Citizenship—New Domains, New Regimes?' in M Freedland and S Sciarra (eds), *Public Services and Citizenship in European Law: Public and Labour Law Perspectives* (Clarendon Press, 1998) 1, 28.

59 See V George, 'Political Ideology, Globalisation and Welfare Futures in Europe' (1998) 27 *Journal of Social Policy* 17.

health systems and the particular challenges that their efficient management ought to meet. It is pointed out that

> were large numbers of insured persons to decide to be treated in other Member States even when the hospitals having contractual arrangements with their sickness insurance funds offer adequate identical or equivalent treatment, the consequent outflow of patients would be liable to put at risk the very principle of having contractual arrangements with hospitals and, consequently, undermine all the planning and rationalisation carried out in this vital sector in an effort to avoid the phenomena of hospital overcapacity, imbalance in the supply of hospital medical care and logistical and financial wastage.[60]

It is in the light of these considerations that the prior authorisation requirement is deemed legitimate in principle. In that respect, the arguments of the Member States which submitted observations before the Court were not in vain. Viewed from this angle, the Court's appears strict in principle and pragmatic in practice: whilst the scope of the free movement provisions is construed broadly, the distinct features of the relevant activities notwithstanding, those features are taken into account once the authority of EC law has been affirmed. This is illustrated by the wide construction of the overriding reasons of public interest that may justify a national restriction on free movement. According to the Court, the maintenance of a balanced medical and hospital service open to all is accepted as such, despite the fact that it is 'intrinsically linked to the method of financing the social security system'.[61] This display of legal principle and pragmatism is hardly a novelty in the Court's caselaw. The area of external relations is a case in point: on the one hand, the political objectives of external trade measures have been held irrelevant to their position as within the scope of EC trade law; on the other hand, the Member States enjoy wide discretion to define their security interests and assess whether these would be served best by deviating from EC law.[62]

In adopting this approach to the application of the principle of free movement to hospital care, the Court does accept the practical implications of national regulatory autonomy in the area of social security. For instance, in acknowledging the right of a Member State to exclude certain treatments from its sickness insurance scheme, the Court opined that whether that treatment was covered by such systems in another Member State was irrelevant. It is interesting that a similar point had been made in *Alpine*

---

[60] Para 106.

[61] Para 73 of the judgment.

[62] See Case C–70/94 *Werner* [1995] ECR I–3189 and Case C–83/94 *Leifer* [1995] ECR I–3231. For the pragmatic approach underpinning the Court's caselaw in the area of external relations, see the influential analysis in T Tridimas and P Eeckhout, 'The External Competence of the Community and the Case-Law of the Court of Justice: Principle Versus Pragmatism' (1994) 14 *Yearbook of European Law* 143.

Investments where the Court, having held that a Dutch measure banning cold-calling in the area of financial services was in principle contrary to Article 49 EC, examined whether that measure was necessary and proportionate in order to maintain the reputation of the national financial sector. It was pointed out that whether less onerous measures were in force in other Member States in order to protect the same public interest was irrelevant to the assessment of the Dutch measure as justified.[63] This parallelism between the judgments in *Alpine Investments* and *Peerbooms* is all the more interesting as in both cases the Court interpreted the scope of Article 49 EC widely before it construed the exercise of national authority in protecting overriding interests of public policy in equally wide terms.[64]

VI INTRODUCING PROCEDURALISATION

Whilst appearing receptive to national concerns about the regulation of hospital care, the Court's assertion that that should fall entirely within the scope of Article 49 EC is of considerable legal significance. The reason for this is that, its wide construction notwithstanding, the exercise of national regulatory autonomy is now subject to control set by EC law. This leads to the second distinctive feature of the judgment in *Peerbooms*, namely the proceduralisation that the Court appears to introduce. Its purpose is twofold, namely to ascertain whether national restrictions are justified and to ensure the effectiveness of the principle of free movement of services. This aspect of the judgment may be better understood in the light of a part of the judgment which is worth citing in full:

> ... in order for a prior administrative authorisation scheme to be justified even though it derogates from such a fundamental freedom, it must, in any event, be based on objective, non-discriminatory criteria which are known in advance, in such a way as to circumscribe the exercise of the national authorities' discretion, so that is it not used arbitrarily ... Such a prior administrative authorisation scheme must likewise be based on a procedural system which is easily accessible and capable of ensuring that a request for authorisation will be dealt with objectively and impartially within a reasonable time and refusals to grant authorisation must also be capable of being challenged in judicial or quasi-judicial proceedings.[65]

---

[63] Case 384/93 *Alpine Investments* [1995] ECR I–1141, para 51.

[64] In *Alpine Investments*, the wide construction of Art 49 EC and the explicit refusal of the Court to apply the *Keck* formula may be explained in the light of the all-encompassing extraterritorial scope of the national measure in question: see D O'Keeffe and A Bavasso, 'Four Freedoms, One Market and National Competence: In Search of a Dividing Line' in D O'Keeffe and A Bavasso (eds), *Liber Amicorum in Honour of Lord Slynn of Hadley. Vol I: Judicial Review in European Union Law* (Kluwer, 2000) 541, 551.

[65] Para 90 of the judgment.

In setting out the procedural requirements pursuant to which national regulatory autonomy should be exercised in order to be deemed legal, the above passage is revealing in various ways. First, it illustrates an approach to the assessment of the legality of national action which is not only heavily focused on procedures, but is also as detailed in character as it is broad in scope. This is borne out by the remaining analysis by the Court, in particular its attempt to define when treatment in a non-contracted hospital is 'necessary' and 'normal'. Second, in proceduralising the assessment of the legality of national regulatory autonomy, the judgment in *Peerbooms* illustrates with unmistakable clarity that the final arbiter in the exercise of the right of the Member States to regulate their sickness insurance system is the Court itself. Therefore, widely though it may be construed, the national power in the area of social security is *de facto* curtailed. Third, the intensity and depth of the procedural requirements laid down in caselaw are bound to be analogous to the intensity of review the Court is prepared to exercise over national regulatory autonomy. The judgment in *Peerbooms* suggests that the latter is likely to be considerable. The definition of what may constitute 'normal' treatment, for instance, is noteworthy: one of the considerations national authorities are asked to take into account is whether the treatment in question 'is covered or not covered by the sickness insurance system of the Member State in which the treatment is provided'.[66] It is recalled that similar considerations are held, in the same judgment, to be irrelevant to a Member State's assessment of what should be covered by its sickness insurance scheme. In other words, a criterion which does not affect the exercise of the national power to regulate their social security system may affect the circumstances in which that system operates within the realm of the principle of free movement.

Finally, there is another parameter whose role is a *conditio sine qua non* of the above, namely the role of national courts. It is recalled that all judgments on healthcare and its status under EC law have been delivered under the preliminary reference procedure. It is not only because national courts are bound to apply the Court's ruling that their role is of utmost importance. As regards the consistency of national rules on healthcare with Article 49 EC, it is the intense proceduralisation introduced by the Court that renders national courts at the centre of effectiveness of the principle of free movement. This is so because the detailed character of the procedural requirements set out by the Court, inevitably, broadens the scope of assessment that the referring court is bound to make under Article 234 EC. However, the proceduralisation apparent in *Peerbooms* does not have the same effect on both the Court and the national courts: in fact, the extent to which the latter may play an active part in the application of Article 49 EC is determined

---

[66] Para 98.

by whether the former would enable them to do so. Is the Court prepared to treat the essential procedural tests it has introduced in its caselaw as questions for the national courts to decide? Or is the detailed character of those requirements too considerable a temptation for it to ignore?

VII THE THIRD PHASE: THE JUDGMENT IN *MÜLLER-FAURÉ*

These questions were addressed in *Müller-Fauré*, a judgment delivered by the full Court.[67] Nine governments submitted observations, along with the Commission and two governments of EEA countries. This reference from the Higher Social Security Court was, again, about the Netherlands sickness insurance scheme and concerned two cases of provision of medical care. The first one involved dental treatment in Germany the cost of which the Fund refused to reimburse on the ground that insured persons were only entitled to treatment itself and not to reimbursement of any related costs, except in exceptional circumstances which did not exist in the case under consideration. The second case was about an arthroscopy carried out in Belgium pending a request for an authorisation by the Fund. That request was eventually rejected and the Fund subsequently declined to reimburse the costs for the treatment which was provided both in a hospital and outside. In particular, it was argued that it had not been established that the patient could not reasonably wait, for medical or other reasons, until the Fund had taken a decision on her application. As for the waiting time for the operation itself, about six months according to the documents before the Court, it was alleged not to have been unreasonable.

The starting point for the Court's analysis was the reaffirmation, often in identical language, of the principles underpinning the applicability of Article 49 EC to medical care. Then, in order to determine whether the national rules in question were objectively justified whilst meeting the requirement of necessity and proportionality, it summarised what might be called 'the national argument' as follows:

> If it were open to patients to get treatment in a Member State other than that in which they are insured, without prior authorisation to that effect, the competent State could no longer guarantee that in its territory there would be a high-quality, balanced medical and hospital service open to all and hence a high level of public health protection.[68]

It is at this juncture that the Court makes a point distinct from its past dicta as it opines that 'an overall approach must necessarily be adopted in relation

[67] Case C–385/99 *Müller-Fauré* [2003] ECR I–4509.
[68] Para 69.

to the consequences of freedom to provide health-related services'.[69] In doing so, it refers explicitly to the distinction between hospital services and non-hospital services as one that 'may sometimes prove difficult to draw'.[70]

A Healthcare within Hospitals

In relation to healthcare provided within hospitals, the Court reaffirmed their distinct nature, reproduced the judgment in *Peerbooms verbatim* and concluded, accordingly, that the prior authorisation system would be justified provided that the procedural conditions already set out would be met. As to whether these conditions were met by the requirement that medical treatment in a Member State other than that of insurance be 'a medical necessity', the Court reaffirmed the *Peerbooms dictum* according to which the crucial issue is whether the same or equally effective treatment could be provided without undue delay in a medical establishment with which the Fund has an agreement. What distinguishes this judgment from prior caselaw is the Court's express reference to waiting lists in the State of insurance. It is worth citing the relevant extract in full:

> ... a refusal to grant prior authorisation which is based not on fear of wastage resulting from hospital overcapacity but solely on the ground that there are waiting lists on national territory for the hospital treatment concerned, without account being taken of the specific circumstances attaching to the patient's medical condition, cannot amount to a properly justified restriction on freedom to provide services. It is not clear from the arguments submitted to the Court that such waiting times are necessary, apart from considerations of a purely economic nature that cannot as such justify a restriction on the fundamental principle of freedom to provide services, for the purpose of safeguarding the protection of public health. On the contrary, a waiting time which is too long or abnormal would be more likely to restrict access to balanced, high-quality hospital care.[71]

B Healthcare beyond Hospitals

In relation to medical care provided in a non-hospital environment, the Court deemed the prior authorisation requirement unjustified too. In particular, it opined that the assertion that the absence of a prior authorisation requirement would result in seriously undermining the financial balance of the Netherlands social security system was not proved. In order to show that the removal of the prior-authorisation requirement would not have

---

[69] Para 74.
[70] Para 75.
[71] Para 92.

devastating implications for the financial viability of the Netherlands social security scheme, the Court pointed out that, bar emergencies, medical care is provided near the place where the patience resides, because familiarity enables him to build a relationship of trust with the provider of the service. Furthermore, it is still within the powers of the Member States to determine the extent of the sickness cover available to insured persons.

C The Distinct Features of a Sickness Insurance Scheme Providing for Benefits in Kind

Finally, in a long part of its judgment, the Court addressed the extent to which its ruling and the removal of the prior authorisation requirement for non-hospital services would undermine the essential characteristics of the Netherlands sickness insurance scheme. The Court proceeded in a twofold manner. First, it made a point of principle: whilst the organisation of national security systems falls within the power of Member states, 'the achievement of the fundamental freedoms guaranteed by the Treaty inevitably requires Member States to make some adjustments. It does not follow that this would undermine their sovereign powers in this field'.[72] Second, it was held that, in practical terms, its construction of medical services as within the scope of Article 49 EC would not undermine the fundamental logic of the Netherlands sickness insurance system. This conclusion was based on certain interrelated arguments: mechanisms for *ex post facto* reimbursement do exist pursuant to Regulation 1408/71 even in Member States whose sickness insurance system is based on benefits in kind;[73] reimbursement would only be sought within the limits of the cover provided by the sickness insurance scheme of the Member State of insurance; and it is pointed out that the Member States are free to fix the amounts of reimbursement to be claimed by patients who received care in another Member State 'provided that those amounts are based on objective, non-discriminatory and transparent criteria'.[74]

VIII REAFFIRMING, CONSOLIDATING AND REFORMING: THE MULTIFARIOUS FUNCTIONS OF *MÜLLER-FAURÉ*

In certain respects, the judgment in *Müller-Fauré* follows the pattern set by prior caselaw illustrated by its considerable emphasis on the economic nature of medical care as a service. This is apparent not only in the confir-

---

[72] Para 102.
[73] Para 104, where reference to cases where it has not been possible to complete the formalities during the insured person's stay in the State other than that of insurance (Art 34 Reg 574/72 lays down the procedure implementing Reg 1408/71) or where authorisation for treatment abroad has been provided pursuant to Art 22(1)(c) Reg 1408/71.
[74] Para 107.

mation of the principles introduced in *Kohll* and reaffirmed in *Peerbooms* but also in more subtle ways. It is noteworthy that, in examining the factors which ought to determine whether treatment in a non-contracted hospital is necessary, the Court reproduces *verbatim* the conditions already laid down in *Peerbooms*:

> The national authorities are required to have regard to all the circumstances of each specific case and to take due account not only of the patient's medical condition at the time when authorisation is sought ... but also of his medical history.[75]

However, there is another condition which is added in *Müller-Fauré* and which had not been mentioned previously, namely

> 'where appropriate, ... the degree of pain or the nature of the patient's disability which might, for example, make it impossible or extremely difficult for him to carry out a professional activity.[76]

It is not so much the manner in which this factor is added, ever so subtly, as the significance it appears to attribute to the practical implications that medical treatment, or the lack thereof, may have on the ability of the patient. Viewed from this angle, what appears to be relevant is the medical condition of the patient as well as its effect on the patient's capacity to carry on as an economic operator. In addition, the economic nature of medical care is also underlined by the Court's construction of remuneration to which reference is made twice in the judgment.[77]

However, the judgment in *Müller-Fauré* is considerably bolder than those delivered in the past. One of its central features is the assessment made by the Court as to whether the removal of the requirement of prior authorisation in respect of services supplied in a Member State other than that of insurance would undermine the financial balance of the Netherlands social security system. The Court does not confine itself to declaring the lack of evidence to that effect; instead, it opines that there is no proof that such removal

> would give rise to patients to other countries in such large numbers, despite linguistic barriers, geographic distance, the cost of staying abroad and lack of information about the kind of care provided there that ... the overall level of public-health protection would be jeopardised.[78]

This extract is most interesting both for its content and style. It is clear that the Court deems the concerns expressed by national governments exaggerated. In doing so, it makes a step further than *Peerbooms* in so far as it

---

[75] Para 90.
[76] *Ibid.*
[77] At paras 39 and 103.
[78] Para 95.

opines that, whilst justifiable, the national restriction was in fact unjustified. In doing so, a hint of irony is apparent, as reference is made to all the
factors which would, in practice, render the cross-frontier supply of healthcare the exception rather than the rule for patients. In practical terms, the
assessment made by the Court does more than merely reject the concerns
expressed by the Member States as unfounded: it expresses a view as to the
extent to which borders are still relevant to the everyday life of EU citizens.
It suggests that, at least as far as their health is concerned, Europeans are
attached to the facilities provided in their own State. It is noteworthy that
all but one of the factors mentioned by the Court are of a practical nature,
related to language, distance and cost rather than irrational preferences or
nationalistic reactions. Following this line of reasoning, the Court reached
exactly the opposite conclusion from that of its Advocate General; relying
upon the considerable movement of health professionals, the territorial
proximity of many Member States and drawing, refreshingly, upon *Le
malade imaginaire*, Advocate General Colomer had suggested that, in the
absence of the prior authorisation requirement, the cross-border provision
of medical services within a hospital environment would, indeed, endanger
the financial viability of national health systems.[79]

In normative terms, in making this assessment within the context of the
preliminary reference procedure, the Court assumes a role that is purported
to be reserved for the referring court. The judgment in *Müller-Fauré* illustrates with unmistakable clarity that the dividing line between the roles of
the referring court and the Court of Justice under Article 234 EC may be
blurred. In terms of the relationship between national and Community judi-
ciary, this course is not without risks. It is recalled that only months before
the Court delivered its judgment in *Müller-Fauré*, a High Court Judge had
declined to follow the conclusion of the judgment the Court had delivered
in response to his reference.[80]

The above attempt to revolt by a national judge is highly unlikely to signal a deterioration in the relationship between national courts and the
Court of Justice; as a matter of fact, it is an isolated case which has already
been overturned on appeal.[81] However, this temporary aberration does not
make the assessment carried out in *Müller-Fauré* any less remarkable. This
is all the more so in the light of the broader context of the free movement
jurisprudence. In the area of free movement of goods, for instance, it is
rarely the case that the Court engages in such a substantive evaluation, leaving this matter, instead, for the referring court. In *Gourmet*, for instance,
the Court refrained from assessing whether the Swedish ban on advertising

---

[79] See paras 51 *et seq* of his Opinion.
[80] Case C–206/01 *Arsenal v Reed* [2003] 1 *Common Market Law Reports* 12. See A Arnull,
'Annotation of Case C–206/01 *Arsenal*' (2003) 40 *Common Market Law Review* 753; G
Davies, 'Of rules and referees' (2003) 28 *European Law Review* 408.
[81] *Arsenal Football Club plc v Mathew Reed* (Judgment of the Court of Appeal, 21 May 2003).

of alcohol was necessary and proportionate. This was a noteworthy case, both because of the overwhelming evidence of the unduly restrictive effects of the national measure and the detailed and compelling analysis of Advocate General Jacobs to that effect—after all, that case was ideally placed for the Court to adjudicate on the necessity and proportionality of the national measure.[82] In other cases, the Court has not only reserved the assessment of the legality of justifiable national barriers to trade for the referring courts, but it also set out in a quite detailed manner the precise parameters that should be taken into account, often entailing a very onerous task for the national court.[83]

In order to appreciate the significance of the assessment made by the Court in *Müller-Fauré*, account ought to be taken of a number of relevant factors. The first factor is the considerable significance of the subject matter of the reference. Whilst the applicability of Article 49 EC is beyond doubt, its practical implications for the national health systems are far from clear. To a certain extent, uncertainty may be inevitable in a decentralised system of adjudication. However, it may seriously undermine the effective application of EC law if persistent in areas of acute political sensitivity and financial importance. The second factor that may have influenced the Court's assessment of the Netherlands rule was the circumstances under which the reference was made in *Müller-Fauré*. The referring court had been specifically asked by the Court registry as to whether the reference should be maintained following the *Peerbooms* judgment, to which it responded in the affirmative. In doing so, the referring court pointed out that the latter judgment had not dealt specifically with the individual features of the Netherlands sickness insurance scheme, neither had it properly defined the notion of 'reasonable time'. This is quite significant: the normative repercussions of its judgments for the nature of the preliminary reference procedure notwithstanding, the referring court did, in fact, require detailed guidance as to how to apply the specific requirements set out in the Court's limited caselaw so as to ascertain the legality of the national measure.[84] It is interesting that another case where the Court carried out a substantive assessment of the legality of the national measure was *Kreil*, that is another preliminary ruling, on the German ban on women's access to the armed forces. This was an area of acute sensitivity for the Member States where the Court had only set out the state of the law in one prior judgment whose implications were not entirely clear.[85] In concluding

---

[82] See P Koutrakos, 'On groceries, alcohol and olive oil: more on free movement of goods after *Keck*' (2001) 26 *European Law Review* 391, 399.

[83] For instance: Case C–368/95 *Familiapress* [1997] ECR I–3689.

[84] It is interesting that both measures examined in *Peerbooms* were subsequently held to be lawful by the referring courts: see E Mossialos and M McKee, *EU Law and the Social Character of Health Care* (PIE-Peter Lang, 2002) 83, 97.

[85] Case C–273/97 *Sirdar* [1999] ECR I–7403.

that the national measure, whilst justifiable, was in fact unjustified, the Court removed uncertainties as to the practical implications of the relevant EC law requirements. It is the same principle that underpins *Müller-Fauré*: having outlined the course of action for the national authorities in the area of cross-border medical services, the Court thought it necessary to familiarise national courts with what was expected of them.

Finally, another reason which may have influenced the Court's decision to engage in a bold assessment of the national measure in *Müller-Fauré* was the reception of its judgment in *Peerbooms* by national authorities.[86] The United Kingdom was one of the Member States whose Government had submitted written observations to the Court in the latter judgment and, yet, in less than two months after the ruling was delivered, it launched a programme of cross-border provision of medical care. This pilot programme involved three National Health Service Trusts from Southeast England sending patients in need of routine operations to French and German hospitals. This programme involved 190 patients and, according to an evaluation report commissioned by the Department of Health, is deemed successful.[87] Furthermore, the institutionalisation of cross-border provision of medical care appears to be at the centre of the future policy of the Department.[88]

Another noteworthy feature of the judgment in *Müller-Fauré* is that the Court appears keen to demonstrate that, in both legal and practical terms, the removal of the prior authorisation requirement would not impinge unduly upon the right of the Member States to regulate their health systems. It does so twice: first, in suggesting that, in any event, Member States would be able to determine the extent of the sickness cover available to insured persons; second, in stressing that removal of the prior authorisation requirement would not undermine the specific features of the Netherlands system which provides for benefits in kind. In essence, the Court makes it clear that, whilst the very considerable power of the Member States to regulate their social security system has been challenged, it is their remaining power to manage that system that is of utmost importance. The line of reasoning underpinning this assumption is in contrast to the position put forward by Advocate General Colomer in his Opinion. He had argued that the requirement that Member States exercise their right to regulate their social security system in accordance with EC law should not become tantamount to challenging their fundamental policy choices.[89]

---

[86] See *The Financial Times* (16 October 2001) p 12.

[87] See K Lowson, P West, S Chaplin and J O'Reilly, *Evaluation of Treating Patients Overseas* (2002) <www.doh.gov.uk/international/evaluationreport.htm>.

[88] See Guidance for Primary Care and Acute Trusts—Treating More Patients and Extending Choice: Overseas Treatment for NHS Patients <http://www.doh.gov.uk/international/overseastreatment.pdf>.

[89] See para 58 of his Opinion.

It is interesting that, whilst the judgment in *Müller-Fauré* removes some of the uncertainty that had surrounded the Court's prior caselaw, it is in relation to those national powers that a degree of uncertainty persists. This is the case, for instance, regarding the right of the Member States to determine the amounts of reimbursement to be claimed by patients receiving care across the border, provided that the relevant criteria are objective, non-discriminatory and transparent. As the regulation of national security systems is now largely shaped within the parameters of EC law, it will be the nuances of the management of those systems that will give rise to further references before the Court of Justice.

IX MARKET INTEGRATION AND SOCIAL PROTECTION

The principles set out in the caselaw examined in this chapter have been more recently reaffirmed by the Court.[90] There can be little doubt that, in principle, patients are the direct beneficiaries of the Court's rulings on healthcare. In particular, they may benefit in two ways: either by becoming active consumers and receiving cross-border medical treatment for which they would expect speedy reimbursement or by benefiting from the momentum that *Peerbooms* and *Müller-Fauré* have produced for Member States in a manner clearly illustrated in the pilot programme launched by the Department of Health in United Kingdom. However, it is noteworthy that the line of reasoning followed by the Court in the relevant judgments is not couched in social welfare terms. It is not the EU citizen for the benefit of whom efficiency and choice should underlie the assessment of the legality of national measures. Instead, any benefits for the citizen accrue from non-social considerations which were objective in nature, namely the mechanical application of the free movement provision of the EC Treaty, the practical realities of everyday life which render cross-border provision of medical care the exception rather than the rule and, in consequence, the insignificant financial implications for the Member States.

In delivering the judgment in *Müller-Fauré* in an 'economic' rather than 'welfare' language, the Court hardly sails in uncharted waters. It is recalled that the starting point in both *Kohll* and *Peerbooms* was the objective construction of remuneration which resulted in a mechanical application of Article 49 EC. This approach is not only reaffirmed in *Müller-Fauré* but is reinforced to a very considerable extent. It was pointed out above how the Court, relying upon the geographical, cultural and language barriers prevailing within the EU, concluded that the prior authorisation requirement for services rendered beyond a hospital environment was not only

---

[90] See Case C–56/01 *Inizan* [2003] ECR I–12403.

illegal in principle but also unjustified. In addition, it stressed the practical significance of the national power to manage the social security system, in particular by determining the level of reimbursement available to insured persons. In order to bring this point home, the Court even made express reference to the amount of money available to insured persons as reimbursement for the cost of their treatment: Ms Müller-Fauré would only be entitled to €221.03 instead of €3,806.35 which was the actual cost of the operation.[91]

In the light of the above, is the argument that the Court has often assumed a 'socially activist role'[92] justified as regards the caselaw on the cross-border provision of healthcare? A response in the affirmative is not inconceivable. Indeed, it has been argued that, in fact, the Court does engage in a balancing act in its free movement jurisprudence, albeit *sub silentio*.[93] However, it is suggested that not only is this not apparent in the cases on healthcare, but also that the judgment in *Müller-Fauré* suggests quite the opposite. As far as medical care provided in a hospital environment is concerned, it was merely the objective construction of remuneration that rendered cross-border movement less cumbersome for citizens. Whilst of apparent significance for individuals,[94] this method of extending the scope of the application of the free movement principle is not tantamount to defining a social welfare right. This becomes apparent in relation to medical care provided beyond a hospital environment. It was pointed out above that, in concluding that the requirement of prior authorisation was unjustified, the Court relied upon its own assessment of what it viewed as objective factors; most importantly, it did so in the absence of arguments to the contrary. This line of reasoning suggests that the benefits bestowed upon individuals following this bold assessment are, in fact, incidental in nature and conditional in effect. In essence, individuals benefit from the existence of objective, non-legal barriers which maintain distinct markets within the single market. It is due to what the Court perceives as *de facto* disunity that the cross-border provision of medical care is interpreted liberally. In a paradoxical manner, fragmentation appears to be the *conditio sine qua non* of integration.

The normative consequences of this line of reasoning are significant and multifarious. On the one hand, if a Member State were to submit specific evidence about the mobility of patients in a future reference, the prior authorisation requirement could be deemed justified. On the other hand, if

---

[91] Para 106 of the judgment.

[92] K Lenaerts and P Foubert, 'Social Rights in the Case-Law of the European Court of Justice' (2001) 28 *Legal Issues of Economic Integration* 267, 293.

[93] See P Davies, 'Market Integration and Social Policy in the Court of Justice' (1995) 24 *Industrial Law Journal* 49, 66 *et seq*, where specific references to caselaw on free movement of goods, state aids and public undertakings.

[94] See D Chalmers, 'The Single Market: From Prima Donna to Journeyman' in J Shaw and G More (eds), *New Legal Dynamics of European Union* (Clarendon Press, 1995) 55, 63.

it were to transpire that a very considerable number of citizens were informed of the Court's pronouncements and, miraculously, fled their own country in order to receive medical treatment in other Member States, the objective factors mentioned by the Court in *Müller-Fauré* might not reflect the reality accurately. If that were to be the case, a *de facto* united market in medical care would provide justifications to national barriers to free movement. Viewed from this angle, the economic language used by the Court suggests that the criterion for the justification of national regulatory measures in the area under discussion would require constant redefinition.

The Court's reluctance to articulate a 'social welfare' line of reasoning may be understood in the light of various considerations, one being the subject-matter of the cases under discussion and the financial implications of judicially-driven market integration for national social security systems. Another consideration might be the fact that the debate as to whether there is a 'European welfare state' as such[95] is, as yet, open. Furthermore, even if there is, it is far from clear which 'values' does a 'European social model' encapsulate.[96] However, most importantly, it is the link between nationals of Member States and their social security system that makes the regulation of the latter controversial. It should not be forgotten that the corollary of the right of individuals to receive medical treatment in another Member State is the duty of the providers of medical services established in the latter not to raise obstacles. From the host Member States' point of view, it is essential that their social security system is not undermined by excessive movement of patients. In general, it is important that individuals should not feel that the capacity of their health systems to provide comprehensive care of a high quality is under threat.[97] Citizens feel safe within the context of the social security system of their State and the Court alluded to that when it indicated that the volume of cross-border movement by recipients of medical services was not very significant. Had the Court defined healthcare services in 'social welfare' terms, it would have entered a political arena of acute sensitivity. In effect, the Court would have risked dissatisfaction not only from national authorities but also EU citizens.

---

[95] See B Schulte, 'The Welfare State and European Integration' (1999) 1 *European Journal of Social Security* 7, 9 *et seq* where reference to the considerable degree of variation in social protection afforded in Member States.

[96] These terms are used in T Hervey, 'Mapping the Contours of European Union Health Law and Policy' (2002) 8 *European Public Law* 69, 72.

[97] It has been argued that the judgments in *Decker* and *Kohll* provided for no defence mechanism against a potential 'medical tourism', hence giving rise to a regulatory 'race to the bottom': T Hervey, 'Social Solidarity: A Buttress Against Market Law?' in J Shaw (ed), *Social Law and Policy in an Evolving European Union* (Hart Publishing, 2000) 31, 42. In referring to the objective reasons which render excessive patient mobility unlikely to arise, the Court appears to suggest that such concerns are exaggerated. For an analysis of the 'race to the bottom' phenomenon, see C Barnard, 'Social dumping and the race to the bottom: some lessons for the European Union from Delaware?' (2000) 25 *European Law Review* 57.

In the light of the above and given that the existing caselaw on cross-border provision of medical care has arisen exclusively from disputes about the rights of the recipients of the service, one should be rather reluctant to deduce a general theory about the Court's approach to the regulation of healthcare under Article 49 EC. However, this note of caution is not to suggest that the improvement of the position of EU patients is insignificant: not only have national governments reacted to the Court's caselaw by incorporating institutionalised cross-border movement as a way of addressing concerns underlying national healthcare systems, but also that caselaw has not passed unnoticed by the Community institutions. The Health Council of 26 June 2002 accepted the suggestion by Public Health Commissioner Byrne and launched a 'high-level process of reflection' on patient mobility and healthcare developments in the EU. The aim is for the reflection process to reach its conclusions by the end of 2003. Commissioner Byrne stated:

> Member States are responsible for their own healthcare systems and will remain so. It is not the aim of this reflection process to change that, but it is an opportunity to reflect and collectively consider the full range of issues affecting health and health systems at European level and to see how best to respond. European Health systems share many common aims, whilst remaining distinctively national. This reflection process is intended to work towards a common vision of how Europe should help to support and foster those aims.[98]

This statement is not only characteristically open-ended, but also contains the term 'vision' which, to a cynical commentator of EC affairs, might appear rather alarming. However, this does not negate the fact that the Court's caselaw has created considerable momentum which is bound to benefit EU citizens.

X CONCLUSION

In legal terms, the existing caselaw on cross-border provision of medical care contains various commendable elements, namely the extension of the application of Article 49 EC, the detailed character of the Court's pronouncements and the rigour which it appears prepared to display in examining the specific context within which national measures are applied. However, the benefits for the legal position of individuals are neither unconditional nor articulated in a 'social welfare' language. In practical terms, the Court's jurisprudence has initiated a dynamic and multi-faceted process which appears to display the main characteristics of the development of the internal market: it has been launched incidentally by the Court

---

[98] Press Release, Health and Consumer Affairs Council (3 December 2002).

of Justice and then developed incrementally on the basis of the interaction between EC and national courts and involving both national and EC administration. It has been argued, in another context, that the development of social rights appears 'not [to be] a consequence of a political conception of the social and economic protection deserved by any European citizen'.[99] The Court's caselaw on cross-border medical care, cautious and bold simultaneously, suggests that this is not necessarily regrettable.

---

[99] M Poiares Maduro, 'Striking the Elusive Balance Between Economic Freedom and Social Rights in the EU' in P Alston (ed), *The EU and Human Rights* (OUP, 1999) 450, 455.

6

Community Competence to Regulate Medical Services

DERRICK WYATT*

I COMMUNITY COMPETENCE TO REGULATE PUBLIC HEALTH

Direct Community competence over public health protection is limited to complementary and incentive measures, but the latter must not include measures of harmonisation.[1] Under the EU Constitution the protection and improvement of public health falls under the complementary competence of the Union (and harmonisation is excluded).[2]

For an example of complementary Community action under Article 152 EC, reference may be made to Decision No 1786/2002/EC of the European Parliament and of the Council of 23 September 2002 adopting a programme of Community action in the field of public health (2003–08). The coverage of the programme and its complementary nature is indicated by the following:

Article 2

Overall aim and general objectives
1. The programme, which shall complement national policies, shall aim to protect human health and improve public health.
2. The general objectives of the programme shall be:
    (a) to improve information and knowledge for the development of public health;

---

* Professor of Law, University of Oxford, Fellow of St Edmund Hall, and Queen's Counsel.
[1] Article 152(4)(c) EC refers to 'incentive measures designed to protect and improve human health, excluding any harmonisation of the laws and regulations of the Member States.' Article 152(5) EC provides that 'Community action in the field of public health shall fully respect the responsibilities of the Member States for the organisation and delivery of health services and medical care'.
[2] Article I–11(5) of the Treaty establishing a Constitution for Europe states inter alia in respect of complementary competences (including the protection and improvement of public health) that 'Legally binding acts adopted by the Union on the basis of the provisions specific to these areas in Part III may not entail harmonisation of Member States' laws or regulations'.

(b) to enhance the capability of responding rapidly and in a coordinated fashion to threats to health;

(c) to promote health and prevent disease through addressing health determinants across all policies and activities.

3.   The programme shall thereby contribute to:

(a) ensuring a high level of human health protection in the definition and implementation of all Community policies and activities, through the promotion of an integrated and intersectoral health strategy;

(b) tackling inequalities in health;

(c) encouraging co-operation between Member States in the areas covered by Article 152 of the Treaty.

The limitations on direct Community competence over public health protection are however to some extent offset by other competences, for example Community competence over the environment. Community policy on the environment shall contribute to 'protecting public health' (Article 174 EC), and much legislation adopted under the environment title has important public health implications, for example, legislation on the quality of drinking water,[3] and the management and transport of wastes.[4]

A less obvious source of legislative competence to protect public health is to be found in Article 95 EC, which allows the adoption of measures to promote the free movement of goods, and freedom to provide services. That this provision might serve as the basis for legislation relating to public health is not surprising in itself; disparities between national rules on the environment, consumer protection and public health are capable of leading to trade barriers. Article 95(3) EC acknowledges that measures adopted on internal market grounds may concern health, safety, environmental protection and consumer protection. Thus for example, if Member States adopt different specifications for the content of products (cosmetics, chemicals, paints, etc) on health, safety, environmental or consumer protection grounds, inter-State trade may be impeded. The adoption of common standards at the European level allows trade in the relevant products to take place. An important contemporary example of the need for harmonisation arising out of the existence of different national rules on public health and the environment concerns the release of genetically modified organisms into the environment.[5] Some measures described and adopted as internal market measures have, however, been thinly disguised public health measures lacking genuine internal market objectives; directives on tobacco advertising, and tobacco products specifications and labelling, are good examples.

---

[3]   Dir 98/83 on the quality of water intended for human consumption, 1998 OJ L330/32; the earlier Dir 80/778 relating to the quality of water intended for human consumption was based on Articles 100 and 235 EC.

[4]   See eg Reg 259/93 on the supervision and control of shipments of waste, 1993 OJ L30/1.

[5]   Dir 2001/18 of the European Parliament and the Council on the deliberate release into the environment of genetically modified organisms, 2001 OJ L106/1.

Thus Directive 98/43/EC[6] prohibited all advertising of tobacco products. The rationale of the Directive was that it would remove obstacles to the cross-frontier provision of services and eliminate distortions of competition. It was annulled by the European Court on the ground that important provisions of the Directive made no genuine contribution to the internal market. Provisions identical to those held invalid by the Court reappeared in a Council Recommendation 2003/54/EC on the prevention of smoking and on initiatives to improve tobacco control, based on Article 152 EC.[7] The Council recommended inter alia that Member States:

Adopt appropriate legislative and/or administrative measures to prohibit, in accordance with national constitutions or constitutional principles, the following forms of advertising and promotion:

(a) the use of tobacco brand names on non-tobacco products or services,
(b) the use of promotional items (ashtrays, lighters, parasols, etc) and tobacco samples,
(c) the use and communication of sales promotion, such as a discount, a free gift, a premium or an opportunity to participate in a promotional contest or game,
(d) the use of billboards, posters and other indoor or outdoor advertising techniques (such as advertising on tobacco vending machines),
(e) the use of advertising in cinemas, and
(f) any other forms of advertising, sponsorship or practices directly or indirectly addressed to promote tobacco products.

The foregoing recommendations mirrored requirements which had been contained in Directive 98/43/EC.

Subsequently, Directive 2001/37[8] regulated (a) the tar nicotine and CO content of cigarettes (b) the labelling of tobacco products (large health warnings) (c) the use of expressions such as 'light' or 'low tar'. The Court of Justice upheld this measure as a genuine internal market measure, though it might be questioned whether the aim of the measure was actually to promote cross-frontier trade in tobacco products, and it is difficult to see how the directive would be likely in practice to promote such trade.

A quite different possibility has emerged more recently; the possibility that the delivery of health care and medical services subject to national social security systems, while recognised as the responsibility of the Member States under Article 152 EC, might nevertheless be regarded as falling within the competences of the Community to regulate the internal market by virtue of the fact that the provision of medical services, including hospital care, might comprise services normally provided for remuneration, within the meaning of Article 49 *et seq* EC.

[6] 1998 OJ L213/12.
[7] 2003 OJ L22/31, point 2.
[8] 2001OJ L194/26.

The provision of medical services has not always seemed an obvious candidate for internal market regulation. Commercial services, such as providing package holidays, could clearly be regulated as internal market matters,[9] but there were some grounds for considering that health care and medical services provided within the framework of national social security schemes might not amount in all cases to services normally provided for remuneration within the meaning of Articles 49 *et seq* EC.[10]

As in so many areas of Community activity, it has been interpretation of the Treaty by the European Court of Justice which has provoked a re-examination of assumptions about the division of powers between the Community and the Member States. In a number of recent cases,[11] the Court of Justice has found that medical services (including hospital care) fall within the internal market provisions on free provision of services. In one of the first of these cases the Court rejected the argument that hospital services cannot constitute an economic activity within the meaning of Article 50 EC of the Treaty, particularly when they are provided in kind and free of charge under the relevant sickness insurance scheme. The Court stated:

> It is settled case-law that medical activities fall within the scope of the Treaty, there being no need to distinguish in that regard between care provided in a hospital environment and care provided outside such an environment (...)
> It is also settled case-law that the special nature of certain services does not remove them from the ambit of the fundamental principle of freedom of movement (...), so that the fact that the national rules at issue in the main proceedings are social security rules cannot exclude application of Articles [49 and 50 EC] of the Treaty.[12]

This has implications for individual patients, who may in certain cases insist that their national health care systems pay for their health care in other Member States. It also has another important implication. It brings the medical services in question within the scope of internal market regulation by the Commission, Council and Parliament under Article 95 EC.

---

[9] Dir 90/314 on package travel, package holidays and package tours, 1990 OJ L158/59, was adopted on the basis of Article 95 EC; the Directive aims to eliminate 'obstacles to the freedom to provide services in respect of packages and distortions of competition amongst operators established in different Member States'.

[10] See Case 263/86 *Humbel* [1988] ECR 5365, paras 17 to 19. The remarks of the Court were in connection with education, but seemed applicable by analogy to the provision of health care.

[11] See in particular Case C–157/99 *B S M Geaets-Smits v Stichting Ziekenfonds VGZ; H T M Peerbooms v Stichting CZ Groep Zorgverzekeringen* [2001] ECR I–5473; and Case C–385/99 *V G Müller-Fauré v Onderlinge Waarborgmaatschappij OZ Zorgverzekeringen UA* [2003] ECR I–4509.

[12] Case C–157/99 *B S M Geaets-Smits v Stichting Ziekenfonds VGZ; H T M Peerbooms v Stichting CZ Groep Zorgverzekeringen* [2001] ECR I–5473 paras 53 and 54.

II PROVISION FOR HEALTH CARE IN THE MEMBER STATES

Health care systems in the Member States may be broadly grouped into two categories.[13] In the first category the cost of treatment is borne by social insurance schemes, and payment is made by these schemes to care providers. In the countries with national health services, delivery of health care and ensuring its access are integrated into one single organisation. Social insurance systems generally offer category based protection on the basis of compulsory insurance (for the employed, self-employed, etc,). Those with incomes below a certain level may be excluded from compulsory insurance. In countries with compulsory social insurance, two systems for meeting medical costs may be distinguished. In one group of countries (Belgium, Luxembourg and France), provision is made for the reimbursement of the cost of health care services. The insured person has a free choice of health care provider. In the other group of countries (Austria, Germany, and the Netherlands), benefits in kind are provided. In these countries, a patient insured under the compulsory health insurance scheme receives the care he needs without charge provided he uses a provider approved by the scheme on the basis of an agreement between the scheme and the service provider. In the countries with national health services, it is the state which ensures access to health services. Generally, the patient makes no payments except for certain standard charges. Coverage is usually universal. Most of these countries fund their systems from taxes (Denmark, Ireland, Finland, Norway, Portugal, Sweden, the United Kingdom). Despite the fundamental differences between the insurance based schemes and the national health schemes, the position of certain countries applying one or other of these schemes has changed considerably over the last twenty years as a result of measures adopted to contain health expenditure. Each model has incorporated management and funding techniques based on the other. The health care systems have thus tended to converge towards hybrid systems. National rules or administrative action, sometimes in conjunction with agreements between funding bodies and care providers, to a greater or lesser extent regulate the coverage of national schemes, the rules for reimbursement or provision of services in kind, and the organisation and provision of medical services by care providers in the systems operating on the 'national health service' model.

---

[13] The account in the text is drawn from the *General Report Produced for the Directorate-General for Employment and Social Affairs of the European Commission,* Association International de la Mutualité (AIM), Palm, Nickless, Lewalle, and Coheur; available on the Commission's web-site: <http://europa.eu.int/comm/internal_market/en/services/services/docs/2003-report-health-care_en.pdf>, pp 16–18.

III POSSIBLE GROUNDS FOR HARMONISATION IN THE INTERNAL MARKET AND THE SCOPE OF HARMONISATION

Several grounds for harmonising national rules on the provision of services may be advanced. One ground for harmonisation might be the aim of eliminating obstacles to the provision of services (even if such obstacles are potential).[14] In the case of medical services, decisions taken by public authorities in Member States following the 'national health service' model, perhaps largely on budgetary grounds, to the effect that certain medical treatment should not be provided by care providers, might be said to amount to a restriction on the provision of services to patients in other Member States who would be entitled to receive such treatment, if available, at the expense of the health scheme to which they are affiliated, if the treatment were not available without undue delay in their country of residence.[15] It is to be noted that the fact that obstacles to the provision of services may be justified is not an argument against harmonisation; on the contrary, harmonisation is principally aimed at eliminating obstacles to the internal market which persist *because* they result from national measures which are consistent with Community law.

Another ground for harmonisation is the elimination of appreciable distortions to the conditions of competition; it is not clear what 'appreciable' means, but it seems from the *Tobacco Advertising* case[16] that distortion of competition is appreciable where differences between national rules affect the location where services are provided, that is to say, the differences are

---

[14] Case C–376/98 *Germany v Parliament and Council* ('Tobacco Advertising') [2000] ECR I–8419; for potential obstacles, see para 86. It is true that in the latter paragraph the Court states that 'the emergence of such obstacles must be likely and the measure in question must be designed to prevent them', but the institutions enjoy a large margin of appreciation in making such assessments.

[15] In Case C–405/98 *Gourmet International Products* [2001] ECR I–1755, the Court regards a restriction on the provision of a service in a Member State as being capable of amounting to a restriction on the freedom to provide services to potential customers in other Member States. The potential 'customer' of a care provider operating within a system following the national health service model would be likely to be a person relying upon Article 22 of Reg 1408/71 on the application of social security schemes to employed persons, to self-employed persons and to members of their families moving within the Community, as amended. Consolidated version, 1997 OJ L28/1, and <http://www.europa.eu.int/eur-lex/en/consleg/pdf/1971/en_1971R1408_do_001.pdf>. It is certainly arguable that the full refunding by the competent institution in the Member State of residence of the benefits in kind provided in another Member State by the relevant institution in that Member State pursuant to Article 36 of Regulation 1408/71 amounts to 'remuneration', so that treatment pursuant to Article 22 of Regulation 1408/71 is in all cases to be regarded as covered by Article 49 EC as well as by the provisions of Regulation 1408/71. That Article 22 of Regulation 1408/71 and Article 49 EC are cumulatively applicable in cases involving the relations between schemes following the national insurance model is recognised by the Court in Case C–368/98 *Abdon Vanbraekel and Others v ANMC* [2001] ECR I–5363, and in Case C–56/01 *Patricia Inizan v Caisse primaire d'assurance maladie des Hauts-de-Seine* [2003] ECR I–12403.

[16] See n 12 above.

sufficient for an undertaking to choose to provide the service in question in one Member State rather than another in order to avoid legal restrictions in the latter Member State.[17] But it is not essential that a difference in the conditions of competition be capable of leading to a transaction taking place in one Member State rather than another for that difference to amount to an 'appreciable' distortion of competition.[18]

More broadly, it appears that harmonisation may also be based on the proposition that if national rules regulating the provision of goods or services vary from country to country, potential recipients of services in one Member State may, through lack of awareness of the degree of protection secured by the rules governing the supply of services in other Member States, be deterred from purchasing such services in a Member State other than their own.[19]

It is to be noted that the power to harmonise is not limited to harmonising binding legal rules. The Treaty recognises that administrative action as well as laws and regulations may be the subject of harmonisation.[20] Where rules or administrative measures adopted by national authorities determine or influence the content of insurance schemes designed to provide health care for the population at large, or influence the range of medical treatment and procedures available to those covered by such schemes, the measures in question could in principle be subject to harmonisation measures under Article 95 EC. It is also to be noted that recommendations by public authorities are recognised as being capable of constituting obstacles to freedom of movement.[21] While recommendations as to the availability or not of certain medical treatments and relating to the standards applicable to available treatment might be entirely justifiable on grounds of public health, this

---

[17] Case C–376/98, n 12, para 110.

[18] Case C–168/00 *Simone Leitner v TUI Deutschland Gmbh & Co KG* [2002] ECR I–2631, at para 21: 'It is not in dispute that, in the field of package holidays, the existence in some Member States but not in others of an obligation to provide compensation for non-material damage would cause significant distortions of competition, given that, as the Commission has pointed out, non-material damage is a frequent occurrence in that field.'

[19] See eg, Dir 93/13 on unfair terms in consumer contracts, 1993 OJ L95/29, 5th 'whereas' clause. The Court described the aims of the First Company Law Directive, 68/151, 1968(I) OJ Sp Ed, p 41, in Case 32/74 *Friedrich Haaga GmbH* [1974] ECR 1205, para 6, as being 'to guarantee legal certainty in dealings between companies and third parties in view of the intensification of trade between Member States following the creation of the common market...' The proposition that legal uncertainty resulting from disparities between national laws can justify harmonisation is potentially a basis for very wide-ranging harmonisation indeed.

[20] Article 95 EC, in common with other provisions for harmonisation, refers to the approximation of 'law, regulation or administrative action...'.

[21] Dir 70/50 on the abolition of measures which have an effect equivalent to quantitative restrictions on imports, 1970(I) OJ Sp Ed, p 17, identifies 'recommendations' as national measures capable of amounting to measures having equivalent effect to quantitative restrictions. In Case 249/81 *Commission v Ireland* [1982] ECR 4005, the Court held that a campaign funded by a Member State to promote the sale of domestic goods with a view to limiting imports amounted to a measure having equivalent effect contrary to Article 28 EC.

would not prevent harmonisation of such administrative measures if they created obstacles to the cross-frontier provision of services or created appreciable distortions of competition.

It is clear furthermore that harmonisation is not confined to situations where adverse effects on the internal market are caused by national rules or administrative action. It is true that Article 95 EC provides for the harmonisation of law, regulation or administrative action, but the 'mischief' which the measure seeks to rectify may have its source in purely private action, or in absence of national rules protecting certain interests of individuals. Thus Directive 75/117 identifies unequal pay for men and women as an obstacle to the internal market, and requires national rules to ensure that collective agreements and wages scales comply with equal pay requirements.[22] Again, the transfer of undertakings directive, which is based on Article 94 EC,[23] and aims to facilitate cross-border mergers, provides for the continuation of rights under employment contracts and collective agreements in the event of the transfer of an undertaking. In this connection it is to be noted that the Court's case-law indicates that obstacles to the free movement of persons may be caused by activities of associations or organisations governed by private law, (for example, sports associations of various kinds),[24] and indeed by the terms of individual contracts of employment.[25] It follows that Article 95 EC could in principle be used to require Member States to adopt national rules to regulate private conduct, such as the terms of health insurance policies, in order to remove obstacles to cross-frontier provision of medical services, and this would clearly be the case where the terms of cover for patients take effect under schemes applying to the general population within a national regulatory framework. A further point to bear in mind is that the alleged effects on the internal market of discrepancies between national rules are often hypothetical or theoretical; it is not generally thought necessary to actually *prove* that actual or potential adverse effects to the provision of services, or distortions in competition, are likely to occur.[26]

---

[22] 1975 OJ L45/19, Article 3(2)(b).

[23] Dir 2001/23, 2001 OJ L82/16.

[24] Case 36/74 *Walrave and Koch v Association union cycliste internationale* [1974] ECR 1405; Case C–415/93 *Union royal belge des Sociétés de football association ASBL v Jean-Marc Bosman* [1995] ECR I–4921.

[25] Case C–281/98 *Roman Angonese v Cassa di Risparmio di Bolzano SpA* [2000] ECR I–4139.

[26] Though the present writer considers that the requirements of proportionality and subsidiarity argue in favour of basing legislation on empirical evidence wherever it is possible to do so. This is supported by the statement in the Subsidiarity Protocol to the effect that 'the reasons for concluding that a Community objective can be better achieved by the Community must be substantiated by...wherever possible, quantitative indicators' (para (4)). This would seem to require the adverse internal market effects of disparities between national laws to be quantified unless it is not possible to undertake such an assessment. In normal circumstances such an assessment would seem entirely possible, and to facilitate application of the principle of proportionality.

IV POSSIBLE APPLICATION OF THE FOREGOING PRINCIPLES AS A BASIS TO HARMONISE STANDARDS OF HEALTH CARE

The possible application of the foregoing principles as a basis for Community regulation of hospital health care may be illustrated by reference to a hypothetical example: a proposed directive (a) requiring certain medical treatment or procedures to be covered by health care schemes in Member States identified in the directive as being intended to provide general health care for the whole population or sections of the population; (b) prescribing as regards care provided in pursuance of such schemes maximum waiting periods for certain in-patient procedures; (c) prescribing minimum periods of in-patient post operative care in respect of said procedures, and (d) prescribing effective judicial remedies for consumers against care providers failing to comply with these requirements. It must be emphasised that the example is chosen in order to provide a framework for a discussion on competence, rather than as a politically probable initiative on the part of the Commission—the present writer is solely concerned with the issue of legal competence rather than engaged in speculation about future policies of the Community institutions.

It has already been noted that the Community institutions have in the past based internal market measures on the need to remove barriers to trade or distortions of competition in circumstances where the barriers or distortions were of a somewhat speculative nature.[27] Furthermore, Article 152 EC, while placing some limit on Community initiatives in the public health field, does not purport to limit the scope of Article 95 EC. The Court has held that if a national measure makes a contribution to the internal market, then it may be based on Article 95 EC, and if it makes such a contribution, then it is permissible for health to make a decisive contribution to the content of the measure in question.[28] It follows that a measure principally concerned with health protection may be regarded as being an internal market measure which can be adopted on the basis of Article 95 EC if it can be regarded as making some *slight* contribution to the internal market, by for instance, eliminating *potential* obstacles to trade in goods or services.

It might be questioned whether the fact that Article 95 EC excludes provisions relating to the free movement of persons[29] might inhibit its application to the provision of services such as hospital services which have a cross-border element principally because recipients cross borders to

---

[27] For example Dir 2001/23, on the approximation of the laws relating to the safeguarding of employees' rights in the event of transfers of undertakings, businesses or parts of undertakings and businesses, 2001 OJ L82/16, and Dir 2001/37 on the manufacture, presentation and sale of tobacco products 2001 OJ L194/26.

[28] Case C–376/98 *Germany v Parliament and Council* ('*Tobacco Advertising*') [2000] ECR I–8419, para 88.

[29] Article 95(2) EC excludes from the application of Article 95(1) EC provisions 'relating to the free movement of persons'.

receive treatment in other Member States. That is not however the case. Provisions relating to the free movement of persons are those provisions which relate to the rights of free movement of employed and self-employed persons. This follows from the text of the Treaty, which distinguishes the free movement of persons from freedom to provide services, and the free movement of capital, in the heading of Title III of Part Three of the Treaty. Title III contains four chapters: workers, establishment, services and capital. It follows that the right of recipients of services to visit another Member State falls within the scope of the chapter on services and does not relate to the free movement of persons within the meaning of Article 95(2) EC.[30] Similarly, the right of persons to cross frontiers to buy goods is covered by the free movement of goods provisions.[31] It is to be noted that part of the rationale of the Unfair Contract Terms Directive (made under Article 95 EC) is to remove discrepancies in national laws which may deter consumers from 'direct transactions for the purchases of goods or services in another Member State'. This reflects the proposition that Article 95 EC may harmonise national rules which affect the cross-frontier purchasing activities of individuals.

The basic arguments underlying a hypothetical draft internal market directive harmonising national rules and administrative action on the matters referred to above would be that actual or potential differences in national provisions might (a) restrict the 'export' of services to out-of-State patients and (b) deter patients from seeking treatment in Member States other than their own. The latter deterrence, as well as adversely affecting the cross-frontier provision of services, might be said to amount to an *appreciable* distortion of competition, since it could lead to services being provided in one Member State rather than another.

The restriction on the 'export' of services could follow from limitations imposed directly on health care providers working within systems which follow the national health service model.[32] Patients covered by a health scheme in one Member State might be deterred from seeking treatment in another Member State, where the treatment is available, but where the waiting list is longer than in their Member State of residence, and/or where the standard of provision of that treatment might be less generous, for example, as regards post operative in-patient care. Patients might indeed be deterred from even considering the possibility of out-of-state treatment because of concern that the above *might* be the case and because of lack of information about the

---

[30] See n 17 above, and text to n 17.
[31] Case 362/88 *GB-INNO-BM v Confédération du commerce luxembourgeois* [1990] ECR I–667, para 8.
[32] General Report produced for the Directorate-General for Employment and Social Affairs of the European Commission, Association International de la Mutualité (AIM), Palm, Nichless, Lewalle, and Coheur; available on the Commission's web-site: <http://europa.eu.int/comm/internal_market/en/services/services/docs/2003-report-health-care_en.pdf>.

actual position in other Member States. The proposition that lack of consumer confidence in the minimum guaranteed standards for the supply of goods and services in other Member States should be regarded as in itself justifying harmonisation is one of which the present writer is sceptical. It is a proposition which can be invoked to justify harmonisation even in the absence of restrictions of a kind prohibited by internal market requirements in the absence of justification. Yet as already noted, it figures in the rationale of existing Community legislation, such as the Unfair Contract Terms Directive, which is based in part on the proposition that consumers in one Member State may be deterred from shopping abroad for goods and services by uncertainty as to whether unfair contract term provision in other Member States might be as protective as in their own.

The appropriate remedy identified in the Unfair Contract Terms Directive is minimum European-wide unfair contract terms provisions, though one might have thought that more information about consumer rights would have provided a less intrusive solution, as would more information about standards of health care in other Member States provide a less intrusive solution to the hypothetical problem under consideration than harmonisation of health care standards. Nonetheless, the argument could be made in the current (hypothetical) context that consumers of health care in one Member State might be deterred from receiving health care in another Member State by the possibility that the relevant required standards of care might be less demanding than in their own. And this reluctance, it might further be said, could be overcome by an overall minimum European standard.

A further ground for harmonisation would be that different standards of care resulting from disparities between national rules or administrative action in the various Member States could lead to distortions in the conditions of competition, since patients and/or agencies of national health care schemes paying for service provision would prefer some services over others as a consequence. It will be noted that distortion of competition must be appreciable, but that condition could be said to be satisfied if the distortion actually determined in which Member State certain patients were given treatment, which could be the case here. It might be said that recourse to the concept of distortion of competition is artificial in this context, since the conditions of competition are not 'normal'. But it might be said on the other hand that as long as the Community institutions considered that the effect of harmonisation was to *reduce* 'abnormalities' and *contribute* to 'normal' conditions of competition, this would be a valid exercise of legislative competence under Article 95 EC. The particular characteristics of systems following the national health service model would not seem to rule out the adoption of measures of harmonisation nor the application of such harmonisation to such systems. On the one hand, patients of care providers operating under such schemes might be deterred from seeking out of state treatment because of the considerations referred to above.[33] On the other hand, patients from other Member States might be deterred from seeking treatment from care providers operating in Member States following the national health service model.[34] In light of these consideration, the distortion of competition argument could be said to apply as much to systems following the national health service model as to the national insurance model.

V SUBSIDIARITY

The question arises as to the extent to which the principle of subsidiarity might inhibit the use of Article 95 EC to legislate as regards the provision of medical services. It is certainly the case that subsidiarity applies to internal market measures,[35] but it seems that if an internal market measure satisfies the test of competence, the requirements of subsidiarity are also satisfied.[36] The present writer regrets that the Court has taken such a half-hearted approach to the application of what could and should be one of the most significant constitutional principle of the European legal order.[37] The Court's failure to breathe life into the principle of subsidiarity accords with a reluctance to take more than perfunctory account of the principle on the part of other Community institutions. It remains to be seen whether involvement of national parliaments in scrutiny for compliance with the principle of subsdiarity[38] can turn the latter principle into a genuine constitutional filter; its intended function yet one which has yet to materialise.

VI CONCLUSION

The present writer has not argued that there is an open and shut case for Community competence to regulate medical services via Article 95 EC. Much would depend on the specific subject matter under consideration. But to the extent that medical services are services within the meaning of Article 49 EC they are in principle open to regulation by measures of harmonisation

---

[33] Even where a national scheme does not provide for reimbursement in respect of care provided, Arts 22 and 36 of Regulation 1408/71 provides for such reimbursement and arguably attracts the application of Art 49 EC even if the latter article would not be otherwise applicable.

[34] The regime for reimbursement under Regulation 1408/71 is also relevant in this context.

[35] Case C–491/01 *The Queen v Secretary of State for Health, ex parte British American Tobacco (Investments) Ltd and Imperial Tobacco Ltd* [2002] ECR I–11453, para 179.

[36] *Ibid* at paras 181–83.

[37] Particularly in a case concerned with the validity of an internal market measure likely to make little positive contribution to the removal of obstacles to the free movement of goods, whose main aim was public health protection.

[38] Draft EU Constitution Article 9(4), and the Protocol on the application of the principles of subsidiarity and proportionality.

adopted by the Community institutions under Article 95 EC. National authorities have taken responsibility to greater or lesser extent to ensure that a range of medical services is available to the general population. Fulfilment of this responsibility is secured via legislation or administrative measures which regulate schemes for reimbursement of the costs of medical services, or which make provision for the direct supply of in-patient and out-patient medical services. Disparities between available treatment in the various Member States, between waiting periods for available treatment, and between the standards of treatment in different Member States, reflecting differences between legal rules and administrative arrangements in the various Member States, could be said, in certain respects, to amount to restrictions on the provision of services and to lead to appreciable distortions in the conditions of competition. This would seem to provide at least the possibility for the institutions to adopt internal market legislation under Article 95 EC harmonising treatments which are available to patients, waiting periods for such treatments, and the standard of delivery of such treatments. Probably the prudent view to take of European competence to regulate health care provision under Article 95 EC, at the present stage of development of Community law, is that such competence cannot in principle be excluded.

7

Impact of European Union Law on English Healthcare Law

JONATHAN MONTGOMERY*

I INTRODUCTION

Traditionally, English healthcare law has been resistant to the idea of patient rights. In relation to access to care, patient entitlements have been avoided in favour of defining the obligations of health authorities and service providers in general terms that have been found by the courts not to be enforceable by individual citizens. However, since the decision in *Peerbooms,* considerable interest has been shown by English media, politicians and lawyers in whether European law requires a more interventionist approach to the regulation of the health service by the courts. If it does, the courts will need to reassess their stance and a radical shift in the basis of judicial oversight will be required.

The matter reached the English domestic courts in a case brought by Mrs Yvonne Watts seeking reimbursement for some of the costs of a hip replacement treatment that she had undergone in France after having been told that she would need to wait approximately one year before the National Health Service (NHS) would be able to carry out the operation. She won her substantive arguments before Munby J in the High Court, although she was denied compensation on the basis that the NHS had been able to offer her an earlier appointment when her condition was reassessed.[1] The implications of this decision for the administration of the NHS were considerable and the Department of Health has appealed against the decision. In February 2004 the issue was referred to the European Court of Justice by the Court of Appeal in the *Watts* case for a ruling on whether UK citizens can choose to avoid the usual waiting times of the National Health Service by travelling abroad and then claiming reimbursement from the local commissioning Primary Care Trust.[2] If this proves to be the case, a fundamental change in

---

* Southampton University.
[1] R (Watts) v Secretary of State for Health [2003] EWHC 2228 (Admin).
[2] R (Watts) v Secretary of State for Health [2004] EWCA Civ 166. For an explanation of the legal structure of the NHS, see J Montgomery, *Health Care Law* (OUP, 2003) Ch 3.

the domestic law on access to health services will have been achieved through the interpretation of the European Treaty. Such a claim to reimbursement would not be entertained in respect of an independent health provider within the UK without prior approval.

The focus of this chapter is the impact of EU law on the domestic law governing access to healthcare in England. It considers the main character-istics of this area of English domestic law and examines the way in which EU law has affected it. It argues that the direct impact of EU law was ini-tially limited and that changes presented as linked to EU matters, were in fact been driven by domestic political agendas. One consequence of this is that the programme of the current Labour administration to 'modernise' the structure of the National Health Service and enhance patient choice may have underestimated the possible impact of EU law. If this is correct, the Department of Health's challenge to the *Watts* case may have limited prospects of keeping EU law at bay even if it is initially successful.

Key aspects of the control of access to health services are examined, including the role of enforceable rights, the functions of prior approval before resources are committed, and the extent to which the scope of state financed services can be limited. In relation to the former, the suggestion is that EU law creates enforceable rights that have previously been resisted. In relation to prior approval, that there is a continuum of such approvals, some more readily amenable to legal control in the name of an open European market than others. In relation to the scope of state financed serv-ices, the impact of European law is less clear, and it is suggested that the full implications of what is at stake have yet to be explored.

II KEY FEATURES OF ENGLISH LAW
ON ACCESS TO HEALTH SERVICES

The United Kingdom is committed to providing a comprehensive health service free at the point of delivery and its legal system contains a range of legal duties aimed to secure that provision.[3] These are defined in terms of both general and specific duties, imposed explicitly upon the Secretary of State for Health, but delegated down to local NHS bodies. These have generally been held not to be intended to benefit individuals, so that actions for compensation in the UK courts for breach of statutory duty have failed.[4] Even when it is accepted that a claimant has legal standing to challenge the carrying out of these public duties, the courts have accepted various argu-ments that serve to protect health service bodies. These include the explicit

---

[3]   National Health Service Act 1977, ss 1–5. These provisions can be seen as the UK's mech-anism for meeting rights of access to healthcare in accordance with the commitments made under the European Social Charter (Revised) 1996, art 13.

[4]   *Re HIV Haemophiliac Litigation* (1990) 41 Butterworths Medico-Legal Reports 171.

statutory wording, which limits obligations to concepts the provision of services 'to such extent as [the Secretary of State] considers necessary to meet all reasonable requirements' (allowing the courts to accept a subjective discretion on the part of the Health Secretary). The courts have even been prepared to read in limitations based on resources as being implied by the context.[5] In summary, it could be said that there is almost no prospect for individuals to enforce rights to receive care under domestic law,

This can be illustrated in a more individualised context by the litigation over treatment of Jaymee Bowen in 1995. Jaymee, aged 10, suffered a relapse in Leukemia, a disease for which she had previously been treated. Her doctors in Cambridge, supported by a second medical opinion from the Royal Marsden Hospital in London, reached the view that further treatment was not in her best interests. Her father, who found support from a doctor in the USA and a professor from the Hammersmith Hospital in London, felt differently. He tried to persuade Cambridge Health Authority to fund additional treatment, and when the Director of Public Health refused to authorise it he brought the matter to court in the process of judicial review. The High Court judge, Laws J, felt that insufficient regard had been paid to the human rights issues raised.[6] However, the Court of Appeal held that judges should not be drawn into disputes over the allocation of resources. They further took the view that the main area of contention was clinical—the question of what treatment was appropriate. On this aspect of the case they also felt that judges should be wary of intervening as clinical matters were properly within the scope of the medical discretion. Although the clinical issues were clearly controversial, in the light of the disagreements exposed by Jaymee's situation, the Court of Appeal took the view that judges should not override the clinical assessment made by the Cambridge Health Authority.[7]

One of the interesting features of the decision on Munby J in the *Watts* case was his candid recognition that Mrs Watts was seeking something that she was not entitled to enforce under domestic law. This was conceded by her counsel.[8] In the cases under English domestic law, the courts had consistently accepted that it was not their role to make judgments about how scarce budgets should be allocated,[9] nor about clinical judgments on the appropriateness[10] or urgency of particular treatments.[11] Yet in the view of

---

[5] *R v Secretary of State for Social Services, W Midlands RHA & Birmingham AHA (Teaching), ex p Hincks* (1980) 1 Butterworths Medico-Legal Reports 93, see esp Lord Denning at 95.

[6] *R v Cambridge DHA, ex p B* [1995] 1 Family Law Reports 1055.

[7] *R v Cambridge HA, ex p B* [1995] 2 All ER 129.

[8] *R (Watts) v Secretary of State for Health* [2003] EWHC 2228 (Admin) para 38.

[9] *R v Cambridge HA, ex p B* [1995] 2 All ER 129; *R v N W Lancashire HA, ex p A* [2000] 2 FCR 525.

[10] *Re J* [1992] 4 All ER 614.

[11] *R v Secretary of State for Social Services, ex p Walker* (1987) 3 Butterworths Medico-Legal Reports 32.

Munby J, this did not preclude the court from concluding that EU law required treatment to be funded despite clinical uncertainty and managerial control over priorities in resource allocation. In the *Watts* case Munby was prepared to determine for himself the clinical question of how urgent the case was, in terms of how long a patient needed to wait until delay was 'undue'. He was not prepared simply to accept the clinical view on this matter expressed by the English doctors. He also showed few qualms about cutting through the Gordian knot of resource allocation decisions by deciding for himself that Yvonne Watts's treatment should be funded. The discomfort of the Court of Appeal with this shift in judicial approach can be seen in the phrasing of the questions referred to the European Court of Justice probing the extent to which intrusion into the management of the NHS was permitted in the name of the EU law. The Court of Appeal defines the questions very much from a provider perspective, raising concern about duties that would 'have the effect of requiring an increase in the National Health Service budget', 'dislocate its system of administering priorities', and entitle patients to 'jump the queue'.[12] Like Laws J in the Cambridge case, Munby J defined the issues from the perspective of the patient.

III ENGLISH LAW ON THE SCOPE OF NHS SERVICES

Given the significance in European law of determining whether a particular treatment is 'among the benefits provided for by the legislation of the member state [in which] the person concern resided',[13] it is important to identify how the scope of entitlement to services under the UK National Health Service is determined. The legal framework for determining the scope of services provided under the NHS has not principally been established through litigation by individual patients. As the previous section has illustrated, such litigation has served to show how reluctant the courts are to intervene in this area, at least prior to the Watts decision. There is, however, specific legislation, with an administrative system to back it up, which serves to define the obligations of the NHS to provide services.

Primary healthcare is guaranteed in the UK by a nationally fixed contract, with standard terms and targets, with general medical practitioners (GPs). This ensures that everyone can be registered with an NHS GP in order to receive 'personal medical services'. The GPs also carry out a gate-keeping role for hospital and community services, referring their patients when they

---

[12] *R (Watts) v Secretary of State for Health* [2004] EWCA Civ 166, para 112.
[13] Article 22(2) of Reg 1408/71 on the application of social security schemes to employed persons, to self-employed persons and to members of their families moving within the Community, as amended. Consolidated version, 1997 OJ L28/1, and <http://www.europa.eu.int/eur-lex/en/consleg/pdf/1971/en_1971R1408_do_001.pdf>.

deem it appropriate. Direct access to NHS hospitals is not available other than for accident and emergency services. This gate-keeping role can be seen as a form of prior consent. Prior consent is also present in relation to access to prescription-only medicines. The need for a prescription plays the twin role of ensuring that potentially harmful medicines can only be obtained under the auspices of a health professional, and also making sure that NHS funds are only committed when such a professional has decided it is appropriate. Although under current Government plans, patients will be given increasing amounts of choice over where they will be referred, there are no plans to remove the referral process.

Considerable state control is exercised over the scope of services that can be funded under the NHS. Clinical and cost effectiveness is monitored by the National Institute for Clinical Excellence,[14] which advises the Government on which drugs should be funded for which purposes. Thus, the drug Viagra, for the treatment of erectile dysfunction, is funded only in very limited circumstances. While the UK Government was successfully challenged for restricting the NHS funding of Viagra through informal means, its right to limit such funding through the appropriate legal measures has been upheld.[15] The Viagra case illustrates one of the complexities of regulating the healthcare market because it draws attention to the interplay between issues of cost control and public policy/morality. Lurking behind the question of the NHS funding of Viagra use is whether the UK wishes to pay for people to achieve sexual satisfaction. The policy adopted by the Government is that this should not be the case unless there is a defined health problem identified by a health professional giving a form of prior approval. Litigation over sex reassignment surgery has indicated that the Government cannot ignore the medical consensus on the definition of health problems,[16] but there remains a significant moral dimension to determining the scope of NHS provision. That scope is driven by public policy not patient demand.

This can be seen further in the way in which the duties of the NHS to provide hospital and community services are defined. The Secretary of State for Health is obliged to promote a 'comprehensive health service' which must include hospital services 'to such extent as he considers necessary to meet all reasonable requirements'.[17] Decisions on what services should be developed lie with Primary Care Trusts, who are given funds to pay for the services needed by the population on whose behalf they commission. Occasionally, as in the Jaymee Bowen case, these decisions are made on an individual basis, but more typically specific volumes of services have been funded, with GPs controlling access by specific patients. One of the prime

---

[14] <www.nice.org.uk>.
[15] *R v Secretary of State for Health, ex p Pfizer* [2003] CMLR 19 (CA), NHS (General Medical Services) Regulations Amendment (No 2) Regulations 1999, SI 1999 No 1627.
[16] *R v NW Lancashire HA, ex p A* [2000] 2 FCR 525.
[17] National Health Service Act 1977, ss 1, 3.

mechanisms for fitting demand in the NHS to the supply of services that have been commissioned has traditionally been the waiting list. In a typically British manner, people have queued for access to services. The speed with which the queue shortened was determined by the supply of the services for which people were waiting. Shortening waiting lists required more of the relevant services to be commissioned. Control of the cost of commissioning could be achieved by limiting supply, with the result that waiting lists were created. Waiting lists are a mechanism for matching the political will to fund services against need. Provided they are managed fairly they can also be a technique for determining clinical priority.

Independently of EU law, waiting is becoming increasingly less acceptable to the British public and politicians. Changes are being introduced to make funding follow patients more closely with a fixed tariff for procedures irrespective of where the procedure is carried out. This will increase patient choice and variety of providers, but will not remove the need to secure a referral from the GP. Some discretion will therefore remain over whether patients are entitled to access services, but control over where those services are accessed will be relaxed.

It can be seen from this summary that English law continues to maintain a system of prior approval to ensure that the NHS funds only those treatments that professionals think suitable. This currently includes managing the time taken to access services as well as which services should be offered. The expected relaxation of the power of referring and receiving doctors to determine where treatment is delivered has important implications in the light of EU law. By liberalising control and introducing a form of market competition between providers, current NHS reforms will make it easier for non-UK health providers to use EU law to demand equal entry to that quasi-market and to be given an equal status in the provision of services to NHS patients as UK providers. Increasing capacity in the health system is also expected to eliminate waiting.

IV THE EARLY RECEPTION OF EU LAW ON ACCESS TO TREATMENT

These developments are likely to move the relationship between law and health services in the UK into a different phase. The initial engagement between UK healthcare law and EU law presented limited concerns to the mechanisms being used to limit the development of patient rights and maintain cost control and public policy in the NHS. Early caselaw established that free movement of persons implied guarantees that existing care could be continued if a worker took up employment in a different Member State.[18] Reciprocal arrangements were developed under the E 112 system to

---

[18] *Re Dialysis Treatment* [1984] 3 CMLR 242.

implement Regulation 1408/71. These developments did little to challenge the basic control mechanisms over health services.

A significant extension occurred with the case of *R v Human Fertilisation and Embryology Authority, ex parte Blood*.[19] In that case the applicant was not permitted to use the sperm of her deceased husband to seek to conceive after his death because she did not have his written consent as required by English law. However, the Court of Appeal suggested that she was nevertheless entitled under EU law to take the sperm to another Member State where the treatment was legal under the banner of freedom to provide and use services. This challenges the ability of individual Member States to control medico-moral policy.[20] Dianne *Blood* sought to do something that the UK legislature had decided should not be permitted. EU law enabled her to evade that policy, although the Court of Appeal hoped that it would not happen in another case because the gathering of the sperm had been illegal. Nevertheless, the right established in the *Blood* case was a negative freedom, to be permitted to seek services abroad. This is very different from the claim made by Yvonne Watts, which was a positive right to be funded to seek services in another Member State. This would not challenge just the power of states to regulate the ethics of healthcare provision, but also their access restrictions and cost control mechanisms.

This is crucially different in that it affects the abilities of states to (a) control budgets and (b) establish clinical/moral norms within their own national boundaries. The earlier cases present less of a threat because they can be dealt with by individual not systemic responses. Continuing kidney dialysis treatment that has already been established in another Member State does not impact on rationing processes any more than occasional aberrations within the national healthcare system. The Court of Appeal in the *Blood* case specifically decided it on the basis that it did not compromise the prevailing national law under which the taking of the sperm that she sought permission to take abroad was, and remained, unlawful. Nor did it force the UK to permit the treatment on its own territory. Thus, the integrity of the legislation controlling the conditions on which assisted conception can be provided was not challenged.

V A HEALTHCARE LAWYER'S READING OF *PEERBOOMS*

From the perspective of a domestic healthcare lawyer, the decision in *Geraets-Smits v Stichting Ziekenfonds VGZ* and *Peerbooms v Stichting Ca Groep Zorgverzekering* was not particularly surprising.[21] Although much

---

[19] [1997] 2 All ER 687.

[20] I explore this issue further in 'Law and the Demoralisation of Medicine' (2005) *Journal of Legal Studies* forthcoming.

[21] Case C–157/99 *B S M Geaets-Smits v Stichting Ziekenfonds VGZ; HTM Peerbooms v Stichting CZ Groep Zorgverzekeringen* [2001] ECR I–5473.

was made of it by the English media, particularly the *Sunday Times*, it did not threaten the ability of health systems to control their allocation of resources. The decision considered the reference in Article 22 Regulation 1408/71 to two reasons for declining to fund services abroad—clinical appropriateness and 'undue delay'—without expressly distinguishing them. On its facts, the case raised only the former issue, clinical appropriateness, and concerned the question whether appropriateness should be defined by reference only to medical opinion in the Member State or whether the European (or international) consensus should be the measure. This can be seen as a mechanism to prevent market barriers being erected by Member States through privileging the opinions of their own professionals over those based elsewhere in the EU. The ECJ decided that a refusal to fund treatment widely regarded as effective elsewhere in the Union in order to force nationals to use local services even though they were less effective was an improper restraint on the market. It was thus aimed to prevent a state social security system from improperly protecting national providers.

The application of this decision to health systems based on direct provision by the state rather than providing funds to use independent providers remained uncertain. Domestic lawyers could be reassured by the explicit statement that 'Community law cannot in principle have the effect of requiring a Member State to extend the list of services paid for by its social insurance system'.[22] This seemed to preserve the controls over the scope of services and individual access to treatment that had been so robustly defended by the UK courts. It was also the case that *Peerbooms* presented no challenge to cost control by waiting list because it did not examine what was meant by 'undue delay'.

Subsequent developments have cast the EU law in a different light. The *Müller-Fauré* case focussed on the concept of 'undue delay' and rejected the idea that waiting lists were a legitimate mechanism to control access to health services.[23] It also concerned a health system where one of the cost and quality control mechanisms was that benefits were provided in kind under contracts between the insurer and providers rather than patients contracting with providers directly and then seeking reimbursement. From an English healthcare lawyer's perspective, aspects of the reasoning of the Court are instructive. It is predicated on a degree of choice that is not granted in the NHS:

> The requirement for prior authorisation where a person is subsequently to be reimbursed for the costs of that treatment is precisely what constitutes... the barrier to freedom to provide services, that is to say, to a patient's ability to

---

[22] Para 87.
[23] Case C–385/99 *V G Müller-Fauré v Onderlinge Waarborgmaatschappij OZ Zorgverzekeringen UA* [2003] ECR I–4509.

go to the medical service provider of his choice in a Member State other than that of affiliation.[24]

The UK system has not traditionally guaranteed patients choice of provider, and although it is moving that way, choices are not a matter of legal entitlement. The Court goes on to say that:

> There is thus no need, from the perspective of freedom to provide services, to draw a distinction by reference to whether the patient pays the costs incurred and subsequently applies for reimbursement thereof or whether the sickness fund or the national budget pays the provider directly.

From an English perspective, what this does is to disregard the fact that choice of provider is not a component of all health systems. To create such a choice is to alter fundamentally the nature of the relationship between the patient and the health service. Once such a choice has been guaranteed, the position adopted by the court is logical—choice should not be restricted to a single Member State. However, this does not provide a justification for the existence of the choice itself. Here lies the fundamental issue for English healthcare jurisprudence.

Ms Müller-Fauré's case also raised crucial questions about the responsibility for determining effectiveness of the services that the state funds. Although it was not discussed by the ECJ in reaching its conclusions, there was also an element of mistrust by Ms Müller-Fauré of the quality of services contracted for in the Netherlands.[25] She thus wished to supplant the Dutch Government's quality control with her own assessment. This can be seen more clearly as an issue in *Inizan v Caisse primaire d'assurance maladie des Hauts-de-Seine*.[26] Ms Inizan sought a type of treatment for back pain that was not funded by her French insurance company. The Court treated the case as one concerning procedures for approval,[27] but in fact it seems to have been a dispute over complementary therapy.[28] The national medical officer believed that the French care was appropriate and effective and that the treatment desired by Ms Inizan was not scientifically recognised.[29] By supporting Ms Inizan, the European Court of Justice required treatment regarded as inappropriate to be funded by the insurance system. Once again, this removes a key control in the system. Where a healthcare

---

[24] Para 103.

[25] See para 24.

[26] Case C–56/01 *Patricia Inizan v Caisse primaire d'assurance maladie des Hauts-de-Seine* [2003] ECR I–0000.

[27] See para 42 rejecting the suggestion that the treatment was not one covered by the scheme. This was true if the treatment was seen as a remedy for back pain, but not if the treatment technique was considered.

[28] This is apparent from paras 17 and 19 of the Advocate General's conclusions.

[29] See para 17.

law perspective regards professional control of which treatments are effective as a significant feature, an analysis based on the market in services subordinates that to patient preference. That feature is perhaps unexceptional in a private health system, where patients spend their own money, but it raises a fundamental challenge in a system such as the NHS which has been so professionally dominated.

VI THE ENGLISH 'RESPONSE'

The story of the reception of this EU law into English domestic law is an interesting one. Initial suggestions that *Peerbooms* was of limited significance were rapidly replaced by the apparent acceptance of the then Secretary of State, Alan Milburn, that the decision was of great importance. In part this may reflect the political importance of the extended campaign by the *Sunday Times* against long NHS waiting lists and its expression of the belief that market providers are consistently more responsive to demand than socialised medical services. More likely this indirect pressure merely reinforced the Government's determination to shorten waiting times, make the NHS more businesslike and increase patient choice. Whatever the immediate cause, the Secretary of State announced on a bank holiday weekend that the ECJ decision required the NHS to re-examine its practice on the funding of overseas treatment.

Steps were quickly taken to establish a pilot scheme to replace the existing E 112 system that had been put into place to implement Regulation 1408/71. This involved selected Primary Care Trusts negotiating contracts with health providers on the European mainland to treat English patients. It is important to note that this did not supplant the traditional English approach of prior approval before services are funded.[30] Eligible patients were contacted by health professionals to invite them to participate. Selection was made by the professionals not the patients, who could merely choose whether to take up the invitation.

Of far greater significance, however, has been the willingness of Munby J to use these developments to enhance the rights of English patients to take the initiative and seek treatment abroad. He reviewed the domestic law and identified the fact that it did not provide patients with the right to demand any particular treatment or to have the NHS fund it from a specific service provider.[31] Patients could merely accept or reject what was offered to them. He then reviewed the impact of human rights law and concluded that this could not provide the foundation for any right to treatment either.[32] Yet EU

---

[30] See the evaluation report at <http://www.doh.gov.uk/international/evaluationreport.htm>.
[31] *R (Watts) v Bedford Primary Care Trust and the Secretary of State for Health* .[2003] EWHC 228 (Admin) paras 38–43.
[32] Paras 44–55.

law, in the interests of ensuring that no barriers were erected by Member States to the freedom to seek and provide services, could give Mrs Watts a right she could not obtain at home. Providers in France are thus better off than independent UK providers, who have no basis on which to offer services and then demand reimbursement.

This raises the intriguing prospect that if the facts of the Jaymee Bowen case were to arise today, her father might have been able to force the NHS to pay for her treatment if he had found a doctor in another Member State who was prepared to treat her. The approach taken in *Peerbooms* and *Inizan* would suggest that the ECJ would not accept that a clinical opinion by the doctors caring for Jaymee should prevail over that elsewhere. The facts that the UK courts would not force the doctors to give her the treatment her father requested and that Jaymee was thought to be dying would combine to make a compelling case that there would be undue delay in administering life saving treatment if the care was not funded. It is conceivable that the NHS would be forced to pay for treatment that the Court of Appeal found it should not be required to provide directly. Whether the key issues in the *Bowen* case are seen to be financial control or clinical appropriateness, the power of the NHS to regulate its work in the way it is accustomed to would be substantially removed.

The Court of Appeal in the *Watts* case has grasped the sea change that Munby's judgment implies.[33] Its reference to the ECJ draws attention to two groups of issues. The first concerns compatibility with the NHS approach to delivering healthcare. What would be the basis of reimbursement, for which there is currently no provision? Are patients entitled to 'jump the queue'? When, if at all, should the NHS fund treatment in another Member State when it would not be obliged to fund it privately in the UK? The second challenges the rationale of the line of ECJ cases themselves. What is the relationship between Article 49 of the Treaty and Article 22 of Regulation 1408/71? Amendment of the latter in 1981 made it clear that the Council intended to enable Member States to protect the integrity of their health systems, but it cannot prevail over the Treaty if that requires a different solution. Can Member States effectively protect their cost containment measures or prioritisation methods or will a ruling on what constitutes undue delay force harmonisation?

This chapter suggests that the outcome of the ECJ reference is crucially important for the shape of English healthcare law and the maintenance of the fundamental principle expressed in *Peerbooms* that Member States should not be forced to extend the scope of their social security systems. It has shown that a move towards enforceable rights to funding for specific care in a foreign place of the patient's choosing would introduce fundamental changes into English healthcare law. This would imply that the

---

[33] *Secretary of State for Health v R (Yvonne Watts)* [2004] EWCA Civ 166.

change should be strongly resisted by the UK government, as it was in the *Müller-Fauré* case. On the other hand, attention has also been drawn to developments in Government policy for the NHS that make the arguments used to resist the impact of European Union law look increasingly vulnerable. It remains to be seen whether Munby J's approach will turn out to constitute a new dawn for NHS law or a wrecking attack on its fundamental principles.

8

EU Citizenship and the Principle of Solidarity

CATHERINE BARNARD[*]

Believing that Europe, reunited after bitter experiences intends to continue along the path of civilisation, progress and prosperity, for the good of all its inhabitants, including the weakest and most deprived; that it wishes to remain a continent open to culture, learning, and social progress; and that it wishes to deepen the democratic and transparent nature of its public life, and to strive for peace, justice and solidarity throughout the world.

Preamble, Treaty establishing a Constitution for Europe[1]

I INTRODUCTION

The principle of 'solidarity' is taking root as a guiding principle of European Community law. The Treaty establishing a Constitution for Europe contains at least five separate references to the term. It appears in the Preamble, and again in the statement of the Union's values[2] and Union's objectives as well as in specific substantive provisions. This is not an unforeseen development: solidarity is a principle of long standing in the constitutions of some of the Member States.[3] It therefore comes as no surprise that the principle has increasingly crept into the lexicon of the Court of

---

[*] Trinity College, Cambridge.

[1] CM 6289/11.

[2] Art-I-2: 'The Union is founded on the values of respect for human dignity, liberty, democracy, the rule of law and respect for human rights... These values are common to the Member states in a society in which pluralism, non-discrimination, tolerance, justice, solidarity and equality prevail.' 'Solidarity' can also be found in the existing Art 2 EC. See also the Poverty Action Programmes designed to combat exclusion and promote solidarity eg The Poverty 4 Programme COM(93) 435 final successfully challenged by the UK in Case C-106/96 UK v Council [1998] ECR I-2729.

[3] See, eg Art 2 of the Italian Constitution which provides: 'The republic recognizes and guarantees the inviolable human rights, be it as an individual or in social groups expressing their personality, and it ensures the performance of the unalterable duty to political, economic, and social solidarity.' See also the Preamble to the French Constitution of 1958 which refers to the 1946 Constitution which provides that 'La Nation proclame la solidarité et l'égalité de tous les Français devant les charges qui résultent des calamités nationales.'

Justice. The focus of this chapter is to examine how the Court has used the principle to establish the parameters of Union citizenship.

II THE USE AND SCOPE OF THE SOLIDARITY PRINCIPLE

In its description of the Union's objectives,[4] the Constitutional Treaty uses the term solidarity in three different ways: firstly, it talks of 'solidarity between generations';[5] secondly, it talks of 'solidarity among Member States', an idea which is given more concrete expression in Article I–42 which requires the Union and its Member States to act jointly in a spirit of solidarity if a Member State is the victim of a terrorist attack or natural or man-made disaster;[6] and thirdly, it refers to 'solidarity and mutual respect among peoples' in respect of the Union's relations with the outside world. The idea of mutual respect underpins the 'solidarity' Title in the Charter of Fundamental Rights.[7] This Title embraces a range of social rights (eg workers' rights to information and consultation, collective bargaining and action, protection in the event of unjustified dismissal, fair and just working conditions, prohibition of child labour and protection of young people at work, social security and social assistance, healthcare, environmental and consumer protection).

'Solidarity' has also being used as a guiding principle in EU legislation. For example, Council Regulation 1101/89[8] helped to achieve a substantial reduction in overcapacity in the inland waterways sector (particularly in the Benelux countries and France and Germany) by introducing a scrapping scheme coordinated at Community level but financed by the industry itself. The Council justified this as a 'solidarity measure that was appropriate and

---

[4]   Art I–3, para 3, provides 'It shall combat social exclusion and discrimination and shall promote social justice and protection, equality between women and men, solidarity between generations and protection of the rights of the child . It shall promote economic, social and territorial cohesion, and solidarity among Member States.' Para 4 reads 'In its relations with the wider world, the Union shall uphold and promote its values and interests. It shall contribute to peace, security, the sustainable development of the Earth, solidarity and mutual respect among peoples, free and fair trade, eradication of poverty and protection of human rights and in particular the rights of the child, as well as to strict observance and development of international law, including respect for the principles of the United Nations Charter.'

[5]   This is particularly the case between those in employment and those in retirement: see eg Case C–50/99 *Podesta v CRICA* [2000] ECR I–4039, para 21.

[6]   See also Reg 2012/2002 establishing the European Union Solidarity Fund, 2002 OJ L311/3, which has been used in cases of the storm and flooding in Malatin in September 2003, the forest fire in Spain in the summer of 2003 and the flooding in Southern France in December 2003: see EP and Council Decision 2004/323, 2004 OJ L104/112.

[7]   To be included in Part II of the Treaty.

[8]   1989 OJ L116/25.

beneficial for the whole sector', an argument that the Court of Justice accepted.[9]

At the heart of these various uses of the principle of solidarity lies the idea, expressed in the Oxford English Dictionary, of 'mutual dependence, community of interests, feelings, and action'. Often solidarity has financial consequences: as Advocate General Fennelly noted in his opinion in *Sodemare*:[10]

> Social solidarity envisages the inherently uncommercial act of involuntary subsidization of one social group by another.[11]

But how has the principle shaped and influenced judgments of the Court? It has been invoked by litigants as a synonym for the duty of cooperation found in Article 10 EC[12] and as a guiding principle to justify the formation of political groupings.[13] It is also frequently called in aid in references from states such as France,[14] where solidarity underpins their social security schemes.[15] But I am particularly interested in two specific and deliberate uses of the term by the Court as it tries to flesh out the principles underpinning the concept of Union citizenship. In the first group of cases, considered in section III below, the Court has used the principle of solidarity *negatively* to defend national social welfare policies against erosion from single market principles. This is what Tamara Hervey describes as solidarity being a 'buttress' against the single market.[16] Here the Court deploys a

---

[9] Joined Cases C–248/95 and C–249/95 *SAM Schiffart GmbH, Heinz Stapf v Germany* [1997] ECR I–4475, para 74.

[10] Case C–70/95 *Sodemare v Regione Lombardia* [1997] ECR I–3395.

[11] Para 29.

[12] Case C–453/00 *Kühne & Heitz NV v Productschap voor Pluimvee en Eieren* (Judgment of 13 January 2004) para 1.

[13] Case C–488/01 P *Jean-Claude Martinez v European Parliament* (Judgment of 11 November 2003), para 38 where Martinez argued that the concept of 'political affinity' in Rule 29 of the European Parliament's Rules of Procedure had to be construed as authorising re-grouping of members beyond national frontiers and favoured the formation of 'ideological solidarity or solidarity of other kinds rather than national affiliations'. See also the earlier application under Article 242: Joined Cases C–486/01 P–R and C–488/01 P–R *Front National and Martinez v Parliament* [2002] ECR I–1843.

[14] For the definitive work, see M Borgetto, *La Notion de Fraternité en Droit Public Français: le Passé, Le Présent et L'Avenir de la Solidarité* (LGDJ, 1993). Joined Cases C–393–94/99 *Institut national d'assurances sociales pour travailleurs indépendants (Inasti) v Claude Hervein* [2001] ECR I–2829, AG Jacobs' Opinion, para 28. This is particularly so in cases involving the French 'national solidarity scheme' which includes family benefits and benefits from the Fonds de Solidarité Vieillesse: eg Case C–169/98 *Commission v France* [2000] ECR I–1049.

[15] The same also seems to apply in Belgium: see eg Case C–75/97 *Belgium v Commission* [1999] ECR I–3671, para 35, where the Court noted that the national law, whose aim was to replace or supplement the income of the worker to protect him from the consequences of certain employment risks, expressed solidarity between workers and employers; Case C–347/98 *Commission v Belgium* [2001] ECR I–3327, AG Alber's Opinion, para 54. It also applies in Germany: Case C-302/98 *Manfred Sehrer v Bundesknappschaft* [2000] ECR I–4585.

[16] T Hervey, 'Social Solidarity: A Buttress Against Internal Market Law?' in J Shaw (ed), *Social Law and Policy in an Evolving European Union* (Hart Publishing, 2000).

strong and robust form of the principle of solidarity to protect nationals (who are usually citizens of the Union but who have not exercised their rights of free movement), and in particular their pension and sickness funds, from the deregulatory tendency of the core Treaty provisions.

By contrast, in the second group of cases, considered in section IV below, the Court has employed the solidarity principle *positively* to impose obligations on the state, this time in respect not of nationals but migrant EU citizens who have exercised their rights of free movement and residence under Article 18(1) EC. It has recognised that, given the existence of the status of EU citizenship, there is now—in certain circumstances—sufficient solidarity between the migrant and the host state taxpayer to require the state to provide some financial support to the migrant. In this context the Court's use of the solidarity principle is more cautious, based—as I will argue—on an incremental approach. By this I mean that the longer the migrant's period of residence and the deeper his or her integration into the community of the host state, the greater the rights he or she enjoys in the host state. The corollary of this is that for those who have recently arrived in the host state, their rights to equal treatment, especially in the key area of social benefits, are more limited since there is very limited solidarity between the migrants and nationals from the host state.

By adopting this incremental approach, I will argue that the Court has shown itself sensitive to the broader political environment in which it is operating and, in particular, the suspicion with which economic migrants are viewed in some quarters. By contrast, in a third group of cases, considered in section V below, the Court has not demonstrated the same degree of sensitivity towards the political and economic issues at stake. In these cases, notably *Gravier*,[17] *Cowan*[18] and *Kohll*[19] the Court considers that the issues raised concern the building of the single market and not migration and so it applies the full rigours of its equal treatment/market access case law.[20] While it could be argued that the Court's decisions were justified since they were delivered in the context of Articles 49 and 50 EC on free movement of services and not Articles 17–21 EC on citizenship, they were, as Advocate General Jacobs pointed out,[21] nascent citizenship cases since they involved those who were not economically active taking advantage of the fundamental Treaty provisions on free movement to gain access to welfare services in other Member States. It will be argued that the Court's failure in these cases to take into account the attenuated concept of solidarity which currently

---

[17] Case 293/83 *Gravier v Ville de Liège* [1985] ECR 593

[18] Case 186/87 *Cowan v Trésor public* [1989] ECR 195.

[19] Case C–158/96 *Kohll v Union des Caisses de Maladie* [1998] ECR I–1931.

[20] This is considered in further detail in C Barnard, The Substantive Law of the EU: The Four Freedoms (OUP, 2004) chs 10–13.

[21] As recognised by AG Jacobs in his Opinion in Case C–274/96 *Criminal Proceedings against Bickel and Franz* [1998] ECR I–7637, para 20.

exists between citizens of the Union may, in the long term, do more damage to any developing sense of solidarity gradually evolving in the European Union than foster it. However, before we examine these issues we shall consider the most well-established use of the solidarity principle by the Court of Justice–as a means of protecting long-established, well-embedded national social welfare provisions against the potentially destabilising influence of fundamental Treaty provisions, especially Articles 81, 82 and 86 EC.

III WHERE THE SOLIDARITY PRINCIPLE IS USED DEFENSIVELY

Pension and other welfare schemes, often privately organised but on a not-for-profit basis, need a constant flow of members to keep them solvent (for example those still in employment paying for those who are retired). In order to ensure this, some employers require all their employees to be members of a particular scheme with which the employer has an agreement, and with no other. This has prompted some to challenge the compatibility of such agreements with Community law, especially the antitrust provisions of the Treaty. This has presented the Court with a dilemma: while keen to remove the barriers to the creation of a single market it is also conscious of the Community's obligations under the social policy provisions of the Treaty[22] and does not want to jeopardise the viability of such schemes with the result that social welfare provision in certain states is undermined.

It is against this backcloth that the Court has developed the principle of national solidarity.[23] According to this principle, where the activity is based on national solidarity, it is not an economic activity and therefore the body concerned cannot be classed as an undertaking to which Community antitrust provisions apply. The approach was first adopted in the case of *Poucet and Pistre*[24] where the Court held that certain French bodies administering the sickness and maternity insurance scheme for self-employed persons engaged in non-agricultural occupations and the basic pension scheme for

---

[22] See, eg Case C–67/96 *Albany International BV v Stichting Bedrijfspensioenfonds Textielindustrie* [1999] ECR I–5751, para 59: 'It is beyond question that certain restrictions of competition are inherent in collective agreements between organisations representing employers and workers. However, the social policy objectives pursued by such agreements would be seriously undermined if management and labour were subject to Article [81(1)] of the Treaty when seeking jointly to adopt measures to improve conditions of work and employment'; Joined Cases C–270/97 and C–271/97 *Deutsche Post v Sievers* [2000] ECR I–929, para 57 on Article 141 EC on equal pay where the Court said that 'the economic aim pursued by Article [141] of the Treaty, namely the elimination of distortions of competition between undertakings established in different Member States, is secondary to the social aim pursued by the same provision, which constitutes the expression of a fundamental human right'.

[23] T Hervey, 'Social Solidarity: A Buttress against Internal Market law?' in J Shaw (ed), *Social Law and Policy in an Evolving European Union* (Hart Publishing, 2000).

[24] Joined Cases C–159/91 and C–160/91 *Poucet and Pistre v AGF and Cancava* [1993] ECR I–637.

skilled trades were not to be classified as undertakings for the purpose of competition law. The schemes, to which affiliation was compulsory, provided a basic pension,[25] regardless of the financial status and state of health of the individual at the time of affiliation. The schemes were also non-funded which meant that they operated on a redistributive basis, with active members' contributions being directly used to finance the pensions of retired members. This is the embodiment of the principle of solidarity.

Solidarity was also reflected in the grant of both pension rights to those who had made no contributions and of pension rights that were not proportional to the contributions paid. There was also solidarity between the various social security schemes, with those in surplus contributing to the financing of those with structural difficulties. The Court therefore stated:

> It follows that the social security schemes, as described, are based on a system of compulsory contribution, which is indispensable for the application of the principle of solidarity and the financial equilibrium of those schemes.
>
> ...[O]rganisations involved in the management of the public social security system fulfil an exclusively social function. That activity is based on the principle of national solidarity and is entirely non-profit-making. The benefits paid are statutory benefits bearing no relation to the amount of the contribution.

The Court concluded: 'Accordingly, that activity is not an economic activity...' and so EC competition law did not apply.

Poucet and Pistre can, however, be contrasted with *FFSA*[26] where the Court found there was insufficient solidarity in the scheme to justify taking it outside the scope of European Community law. The case concerned a French supplementary retirement scheme for self-employed farmers.[27] Membership of the scheme was optional and, unlike *Poucet*, the scheme operated on a capitalisation (rather than a redistributive) basis which meant that the benefits depended solely on the amount of contributions paid by the recipients and the financial results of the investments made by the managing organisation. On these facts the Court concluded that the managing body carried on an economic activity in competition with life assurance companies and so the Community competition rules, in particular Article 81 EC, applied. Neither the social objective pursued (it was created by the Government in order to protect a population whose income was lower and

---

[25] These are helpfully summarised by AG Jacobs in his Opinion in Case C–67/96 *Albany International BV v Stichting Bedrijfspensioenfonds Textielindustrie* [1999] ECR I–5751, para 317.

[26] Case C–244/94 *Fédération Française des Sociétés d'Assurances* [1995] ECR I–4013 discussed by P Laigre, 'L'intrusion du droit communautaire de la concurrence dans le champ de la protection sociale' [1996] *Droit Social* 82.

[27] Case C–67/96 *Albany* [1999] ECR I–5751, para 325.

whose average age was higher than those of other socio-economic categories and whose basic old-age insurance was not sufficient), nor the fact that it was non-profit-making, nor the requirements of solidarity (for example, contributions were not linked to the risks incurred and there was no prior questionnaire or medical examination and no selection took place) altered the fact that the managing organisation was carrying on an economic activity.

In the light of *FFSA* it is not surprising that the Court found in *Albany*[28] that a pension fund charged with the management of a supplementary pension scheme set up by a collective agreement concluded between organisations representing employers and workers in a given sector, to which affiliation had been made compulsory by the public authorities for all workers in that sector, was an undertaking within the meaning of Article 81 et seq. of the Treaty. It noted that, like *FFSA*, the scheme operated in accordance with the principle of capitalisation, in respect of which it was subject, like an insurance company, to supervision by the Insurance Board; and, as with *FFSA*, the Court added that neither the fact that the fund was non-profit making, nor that it pursued a social objective, nor that it demonstrated elements of solidarity affected this conclusion.[29] On the other hand, the Court recognised that the solidarity elements did justify the exclusive right of the fund to manage the supplementary scheme under Article 86(2) EC and so there was no breach of Articles 82 and 86 EC respectively.

Although the Court's initial enthusiasm for the principle of solidarity seemed rather to have cooled after *FFSA*, the principle was again successfully invoked in *Sodemare*.[30] The Court ruled that Articles 43 and 48 EC on freedom of establishment did not preclude a Member State from allowing only non-profit-making private operators to participate in the running of its social welfare system by concluding contracts which entitled them to be reimbursed by the public authorities for the costs of providing social welfare services of a healthcare nature. Having noted that Community law did

---

[28] Case C–67/96 *Sodemare v Regione Lombardia* [1999] ECR I–5751, para 87.

[29] The solidarity was reflected by the obligation to accept all workers without a prior medical examination, the continuing accrual of pension rights despite exemption from contributions in the event of incapacity for work, the discharge by the fund of arrears of contributions due from an employer in the event of the latter's insolvency and by the indexing of the amount of the pensions in order to maintain their value. The principle of solidarity was also apparent from the absence of any equivalence, for individuals, between the contribution paid, which is an average contribution not linked to risks, and pension rights, which are determined by reference to an average salary. Such solidarity makes compulsory affiliation to the supplementary pension scheme essential. Otherwise, if 'good' risks left the scheme, the ensuing downward spiral would jeopardise its financial equilibrium (para 75). This would increase the cost of pensions for workers, particularly those in small and medium-sized undertakings with older employees engaged in dangerous activities, to which the fund could no longer offer pensions at an acceptable cost (para 108).

[30] Case C–70/95 *Sodemare v Regione Lombardia* [1997] ECR I–3395.

not detract from the powers of the Member States to organise their social security systems[31] the Court added:

> It is clear from the documents before the Court that that system of social welfare, whose implementation is in principle entrusted to the public authorities, is based on the principle of solidarity, as reflected by the fact that it is designed as a matter of priority to assist those who are in a state of need owing to insufficient family income, total or partial lack of independence or the risk of being marginalized, and only then, within the limits imposed by the capacity of the establishments and resources available, to assist other persons who are, however, required to bear the costs thereof, to an extent commensurate with their financial means, in accordance with scales determined by reference to family income.[32]

The Court accepted the Italian government's reasoning that since non-profit making private operators, by their very nature were not influenced by their need to derive profit from the provision of services, they could pursue social aims as a matter of priority. Thus, in *Sodemare* the Court used the principle of solidarity to reinforce its view that Community law was not just about unrestricted access for all economic operators to the market in other Member States and so found that there was no breach of Community law and Articles 43, 48 and 49 EC in particular.

Since *Sodemare* the Court has carefully examined the facts of individual cases to consider whether there is a sufficient degree of solidarity to justify a finding that the activity is not economic, so falling outside the scope of Community law, or insufficient solidarity and so falling within Community law. For example, in *AOK*[33] the Court found that the sickness funds in the German statutory health insurance scheme were involved in the management of the social security system where they fulfilled 'an exclusively social function which is founded on the principle of national solidarity and is entirely non-profit-making'.[34] Since the funds were obliged by law to offer their members essentially identical benefits, irrespective of contributions,

---

[31] Para 27.

[32] Para 29.

[33] Joined Cases C–264/01, C–306/01, C–354/01 and C–355/01 *AOK Bundesverband, Bundesverband der Betriebskrankenkassen (BKK), Bundesverband der Innungskrankenkassen, Bundesverband der landwirtschaftlichen Krankenkassen, Verband der Angestelltenkrankenkassen eV, Verband der Arbeiter-Ersatzkassen, Bundesknappschaft and See-Krankenkasse v Ichthyol-Gesellschaft Cordes, Hermani & Co* (C–264/01), *Mundipharma GmbH* (C–306/01), *Gödecke GmbH* (C–354/01) and *Intersan, Institut für pharmazeutische und klinische Forschung GmbH* (C–355/01) (Judgment of 16 March 2004). See also Case C–218/00 *Cisal di Battistello Venanzio & C Sas v Istituto nazionale per l'assicurazione contro gli infortuni sul lavoro* [2002] ECR I–691 concerning compulsory insurance against accidents at work and occupational diseases; Case C–355/00 *Freskot AE v Elliniko Dimosio* [2003] ECR I–5263; Case T–319/99 *FENIN v Commission* [2003] ECR II–357 concerning the bodies which run the Spanish national health system.

[34] Para 51.

they were bound together in a type of community founded on the basis of solidarity which enabled an equalisation of costs and risks between them and they did not compete with one another or private institutions,[35] the Court considered that they fell on the *Poucet and Pistre* side of the line and so their activity could not be regarded as economic in nature. On the other hand, in *Wouters*[36] the Court said that because a professional regulatory body such as the Bar of the Netherlands was neither fulfilling a social function based on the principle of solidarity nor exercising powers which were typically those of a public authority, it did engage in an economic activity and so was subject to Community law.

This brief review shows that in respect of its non-mobile citizens, the Court has used the solidarity principle to ensure that Community Law does not have the effect of eroding their standard of living and quality of life.[37] If it were otherwise, the very legitimacy of EC law would be undermined. In this way the principle of solidarity has reinforced the principle of subsidiarity—the local provision of services and facilities has been preserved from the reach of European Community law. In the next section we consider a different and more positive function of the principle of solidarity— to require the host state to extend benefits already enjoyed by nationals to migrant citizens, all in the name of Union citizenship.

IV WHERE THE SOLIDARITY PRINCIPLE IS USED POSITIVELY

In *Grzelczyk* the Court made its important observation about the nature of EU citizenship. It said:

> Union citizenship is destined to be the fundamental status of nationals of the Member States, enabling those who find themselves in the same situation to enjoy the same treatment in law irrespective of their nationality, subject to such exceptions as are expressly provided for.[38]

This suggests that migrant EU citizens, including those who are not economically active, have the right to claim all benefits available in the host state on the same terms as nationals, unless the benefits are expressly

---

[35] Paras 51–53.

[36] Case C–309/99 *Wouters, Savelbergh, Price Waterhouse Belastingadviseurs BV v Algemene Raad van de Nederlandse Orde van Advocaten* [2002] ECR I–1577, para 58. See also Case C–55/96 *Job Centre Coop Arl* [1997] ECR I–7119.

[37] Cf Art 2 EC.

[38] Case C–184/99 R *Grzelczyk v Centre public d'aide social d'Ottignies-Louvain-la-Neuve* [2001] ECR I–6193, para 31, echoing AG La Pergola in Case C–85/96 *Martínez Sala* [1998] ECR I–2691, para 18.

excluded by Community law.[39] This is the so-called 'perfect assimilation' approach.[40] This suggests that migrant EU citizens are entitled to full equal treatment from day one of their arrival in the host state. However, in this section I will suggest that, when looked at carefully, the cases do not actually support the full assimilationist approach. In fact, the caselaw suggests an incremental approach to residence and equality—the longer migrants reside in the Member State, the greater the number of benefits they receive on equal terms with nationals and this is justified in the name of integration and solidarity.

In this section I therefore argue that there is a spectrum of situations. At one end lie those migrants who have legally resided in the host state for many years ('long-term residents'): because they are fully assimilated into the community of the host state they enjoy full equal treatment with nationals based on the principle of *national* solidarity (solidarity between nationals) which they benefit from on the basis of their long period of residence. Further along the spectrum lie those who have been legally resident in the host state for a number of years ('medium-term residents'). They will also enjoy equal treatment with nationals but this time equality is based on *transnational* solidarity (solidarity between nationals and migrants). However, given their medium-term resident status, this equal treatment may be limited to certain benefits and for certain periods. At the far end of the spectrum are those who have just arrived or who have recently arrived in the host state. They will enjoy only limited equal treatment with nationals due to the virtual absence of solidarity between the newly arrived migrant and the resident.

The incremental approach to the principle of equal treatment suggested by the caselaw was also recognised by Advocate General La Pergola in *Stöber.* He said that the ultimate purpose of the citizenship provisions was to bring about *increasing* equality between citizens of the Union, irrespective of their nationality.[41] This incremental approach also underpins the Directive on Citizens' Rights.[42] The Directive envisages three categories of migrants. The first group are those wishing to enter the host state for up to three months. They are not subject to any conditions (eg as to resources, medical insurance) other than holding a valid identity card or passport. They enjoy the right to reside in the host State for themselves and their families and the right to equal treatment but they have no entitlement to social assistance during the first three months of their stay.

---

[39] An example of an express exclusion is maintenance grants for students in Art 3 of Dir 93/96 on the right of residence for students, 1993 OJ L317/59.

[40] A Iliopoulou and H Toner (2002) 39 *Common Market Law Review* 609, 616. See also Case C–214/94 *Ingrid Boukhalfa v Bundesrepublik Deutschland* [1996] ECR I–2253, para 63 and S Friess and J Shaw, 'Citizenship of the Union: First Steps in the European Court of Justice' (1998) 4 *European Public Law* 533.

[41] Joined Cases C–4 and 5/95 *Stöber and Pereira* [1997] ECR I–511, para 50.

[42] Dir 2004/38/EC 2004 OJ L158/77.

The second group are those residing in the host state for more than three months. They have a 'right to residence' if:

— They are workers or self-employed persons in the host state; or
— They have sufficient resources for themselves and their family members not to become a burden on social assistance in the host Member State during their stay and have comprehensive sickness insurance cover in the host Member State; or
— They are students enrolled at an accredited establishment for the principal purpose of following a course of study, including vocational training, have comprehensive sickness insurance cover in the host Member State and assure the relevant authorities that they have sufficient resources to avoid becoming a burden on the social assistance scheme of the host state during their stay; or
— They are family members of a Union citizen who satisfies one of the conditions above.[43]

They have the right to engage in gainful activity and the right to equal treatment but Member States are not obliged to provide maintenance grants to migrants unless they are workers, self-employed, or members of their family.

The third group concerns those legally residing in the host state for a continuous period of more than five years.[44] These citizens (and their family members who are not nationals but who have resided with the Union citizen for five years) will have the right of permanent residence. None of the conditions applicable to the second group apply to those seeking permanent residence. Continuity of residence will not be affected by temporary absences[45] and, once acquired, the right of permanent residence can be lost only through absence from the host Member State for a period exceeding two years at a time. As with the second group, the third group also enjoy the right to work and to equal treatment. In addition, they can enjoy student maintenance in the form of grants or loans.[46] As we shall see, the Court's caselaw broadly anticipates these different positions.

---

[43] Art 7.
[44] There are certain exceptions to the five year rule, eg those reaching pension age or suffer a permanent incapacity or frontier workers.
[45] The right to permanent residence will not be lost if the absences do not exceed a total of six months a year or twelve months at for important reasons such as compulsory military service, serious illness, pregnancy and childbirth, study or vocational training, or a work assignment in another Member State or a third country.
[46] Those with the right of residence and who are engaged in gainful activity may also have the right to students maintenance.

A The Incremental Approach to Residence and Equal Treatment

1 Long-term residents

Martínez Sala[47] concerns the first situation, that of a long term resident. She was a Spanish national who had spent most of her life in Germany, having lived there since 1968 when she was 12 years old. She had various jobs and various residence permits in that time. When she gave birth in 1993 she did not have a residence permit but she did have a certificate saying that an extension of the permit had been applied for. The German authorities refused to give her a child-raising allowance on the grounds that she was not a German national nor did she have a residence permit. If she had been a worker she would have been entitled to the benefit as a social advantage under Article 7(2) of Regulation 1612/68.

Given her background, it was unlikely that she was a worker (or an employed person within the meaning of Regulation 1408/71).[48] The Court therefore considered her situation under the citizenship provisions. It said that, as a national of a Member State lawfully residing in the territory of another Member State, Martínez Sala came within the personal scope of the citizenship provisions.[49] She therefore enjoyed the rights laid down by Article 17(2) EC which included the right not to suffer discrimination on grounds of nationality under Article 12 EC in respect of all situations falling within the material scope of the Treaty.[50] This included the situation where a Member State delayed or refused to grant a benefit provided to all persons lawfully resident in the territory of that State on the ground that the claimant did not have a document (a residence permit) which nationals were not obliged to have.[51] On this basis the Court concluded that Martínez Sala was suffering from direct discrimination on the grounds of nationality contrary to Article 12 EC[52] and since it was direct discrimination it could not be objectively justified.[53]

2 Medium-term residents

Grzelczyk[54] concerns the second situation—of someone who has been lawfully resident in the host state for a shorter period of time. Grzelczyk, a French national studying at a Belgian university, supported himself

---

[47] Case C–85/96 M M *Martínez Sala v Freistaat Bayern* [1998] ECR I–2691.
[48] It was for the national court to make the final decision.
[49] Para 61.
[50] Para 62.
[51] *Ibid.*
[52] Para 64.
[53] *Ibid.*
[54] Case C–184/99 R *Grzelczyk v Centre public d'aide social d'Ottignies-Louvain-la-Neuve* [2001] ECR I–6193.

financially for the first three years of his studies but then applied for the minimex (the Belgium minimum income guarantee) at the start of his fourth and final year. While Belgian students could receive the benefit, migrant students could not[55] and so Grzelczyk suffered (direct) discrimination contrary to Article 12 EC.[56] Grzelczyk, a citizen of the Union, could rely on Article 12 in respect of those situations which fell within the material scope of the Treaty[57] which included those situations involving 'the exercise of the fundamental freedoms guaranteed by the Treaty and those involving the exercise of the right to move and reside freely in another Member State, as conferred by Article [18(1)] of the Treaty'.[58]

It therefore looked like Grzelczyk was going to succeed. However, the Court then turned to consider the limits laid down in the Residence Directives, in particular the limits imposed by Article 1 of the Students' Directive 93/96 which required the migrant student to have sufficient resources. The Court said that while a Member State could decide that a student having recourse to social assistance no longer fulfilled the conditions of his right of residence and so could withdraw his residence permit or decide not to renew it,[59] such actions could not be the *automatic* consequence of a migrant student having recourse to the host State's social assistance system.[60] The Court continued that beneficiaries of the right of residence could not become an 'unreasonable' burden on the public finances of the host State.[61] Therefore, the Belgian authorities had to provide some temporary support (the minimex) to the migrant citizen, as they would to nationals, given that there exists 'a certain degree of financial solidarity' between nationals of a host Member State and nationals of other Member States.[62] However, that support would continue only for so long as the student did not become an unreasonable burden on public finances. Thus, in the name of financial solidarity between EU citizens, Grzelczyk could receive the minimex for a certain period of time (i.e until he became an unreasonable burden).

Baumbast[63] is another example of a case involving medium term residence. He was a German national who had been working in the UK and continued residing there with his family once his work in the EU had ceased. While he had sufficient resources for himself and his family, his German medical insurance did not cover emergency treatment in the UK,

---

[55] Para 29.
[56] Para 30.
[57] Para 32.
[58] Para 33, citing Case C–274/96 *Bickel and Franz* [1998] ECR I–7637.
[59] Para 42.
[60] Para 43.
[61] Para 44.
[62] *Ibid*.
[63] Case C–413/99 *Baumbast and R v Secretary of State for the Home Department* [2002] ECR I–7091.

as required by Directive 90/364 on persons of independent means.[64] For this reason the British authorities refused to renew his residence permit. The Court said that he could rely on his directly effective right to reside under Article 18(1) EC but this right had to be read subject to the limitations laid down in the Residence Directives.[65] It then qualified this remark by adding that the limitations and conditions referred in Article 18(1) EC had to be applied 'in compliance with the limits imposed by Community law and in accordance with the general principles of that law, in particular the principle of proportionality'.[66] It concluded that, given neither Baumbast nor his family had become a financial burden on the state, it would amount to a disproportionate interference with the exercise of the right of residence if he were denied residence on the ground that his sickness insurance did not cover the emergency treatment given in the host Member State.[67]

The careful articulation of the proportionality principle in Baumbast helps to explain Grzelczyk: Grzelczyk could not be refused a minimex under Article 1 of Directive 93/96 because he had been lawfully residing in Belgium for three years during which time he had had sufficient resources (and medical insurance). Now that he was suffering 'temporary difficulties' it would be disproportionate to deny him the minimex (and so prevent him from finishing his studies). Therefore, Grzelcyzk and Baumbast, both medium-term residents, received the benefit (the minimex in the case of Grzelczyk) and the entitlement to the benefit (access to emergency health-care in the case of Baumbast) for a temporary period on the same terms as nationals. So the Court appears to be using the concept of citizenship to limit the use of the derogations expressly provided for by Article 18(1) EC.

This does, however, beg the question as to why the Residence Directives were not raised in *Martínez Sala*. One explanation may be oversight. Another may be that, because she was such a long-term resident the Court thought that the Residence Directives did not apply to her. Some support for this view can be found in Advocate General Geelhoed's opinion in *Ninni-Orasche*.[68] Mrs Ninni-Orasche, an Italian, married an Austrian national in 1993. Under Austrian law she was given leave to enter and reside in Austria.[69] She did various casual jobs until 1996 when she started studying at an Austrian university. The Austrian authorities refused her study finance because she did not satisfy the criteria laid down in *Lair*.[70]

---

[64] Para 88. See also Case T-66/75 *Hedwig Kuchlenz-Winter v Commission* [1997] ECR II-637, paras 46–47.
[65] Case C–413/99 *Baumbast and R v Secretary of State for the Home Department* [2002] ECR I-7091, para 90.
[66] Para 91.
[67] Para 93.
[68] Case C–413/01 *Franca Ninni-Orasche v Bundesminister für Wissenschaft, Verkehr und Kunst* [2003] ECR I-0000.
[69] Para 81.
[70] Case 39/86 *Lair* [1988] ECR 3161.

The Advocate General said that she could not rely on the Students' Directive 93/96 to obtain the finance because, unlike Grzelczyk, she was just starting her course and Article 3 of the Directive expressly precluded her from obtaining maintenance grants in the host state.

However, he then considered her other capacity—that of legal resident, living in another Member State 'in a capacity which is not connected primarily with the exercise of the fundamental economic freedom'.[71] In other words, she had potentially indefinite residence in Austria—as the spouse of a national—and this made her more Austrian than Italian. When viewed from this perspective, he said, the restrictions contained in Article 18(1) EC did not apply. He continued that Article 17 EC, read in conjunction with Article 12 EC, alone applied and they could 'in specific circumstances, confer a right to equal treatment even where social advantages which are not granted under the directives on residence are concerned'.[72] He emphasised the importance of education and said that there were no reasons why Mrs Ninni-Orashe could not be treated like a national, especially because, in her case, there was no hint of abuse of Community law rights. He referred to the need for a minimum degree of financial solidarity towards those residents who are students but holding the nationality of another Member State and concluded that a resident like Mrs Ninni-Orasche with a 'demonstrable and structural link to Austrian society' could not be treated in Austria 'as any other national of a third country'.[73] For this reason, he said that she enjoyed the right to equal treatment unless unequal treatment could be objectively justified.[74]

Advocate General Geelhoed's reference to 'a minimum degree of financial solidarity' suggests that Mrs Ninni-Orasche is benefiting from the principle of national solidarity which underpins national welfare systems (national taxpayers pay their taxes which help to provide benefits for their fellow nationals who are in need). The same could be said of Martínez Sala: as a long-term resident fully integrated into the host State's community the Court required her to be treated like nationals. *D'Hoop*[75] can probably be explained on a similar basis. D'Hoop, a Belgian national, completed her secondary education in France.[76] When she finished her university studies

---

[71] Para 91.

[72] Para 92.

[73] Para 96.

[74] Para 98.

[75] C–224/98 *D'Hoop v Office national de l'emploi* [2002] ECR I–6191.

[76] One of the questions raised in the case was that since D'Hoop's education took place in 1991, could the discrimination alleged be assessed in the light of the provisions on citizenship of the Union which entered into force subsequently. The Court said that the case did not concern the recognition of Community law rights acquired before the entry into force of the provisions on citizenship of the Union, but related to an allegation of current discriminatory treatment of a citizen of the Union. It said that the provisions on citizenship of the Union were applicable as soon as they enter into force. Therefore they had to be applied to the present effects of situations arising previously (citing Case C–195/98 *Österreichischer Gewerkschaftsbund* [2000] ECR I–10497, paras 54 and 55, and Case C–290/00 *Duchon* [2002] ECR I–3567, paras 43 and 44).

in Belgium her request to the Belgian authorities for a tideover allowance[77] was refused on the grounds that she had not received her secondary education in Belgium. The Court of Justice said that as a free mover she fell within the material scope of the Treaty provisions.[78] It then said that it would be incompatible with the right of freedom of movement if a citizen, in the Member State of which he was a national (Belgium), received treatment 'less favourable than he would enjoy if he had not availed himself of the opportunities offered by the Treaty in relation to freedom of movement'.[79] Reducing this case to its bare facts we can see that a Belgium woman with Belgian parents living in Belgium was entitled to a benefit paid to other Belgians. This should come as no surprise: there is sufficient national solidarity.

The fact that both Grzelczyk and Baumbast received any benefits at all (despite the limitations laid down in the Directive) can, I think, also be explained on the basis of solidarity—the very principle the Court relied on in *Grzelczyk*. As we have seen, the Court noted that, as a result of the creation of Union citizenship, there was now sufficient solidarity—this time *transnational* solidarity (nationals taxpayers pay their taxes to help provide benefits for their fellow nationals in need *and* for migrant EU citizens who are in temporary need)—to justify requiring the host state to give the benefits for a limited period to those medium-term residents in temporary difficulty.[80] The same principle must also be true of Baumbast whose situation is broadly similar to that of Grzelczyk.

3 New arrivals

The corollary of these arguments is that while Article 18(1) EC gives newly arrived migrants the right to move and reside freely in the host State[81] there is insufficient solidarity between the newly arrived migrant and the host state taxpayer to justify requiring full equal treatment in respect of social welfare benefits (such as the minimex) although they might receive some social advantages on a non-discriminatory basis, particularly those granted on a one-off basis (eg court translation services, as in *Bickel and Franz*,[82] free admission to museums, as in *Commission v Spain*).[83] The view that

---

[77] This is a type of unemployment benefit granted to young people who have just completed their studies and are seeking their first employment.
[78] Para 29.
[79] Para 30.
[80] Case C–184/99 R *Grzelczyk v Centre public d'aide social d'Ottignies-Louvain-la-Neuve* [2001] ECR I–6193, para 44.
[81] See also AG Geelhoed in Case C–413/01 *Franca Ninni-Orasche v Bundesminister für Wissenschaft, Verkehr und Kunst* [2003] ECR I–0000, para 87.
[82] Case C–274/96 *Bickel and Franz* [1998] ECR I–7637.
[83] Case C–45/93 *Commission v Spain* [1994] ECR I–911; Case C–388/01 *Commission v Italy* [2003] ECR I–721, para 12.

there is a direct link between length of residence and solidarity is confirmed by Advocate General Geelhoed in *Ninni-Orasche*. He says:[84]

> In my view, the principle of a minimum degree of financial solidarity can, in specific, objectively verifiable circumstances, create a right to equal treatment.
>
> This is so where an EU national has already resided legally for a *considerable time* in another Member State in a capacity which is not connected primarily with the exercise of the fundamental economic freedoms granted by the Treaty and where the residence permit is also not dependent on university studies which the person concerned has commenced in the host state. I consider that such a situation must, for a number of reasons, be placed within the scope of the Treaty, with the result that the EU national acquires the right to equal treatment in law.[85]

This view seems to be shared by Advocate General Ruiz-Jarabo Colomer in *Collins*.[86] Collins, who was Irish, arrived in the United Kingdom and promptly applied for a job-seeker's allowance which was refused on the grounds that he was not habitually resident in the UK. The Advocate General distinguished *Grzelczyk*[87] and concluded that Community law did not require the benefit to be provided to a citizen of the Union who entered the territory of a Member State with the purpose of seeking employment while lacking any connection with the state or link with the domestic employment market.[88]

The Court reached much the same conclusion as its Advocate General, but without reference to the language of solidarity. It made clear that, as a *work seeker*, the rights Collins enjoyed under Article 39 EC and Regulation 1612/68 were limited to equal treatment in respect of access to employment; he did not enjoy equal treatment in respect of social (financial) advantages. The Court then considered the effect of its recent caselaw on citizenship. Having referred to its decision in *Grzelczyk*, the Court said that 'in view of the establishment of citizenship of the Union', it was no longer possible to exclude from the scope of Article 39 EC benefits of a 'financial nature intended to facilitate access to employment in the labour market of a Member State'.

---

[84] Case C–413/01 *Franca Ninni-Orasche v Bundesminister fürr Wissenschaft, Verkehr und Kunst* [2003] ECR I–0000, paras 90–91.

[85] Emphasis added.

[86] Case C–138/02 *Brian Francis Collins v Secretary of State for Work and Pensions* (Judgment of 23 March 2004). See also AG Geelhoed's Opinion in Case C–413/01 *Franca Ninni-Orashe v Bundesminister für Wissenschaft, Verkhr and Kunst* [2003] ECR I-0000, para 86 where he highlighted the 'specific circumstances' of Grzelczyk in comparison with the newly arrived Mrs Ninni-Orasche.

[87] Case C–138/02 *Brian Francis Collins v Secretary of State for Work and Pensions* (Judgment of 23 March 2004) Para 66. See also the AG's opinion in case C-413/01 *Franca Ninni–Orashe v Bundesminister für Wissenschaft, Verkhr und Kunst* [2003] ECR I–0000, para 86 where he highlighted the 'specific circumstances' of Grzelczyk in comparison with the newly arrived Mrs Ninni-Orasche.

[88] Para 76.

The Court then subjected the 'habitual residence' requirement to a conventional discrimination analysis. It noted that because the rule disadvantaged those who had exercised their rights of free movement (it was therefore essentially an indirectly discriminatory requirement) it would be lawful only if the UK could justify it based on objective considerations unrelated to nationality and proportionate to the aim of the national provisions. Following *D'Hoop*,[89] the Court accepted that it was legitimate for a national legislature to wish to ensure that there was a genuine link between the person applying for the benefit and the employment market of that state, and that the link could be determined by establishing that the claimant has 'for a reasonable period, in fact genuinely sought work' in the UK. The Court added that while the residence requirement was appropriate to attain the objective it was only proportionate if it rested on clear criteria known in advance, judicial redress was available and the period of residence must not be excessive. In other words, only once migrants are at least partially integrated into the host state's community can they enjoy these benefits—presumably on the basis of some limited transnational solidarity, as with the medium-term residents.

The basis for such transnational solidarity lies in the fact that the principle of citizenship of the Union is common to both nationals and migrants alike. When viewed from this perspective the principle of citizenship provides the means as well as the ends: the means because it justifies using the solidarity principle to give migrants—even temporary migrants—rights; the ends because true Union Citizenship will only be realised when there is genuine solidarity between the citizens of all 25 Member States of the kind found in the national systems. We can therefore see a process of boot-strapping taking place—citizenship (imposed from above) is used to justify taking limited steps in the name of solidarity and solidarity is being used from the bottom up to foster a growing sense of citizenship. This is particularly so in the field of education where, as Advocate General Geelhoed noted in *D'Hoop*:

> European integration has created an environment conducive to transnational education. Inter-state education is, moreover, viewed as an important instrument in promoting mutual solidarity and tolerance as well as the dissemination of culture throughout the European Union.[90]

However, the Court does seem to recognise that this process needs to be taken slowly: if it expects too much of citizenship as a means it might—in the long term—frustrate citizenship as an ends. In other words, if the Court were to require full equality of treatment in respect of all migrants from day one of their arrival in the host state this would be appreciated

---

[89] Case C–224/98 *M N D'Hoop v Office national d'emploi* [2002] ECR I–6191.
[90] *Ibid*, para 41.

by the migrant citizens but not by the non-migrant citizens (the national taxpayers) in the host State. Indeed such moves could well generate such hostility and anti-migrant feeling among host State nationals that, far from fostering a sense of Union citizenship, it reinforces a sense of nationalism and xenophobia.

The Court's sensitivity to these issues in its caselaw on citizenship can be contrasted directly with its robust attitude to Article 49 EC cases on students and healthcare which, it considers, concern the single market but which directly impact on citizenship rights. In these contexts the Court has not considered the issue in terms of transnational solidarity. Instead, it has focused on its concern to ensure market access and equal treatment. Long term, these decisions might have a serious impact on citizenship building.

V THE ABSENCE OF AN AWARENESS OF SOLIDARITY: STUDENTS AND HEALTHCARE

State provision of education and healthcare form the core of the modern welfare state. In respect of public education,[91] we used to be able to say that this field was not subject to the rigours of the rules on the single market because, in the words of *Humbel*,[92] the funding came from the public purse and the state was not 'seeking to engage in gainful activity but is fulfilling its duties towards its own population in the social, cultural and educational fields'. However, in *Gravier*[93] the Court brought vocational training within the scope of Community law. It said that:

> Access to vocational training is in particular likely to promote free movement of persons throughout the Community, by enabling them to obtain a qualification in the Member State where they intend to work and by enabling them to complete their training and develop their particular talents in the Member State whose vocational training programmes include the special subject desired.[94]

Having done this the Court then said that migrant and non-migrant students should be charged the same fees in respect of vocational training. Failure to do so constituted discrimination on the grounds of nationality prohibited by Article 12 EC.

---

[91] Cf private education: Case C–109/92 *Wirth v Landeshauptstadt Hannover* [1993] ECR I–6447.

[92] Case 263/86 *Belgium v Humbel* [1988] ECR 5365.

[93] Case 293/83 *Gravier v Ville de Liège* [1985] ECR 593 where the Court also confirmed that the principle of non-discrimination contained in Art 12 EC applied to fees but not to maintenance grants.

[94] Para 24.

A similar issue has arisen in respect of healthcare. In *Geraets-Smits and Peerbooms*[95] some of the Member States relied on *Humbel* to argue that hospital services were also 'special'[96] and did not constitute an economic activity within the meaning of Article 50 EC because patients received care in a hospital without having to pay for it themselves.[97] Indeed, in *Geraets-Smits* the Advocate General cited the principle of national solidarity in *Poucet and Pistre* before concluding that the healthcare benefits in kind provided to the insured by the Dutch compulsory sickness scheme 'lack the element of remuneration and are therefore not services within the meaning of Article [50] of the EC Treaty'.[98]

Once again, the Court disagreed. It said that, despite the special nature of the services, Community law still applied.[99] Then the Court said that the payments made by the sickness insurance funds under contractual arrangements between the funds and the hospitals were consideration for the hospital services, even if payable at a flat rate. For this reason they 'unquestionably represent remuneration for the hospital which receives them and which is engaged in an activity of an economic character'.[100] Medical services, including hospital services, were therefore subject to the rigours of Community law, including the principles of equal treatment and market access. Therefore, in *Kohll*[101] the Court said that a national rule requiring prior authorisation for treatment abroad but not in respect of treatment received domestically breached Article 49 EC because it had the effect of making the provision of services between Member States more difficult than the provision of services purely within one Member State.[102]

But what of the solidarity implications of these judgments? This issue was raised directly in the early case of *Cowan*.[103] A British tourist attacked and robbed outside a metro station in Paris was refused criminal injuries compensation on the grounds that he was neither a French national nor a resident

---

[95] Case C-157/99 *Geraets-Smits and Peerbooms* [2001] ECR I-5473.

[96] Para 54. See also the AG's Opinions in Case C-368/98 *Vanbraekel v ANMC* [2001] ECR I-5363.

[97] Albeit that in an insurance-based system such as that in the Netherlands all or part of the cost of the treatment was paid for directly by the relevant sickness scheme to the healthcare provider.

[98] Case C-157/99 *Geraets-Smits and Peerbooms* [2001] ECR I-5473, AG's Opinion, para 32.

[99] *Ibid*, para 54.

[100] See n 98 above, para 58.

[101] Case C-158/96 *Kohll v Union des Caisses de Maladie* [1998] ECR I-1931. For the parallel case on goods, see Case C-120/95 *Decker v Caisse de maladie des employés privés* [1998] ECR I-1831.

[102] Case C-158/96 *Kohll v Union des Caisses de Maladie* [1998] ECR I-1931, para 33. See also Case C-381/93 *Commission v France (Maritime Services)* [1994] ECR I-5145, para 18: 'the provision of maritime transport services between Member States cannot be subject to stricter conditions than those to which analogous provisions of services at domestic level are subject'.

[103] Case 186/87 *Cowan v Le Trésor Public* [1989] ECR 195. See also Case 63/86 *Commission v Italy (Social Housing)* [1988] ECR 29, para 19; and Case C-484/93 *Svensson* [1995] ECR I-3955.

in France. At the hearing the French Government argued that because the case concerned a right to compensation, 'a right which is a manifestation of the principle of national solidarity', such a right presupposes a closer bond with the State than that of a recipient of services, and for that reason it could be restricted to persons who were either nationals of that State or foreign nationals resident on the territory of that State.[104] In other words, given the absence of a sufficient degree of solidarity between national taxpayers and the temporary migrant, the French government argued that Cowan should not receive compensation. The Court firmly rejected this argument:

> That reasoning cannot be accepted. When Community law guarantees a natural person the freedom to go to another Member State the protection of that person from harm in the Member State in question, on the same basis as that of nationals and persons residing there, is a corollary of that freedom of movement. It follows that the prohibition of discrimination is applicable to recipients of services within the meaning of the Treaty as regards protection against the risk of assault and the right to obtain financial compensation provided for by national law when that risk materializes. The fact that the compensation at issue is financed by the Public Treasury cannot alter the rules regarding the protection of the rights guaranteed by the Treaty.[105]

In *Gravier* the Belgian government also relied on the absence of a sufficient degree of solidarity between Belgian taxpayers and migrant students to justify demanding additional tuition fees from foreign students.[106] It said that due to the imbalance between the number of foreign students studying in Belgium and the number of Belgian students living abroad (a fact that the Commission acknowledged) this had serious consequences for the national education budget. This fact compelled the Belgian government to ask students who were 'nationals of other Member States and who normally do not pay taxes in Belgium' to make a proportional contribution to the cost of education. As we have seen, these arguments were unsuccessful. Yet, these very arguments go to the heart of the sensitivities recognised by the Court in its caselaw on Article 18(1) EC. Viewed through the citizenship spectrum outlined above, because these students were newly arrived in the host State there would be good grounds for refusing full equal treatment to them due to the insufficient community of interests between nationals and migrants.

However, because the Court considered that these cases concerned single market issues (the freedom to travel to receive a service) the Court demonstrated no sensitivity to the solidarity arguments. It merely applied its non-discrimination/market access analysis with full rigour and inevitably found the national rules to be discriminatory and thus unlawful. While the

---

[104] Case 186/87 *Cowan v Le Trésor Public* [1989] ECR 195, para 16.
[105] Para 17.
[106] Case 293/83 *Gravier v City of Liège* [1985] ECR 593.

result of judgments such as *Cowan*, *Gravier* and *Kohll* might be to make
the migrant tourist/student/healthcare seeker feel more communautaire, it
also has the effect of imposing greater burdens—not on the EU (the granter
of the rights)—but on the exchequers of the states most affected. In the case
of student migration, this is particularly a problem in countries such as
Belgium and the UK which are net recipients of students.[107] In 2001–02
(with a Union of 15) there were approximately 80,000 students from other
EU countries studying in the UK (excluding EU students on exchange programmes),[108] nearly 50,000 of whom were undergraduates.[109] This migration raises two issues: the availability of places and the cost.

In respect of the number of places, every incoming migrant EU student
will take the place which might have been occupied by a domestic student.[110] In respect of cost,[111] the reality is that (poor and usually non-
mobile) taxpayers from the host countries are supporting the education of
(middle class) students from other Member States with whom they share little by way of community of interests.[112] These taxpayers cannot even com-
fort themselves with the argument that these better educated students will
contribute more to the economies of the host State since 75 per cent of them
subsequently return to their home state[113] and, of those who remain, many

---

[107] The UK is the most popular country of study among EU students, making it the largest net
importer of students within the EU: L Ashton, 'Projecting demand for UK higher education from the Accession Countries' <http://www.hepi.ac.uk/articles>.

[108] *Ibid*: this is about 5% of students in UK higher education institutes.

[109] *Ibid*.

[110] See the comments of the Sir Howard Newby, chief executive of the Higher Education
Funding Council for England reported by L Lightfoot, 'Students face EU fight for Places',
Daily Telegraph, 4 March 2004, 1. He said that 'We expect to admit students on their
merit. Most universities take the view that they want the most talented students almost
irrespective of their origins. If they come from Estonia as opposed to Egham, that is a matter for them'. This problem has been brought into sharp focus by enlargement. A report
form the Higher Education Policy Institute (http://www.hepi.ac.uk/articles) predicted that
30,000 students will arrive from the accession countries and that this is 'likely to increase
competition for places. (...) If the government does not provide the extra places, some of
these will be displacing UK students'.

[111] Recent reports in the British press suggested that it would cost £900 million a year to educate EU students in British universities, a figure expressly rejected by Alan Johnson, the
Minister for Higher Education who suggested a figure of around £30 million: Letter to *The
Times*, 4 February 2004, 19. For a flavour of the debate, see L Clark, 'Britain faces huge
bill for upkeep of students from EU' *Daily Mail*, 22 March 2004, 2.

[112] See eg, S Bush, 'University Admissions and Fees', *Report for the Campaign for Real
Education* March 2004, 6–7: 'While most parents will probably accept a limited degree of
subsidy to fully deserving British students, they will draw the line at subsidising EU students. (...) If, under the provisions of the HE Bill, students from the ten EU accession countries (with average wages in these countries ranging from one-tenth to one-third of the
UK's) have the parental income test applied to them, one can expect that virtually all will
qualify for fee rebates and maintenance bursaries, which the government is now proposing
to offer in cash "upfront". In effect these students will obtain a free British university education for a wide range of courses.'

[113] Although one newspaper reported, in respect of the debate on enlargement, that 'the net
benefit to the UK from the arrival of students from the accession countries through extra

do so for only a relatively short period of time.[114] If this were widely known it could do more to harm the nascent development of EU citizenship in countries such as the UK and Belgium than to foster it. Similar issues may well arise in respect of healthcare, this time raising issues for home—rather than host—States. If their health budget is being diverted to fund operations for nationals in other states this may have serious consequences for the comprehensive provision of healthcare in the home state. Once again this may well have damaging consequences for the 'citizenship' feelings experienced by non-mobile EU citizens wanting operations in their own countries. It might also arouse feelings of hostility on the part of the population of the host states if, as a result of providing operations for migrants, their own nationals are forced to wait.

It is perhaps for this reason that the Court has started to impose some limits on its own judicial developments. For example, in *Brown*[115] it distinguished tuition fees from maintenance grants and confined its ruling in *Gravier* to assistance intended to cover registration or other fees.[116] In respect of 'assistance given to students for maintenance and training' it said that, at the current stage of development of Community law, this fell in principle outside the scope of the EC Treaty for the purposes of Article 12 EC.[117] The healthcare needs of the home state were also recognised by the Court in *Geraets-Smits and Peerbooms*[118] this time through the careful use of the public interest justifications. The Court found that, in principle, a system of prior authorisation was 'both necessary and reasonable' on public health grounds in order to guarantee a 'rationalised, stable, balanced and accessible supply of hospital services'.[119] However, it said that the final decision whether the authorisation requirement could be justified depended on procedural and substantive grounds. It then gave detailed consideration to the procedural and substantive conditions which could be used.[120]

---

taxes paid by students after graduating—was estimated at £80 million a year'; T Miles, 'Warnings over Influx of EU college Students', *The Evening Standard*, 4 March 2004, 24. For more detailed discussion of the cost benefit analysis, see L Aston, 'Projecting demand for UK higher education from Accession Countries' <http://www.hepi.ac.uk/articles>.

[114] L Aston, 'Projecting demand for UK higher education from Accession Countries', <http://www.hepi.ac.uk/articles>.

[115] Case 197/86 *Brown v Secretary of State for Scotland* [1986] ECR 3205.

[116] Case 293/83 *Gravier v City of Liège* [1985] ECR 593.

[117] Although the reference in Case C–209/03 *The Queen on the Application of Dany Bidar against 1) London Borough of Ealing, 2) Secretary of State for Education*, case still pending, aims to challenge this distinction.

[118] Case C–157/99 *B S M Geraets-Smits v Stichting Ziekenfonds, VGZ and H T M Peerbooms v Stichting CZ Groep Zorgverzekeringen* [2001] ECR I–5473.

[119] Paras 80–81.

[120] See further, C Barnard, *The Substantive Law of the EU: The Four Freedoms* (OUP, 2004) 362–69; E Spaventa, 'Public Services and European Law: Looking for Boundaries' (2002–03) 5 *Cambridge Yearbook of European Legal Studies* 271.

VI CONCLUSIONS

In his classic work on (British) citizenship,[121] Marshall argued that citizenship involves full membership of the community which has gradually been achieved through the historical development of individual rights, starting with civil rights (basic freedoms from state interference), followed by political rights (such as electoral rights) and most recently social rights (including rights to education, healthcare, unemployment insurance, and old age pensions—the rudiments of a welfare state). The rather motley collection of 'citizenship' rights provided in Part Two of the EC Treaty falls far short of this. In part this is due to the European Community's lack of competence, particularly in fields connected with the welfare state, and in part to the principle of subsidiarity—can and should the European Community be attempting to replicate welfare state provision which is already extensively and expensively provided for at national level? The striking feature of the case law discussed in this chapter is that it contains a tacit recognition that welfare state is—and will remain—a largely domestic matter and that the Court is prepared to use the solidarity principle to safeguard the welfare state from the most excessive challenges made by Community anti-trust law. However, the flip side of this coin is that since welfare state issues are considered largely domestic matters then, in the interests of creating Union citizenship, host states may need to extend their provision to migrants. This highlights one of the (many) conundrums of EU citizenship: rights intended to foster a commitment to the Union are actually being exercised against the Member States. For many, this is wholly justifiable. As Advocate General Ruiz-Jarabo Colomer said in his opinion in *KB*:

> If we want Community law to be more than a mere mechanical system of economics and to constitute instead a system commensurate with the society which it has to govern, if we wish it to be a legal system corresponding to the concept of social justice and European integration, not only of the economy but of the people, we cannot fail to live up to what is expected of us.[122]

However, for those who are footing the bill—and seeing little in return—this might serve to kindle the flames of hostility to a project of citizenship-building which is being carried out in their name. So long as the Court insists on seeing the caselaw in terms of the citizenship/single market dichotomy, it risks aggravating, rather than alleviating, this problem.

---

[121] T H Marshall, *Citizenship and Social Class* (CUP, 1950, reprinted Pluto Press, 1991), 28–29.

[122] Case C–117/01 *KB v The National Health Service Pensions Agency and the Secretary of State for Health* (Judgment of 7 January 2004), para 80, using the words of AG Tesauro in his Opinion in Case C–13/94 *P v S Cornwall County Council* [1996] ECR I–2143, who in turn paraphrased the words of AG Trabucchi in Case 7/75 *Mr and Mrs F v Belgium* [1975] ECR 679, point 6.

9

'Wish You Weren't Here…' New Models of Social Solidarity in the European Union

MICHAEL DOUGAN & ELEANOR SPAVENTA[*]

I INTRODUCTION: THE EUROPEAN UNION AS A MULTI-LEVEL WELFARE SYSTEM

It is trite to observe that, even though responsibility for welfare provision remains primarily in the hands of the Member States, Community law nevertheless has a significant impact upon the domestic systems of social protection. Indeed, we have grown used to the idea that the European Union now constitutes a multi-level welfare system characterised by a complex combination of local, national and Community policies. This is sometimes expressed in the notion that the Member States are now 'semi-sovereign welfare states' whose choices about how to provide for the social well-being of their own citizens are increasingly constrained *not only* by obvious factors such as the demographic pressures posed by an aging population and the need to compete within the globalising economy *but also* by the pervasive influence of the Union—which has not, however, evolved into a 'newly sovereign welfare state' determining for itself the conditions under which we pay taxes and receive benefits.[1] As a result, the idea of social solidarity can no longer be treated simply as a national or local monopoly. It also has a vital Community component.[2]

---

[*] University of Liverpool and University of Birmingham (respectively). We are very grateful to participants at the Cambridge *Social Welfare* conference (June 2003) for their helpful comments.

[1] In particular: S Leibfried and P Pierson, 'Social Policy: Left to Courts and Markets?' in H Wallace and W Wallace (eds), *Policy-Making in the European Union* (OUP, 2000).

[2] And, of course, an important international component: consider, eg the European Convention on Social and Medical Assistance (11 December 1953), the European Social Charter (18 October 1961) and the Revised European Social Charter (3 May 1996). On the Council of Europe's international instruments concerning social protection, and their

When analysing this Community component, it is perhaps inevitable that the Union lacks either any clear organising concept of social solidarity for itself, or any coherent approach to those national concepts of welfare provision with which it must interface.[3] Instead, social solidarity trickles through different Treaty provisions in different forms and in different ways—creating a veritable kaleidoscope of welfare rights and principles.

Within this kaleidoscope, it is tempting to focus on the Community's contribution to multi-level social solidarity in *negative terms*, that is, how far the core Treaty provisions on economic policy threaten national choices about social protection. For example, domestic structures for the delivery of welfare benefits and services may be found to act as barriers to the effective operation of the Internal Market (under the provisions concerning the free movement of goods or services, and also the rules on competition law or state aids) and thus require objective justification under the appropriate public interest derogations.[4] National welfare choices are also put under more indirect types of pressure by the process of European economic integration. For example, free movement might act as an invitation for undertakings to engage in social dumping, inspired by differences in the contributions and general taxation intended to fund national social security systems, in turn tempting the Member States to engage in a destructive cycle of regulatory competition which will eventually undermine high standards of welfare protection.[5] Moreover, there are concerns that the Growth and Stability Pact intended to consolidate the final stage of monetary union may have a negative impact upon the financing and planning of the domestic social protection systems, when Member States prefer cutting back on welfare expenditure (rather than increasing taxes) as a means of meeting the excessive budget deficit threshold of 3 per cent GDP.[6]

---

potential (indirect) relevance within an EU legal context (thanks to Art 34 of the Charter of Fundamental Rights of the European Union, OJ 2000 C364/1), see further: J Tooze, 'Social Security and Social Assistance' in T Hervey and J Kenner (eds), *Economic and Social Rights under the EU Charter of Fundamental Rights: A Legal Perspective* (Hart Publishing, 2003).

[3] In this regard, the new Constitutional Treaty, for all its references to solidarity, seems unlikely *of itself* to herald any greater coherence.

[4] Consider, in particular, the effect of Art 49 EC on health care provision: eg Case C–158/96 *Kohll v Union des Caisses de Maladie* [1998] ECR I–1931; Case C–368/98 *Abdon Vanbreakel and others v Alliance nationale des mutualités chrétiennes* [2001] ECR I–5363; Case C–157/99 *BSM Geraets-Smits v Stichting Ziekenfonds VGZ* and *Peerbooms v Stichting CZ Groep Zorgverzekeringen* [2001] ECR I–5473; Case C–385/99 *Müller-Fauré v Onderlinge Waarborgmaatschappij OZ Zorgverzekeringen UA*, and *van Riet v Onderlinge Waarborgmaatschappi ZAO Zorgverzekeringen* [2003] ECR I–4509; Case C–56/01 *Patricia Inizan v Caisse primaire d'assurance maladie des Hauts-de-Seine* [2003] ECR I–12403.

[5] Eg L Delsen, N van Gestel and J van Vugt, 'European Integration: Current Problems and Future Scenarios' in J van Vugt and J Peet (eds), *Social Security and Solidarity in the European Union* (Physica-Verlag, 2000).

[6] See the contribution by Mića Panić in this collection.

Against that background, the Union has often been accused of suffering from a form of 'constitutional asymmetry': the legal tools employed in pursuit of economic efficiency far outweigh those available in the cause of social justice—and have the potential to ride roughshod over the complex bargains struck by domestic actors in the exercise of their residual welfare competences.[7] However, the kaleidoscope is much more nuanced than this analysis would suggest. In fact, Community law also makes a significant *positive contribution* to social provision within the European Union. Indeed, one can identify the emergence of new and peculiarly supranational models of solidarity which support and supplement (rather than threaten or undermine) the domestic welfare states. This chapter will focus upon one aspect of this dynamic contribution: the rights to free movement and equal treatment enjoyed by Union citizens who visit another Member State on a temporary basis. In particular, we will investigate how far such individuals should be entitled to claim access to welfare benefits provided by the host society on the same terms as own nationals or other lawful residents—and what sort of legal framework is emerging from the Court of Justice and the Community legislature to address this controversial issue.

Many commentators champion the evolution of a 'European social citizenship', whereby the process of 'ever closer union' encourages novel expectations of social solidarity based upon the shared identity of Union citizenship. In the absence of extensive redistributive or harmonising competences in the sphere of welfare provision, the most effective mechanism by which the Community might realise such ambitions is by employing the principle of equal treatment to guarantee that migrant Union citizens are assimilated into the social protection systems of their host societies. However, this process of assimilation directly challenges the traditional link between an individual's legitimate right to claim welfare support and her/his recognised membership of the Member State's own solidaristic community—thereby raising questions about how far the common bond of Union citizenship can really act as a substitute for accepted ties of belonging based upon nationality or economic contribution. While the Court has already defined the basic parameters of this challenge as regards resident but economically inactive migrant Union citizens, the legal situation seems more uncertain when it comes to Union citizens who are merely visiting another Member State on a temporary basis. We identify two main models which could provide the basis for future developments.

The first (and more orthodox) is an 'objective justification approach': *all* migrant Union citizens are entitled to claim equal treatment as regards *all* benefits falling within the material scope of the Treaty—thus forcing the

---

[7] Eg B Schulte, 'The Welfare State and European Integration' (1999) 1 *European Journal of Social Security* 7; F Scharpf, 'The European Social Model: Coping With the Challenges of Diversity' (2002) 40 *Journal of Common Market Studies* 645.

host society *in every case* to defend restrictions on access to its social protection system, especially residency requirements, by reference to a valid public interest requirement and the principle of proportionality. The second (and more novel) is a 'comparability approach': temporary visitors should be entitled to equal treatment as regards benefits falling within the material scope of the Treaty *only* once it has been verified that they are in a comparable situation to own nationals and other lawful residents. In particular, when it comes to social benefits which represent an expression of solidarity by the domestic welfare community *towards its own members*, temporary visitors might well be found to be in a non-comparable situation; if that is the case any difference in treatment—including that arising from the application of a residency requirement—would not give rise to discrimination which the host state needs to justify. We will argue that the comparability approach has several significant advantages over the objective justification model. Moreover, the relevance of this comparability approach is not diminished *even after* the adoption in spring 2004 of Directive 2004/38 on free movement for Union citizens, which purports to address—but in our view, only incompletely—the relationship between temporary visitors and the host state's social assistance benefits.[8]

II SOCIAL SOLIDARITY: COMMUNITY AND MEMBERSHIP

Social solidarity, at least as it is understood in Europe, represents an assumption of welfare responsibilities between the members of a particular community. Solidarity systems are based, in particular, upon a principle of subsidisation: a proportion of the wealth generated or enjoyed by certain members of a group is placed at the disposal of public institutions in order to satisfy the social needs of other members of the group.[9]

Solidarity and *community* are in fact closely related concepts, and this is true for two main reasons. The first is primarily moral in nature. Social protection measures promote the redistribution of society's wealth, contrary to the outcomes which would result from the free operation of market forces. Such redistributory policies, especially those offering non-contributory benefits and services paid for out of general taxation, are perceived as being

---

[8]   Dir 2004/38 on the right of citizens and their family members to move and reside freely within the territory of the Member States, 2004 OJ L158/77.

[9]   Consider, in particular, AG Fennelly in Case C–70/95 *Sodemare* [1997] ECR I–3395, para 29: social solidarity 'envisages the inherently uncommercial act of involuntary subsidisation of one social group by another'. Similarly, eg A Winterstein, 'Nailing the Jellyfish: Social Security and Competition Law' [1999] *European Competition Law Review* 324; T Hervey, 'Social Solidarity: A Buttress Against Internal Market Law?' in J Shaw (ed), *Social Law and Policy in an Evolving European Union* (Hart Publishing, 2000); S O'Leary, 'Solidarity and Citizenship Rights in the Charter of Fundamental Rights of the European Union' in *Collected Courses of the Academy of European Law 2003* (OUP, forthcoming).

'morally demanding' (or perhaps 'compelling'). They are thus dependent upon a diffuse sense of social solidarity, which is nevertheless sufficiently powerful to persuade people to engage in the necessary process of subsidisation, of the sort which only derives from the existence of a common identity, forged through shared social and cultural experiences, and institutional and political bonds.[10] The second reason is largely financial in character. The redistribution of wealth, particularly through the provision of non-contributory welfare benefits and services, also requires a realistic management of society's available resources. The competent public authorities must strike a balance between the number of people potentially able to claim social support, and the number of people actually able to pay for it. After all, if demand for welfare benefits were to outstrip the revenues capable of supporting them, the financial balance of the solidarity system could be seriously jeopardised.[11]

This marriage between *solidarity* and *community*, compelled by the need to construct a moral argument capable of justifying subsidisation, and by the budgetary realities of matching welfare demand and supply, has begotten an important conceptual progeny of its own. It becomes necessary to identify precise parameters of *membership*—defining which individuals *belong* to the collectivity (and are thus entitled to stake claims to its welfare support), and which individuals are *excluded* from the collectivity (and therefore unable to make out a legitimate case for social protection). In other words, 'the right of an individual to claim membership of a particular community is crucial if that individual is to gain access to a community's collective welfare arrangements'.[12]

Social solidarity can represent a manifestation of this collective identity, and thus reflect its inherent thresholds of membership and belonging, at several different levels. The most important is the state. After all, the bonds of national identity and citizenship are inseparable from the diffuse sense of social solidarity which fuelled the evolution of the modern European welfare states, and continues to provide the moral backbone which supports and justifies their social protection systems.[13] But other levels of solidarity also play an important role: for example, local (such as welfare provision organised by the region or commune), functional (as with social protection

---

[10] In particular, T Faist, 'Social Citizenship in the European Union: Nested Membership' (2001) 39 *Journal of Common Market Studies* 37. Also, eg G Majone, 'The European Community Between Social Policy and Social Regulation' (1993) 31 *Journal of Common Market Studies* 153.

[11] See further, on the conceptual foundations of social solidarity, K Tinga and E Verbraak, 'Solidarity: An Indispensable Concept in Social Security' in J van Vugt and J Peet (eds), *Social Security and Solidarity in the European Union* (Physica-Verlag, 2000).

[12] P Dwyer, *Welfare Rights and Responsibilities: Contesting Social Citizenship* (Policy Press, 2000) p 187.

[13] Eg AP van der Mei, *Free Movement of Persons within the European Community: Cross-Border Access to Public Benefits* (Hart Publishing, 2003) Ch 1.

schemes supported by employers and employees), or inter-generational (such as pensions systems whereby current workers contribute to the welfare needs of persons who have already retired). And also supranational—especially in a complex governance system such as the Union, which has the effect of 'nesting' individuals into several overlapping strata of collective political and cultural consciousness.[14] Within such a system, different ideas of 'community' can emerge—each carrying its own definitions of membership, and its own expectations of social solidarity. In particular, many commentators anticipate the consolidation of a 'European social citizenship', which will act as a counterweight to the traditional economic constitution embodied in the Internal Market, whereby the sense of identity and mutual responsibilities which derive from the nationality of a Member State are supplemented by a new bond, carrying its own welfare rights and obligations, based upon the common heritage accrued through the process of 'ever closer' integration.[15]

Of course, controversies can arise *within* any single level of solidarity about where best to pitch its own thresholds of belonging and exclusion. For example, at the domestic level, a refusal to recognise certain forms of welfare need can effectively exclude many individuals from membership of the solidaristic community; and indeed, national welfare systems can be organised in a manner which systematically discriminates against disadvantaged groups such as women, ethnic minorities and homosexuals.[16] Similarly, at the supranational level, when qualification for the status of Union citizen relies exclusively upon the claimant possessing the nationality of a Member State in accordance with the latter's own rules, it can be argued that long term resident third country nationals are unfairly excluded from membership of the Union's own fledgling solidaristic community.[17] But more important for present purposes is the idea that controversies can also result from the interaction *between* different levels of solidarity, especially as regards relations between the Union and its Member States, thanks to the

---

[14] In particular, T Faist, 'Social Citizenship in the European Union: Nested Membership' (2001) 39 *Journal of Common Market Studies* 37.

[15] On social citizenship and the role of Union citizenship, eg M Everson, 'The Legacy of the Market Citizen' in J Shaw and G More (eds), *New Legal Dynamics of European Union* (Clarendon Press, 1995); D O'Keeffe and M Horspool, 'European Citizenship and the Free Movement of Persons' (1996) XXXI *The Irish Jurist* 145; S Douglas-Scott, 'In Search of Union Citizenship' (1998) 18 *Yearbook of European Law* 29. For contextual discussion of the broader relationship between social citizenship and welfare provision in social policy theory, eg N Harris, 'The Welfare State, Social Security, and Social Citizenship Rights' in N Harris et al (eds), *Social Security Law in Context* (OUP, 2000).

[16] Though, of course, Community law can have a positive impact here, eg Dir 79/7 on the progressive implementation of the principle of equal treatment for men and women in matters of social security, 1979 OJ L6/24; Dir 2000/43 implementing the principle of equal treatment between persons irrespective of racial or ethnic origin, 2000 OJ L180/22. Cf. Art 3(3) Dir 2000/78 establishing a general framework for equal treatment in employment and occupation, 2000 OJ L303/16.

[17] See recently, eg European Economic and Social Committee, *Opinion on Access to European Union Citizenship*, 2003 OJ C208/76. However, note the provisions of Dir 2003/109 concerning the status of third country nationals who are long term residents, 2004 OJ L16/44.

perennial question of competence: how might the Community actually go about fulfilling the novel expectations of social solidarity which many associate with the promotion of a 'European social citizenship'?

III FULFILLING EXPECTATIONS
OF SUPRANATIONAL SOCIAL SOLIDARITY

One possibility can be discounted immediately: the idea that the Union should act as a federal welfare state, enjoying general tax-and-spend redistributive competences. It is true that the Union does undertake limited redistributive functions. Consider, for example, the common agricultural policy, which organises on a Community-wide scale a system of collective responsibility for the social needs of farmers, operating in blatant defiance of the economic demands of the market;[18] or the structural funds, whereby significant sums of money are transferred from the more to the less affluent countries and regions, in pursuit of greater economic and social cohesion.[19] Of course, neither system of 'Community solidarity' is perfect. The CAP's traditional focus upon price support for agricultural production has tended to benefit big agricultural holdings, particularly in northern Europe (though the 2003 reforms decoupling income support from agricultural production, and reducing direct income payments for larger farms, might help to make the system more equitable).[20] Meanwhile, the structural funds have long been criticised on the grounds that the sums involved are not large enough to make any serious contribution to the elimination of persistent regional disparities; and have in fact tended to benefit the rich rather than the poor even within recipient regions by alleviating the need to increase tax revenues.[21] But in any case, the CAP and structural funds are hardly precedents for any realistic prospect of the Union acquiring general competence to provide for the population's social needs based upon classic risks such as unemployment, old age, illness or disability—and the reasons are not hard to find. Just as the bond of nationality constitutes an essential component of the diffuse sense of solidarity underpinning the Member States' social protection systems, so the lack of any comparable sense of collective identity at the supranational level, strong enough to provide popular support for the construction of a genuine European welfare system, acts as a serious obstacle against the attribution of

---

[18] Further, eg E Rieger, 'The Common Agricultural Policy: Politics Against Markets' in H Wallace and W Wallace (eds), *Policy-Making in the European Union* (OUP, 2000).

[19] Further, eg D Allen, 'Cohesion and Structural Funds: Transfers and Trade-Offs' in H Wallace and W Wallace (eds), *Policy-Making in the European Union* (OUP, 2000).

[20] In particular: Reg 1782/2003 establishing common rules for direct support schemes under the common agricultural policy and establishing certain support schemes for farmers, 2003 OJ L270/1.

[21] Eg, G Majone, 'The European Community Between Social Policy and Social Regulation' (1993) 31 *Journal of Common Market Studies* 153.

more far-reaching redistributive functions to the Union.[22] Put crudely: it is far from clear that Polish taxpayers would be prepared to pay for the unemployment benefits of French citizens living in France; or that Irish taxpayers would be happy to fund healthcare for Greek nationals residing in Greece.

Another possibility fares little better. In certain fields of social policy, such as labour law, the Community's activities are largely regulatory (rather than redistributive) in nature—and often involve the harmonisation of national laws, thus permitting the Community to promote common standards of social protection across the Member States. And indeed, the Treaty has been used to adopt certain harmonising measures directing the Member States about how to allocate their own welfare resources: consider, for example, Regulation 1408/71 on the cross-border coordination of the national social security systems;[23] Directive 79/7 on equal treatment between men and women as regards social security benefits;[24] and Directive 2003/8 establishing minimum common principles for legal aid in cross-border disputes, intended to facilitate access to justice for less well-off members of society.[25] But by-and-large, the scope for approximating national welfare rules is very limited. After all, the Treaty expressly precludes the adoption of harmonising measures to combat social exclusion or to modernise social protection for citizens other than workers; and requires that, in any case, Community action in the social sphere must not affect the right of Member States to define the fundamental principles and maintain the basic financial equilibrium of their own social security systems.[26] Those limitations on Community competence perhaps reflect more fundamental political and logistical obstacles to the harmonisation of national welfare regimes, especially given the myriad differences which continue to separate the Member States when it comes to the basic character, detailed structure and cultural context of their social protection systems.[27] It is true that the Community has steadily increased the range of its 'new governance' ventures, aimed at informing and influencing national

---

[22] Eg, M Rhodes, 'Defending the Social Contract: The EU Between Global Constraints and Domestic Imperatives' in D Hine and H Kassim (eds), *Beyond the Market: the EU and National Social Policy* (Routledge, 1998). Cf MP Maduro, 'Europe's Social Self: The Sickness Unto Death' in J Shaw (ed), *Social Law and Policy in an Evolving European Union* (Hart Publishing, 2000).

[23] Reg 1408/71 on the application of social security schemes to employed persons and their families moving within the Community (last consolidated version published at 1997 OJ L28/1). See now: Reg 883/2004 on the coordination of social security systems, 2004 OJ L200/1 (partially repealing and replacing Reg1408/71).

[24] Dir 79/7 on the progressive implementation of the principle of equal treatment for men and women in matters of social security, 1979 OJ L6/24.

[25] Dir 2003/8 to improve access to justice in cross-border disputes by establishing minimum common rules relating to legal aid for such disputes, 2003 OJ L26/41. The Commission's original proposal was even more solidaristic in nature, since it would have covered not only cross-border but also wholly internal situations: COM(2002) 13 Final.

[26] In particular: Arts 137(2) and (4) EC. Also: Art 18(3) EC.

[27] Eg M Rhodes, 'Defending the Social Contract: The EU Between Global Constraints and Domestic Imperatives' in D Hine and H Kassim (eds), *Beyond the Market: the EU and National Social Policy* (Routledge, 1998).

welfare choices, and encouraging Member States to converge around certain core values and standards: consider, for example, the open method of coordination in the modernisation of social protection, as an integral part of the (post-Lisbon European Council) Social Policy Agenda.[28] Ultimately, however, the lack of extensive harmonising competences makes it difficult to identify a truly effective vehicle by which the Community might articulate any genuinely supranational framework of social solidarity.

That leaves one final option. It remains open for the Union to fall back upon its admittedly less ambitious but still tried-and-tested 'assimilation model': guaranteeing equal treatment between Community and own nationals, so that foreign migrants are fully integrated into the solidarity system of their host society, but without otherwise questioning the competence of each Member State to determine its own welfare choices (or the persistence of differences between the forms and levels of social protection available across the Union territory) provided they apply without unjustified discrimination on grounds of nationality. The assimilation model is therefore based upon the principle of subsidisation—but the relevant subsidies do not take the form of direct wealth transfers between social groups organised at the Community level. Subsidisation relies instead upon a model of vicarious responsibility: novel expectations of social solidarity engendered at the supranational level are actually discharged (in the sense of paid for) by the Member States through their domestic welfare budgets. For that reason, the assimilation model directly challenges—or at least seeks actively to redefine and reshape—traditional national thresholds of belonging to and exclusion from the solidaristic community. This challenge has been mounted in two main phases.

The first phase—already well consolidated—concerns the interaction between domestic thresholds of belonging/exclusion traditionally based upon nationality; and a supranational assimilation model originally focused upon engagement in an economic activity—especially through the free movement of workers and freedom of establishment. Experience has highlighted an inherent tension between (on the one hand) the mobility needs of the Common Market, including the desire to guarantee equal access to social benefits as a means of ensuring that such mobility is efficacious in practice; and (on the other hand) the collective identity of the solidaristic community which grew from within, or at least alongside, the European nation state, whereby countries were sometimes willing to appropriate the labour of migrant workers without offering them access to certain welfare benefits in return.[29] This is true less of contributory benefits, or those linked

---

[28] See in particular: Commission, *A Concerted Strategy for Modernising Social Protection*, COM(1999) 347 Final; Presidency Conclusions of the Lisbon European Council (23–24 March 2000); Commission, *Social Policy Agenda*, COM(2000) 379 Final.

[29] Consider the national attitudes revealed in disputes such as Case 32/75 *Fiorini v SNCF* [1975] ECR 1085; Case 63/76 *Inzirillo* [1976] ECR 2057; Case 65/81 *Reina* [1982] ECR I–33; Case 261/83 *Castelli* [1984] ECR 3199.

to one's status as a worker, than of non-contributory benefits funded from the public purse that (as we have noted) are usually dependent upon a morally demanding sense of diffuse solidarity—for which purpose, the collective identity has historically been defined by nationality, and the individual's claim to welfare support thus evidenced by her / his status as a national citizen. The Community institutions have consciously set out to deconstruct those thresholds for membership, insofar as they adversely affect economically active migrants by virtue of their nationality. In particular, that is the basis for the guarantee of equal treatment as regards tax and social advantages for foreign workers (whether or not they are resident within the relevant Member State) contained in Article 7(2) Regulation 1612/68.[30] In such situations, a direct contribution to the economic life of the host community enables the foreign worker to overcome the exclusive nature of the group identity, and to benefit from the assimilation model as regards access to (even non-contributory, non-employment related) social benefits.

The second phase—still in its infancy—concerns the interaction between (on the one hand) these new domestic thresholds of belonging, whereby a Member State offers membership of its solidaristic community to all those, regardless of nationality, who make an economic contribution to public resources; and (on the other hand) a supranational assimilation model which has begun to question whether *even that requirement* can act as a legitimate barrier to the social integration of migrant Community nationals. This new interaction has been triggered, in particular, by the introduction of Union citizenship under Article 17 EC, together with rights to free movement for Union citizens under Article 18 EC, and the concomitant entitlement to equal treatment contained in Article 12 EC. These provisions offer a potentially fruitful opportunity to those who advocate the further development of the Community's own autonomous contribution to a multi-level welfare system. The Union may well lack the deep-rooted popular consciousness required to generate a diffuse sense of social solidarity and in turn capable of facilitating the attribution to the Community of extensive redistributive competences. And the Union has not been entrusted with the legal competence required to harmonise the framework within which Member States themselves collect and spend welfare revenue, or organise the provision of basic social benefits and services for their populations. But it is nevertheless possible that Union citizenship will provide a sufficiently cohesive collective identity to justify the assimilation of foreign migrants into the existing domestic welfare systems—so that even those who cannot claim membership of the national solidaristic community on the basis of

---

[30] Reg 1612/68 on freedom of movement for workers within the Community, 1968 OJ L257/2. Cf equivalent principles developed as regards self-employed persons under Art 43 EC, eg Case 305/87 *Commission v Greece* [1989] ECR 1461; Case C–337/97 *Meeusen* [1999] ECR I–3289; Case C–299/01 *Commission v Luxembourg* [2002] ECR I–5899.

their nationality or economic contribution would still enjoy the full range of social protection benefits offered by each Member State, and indeed so that the latter willingly accepts its role as an agent in promoting (and funding) a specifically 'European social citizenship'.[31]

However, this mismatch between the Community's potential welfare aspirations, and its actual competence to fulfil them, gives rise to tensions which are surely even more acute than before, going to the very foundations of the solidarity-community-membership triptych. In the first place, there is a sense that Community law might arbitrarily stretch, to beyond its tolerable limit, the moral argument underpinning the acceptance by the national (or local) community of mutual social responsibilities through the process of subsidisation.[32] Indeed, especially when it comes to non-contributory benefits and services funded from general (or local) taxation, it is not clear that the psychological web of fraternal responsibility which justifies and supports public welfare provision will be strong enough to catch not only the foreigner who participates in economic life, but also the foreigner who does not so contribute.[33] In the second place, there is also a feeling that any overly ambitious attempt by the Union to grant unconditional rights to free movement and residency to its own citizens, then simply assimilate them into the domestic systems of social protection, could threaten to undermine the delicate financial stability of national welfare states, by significantly increasing the potential number of people who might receive solidarity support relative to the actual number of people who contribute to its financing—especially given that the burdens of non-economic migration are not spread evenly across the Member States.[34]

---

[31] On the broader role of equal treatment as a general principle of Community law, including its transformation from an economic facilitator to an individual social right, eg K Lenaerts, 'L'égalité de traitement en droit communautaire: un principe unique aux apparences multiples' (1991) 26 *Cahiers de Droit Européen* 3; G de Búrca, 'The Role of Equality in European Community Law' in A Dashwood and S O'Leary (eds), *The Principle of Equal Treatment in EC Law* (Sweet & Maxwell, 1997); G More, 'The Principle of Equal Treatment: From Market Unifier to Fundamental Right?' in P Craig and G de Búrca (eds), *The Evolution of EU Law* (OUP, 1999).

[32] Cf J Steiner, 'The Right to Welfare: Equality and Equity Under Community Law' (1985) 10 *European Law Review* 21; C Tomuschat, 'Annotation of Sala' (2000) 37 *Common Market Law Review* 449.

[33] Consider the public debate, across many of the old Member States, over free movement rights for the citizens of the newly acceding Member States, in the few months before enlargement on 1 May 2004: potential contributors as well as potential non-contributors were treated with derision in the popular press as 'spongers' and 'welfare tourists', prompting many governments to introduce or reinforce restrictions on residency and equal treatment rights pursuant to (but sometimes only dubiously in accordance with) the Accession Treaty 2003.

[34] Consider, for example, the migration patterns associated with cross-border education, whereby certain countries are clearly net importers or net exporters of students, as discussed by S O'Leary, *The Evolving Concept of Community Citizenship: From the Free Movement of Persons to Union Citizenship* (Kluwer Law, 1996) Ch 5; and by C Barnard in this book; cf also the chapter by A P van der Mei in this book.

IV RESIDENT ECONOMICALLY INACTIVE MIGRANT
UNION CITIZENS

Such tensions are most obvious when one considers the situation of economically inactive migrant Union citizens *residing* in another Member State
on a stable and continuous basis. After all, this raises the prospect of individuals, who cannot claim membership of the solidaristic community on the
basis of their nationality or economic contribution, nevertheless staking
potentially long-term claims to possibly significant levels of welfare support,
simply on the basis of their membership of the 'European community'.[35]

We now have a sufficient mass of caselaw to be able to map out the
Court's general response to this issue. It was established in *Sala* that
Community nationals lawfully residing in the territory of another Member
State come within the personal scope of the Treaty provisions on Union cit-
izenship.[36] This is true of Community nationals living within the host ter-
ritory on the basis of purely domestic immigration rules.[37] But it is also true
of Community nationals residing in the Member State on the basis of the
Treaty.[38] In this regard, the Court established in *Baumbast* that Article 18
EC creates a directly effective right to residency for all Union citizens.[39]
However, the Treaty itself expressly refers to the existence of certain limitations and conditions upon the exercise of that right to residency as laid
down under Community law. Those limitations and conditions include the
requirement, laid down in secondary Community legislation, that Union
citizens must possess sufficient resources and comprehensive medical insurance.[40] Nevertheless, the Community courts will interpret such provisions
restrictively, as with all exceptions and limitations imposed upon the fundamental freedoms upheld by the Treaty.[41] Moreover, the Member States,
for their part, are obliged to enforce such provisions in accordance with the
general principles of Community law and (in particular) the principle of
proportionality. This entitles resident economically inactive migrant Union
citizens to expect a degree of financial solidarity from their host society,

---

[35] Though the Union's relatively low long-term mobility rates make it possible to argue that
rights of equal treatment for lawfully resident migrants will not in practice have a destabilising impact upon national solidarity systems: see, eg A P van der Mei, 'Residence and the
Evolving Notion of European Union Citizenship' (2003) 5 *European Journal of Migration
and Law* 419.

[36] Case C–85/96 *M M Martínez Sala v Freistaat Bayern* [1998] ECR I–2691.

[37] *Ibid.*

[38] Case C–184/99 *R Grzelczyk v Centre public d'aide social d'Ottignies-Louvain-la-Neuve*
[2001] ECR I–6193.

[39] Case C–413/99 *Baumbast and R v Secretary of State for the Home Department* [2002] ECR
I–7091.

[40] In particular: Dir 90/364 on the right of residence, 1990 OJ L180/26; Dir 90/365 on the right
of residence for employees and self-employed persons who have ceased their occupational
activity, 1990 OJ L180/28; Dir 93/96 on the right of residence for students, 1993 OJ L317/59.

[41] Eg AG Cosmas in Case C–378/97 *Wijsenbeek* [1999] ECR I–6207; AG Tizzano in Case
C–200/02 *Chen and Zhu* (Opinion of 18 May 2004; Judgment of 19 October 2004).

particularly where their welfare needs are temporary and / or limited in character, having regard to their degree of integration into the Member State.[42]

For these purposes, as established in *Sala*, Article 17(2) EC attaches to the status of Union citizen the rights and duties laid down by the Treaty, including the right contained in Article 12 EC not to suffer discrimination on grounds of nationality within the material scope of the Treaty.[43] The Court has demonstrated that it will adopt an extremely broad approach in this regard: *any benefit* which falls within the material scope of *any provision* of Community law will be caught by the combined effects of Articles 17 and 12 EC, and must be offered on an equal basis to lawfully resident migrant Union citizens. There is no need to demonstrate some direct or tangible link between one's enjoyment of the benefit claimed and the exercise of any specific right to residence *qua* Union citizen. For example, in *Sala* itself, a non-contributory child-raising allowance which fell within the scope of Community law both as a family benefit under Article 4(1)(h) Regulation 1408/71, and as a social advantage under Article 7(2) Regulation 1612/68, was automatically treated as falling within the material scope of the Treaty for the purposes of Article 12 EC; discriminatory qualifying criteria could thus be challenged by the claimant, even if she was not an insured person entitled to rely upon Regulation 1408/71, nor a worker entitled to benefit from Regulation 1612/68, simply on the basis that she was a lawfully resident migrant Union citizen.[44]

As regards all benefits falling within the material scope of Article 12 EC, it is possible to challenge both direct discrimination and indirect discrimination on grounds of nationality—including domestic rules which make access to social advantages conditional upon (for example) a certain period of residence, or prior education, within the host territory.[45] However, as the Court held in *Grzelczyk*, the resident economically inactive migrant Union citizen's expectation of financial solidarity from her/his host society cannot in any case justify the claimant becoming an unreasonable burden upon the public finances of the

---

[42] Further: M Dougan and E Spaventa, 'Educating Rudy and the (non-)English Patient: A Double-Bill on Residency Rights under Article 18 EC' (2003) 28 *European Law Review* 699. Also, eg C Jacqueson, 'Union Citizenship and the Court of Justice: Something New Under the Sun? Towards Social Citizenship' (2002) 27 *European Law Review* 260.

[43] Case C–85/96 *M M Martínez Sala v Freistaat Bayern* [1998] ECR I–2691.

[44] Similarly, eg with the minimex as a social advantage under Art 7(2) Reg 1612/68 in Case C–184/99 *R Grzelczyk v Centre public d'aide social d'Ottignies-Louvain-la-Neuve* [2001] ECR I–6193; and with the tide-over allowance for young people seeking their first employment again as a social advantage under Art 7(2) Reg 1612/68 in Case C–224/98 *M N D'Hoop v Office national d'emploi* [2002] ECR I–6191. Consider also earlier caselaw such as Case 293/83 *Gravier v City of Liège* [1985] ECR 593; though cf the more restrictive approach in judgments like Case 39/86 *Lair* [1988] ECR 3161.

[45] Consider, eg Case C–299/01 *Commission v Luxembourg* [2002] ECR I–5899 (given period of residence); Case C–224/98 *M N D'Hoop v Office national d'emploi* [2002] ECR I–6191 (prior education).

host state.[46] In that event, the national authorities remain competent to terminate the individual's right to residency altogether.[47] By these means, the Union citizen's apparently very broad right to non-discrimination is subject to certain inherent limits: an individual may only claim access to welfare benefits within the basic parameters imposed by the unreasonable financial burden test, beyond which the Member State is entitled to repudiate her/his lawful immigration status, and with it any further entitlement to equal treatment.[48]

The Court's general approach has been adapted to other categories of Union citizen who can be considered lawfully resident within the host state, but whose rights under Article 18 EC are not limited by reference to the requirements of sufficient resources and health insurance, and whose immigration status is therefore not dependent upon staying on the right side of the 'unreasonable burden' principle. For example, Union citizens who arrive in another Member State in search of employment have a right to stay under Article 39 EC for a reasonable period of time, and in any case for so long as they are still actively seeking work and have genuine chances of being engaged.[49] The Court held in *Collins* that such Union citizens, being lawfully present in another Member State, are entitled to claim equal treatment under Article 39 EC, read in conjunction with Article 12 EC, as regards non-contributory benefits such as jobseeker's allowance intended to facilitate access to employment in the host labour market.[50] This time, the workseekers' right to residency—and therefore her/his right to equal treatment—is not conditional upon making only *Grzelczyk*-style reasonable demands upon the public purse. The duration of the Union citizen's expectation of equal treatment as regards access to welfare support is limited only by the claimant ceasing to make genuine efforts to become engaged and thereby losing any right to stay lawfully within the host state. There is much to be said for this approach, for example, in ensuring that the workseeker's right to free movement has practical rather than just theoretical value, and in encouraging greater labour mobility to help fill skills shortages within the Internal Market.[51] But one must also recognise that the Court has pushed back one step further the threshold of belonging/exclusion by which

---

[46] As referred to in the preamble to each of Dir 90/364, Dir 90/365 and Dir 93/96.

[47] See above n 38.

[48] Consider, eg Case C–456/02 *Trojani* (Opinion of 19 February 2004; Judgment of 7 September 2004).

[49] Eg Case C–292/89 *ex parte Antonissen* [1991] ECR I–745; Case C–344/95 *Commission v Belgium* [1997] ECR I–1035.

[50] Case C–138/02 *Collins v Secretary of State for Work and Pensions* (Judgment of 23 March 2004). Here, the British habitual residency requirement was indirectly discriminatory, and had to be objectively justified, by the need for a 'real link' between the claimant and the national employment market: see further below.

[51] Even if the eventual outcome of the objective justification process as undertaken in *Collins* is that workseekers enjoy no right to seek social support during their initial residency—which is arguably when some claimants might need it most. Further, eg M Dougan, 'Free Movement: The Workseeker as Citizen' (2001) 4 *Cambridge Yearbook of European Legal Studies* 93.

Member States regulate access to their public welfare systems—a perfect illustration of the assimilation model being used to reshape diverse national conceptions of diffuse solidarity, not *from within* but *from above*, in pursuit of a new Community framework of welfare expectations based upon the common bond of Union citizenship.[52]

V THE SITUATION OF TEMPORARY VISITORS

The Court is clearly getting to grips with the friction between conceptions of belonging to / exclusion from the national welfare society, and the prospect of the full rigour of the Community's assimilation model being extended to cover resident but economically inactive migrant Union citizens. Yet the proper legal situation is not nearly so well explored when it comes to *temporary visitors*, that is, economically inactive migrants who do not ordinarily live, and have no desire to establish their usual residence, within the host state.[53] As a matter of policy, we accept that Community law should surely place limits to the integration of temporary visitors into national (or local) solidarity systems—recognising that the ambitions harboured in certain quarters towards creating a supranational model of social citizenship must be reconciled with the limited political and financial ability of the EU (as presently configured) to do so; and therefore that the Treaty must avoid the risk of undermining either the social cohesion or the financial equilibrium of those national (and local) solidarity systems with which it must necessarily interact. The question is how to devise a legal framework capable of accommodating this policy.

In this regard, it is useful to begin by recalling that the equal treatment rights of temporary visitors have traditionally been constrained by the legal capacity in which such Community nationals exercise their entitlement to free movement. Most of the relevant caselaw concerns economic service recipients, and especially cross-border tourists, falling within the personal scope of Article 49 EC.[54] It is clear that, as well as governing the conditions

---

[52] Note that Dir 2004/38 on the right of citizens and their family members to move and reside freely within the territory of the Member States, 2004 OJ L158/77 will extend the 'limitations and conditions' currently imposed upon exercise of the rights to residence and equal treatment of economically inactive migrants: such Union citizens will have no right to equal treatment as regards social assistance during their first three months' residency; indeed, in the case of workseekers, this derogation from the principle of non-discrimination will apply for so long as they are still seeking employment (in apparent contradiction of the judgment in *Collins*). However, we will suggest (below) that the picture is not so clear as the simple text of Dir 2004/38 would suggest.

[53] One should acknowledge, but for present purposes need not explore, the factual and definitional problems which can arise in distinguishing lawful residency from a mere lawful presence in the national territory. Consider, in the EC law context, eg Case 76/76 *Di Paolo v Office National de l' Emploi* [1977] ECR 315; Case C–102/91 *Knoch v Bundesanstalt für Arbeit* [1992] ECR I–4341. Similarly, in an English legal context, eg P Smart, 'Ordinarily Resident: Temporary Presence and Prolonged Absence' (1989) 38 *International and Comparative Law Quarterly* 175.

[54] Eg, Case 286/82 *Luisi and Carbone* [1984] ECR 377.

for enjoyment of the economic services whose receipt justifies the claimant's right to free movement within the host territory in the first place, Community law also makes provision for the enjoyment of certain incidental social advantages funded by the Member State. For these purposes, however, the Court has articulated a relatively limited conception of the range of benefits actually caught by the Treaty—certainly much more limited than the definition adopted as regards Article 7(2) Regulation 1612/68—and therefore of the potential field of application of the principle of non-discrimination on grounds of nationality.[55] Certainly, the material scope of Article 49 EC is understood to embrace benefits directly linked to enjoyment of the economic services which the claimant has entered the territory to receive: for example, the tariffs for entry into publicly-run museums and galleries at issue in *Commission v Spain* and *Commission v Italy*, which tangibly affect the position of cross-border tourists in their capacity as such.[56] Beyond that, the Court has gone no further than finding service recipients entitled to equal treatment as regards access to criminal injuries compensation;[57] and the language in which penal proceedings are conducted.[58]

As regards such social advantages, the temporary visitor is entitled to challenge, on the basis of Article 49 EC, domestic restrictions which directly or indirectly discriminate on grounds of nationality—including (in particular) residence requirements which inevitably favour own nationals over foreign citizens, especially when the latter travel as temporary visitors.[59] However, few commentators seem to believe that Article 49 EC confers any right upon migrant service recipients to claim equal treatment as regards welfare benefits *per se* within the host territory. In the first place, surely such benefits are not among the range of incidental social advantages falling within the material scope of Article 49 EC: their enjoyment can hardly be seen as directly linked to the effective exercise of free movement rights by economic service recipients such as tourists.[60] In the second place, the

---

[55] Note that the Court has hinted at a more generous approach to the range of social advantages potentially covered by Art 49 EC when it comes to service providers, eg access to social housing as addressed in Case 63/86 *Commission v Italy* [1988] ECR 29 (though the Court also noted that, in most cases, service providers will not satisfy the conditions, even of a non-discriminatory nature, bound up with the objectives of national legislation on social housing).

[56] Case C–45/93 *Commission v Spain* [1994] ECR I–911 (state-run museums); Case C–388/01 *Commission v Italy* [2003] ECR I–721 (locally-run museums).

[57] Case 186/87 *Cowan v le Trésor Public* [1989] ECR 195.

[58] Case C–274/96 *Bickel and Franz* [1998] ECR I–1121.

[59] As in Case C–274/96 *Bickel and Franz* [1998] ECR I–1121.

[60] In particular: P Craig and G de Búrca, *EU Law: Text, Cases and Materials* 3rd edn (OUP, 2003) pp 812–14. Cf F Weiss and F Wooldridge, *Free Movement of Persons Within the European Community* (Kluwer Law International, 2002) p 124. For an indication that there are indeed limits to the Court's functional approach to equal treatment as regards social advantages, for the purposes of enhancing the exercise of economic rights to free movement, consider Case C–291/96 *Grado and Bashir* [1997] ECR I–5531.

availability of publicly funded services cannot constitute provision of the primary economic service whose receipt is constitutive of the claimant's entire right to free movement within the relevant Member State. It is true that the Court in judgments such as *Peerbooms* and *Müller-Fauré* has adopted a relatively fluid interpretation of the relationship between the provision of publicly funded benefits in one's *home state*, and obstacles to the receipt of private economic services within another country, for the purposes of liberalising the cross-border availability of healthcare.[61] However, this caselaw does not call into question the established principle that social advantages subsidised entirely from the public purse by the *host state* cannot in themselves constitute the provision of an economic service for the purposes of Community law.[62] For these two reasons, it is thought safe to assume that host states are entitled (in effect) to discriminate directly or indirectly on the basis of nationality as regards access to welfare benefits, particularly through the imposition of residency requirements, without exposing themselves to the possibility of legal challenge by adversely affected temporary visitors relying upon Article 49 EC.[63]

But the situation of temporary visitors must be reassessed according to the new legal capacity in which such Community nationals now exercise their right to free movement. In particular, how does Union citizenship affect the right to equal treatment enjoyed by temporary visitors within their host society? It is possible to identify two main approaches: the first accepts that temporary visitors should enjoy extensive rights to equal treatment within the host society, so that discriminatory restrictions on their access to welfare benefits must always be objectively justified in accordance with a valid public interest requirement and the principle of proportionality; whereas the second argues in favour of a closer analysis of whether temporary visitors should actually be considered in a comparable situation to own nationals and other lawful residents, before Member States are placed under any obligation to justify apparently discriminatory restrictions on access to their social solidarity benefits. We will now assess each of these approaches in turn.

---

[61] Case C–157/99 *BSM Geraets-Smits v Stichting Ziekenfonds VGZ* and *Peerbooms v Stichting CZ Groep Zorgverzekeringen* [2001] ECR I–5473; Case C–385/99 *Müller-Fauré v Onderlinge Waarborgmaatschappij OZ Zorgverzekeringen UA,* and *van Riet v Onderlinge Waarborgmaatschappi ZAO Zorgverzekeringen* [2003] ECR I–4509; for a critique of the Court's reasoning cf E Spaventa, 'Public Services and European Law: Looking for Boundaries' (2002–2003) 5 *Cambridge Yearbook of European Legal Studies* 271.

[62] In particular: Case 263/86 *Humbel* [1988] ECR 5365; Case C–109/92 *Wirth* [1993] ECR I–6447.

[63] Though several authors pointed out that the scope of equal treatment as regards social advantages under Art 49 EC was, to be fair, unstable and open to more expansive future interpretation (especially given the tenuous link between the receipt of tourist services and access to criminal injuries compensation in *Cowan*), eg S Weatherill and P Beaumont, *EU Law* (Penguin Books, 1999) pp 704–6.

VI TEMPORARY VISITORS:
THE OBJECTIVE JUSTIFICATION APPROACH

A Equal Treatment for Temporary Visitors

On the basis of the Court's caselaw since 1998, there is significant support for the view that temporary visitors have become entitled to move across the Member States *qua* Union citizens, exercising directly effective rights under Article 18 EC; and as such, are able to rely upon the principle of non-discrimination contained in Article 12 EC as regards all matters falling within the material scope of Community law.[64] The argument runs as follows.

If Community nationals *lawfully residing* in the territory of another Member State (including those lawfully resident by virtue of the Treaty) come within the personal scope of the provisions on Union citizenship under Article 17 EC, so too should Community nationals *lawfully visiting* the territory of another Member State. After all, they too count among the beneficiaries of Article 18 EC, which refers to a right not only to reside, but also simply to move across the entire Community territory. That proposition is supported by the judgment in *Bickel and Franz*: besides observing that Article 49 EC covers all Community nationals who visit another Member State where they intend or are likely to receive services, and are thus free to visit and move around within the host territory, the Court also noted that Article 18 EC confers upon every Union citizen the right to move freely across the Community.[65] That point was reinforced by judgments such as *Grzelczyk* and *D'Hoop*: referring back to *Bickel and Franz*, the Court held that the situations falling within the personal scope of Community law include exercise of the fundamental freedoms guaranteed by the Treaty and, in particular, the freedom to move within the territory of the Member States under Article 18 EC.[66]

It is true that the Court often adopts a default approach to the application of Article 18 EC, refusing to address the legal impact of Union citizenship insofar as disputes can adequately be resolved through reliance upon traditional free movement provisions such as Articles 39, 43 and 49 EC.[67]

---

[64] For endorsement (and further detailed analysis) of this objective justification approach to equal treatment as regards welfare benefits and services for temporary visitors *qua* Union citizens, consider A P van der Mei, *Free Movement of Persons within the European Community: Cross-Border Access to Public Benefits* (Hart Publishing, 2003) Ch 6, esp pp 461–80.

[65] Case C–274/96 *Bickel and Franz* [1998] ECR I–1121, para 15.

[66] Case C–184/99 *R Grzelczyk v Centre public d'aide social d'Ottignies-Louvain-la-Neuve* [2001] ECR I–6193, para 33; Case C–224/98 *M N D'Hoop v Office national d'emploi* [2002] ECR I–6191, para 29. Also, eg Case C–148/02 *Garcia Avello* [2003] ECR I–11613, para 24; Case C–224/02 *Pusa* (Judgment of 29 April 2004), para 17.

[67] Eg, Case C–100/01 *Ministre de l'Intérieur v A O Olazabal* [2002] ECR I–10981 on Art 39 EC; Case C–193/94 *Skanavi* [1996] ECR I–929 on Art 43 EC; Case C–92/01 *Stylianakis* [2003] ECR I–1291 on Art 49 EC.

However, this is unlikely to mean that temporary visitors, since they remain entitled to free movement under the specific provisions of Article 49 EC, will in practice be unable to rely upon the Union citizenship provisions.[68] In particular, the Court seems happy to consider the legal effects of Article 18 EC in situations where this provision is capable of enhancing appreciably the scope or quality of the rights enjoyed by Union citizens, as compared to those derived from other legal bases upon which the claimant might theoretically also rely. For example, the Court held in *Grzelczyk* that there is nothing in the Treaty text to suggest that students who are Union citizens, when they move to another Member State to study there, lose the rights which the Treaty confers upon Union citizens—including the right to equal treatment as regards welfare benefits falling within the material scope of Community law.[69] This was true, regardless of the fact that such students could have been said already to enjoy a legal basis for their right to residency under Article 12 EC and Directive 93/96.[70] Similarly, the Court held in *Collins* that the workseeker's inability to challenge discrimination as regards financial benefits under Article 39 EC and Regulation 1612/68, as established in judgments such as *Lebon*,[71] had to be updated in the light of the introduction of Union citizenship and developments in the scope of the principle of equal treatment under Article 12 EC—permitting migrant workseekers to claim access to financial benefits such as jobseeker's allowance.[72] This was true, regardless of the fact that such workseekers could have been said to enjoy a legal basis for their right to residency under Article 39 EC, as construed in judgments such as *ex parte Antonissen*.[73] By analogy, temporary visitors should also be entitled to rely on the Treaty to enjoy the rights which Community law confers upon Union citizens—regardless of (and in addition to) any other rights they might enjoy under provisions such as Article 49 EC.

With the fact that temporary visitors now fall within the personal scope of Article 17 EC, continues the argument, should come all the rights and duties laid down by the Treaty which, according to the judgment in *Sala*, are inseparably linked to the status of Union citizen—including the right to equal treatment under Article 12 EC across the material field of application of Community law.[74] For these purposes, why should the Court follow any-

---

[68] Not least because judicial practice has never been entirely consistent on this matter: the Court does sometimes mention Art 18 EC as an independent source of legal rights, even when traditional free movement provisions alone could have resolved the relevant dispute, eg Case C–274/96 *Bickel and Franz* [1998] ECR I–7637; Case C-135/99 *Elsen* [2000] ECR I–10409.

[69] See above n 38.

[70] Case C–357/89 *Raulin* [1992] ECR I–1027 on Art 12 EC; Dir 93/96 on the right of residence for students, 1993 OJ L317/59.

[71] Case 316/85 *Lebon* [1987] ECR 2811.

[72] Case C–138/02 *Collins v Secretary of State for Work and Pensions* (Judgment of 23 March 2004).

[73] Case C–292/89 *ex parte Antonissen* [1991] ECR I–745.

[74] Cf Case C–274/96 *Bickel and Franz* [1998] ECR I–7637, para 16.

thing other than the same broad conception of 'material scope' it adopts as regards lawfully resident migrants? In particular, why should there be the need to demonstrate any particular link between one's right to enjoyment of the benefit claimed and the effective exercise of one's right to free movement *qua* Union citizen? It is therefore possible that temporary visitors are now entitled to equal treatment, under Article 12 EC, as regards access to whatever welfare benefits fall within the material scope of any provision of Community law—including the vast range of social advantages generally covered by Article 7(2) Regulation 1612/68.[75]

This line of argument can be clearly discerned in the Commission's 2003 revised proposal for a directive on the rights of citizens of the Union and their family members to move and reside freely within the territory of the Member States.[76] This proposal recognised two categories of temporary visitor: first, draft Article 6 offered a blanket right of up to six months' residency for all Union citizens, without the host state being able to impose any conditions whatsoever; and secondly, draft Article 7 envisaged a right of residency for more than six months for those Union citizens who are service recipients in the sense of Article 49 EC. For both these categories of temporary visitor, draft Article 21 guaranteed equal treatment by the host state with its own nationals 'in areas covered by the Treaty'.

The Commission had originally proposed that Union citizens exercising their free movement rights, but who were not engaged in some gainful activity in either an employed or a self-employed capacity, and had not yet acquired the right of permanent residency in accordance with the draft directive, should not be entitled to equal treatment as regards entitlement to social assistance.[77] However, that limitation was erased from the revised proposal on the grounds that, in the light of the judgment in *Grzelczyk*, it would be retrogressive in relation to the evolving *acquis communautaire* to exclude those economically inactive Union citizens without a right of permanent residence from access to welfare assistance.[78] But for these purposes, the draft directive drew no distinction between economically inactive Union citizens ordinarily resident within the host state (for example) as students or retired persons; and those who are better seen merely as temporary visitors either relying upon the blanket right to six months' residency, or qualifying to stay for longer as service recipients. In the Commission's view, *every* migrant Union citizen should be entitled to equal treatment within the

---

[75] Cf S Fries and J Shaw, 'Citizenship of the Union: First Steps in the European Court of Justice' (1998) 4 *European Public Law* 533, who observe that 'after the ECJ's judgment in *Martínez Sala*, it would appear that something close to a universal non-discrimination right including access to all manner of welfare benefits has now taken root in Community law as a consequence of the creation of the figure of the Union citizen' (at p 536).

[76] COM(2003) 199 Final.

[77] COM(2001) 257 Final, draft Art 21(2).

[78] COM(2003) 199 Final, pp 7–8.

host territory across the material scope of Community law, *even* as regards welfare benefits.[79]

Following that line of analysis, it would seem difficult to identify many limits to the scope of the right to equal treatment enjoyed by temporary visitors. In particular, such Union citizens would be offered the opportunity to challenge restrictions which they could not otherwise have queried in another legal capacity under the traditional free movement provisions: social advantages not available to the temporary visitor *qua* service recipient under Article 49 EC could now be opened up to claimants *qua* Union citizen under Articles 18 and 12 EC. The onus would therefore fall on Member States to attempt to justify any restriction which directly or indirectly discriminates on grounds of nationality—including residency requirements of the sort which commonly regulate access to solidarity benefits at the national or local level.[80]

B Objective Justifications for Discrimination

In particular, indirect discrimination must be justified in accordance with an imperative requirement and the principle of proportionality. For these purposes, the Court in *D'Hoop* recognised that it was legitimate, in the case of a special unemployment benefit for young people seeking their first job, for Member States to insist on the existence of a 'real link' between the claimant and the geographic employment market.[81] Such a real link could (in principle) be made dependent upon the claimant having completed her/his education within the national territory—even though such a requirement is clearly indirectly discriminatory against migrant Union citizens.[82] The same approach was adopted in *Collins*. Here, the Court accepted that a habitual residency requirement is (in principle) appropriate for the purpose of ensuring that some connection exists between those who claim a non-contributory jobseeker's allowance and the competent state's employment market.[83] Although both judgments concerned benefits directly related to the individual's future participation in the economic life of the host society, it seems likely that a similar approach will extend to other

---

[79] The only exception was to have been maintenance grants for migrant students (until they acquired the right of permanent residency): COM(2003) 199 Final, draft Art 21(2).

[80] For examples of residency requirements as indirect discrimination in free movement disputes, consider Case C–111/91 *Commission v Luxembourg* [1993] ECR I–817; Case C–299/01 *Commission v Luxembourg* [2002] ECR I–5899.

[81] Case C–224/98 *M N D'Hoop v Office national d'emploi* [2002] ECR I–6191.

[82] However, the principle of proportionality required that the Member State took into account the claimant's most recent (university) education, rather than recognising only secondary education.

[83] Case C–138/02 *Collins v Secretary of State for Work and Pensions* (Judgment of 23 March 2004).

types of welfare benefits intended to cover more universal social risks, such as disability allowances or healthcare provision.[84] By these means, Member States will have a principled doctrinal defence for their insistence that claimants demonstrate some genuine nexus with the national territory before being able to access a whole range of social provisions. More fundamentally, the Court's idea of a 'real link' between claimant and host society can be understood as referring to our first, *moral*, argument—respecting the diffuse psychological sense of fraternity and concomitant assumption of mutual welfare responsibilities—that underpins the solidarity-community-membership triptych.

Furthermore, although it is settled Community law that purely economic goals can never constitute a valid imperative requirement,[85] Member States may legitimately take account of certain financial considerations when attempting to justify indirectly discriminatory barriers to free movement on broader public interest grounds. In particular, the Court in judgments like *Kohll* and *Peerbooms* was prepared to accept that the possible risk of seriously undermining the financial balance of the social security system may constitute an overriding reason in the general interest capable of justifying a barrier to the exercise of fundamental Treaty freedoms; and also recognised that maintaining an adequate standard of welfare provision for the benefit of the entire population (*in casu*, in the field of public health, though the same approach could, in principle, apply to other forms of social protection) is inextricably linked to the Member State's ability to exercise effective control over its levels of financial expenditure.[86] This in turn implies that the competent public authorities must be in a position to curtail the range of individuals (and especially foreign migrants) capable of staking claims against its social solidarity system.[87] The need to preserve the budgetary balance of the welfare state not only provides the Member

---

[84] Consider other judgments in which the Court acknowledges the legitimacy (in principle) of some sort of link between the claimant, the disputed benefit and the social environment of the competent state, eg Case 313/86 *Lenoir* [1988] ECR 5391. In particular, the caselaw on hybrid benefits under Reg 1408/71 (where the claimant had to demonstrate a link to the national social security system, even if that link need not have been based on residency), eg Case 1/72 *Frilli* [1972] ECR 457; Case C–356/89 *Newton* [1991] ECR I–3017. Similarly, the caselaw on special non-contributory benefits under Reg 1408/71 (where the Court analysed the legislative amendments indeed making residency the required link to the national social security system), eg Case C–20/96 *Snares* [1997] ECR I–6057; Case C–297/96 *Partridge* [1998] ECR I–3467. Finally, the caselaw on ex-workers who are no longer resident in the competent state, but still seek access to social advantages, the latter not being linked to their previous contract of employment, eg Case C–43/99 *Leclere* [2001] ECR I–4265; Case C–33/99 *Fahmi* [2001] ECR I–2415.

[85] Eg, Case C–398/95 *SETTG* [1997] ECR I–3091.

[86] Case C–158/96 *Kohll v Union des Caisses de Maladie* [1998] ECR I–1931; Case C–157/99 *BSM Geraets-Smits v Stichting Ziekenfonds VGZ* and *Peerbooms v Stichting CZ Groep Zorgverzekeringen* [2001] ECR I–5473.

[87] Consider also the Court's approach to protecting the stability of national social protection systems in judgments such as Case C–356/89 *Newton* [1991] ECR I–3017.

States with another principled legal defence to indirectly discriminatory qualifying criteria, but again corresponds, more fundamentally, to our second, *financial*, argument—maintaining a realistic equilibrium between welfare supply and demand—that weds together the concepts of solidarity, community and membership.

C Problems With the Objective Justification Approach

Even employing an objective justification approach, it seems unlikely that the Court would in practice allow temporary visitors to free ride on the welfare systems of other Member States. Nevertheless, one should still query whether this objective justification approach is entirely satisfactory. We would argue that there are considerable practical and conceptual problems in requiring automatic judicial scrutiny over rules which make non-contributory social benefits conditional upon requirements such as residency within the national territory.

First, the imperative requirements doctrine requires the national courts to undertake an assessment of the proportionality of the disputed domestic rules. This assessment might be workable enough when the Treaty permits us clearly to identify the conflicting interests which must be balanced one against the other: for example, eliminating protectionist and discriminatory trade practices, versus respecting national regulatory traditions. But history tells us that, even within the framework of economic integration, this proportionality assessment is difficult and inevitably more subjective when the yardstick against which the exercise of national regulatory competence must be evaluated becomes more blurred: recall the problems encountered by the English courts when assessing the proportionality of the Sunday trading rules, expected to balance the relative merits of protecting cultural traditions and the freedom to exercise an economic activity.[88] How much more difficult will the proportionality assessment become when the scales are weighed between promoting some form of *non-economic* European integration and protecting the national welfare systems? Indeed, in the field of equal treatment for Union citizens—particularly when it comes to an imperative requirement as abstract as the 'real link', which demands an exploration of its own moral relevance to the cultural fabric of the welfare society as the finale to any proportionality assessment—the national courts will be expected to navigate their way through a framework of values which is much less tangible than anything we have encountered under Articles 28, 39, 43 or 49 EC. More likely, the notion of the 'real link' will end up serving its time as an intellectually impoverished substitute for the sort of rigorous analysis of the meaning of social solidarity within Europe's

---

[88] Further, eg A Arnull, 'What Shall We Do on Sunday?' (1991) 16 *European Law Review* 112.

multi-level welfare society now called for by combined effect of Articles 18 and 12 EC. Worse still, the principle that Member States may insist upon a 'real link' between certain benefits and certain claimants might simply become a smokescreen for highly subjective judgments, made by the courts, about which Union citizens do or do not deserve public support.[89]

Secondly, the proportionality assessment—particularly when applied to the imperative requirement of preserving the financial integrity of the welfare system—might well pose important practical problems. If disputes over access to social benefits by temporary visitors were to be assessed having sole regard to the particular claim before the court, then a residency requirement would *never* be justified—since a single individual would not be capable of endangering the balance of a national welfare system. To avoid this result, analysis should focus on the potential cumulative effect of multiple claims—as the Court itself recognised in *Müller-Fauré* in respect of the cross-border provision of healthcare services.[90] Yet it is hardly thinkable that national courts would have the resources to engage in a detailed statistical and budgetary analysis of the consequences of such possible demands for welfare benefits by temporary visitors. It is much more likely that the proportionality of residency requirements would be carried out having regard to purely speculative factors. Again, the approach in *Müller-Fauré* is enlightening: the Court felt able to state, on the basis of an intuitive assessment, without the apparent support of any empirical research—and within the context of non-contentious proceedings under an Article 234 EC reference—that the removal of any prior authorisation requirement for non-hospital treatment abroad would not jeopardise the financial balance of the national healthcare system.[91]

Both these problems are made worse by the risk of inconsistency in the uniform application of Community law by the national courts. Given the difficulties involved in assessing the proportionality of residency requirements as regards welfare benefits, the end result reached by domestic judges is very likely to vary—especially across different Member States—according to the manner in which the welfare system is organised, and the way in which social provision itself is culturally perceived.

One final difficulty concerns not so much the proportionality assessment as the underlying conceptual framework of the objective justification approach. This framework necessarily implies that, in principle, and subject

---

[89] For criticisms of the vague and malleable nature of the 'real link' concept: S O'Leary, 'Solidarity and Citizenship Rights in the Charter of Fundamental Rights of the European Union' in *Collected Courses of the Academy of European Law 2003* (OUP, forthcoming).

[90] Case C–385/99 *Müller-Fauré v Onderlinge Waarborgmaatschappij OZ Zorgverzekeringen UA, and van Riet v Onderlinge Waarborgmaatschappi ZAO Zorgverzekeringen* [2003] ECR I–4509, para 74.

[91] Further: E Spaventa, 'Public Services and European Law: Looking for Boundaries' (2002–03) 5 *Cambridge Yearbook of European Legal Studies* 271.

only to justified exceptions, national welfare provisions *should* be available to *all* Union citizens in *all* Member States, regardless of nationality or contribution, and merely by virtue of Articles 18 and 12 EC. If this is true, it is no longer the case that Community law is gradually reshaping national thresholds of belonging to or being excluded from the welfare society. Something altogether more dramatic is occurring: Union citizenship is being *elevated above*, and *superimposed upon*, the notion of national solidarity. Indeed, the very fact that a Member State must always justify restrictions on access to social benefits by visitors suggests that the Union citizen *as such* has been catapulted in the host welfare society. This bold extension of the assimilation model may well bring Union citizenship a big step closer to fulfilling its destiny as the 'fundamental status of the nationals of the Member States'.[92] But it is far from evident that such a development tallies with current reality within Europe's multi-level welfare system, where the Member States still legitimately claim primary sovereignty over welfare provision.

Yet if the objective justification approach does not emerge as an entirely satisfactory conceptual tool to deal with the problem of equal treatment for temporary visitors, where is the solution to be found? In our opinion, a more careful assessment of whether discrimination exists *at all* might provide us with a more rigorous framework for analysis.

circumvent earlier flows.

VII TEMPORARY VISITORS: THE COMPARABILITY APPROACH

A Assessing the Very Existence of Discrimination

Discrimination arises when two comparable situations are treated differently, or two non-comparable situations are treated similarly.[93] If the situations are not comparable, any disparity in treatment does not give rise to discrimination (and does not need to be justified).[94]

---

[92] Eg, Case C–184/99 *R Grzelczyk v Centre public d'aide social d'Ottignies-Louvain-la-Neuve* [2001] ECR I–6193, para 31; Case C–224/98 *M N D'Hoop v Office national d'emploi* [2002] ECR I–6191, para 28; Case C–413/99 *Baumbast and R v Secretary of State for the Home Department* [2002] ECR I–7091, para 82.

[93] Eg, Case C–137/00 *The Queen v The Competition Commission, Secretary of State for Trade and Industry and The Director General of Fair Trading, ex parte Milk Marque Ltd and National Farmers' Union* [2003] ECR I–7975, para 126.

[94] The assessment of whether two products are comparable is essential in order to establish the existence of discriminatory taxation in relation to Art 90 EC (where the Court has held that the lack of any comparator altogether excludes the existence of discrimination), eg Case C–47/88 *Commission v Denmark* [1990] ECR I–4509; Case C–383/01 *De Danske Bilimportører v Skatteministereriet, Told-og Skattestyrelsen* [2003] ECR I–6065. The notion of comparability was used to exclude discrimination, *inter alia*, in the following cases: Case C–14/01 *Molkerei Wagenfeld Karl Niemann GmbH & Co KG v Bezirksregierung Hannover* [2003] ECR I–2279; Case C–137/00 *R v The Competition Commission, ex parte Milk Marque Ltd* [2003] ECR I-7975. See also the tax caselaw under Art 43 EC, eg Case C–279/93 *Finanzamt Köln-Altstadt v Roland Schumacker* [1995] ECR I–225; Case

In economic free movement cases, comparability is usually taken for granted: the situation of the national worker or self-employed person and the foreign worker or self-employed person is deemed to be comparable, and therefore not specifically assessed by the Court. Nonetheless, even as regards economic migrants, there are disputes in which the Court has had recourse to a prior analysis of comparability in order to exclude the existence of discrimination, and thereby avoid any assessment of whether the disputed national rules pursued a legitimate aim in a proportionate manner. For example, the claimant in *Kaba* argued that British rules prescribing different time-scales for a spouse to gain indefinite leave to remain, depending upon whether the main right-holder was a person 'present and settled' in the United Kingdom or a Community worker, were discriminatory. However, the Court found that the situation of a Community worker is *not comparable* to that of a person present and settled in the United Kingdom, since the former's right to residence within the national territory is not unconditional. Consequently, Member States are entitled to take into account this *objective difference* when laying down their immigration rules—without having to undergo judicial scrutiny in accordance with the objective justification model.[95] Conversely, *Ferlini* concerned the application of Article 12 EC to the fees demanded by a group of private hospitals from a Community official who was not insured under the national social security system (such fees being higher than those charged to insured persons). In order to assess whether Article 12 EC applied at all, the Court first assessed the comparability of the claimant's situation with that of an insured person. Only after being satisfied that such comparability existed did the Court proceed to analyse the hospitals' purported justification for the discriminatory difference in treatment.[96]

In the citizenship free movement cases too, there are judgments where the issue of comparability between own nationals and migrant Community nationals has played a more explicit role in the Court's reasoning. For example, the Court in *Sala* observed that, since the claimant had been

---

C-391/97 *Frans Gschwind v Finanzamt Aachen-Außenstadt* [1999] ECR I–5451; Case C-234/01 *A Gerritse v Finanzamt Neukölln-Nord* [2003] ECR I–5933. The question of whether two categories of persons are in a comparable situation (and must for that reason enjoy some sort of social advantage under the same conditions) is a question involving the interpretation of Community law over which the Court of Justice has the final say, eg Case C–466/00 *A Kaba v Secretary of State for the Home Department* (Kaba II) [2003] ECR I–2219, para 44.

[95] Case C–356/98 *A Kaba v Secretary of State for the Home Department* (Kaba I) [2000] ECR I–2623, upheld in Case C–466/00 *A Kaba v Secretary of State for the Home Department* (Kaba II) [2003] ECR I–2219. However, the Court's reasoning in *Kaba I* has been strongly criticised: see S Peers, 'Dazed and Confused: Family Members' Residence Rights and the Court of Justice' (2001) 26 *European Law Review* 76.

[96] Case C–411/98 *A Ferlini v Centre Hospitalier de Luxembourg* [2000] ECR I–8081. Consider also, eg Joined Cases C–49/98, C–50/98, C–52/98 to C–54/98 and C–68/98 to C–71/98 *Finalarte* [2001] ECR I–7831.

authorised to reside in Germany in accordance with domestic immigration legislation, she was to be considered in the same position as a German national residing in the national territory. On that basis, the claimant was entitled to rely on Article 12 EC as regards a non-contributory child-raising benefit, in principle reserved to those permanently or ordinarily resident in the Member State, so as to challenge certain directly discriminatory qualifying criteria.[97] Similarly, the Court in *Grzelczyk* began its substantive analysis of the case by observing that a student of Belgian nationality who found him/herself in exactly the same circumstances as the claimant would have satisfied the conditions for obtaining the disputed minimum subsistence benefit. The fact that the claimant was not of Belgian nationality constituted the only bar to his application for welfare support, and it was therefore clear to the Court that the case was one of discrimination based solely on the ground of nationality.[98] Conversely, the Court in *Garcia Avello* had recourse to the notion of comparability, this time to establish that identical treatment by the Member State of two situations which could not in fact be considered comparable amounted to discrimination which then needed to be justified.[99] And more generally, the Court throughout its citizenship caselaw seems (consciously) to have left open the door to a more extensive future role for the comparability question:

> Union citizenship is destined to be the fundamental status of nationals of the Member States, **enabling those who find themselves in the same situation** to enjoy the same treatment in law irrespective of their nationality, subject to such exceptions as are expressly provided for.[100] *Grzelczyk*

Clearly, comparability is often assumed—but it is not ignored altogether.

B Comparability and Temporary Visitors

This framework—based upon a prior assessment of comparability, though incorporating a set of refutable presumptions—could be usefully adopted in relation to claims over social advantages by migrant Union citizens.

To begin with, Union citizens who are lawfully resident in another Member State should, as a matter of principle, be considered in a comparable situation to own nationals, and therefore entitled to equal treatment

---

[97] Case C–85/96 *M M Martínez Sala v Freistaat Bayern* [1998] ECR I–2691.
[98] See n 38 above.
[99] Case C–148/02 *Garcia Avello* [2003] ECR I–11613. Consider also, eg AG Ruiz-Jarabo Colomer in Case C–386/02 *Baldinger* (Opinion of 11 December 2003; Judgment of 16 September 2004); AG Geelhoed in Case C–456/02 *Trojani* (Opinion of 19 February 2004; Judgment of 7 September 2004).
[100] Case C–184/99 *Grzelczyk* [2001] ECR I–6193, para 31 (emphasis added). Also, eg Case C–224/98 *M N D'Hoop v Office national d'emploi* [2002] ECR I–6191, para 28; Case C–138/02 *Collins v Secretary of State for Work and Pensions* (Judgment of 23 March 2004), para 61; Case C–224/02 *Pusa* (Judgment of 29 April 2004), para 16.

(subject to justifications) in respect of all benefits.[101] Moreover, other Union citizens who are not resident but nevertheless have a 'real link' to the host territory may also be treated as being in a comparable situation to own nationals and lawful residents. This is the case particularly for frontier workers, who enjoy equal treatment as regards all social advantages falling within Article 7(2) Regulation 1612/68, and are therefore entitled to challenge discriminatory requirements imposed by the host state—demonstrating that membership of the solidaristic community may be established by means other than residency.[102] It might even be the case that, in relation to certain other non-residents, the introduction of Union citizenship shifts the focus away from a purely market-oriented notion of belonging, whereby entitlement to benefits is a direct result of the economic output produced by the frontier worker, towards a broader notion of inclusion, whereby entitlement to benefits is recognised also for those whose claim to membership of the solidaristic community can be established through non-economic links: for instance, by performing unpaid activity in the context of charitable work.

However, as regards other non-residents—temporary visitors *stricto sensu*—the situation is more complex, and comparability needs to be established before a finding of discrimination can be made. For these purposes, an assessment of whether the two situations are comparable will necessarily depend upon the type of benefit claimed. Broadly speaking, we can distinguish benefits paid by the public purse into three categories: those which arise from the discharge of *public order duties* pertaining to the state's sovereignty; those which arise out of the state's choice to use public funding to foster *non-solidaristic* policy objectives; and those which indeed reflect a *link of solidarity* between community and individual.

Benefits arising from the discharge of public order duties would include, for instance, defence, police, and the administration of justice, that is, areas which are usually considered the key element of sovereignty and where the state claims an absolute monopoly. Here, the state owes similar duties towards all those who are subject to its jurisdiction and/or present within its territory, and therefore comparability between residents and non-residents should be easily established.[103] Take the social advantage at issue in Cowan: the French compensation scheme for victims of crime resulted from the state's acknowledgment of failures in its policing duties—borne towards

---

[101] Except for those which are still linked to the notion of nationality: consider, eg Case 207/78 *Even* [1979] ECR 2019; Case C–315/94 *Peter de Vos* [1996] ECR I–1417; Case C–356/98 *A Kaba v Secretary of State for the Home Department* (Kaba I) [2000] ECR I–2623; upheld in Case C–466/00 *A Kaba v Secretary of State for the Home Department* (Kaba II) [2003] ECR I–2219.

[102] Eg, Case C–57/96 *Meints* [1997] ECR I–6689; Case C–337/97 *Meeusen* [1999] ECR I–3289.

[103] Cf the idea of the state's 'night-watch' duties as developed in AP van der Mei, *Free Movement of Persons within the European Community: Cross-Border Access to Public Benefits* (Hart Publishing, 2003) Ch 1.

residents and non-residents alike—so that such a benefit could not be made conditional upon residency, even though it is entirely funded from the public purse.[104] Or consider the social advantage at issue in *Bickel and Franz*: the language used in criminal proceedings directly related to the rules of procedure in the administration of justice—a public law duty borne by the Italian state towards residents and non-residents alike—which could not be made dependent upon residency within the local territory.[105] This is not to say that such indirect discrimination can never be justified, only to observe that it must be justified, by reference to an imperative requirement plus the principle of proportionality.

The second category of benefits are those which, again funded from the public purse, *neither* represent a discharge by the state of its fundamental public order duties *nor* reflect a link of solidarity between the community and the individual. The state may be seeking to fulfil certain social policy objectives (such as the preservation and dissemination of the collective heritage), but it is not assuming responsibility for the basic physical and economic well-being of the members of *its* community. In such cases, comparability should also readily be established. Take, for example, *Commission v Spain* and *Commission v Italy*, where the Court extended the principle of non-discrimination to cover the conditions for entry into museums, accepting (as we have seen) that there was a close link to the reception of economic services as a tourist, thus triggering the joint application of Articles 49 and 12 EC.[106] Following the direct effect of Article 18 EC, a different and more consistent framework of analysis should be adopted. The tourist *qua* Union citizen clearly falls within the personal scope of the Treaty, and museum entry conditions clearly fall within the material scope of the Treaty. Thus, so long as the situations are comparable, the principle of equal treatment applies and any residency requirement needs to be justified. Given that entry into museums is clearly not a manifestation of solidarity premised upon membership of the national community, but an aspect of broader cultural and educational policy objectives, there is no reason why a non-resident tourist should be considered in any way different from a resident tourist.[107]

Finally, there are those benefits which indeed stem from a link of social solidarity: for example, subsistence benefits like income support, disability allowances, and non-emergency healthcare. Such benefits truly reflect the assumption of responsibility by the community towards *its* weaker mem-

---

[104] Case 186/87 *Cowan v le Trésor Public* [1989] ECR 195.
[105] Case C–274/96 *Bickel and Franz* [1998] ECR I–1121.
[106] Case C–43/93 *Commission v Spain* [1994] ECR I–911; Case C–388/01 *Commission v Italy* [2003] ECR I–721.
[107] Case C–388/01 *Commission v Italy* [2003] ECR I–721 suggests that, in these cases, the Member State would have to justify the disparate treatment, for instance, by establishing a clear link between contribution through taxation and the relevant benefit.

not comparable (handwritten margin note)

bers, and the situation of the resident should in principle be considered non-comparable to that of the non-resident, who does not *belong* to the host society. In such cases, therefore, Member States should in principle be allowed to 'distinguish' on grounds of residency without having to rely on the imperative requirements doctrine, or undergo the proportionality assessment. Imagine that a French tourist presents herself at a London hospital asking for treatment—free at the point of delivery—in respect of her chronic arthritic pains. She is told that such non-emergency healthcare is reserved only to residents of the United Kingdom. Can she claim that, as a migrant Union citizen exercising rights to free movement under Article 18 EC, she is the victim of indirect discrimination contrary to Article 12 EC, which the Member State must now objectively justify? We believe not. Since the benefit is an expression of social solidarity, the claimant's situation should not be considered comparable to that of members of the relevant community of reference, and the residency requirement would be safe from scrutiny.

C Benefits of the Comparability Approach

Evidently, both the objective justification and the comparability approach acknowledge that, until the Community acquires and exercises more extensive competences in the fields of taxation and social welfare, Union citizenship must be based on the principle of co-existence between the different—and potentially competing—elements of the Union's multi-level solidarity system. In particular, both models recognise that Member States are entitled to distinguish between own nationals and other lawful residents (on the one hand) and temporary visitors (on the other hand) in cases which presuppose a minimum threshold of belonging before the host community should be asked to assume responsibility for the provision of welfare benefits. Therefore, both approaches help to avoid a situation in which Community law fundamentally challenges basic societal choices which flow from the link binding together members of a solidaristic community; and ensure that the emerging framework of free movement rights and equal treatment for Union citizens does not endanger the financial viability of valuable public services. The main *difference* between the two models lies in the fact that the objective justification approach treats the necessity of a 'real link' between claimant and host society as a legitimate defence for indirect discrimination; whilst the comparability approach considers that the absence of such a link is sufficient to exclude the existence of discrimination altogether.

It is true that, since each model is focused on establishing the existence of a 'real link', the same factors (such as the nature of the benefit under dispute and its mode of funding, or the claimant's past and present relationship with the host society) can be relevant in both the objective justification and the comparability approach. Against that background, the very validity of comparability as a conceptual model has been questioned in the scholarship. For instance, de Búrca has argued that, whilst the comparability approach provides a defence which is substantially equivalent to that available under the objective justification approach, the former has the undesirable effect of enabling Member States to avoid offering a clear articulation of the policy reasons justifying an apparent difference in treatment. Furthermore, the choice between a comparability approach and a justificatory approach affects the burden of proof: in the former case, it is for the claimant to establish the existence of discrimination, and therefore to prove that the two situations are comparable; whereas in the latter case, it is for the defendant Member State to prove that the rules pursue a legitimate policy objective in a proportionate fashion.[108]

Those might well be valid criticisms. Nonetheless, it is important to bear in mind that de Búrca raises them in the context of trade law. In the case of trade restrictions, the aim of liberalisation is clearly sanctioned by the EC Treaty (and the WTO agreement). In this context, it is easier to argue that the onus should fall on the Member State to justify the proportionality of its regulatory standards, once a barrier to movement has been identified. Yet even here, to endorse the objective justification approach, without paying due regard to the need to conduct an *a priori* assessment of the very existence of discrimination, reflects preconceptions about the relative importance of competing policy objectives which are hardly uncontested.[109] This problem becomes even more acute in the field of social welfare, where the normative vision for the interplay between the national solidarity systems, as well as the nature and extent of the Union's own social policy ambitions, is much more ambiguous. Here, the postulate of equal treatment—that the temporary visitor is automatically entitled to the same level of solidaristic support as any own national or other lawful resident—challenges too hastily basic assumptions about the allocation of mutual responsibilities between *citizens* and *societies*. By contrast, the comparability approach—as well as avoiding the difficulties inherent in applying the principle of proportionality—seems better equipped to reconcile the effects of Union citizenship with the very notion of a *national* solidaristic community. In particular, focusing more rigorously on the issue of comparability allows us to question the conceptual desirability of

---

[108] G de Búrca, 'Unpacking the Concept of Discrimination in EC and International Trade Law' in C Barnard and J Scott (eds), *The Law of the Single European Market: Unpacking the Premises* (Hart Publishing, 2002).

[109] Consider, eg the problems arising in free movement of goods in relation to (discriminatory) environmental policies. In particular, see Case C–2/90 *Commission v Belgium (Wallonian Waste)* [1992] ECR I–4431, where the Court used the non-comparability approach in a rather artificial way (cf para 36); and the confused ruling in Case C–379/98 *PreussenElektra AG v Schleswag AG* [2001] ECR I–2099. Further: E Spaventa, 'On Discrimination and the Theory of Mandatory Requirements' (2000) 3 *Cambridge Yearbook of European Legal Studies* 457.

superimposing onto the Member States, without more ado, a novel set of binding welfare values based on the assimilation model—a set of values which may not tally with the basic thresholds of belonging which are a defining characteristic of any morally and financially self-sustaining solidarity system.

VIII THE IMPACT OF DIRECTIVE 2004/38

How does all this fit in with the relevant provisions of Directive 2004/38,[110] the new regime on free movement for Union citizens adopted by Council and Parliament in spring 2004?

Article 6 Directive 2004/38 provides that all Union citizens shall enjoy a right of residence for up to three months in any of the Member States 'without any conditions'.[111] This is the first time that the residency status of Union citizens simply *qua* visitors—and regardless of their economic status—has been codified in secondary legislation.[112] It confirms the view— which, as we have seen, was already evident from the Court's caselaw—that temporary visitors fall within the personal scope of Article 18 EC on the basis of their right to move freely across the Community. However, whilst Article 6 is phrased in an unconditional fashion, the new regime is not in fact as generous as it seems (or as the Commission's 2003 revised proposal had suggested). Two caveats have been imposed. First, Article 14 Directive 2004/38 makes retention of even the temporary right of residence expressly conditional upon its beneficiary not becoming an unreasonable burden upon the host society—thus extending the Court's caselaw beyond long term economically inactive migrants such as *Grzelczyk*, so as also to cover short term economically inactive Union citizens.[113] Secondly, under Article 24 of Directive 2004/38—which sets out a general principle of equal treatment for all lawfully resident Union citizens as regards all benefits falling within the scope of the Treaty—Member States are not obliged to confer entitlement to social assistance during the first three months' residence of any

---

[110] Dir 2004/38 on the right of citizens and their family members to move and reside freely within the territory of the Member States, 2004 OJ L158/77.

[111] Council and Parliament therefore rejected the Commission's 2001/2003 proposal for a general right to residency of six months' duration.

[112] Cf Art 4(2) Dir 73/148, 1973 OJ L172/14 on short term service providers and recipients under Art 49 EC; and caselaw such as Case C–292/89 *ex parte Antonissen* [1991] ECR I–745 on workseekers under Art 39 EC.

[113] Something which is not necessarily appropriate to such short term residents: consider the remarks of AG Geelhoed in Case C–456/02 *Trojani* (Opinion of 19 February 2004; Judgment of 7 September 2004) paras 64–65 Opinion. Indeed, as regards temporary visitors, the steps required to secure expulsion from the national territory may take longer than the claimant's projected residence (cf the situation of students as discussed by J-P Lhernould, 'L'accès aux prestations sociales des citoyens de l'Union européenne' [2001] *Droit Social* 1103).

economically inactive Union citizen.[114] Directive 2004/38 thus allows for the exclusion of any right to equal treatment as regards social assistance for the entire duration of the temporary visitor's sojourn in the host society pursuant to Article 6.

On that basis, it could be argued that the basic problem analysed in this chapter—that of temporary visitors using their newfound status as migrant Union citizens to gain access to the solidarity benefits of the host society—has been effectively resolved by Directive 2004/38: without having to make any specific choice between the objective justification approach or the comparability model, the Community legislature has simply decreed that temporary residents (i.e. visitors) can be legitimately excluded from the right to equal treatment in relation to social assistance within the host state. Even if the reasoning process is very different, at least the end-result envisaged by Directive 2004/38 seems in keeping with the underlying policy objective—that of preserving the thresholds of belonging and exclusion which define the fundamental characters and preserve the financial balance of the national solidarity systems—which led us to prefer the comparability model over the objective justification approach in our analysis above. All's well that ends well: should we not be satisfied? If only things were that simple. Further reflection in fact reveals two potential problems with the scheme embodied in Directive 2004/38.

The first concerns the meaning of 'social assistance'. Directive 2004/38 does not offer any precise definition of this term, even though the matter is crucial to the effective operation of Article 24. One possibility would be to look for inspiration from the parallel expression found in Article 4(4) Regulation 1408/71.[115] In the latter context, the Court has construed the term 'social assistance' narrowly, so as to cover only means-tested benefits offered by the public authorities on a discretionary basis.[116] If that definition were to be adopted also as regards Directive 2004/38, then we could hardly treat the derogation contained in Article 24 as comprehensive in its

---

[114] Not just those relying upon the general three-month right to residency under Art 6 Dir 2004/38; but also longer-term economically inactive residents covered by Art 7 Dir 2004/38. Workseekers with an extended temporary right to residency under Art 14(4)(b) Dir 2004/38 are excluded from equal treatment as regards social assistance throughout the duration of their search for employment: Art 24(2) Dir 2004/38.

[115] See now Art 3(5) Reg 883/2004 on the coordination of social security systems, 2004 OJ L200/1 (partially repealing and replacing Reg 1408/71).

[116] Consider, eg Case 79/76 *Fossi* [1977] ECR 667. Bear in mind that not every benefit which falls outside the material scope of Reg 1408/71 should automatically be considered 'social assistance' within the meaning of Art 4(4): consider, eg benefits granted as of right but which do not relate to one of the specific contingencies listed in Art 4(1) (as in Case 249/83 *Hoeckx* [1985] ECR 982; Case 122/84 *Scrivner* [1985] ECR 1029); and also hybrid benefits (as identified in the Court's caselaw before the introduction of special non-contributory benefits under Art 4(2a)) where the claimant was not previously subject to the social security legislation of the relevant Member State (as in Case 1/72 *Frilli* [1972] ECR 457; Case C–356/89 *Newton* [1991] ECR I–3017).

attempt to prevent economically inactive Union citizens, relying upon the right of temporary residency under Article 6, from claiming equal treatment as regards welfare benefits and other social services. Apart from the relatively narrow category of discretionary social assistance, temporary visitors would still be entitled to rely on Article 12 EC (and indeed the general principle of equal treatment otherwise referred to in Article 24 Directive 2004/38) to seek access to the host state's welfare system. And so it would still be necessary for the Court to decide whether to adopt a straightforward objective justification approach (with all the practical and conceptual problems that would raise); or whether to treat such migrant Union citizens as being in a non-comparable situation to own nationals and other lawful residents (exempting the Member State from any obligation to justify its differential treatment).

However, it seems more likely that the term 'social assistance' as used in Article 24 Directive 2004/38 is intended to have its own autonomous meaning, indeed covering any non-contributory welfare benefit or service which would amount to an encumbrance upon the public purse.[117] But this merely leads on to our second potential problem with the new free movement regime. Secondary legislation must conform to and be interpreted in the light of the Treaty (as interpreted by the Court).[118] For these purposes, the judgments in *Grzelczyk* and *Baumbast* fundamentally altered the legal relationship between the Treaty, the Community legislature and the Member States in the field of Union citizenship. All measures which regulate the right to free movement—including Directive 2004/38—act as limitations and conditions upon the citizen's fundamental freedom under Article 18 EC; and Member States are required to apply those limitations and conditions in accordance with the general principles of Community law and, in particular, the principle of proportionality. Thus, we are back to square one: whatever the black-letter terms of Article 24 Directive 2004/38, it will remain open to a temporary resident (ie visitor) to argue that her/his exclusion from equal treatment as regards social assistance benefits strikes an unfair balance between, on the one hand, effective enjoyment of the Union citizen's right to free movement and, on the other hand, the Member State's legitimate interest in protecting its welfare system against inequitable claims. The bottom line is that, for so long as the Court is willing to pursue the logic of *Grzelczyk* and *Baumbast*, neither the Community legislature nor the Member States enjoy the competence to dictate that any category of

---

[117] And, of course, which the claimant does not qualify for *qua* insured person under Reg 1408/71 / Reg 883/2004. Cf Dir 2003/109 concerning the status of third country nationals who are long term residents, 2004 OJ L16/44: Art 11(1) and (4), read in conjunction with Recital 13 of the Preamble, does not suggest that the Council intended the term 'social assistance' to be limited only to discretionary, means-tested benefits.

[118] From innumerable cases, eg Case 41/84 *Pinna* [1986] ECR 1 on conformity; Case C–114/01 *AvestaPolarit Chrome Oy* [2003] ECR I–8725 on interpretation.

Union citizen should be definitively excluded from enjoying equal treatment as regards any benefit falling within the material scope of the Treaty. And therefore any welfare rule is potentially subject to scrutiny in terms of proportionality, with all the problems that that might entail.

And so, despite the best efforts of Council and Parliament, Directive 2004/38 cannot simply have extinguished the problem of how far temporary visitors are entitled to claim equal treatment with own nationals and other lawful residents when it comes to welfare benefits available within the host territory. As soon as the claimant invokes the reasoning in *Grzelczyk* and *Baumbast*, it will become necessary to look beyond the bare text of Article 24 and ask once again what is the most appropriate doctrinal framework to exclude migrant Union citizens from access to social support from a national solidarity system to which they do not belong: an objective justification approach or the comparability model? But in this regard, the adoption of Directive 2004/38 (while it may not have solved the problem of temporary visitors exactly as its authors intended) does add one more argument for supporting the comparability model over the objective justification approach.

If the Court were eventually to adopt an objective justification approach to temporary visitors who were attempting to overreach the provisions of Directive 2004/38 by reference to the reasoning in *Grzelczyk* and *Baumbast*, then the national authorities would be required to assess, on a case-by-case basis, why this particular individual should be denied equal treatment as regards social assistance in these particular circumstances. For these purposes, the claimant's case might even seem bolstered by the fact that the safeguard provision contained in Article 14 Directive 2004/38 offers Member States the chance to terminate the right to temporary residency, should application of the principle of equal treatment transform the claimant into an unreasonable financial burden. In such circumstances, one might suppose that the possibility of temporary visitors using the principle of proportionality to access limited welfare benefits within the host society, even during their three months' sojourn and despite the express terms of Article 24 Directive 2004/38, should not be viewed too seriously.

But perhaps the legitimate national interests embodied in Directive 2004/38 go further than this argument would acknowledge. Through the derogation contained in Article 24, Council and Parliament have clearly sought to eliminate *any* risk of welfare tourism. Indeed, the problem is not so much a matter of the claimant becoming an unreasonable burden, but of any claimant being a 'burden' (even if a reasonable one). Thus, Directive 2004/38 recognises that any claim (however small) draws away from the resources which have been allocated to the needs of a given welfare society—by its members, for its members. That is a political statement about the value of belonging to a community of interests, as a precondition to enjoying access to that community's solidaristic support, which we should still strive to accommodate. If the Court were to adopt the view that, when it comes to welfare benefits, temporary visitors are not automatically in a comparable situation with own nationals and other settled residents, then even if the migrant Union citizen were to invoke the principle of proportionality embodied in *Grzelczyk* and *Baumbast*, it would in the end offer the claimant little assistance: the underlying principle of equal treatment would still not be activated, and the Member State would not be compelled to offer any defence of its differential treatment. By this route, the caselaw on Union citizenship need not have the effect of undermining the delicate compromise reached by Council and Parliament as regards the mutual allocation of responsibilities between the national solidarity systems. Indeed, the comparability model emerges as the most effective way of ensuring that the derogation contained in Article 24 Directive 2004/38 proves effective in practice.

IX CONCLUSIONS

When Marshall included social rights alongside civil and political rights in his threefold classification of the entitlements pertaining to national citizenship,[119] perhaps he did not fully foresee how the later twentieth century would witness the gradual disaggregation of those traditional components of national citizenship.[120] Particularly in the Member States of the European Economic Community-turned-European Union, the forces of cross-border migration—facilitated at first by the goal of closer economic integration, then also by the ambition of greater political union—have shown us that it is perfectly possible for foreigners to enjoy extensive expectations of welfare protection within their host society, without necessarily sharing in the political rights and responsibilities which are often reserved to own nationals.[121] This process reminds us that the concept of social solidarity is not a constant or given, but dynamic and up for renegotiation. In particular, under the influence of Union citizenship, and through the medium of the assimilation model, social solidarity is undoubtedly becoming less statist and more cosmopolitan in its orientation. The question is:

---

[119] T H Marshall, *Citizenship and Social Class* (CUP, 1949, reprinted Pluto Press, 1991).

[120] As observed by S Benhabib, 'The Rights of Others: Aliens, Residents and Citizens', paper presented at *Migrants, Nations and Citizenship*, conference organised by the Centre for Research in the Arts, Social Sciences and Humanities (University of Cambridge, 5–6 July 2004).

[121] Though even that Marshallian assumption is being increasingly unbundled from the institution of domestic citizenship: consider the voting and candidature rights of migrant Union citizens in municipal and European Parliamentary elections as provided for under Art 19 EC. Also: J Shaw, 'Political Participation of Non-EU Nationals in the EU of 25: Preliminary Observations', paper presented at *Migrants, Nations and Citizenship*, conference organised by the Centre for Research in the Arts, Social Sciences and Humanities (University of Cambridge, 5–6 July 2004).

just how far can the common identity provided by Union citizenship justify the assimilation of economically inactive migrants into the traditional welfare societies of the Member States? Because, on another view, the primary reference point for social solidarity, linked essentially to national identity, remains relatively resilient and prone to self-assertion—especially when the Member State's own definitions of membership appear to be redefined 'from above' by Brussels and Luxembourg (rather than 'from within' by the domestic experience of social change and political debate).[122]

This fundamental tension is bound to saturate any analysis of how the introduction of Union citizenship has affected the legal status of temporary visitors. Before, under Article 49 EC, such migrants enjoyed only limited rights to equal treatment within the host state under Community law. Now, under Articles 18 and 12 EC, temporary visitors might appear to enjoy much more extensive rights to equal treatment. However, we have argued that Union citizenship should not seek to deconstruct altogether the thresholds of belonging and exclusion underpinning the domestic/national welfare settlement. Otherwise, one would risk substituting a sense of popular acceptance (however tacit) with a sense of widespread alienation for a legal construct which is still perceived as far removed from many individuals' core cultural and emotional ties. The prime objective of Union citizenship should be to create a new model of inclusion which complements rather than replaces existing notions of national citizenship.[123] And for these purposes, we should not pretend that all Union citizens are equal claimants vis-à-vis the national solidaristic community.

What is the most convincing conceptual architecture by which our legal discourse can accommodate this differentiation between Union citizens? The idea of a 'real link' is emerging as the key concept in mediating between rights to equal treatment for migrant Union citizens and the Member State's legitimate interest in protecting its social welfare system. But one key issue which remains to be clarified is how far that concept should play a role *only* in the endgame of an objective justification approach; or (as we have argued) *also* in the elaboration of a more doctrinally rigorous comparability model. By taking comparability between residents and non-residents for granted, the objective justification approach challenges the basic assumption that there is something *unique* about community membership which justifies individual sacrifices for the common good. For this reason, it has

---

[122] Though such processes are, of course, far from mutually exclusive: consider German debates in the 1990s over the local voting rights of non-citizens (where domestic considerations of membership and sovereignty interacted with the post-Maastricht Community rules on the electoral rights of Union citizens); as referred to by S Benhabib, 'The Rights of Others: Aliens, Residents and Citizens', paper presented at *Migrants, Nations and Citizenship*, conference organised by the Centre for Research in the Arts, Social Sciences and Humanities (University of Cambridge, 5–6 July 2004).

[123] Cf the text of Art 17 EC.

been submitted that, when it comes to welfare benefits and services which are an expression of social solidarity by the community towards *its* members, temporary visitors should not automatically be equated to own nationals, lawful residents and others who (by whichever means) manage to establish a persuasive link of belonging to the host society. In practical terms, this might look a little like reinventing the wheel: the temporary visitor *qua* Union citizen can claim equal treatment as regards access to the same sorts of social advantages (such as museum entry fees, criminal injuries compensation, and the conduct of penal proceedings) as she/he could expect *qua* service recipient under Article 49 EC. But reinventing the wheel in this manner became necessary when, first, the Member States created the institution of Union citizenship; then, secondly, the Court of Justice infused that institution with powerful legal potential. And reinventing the wheel in this manner seems entirely appropriate if, whilst accepting the rapid pace of change in our multi-level welfare society, we are to acknowledge not only the financial but also the moral imperatives which continue to lie at the very foundation of European social solidarity.

10

EU Law and Education: Promotion of Student Mobility versus Protection of Education Systems

ANNE PIETER VAN DER MEI*

I INTRODUCTION

In the course of the last two decades, the European Community has achieved much in promoting cross-border access to education.[1] In the original EEC Treaty no mention was made of educational rights for the beneficiaries of the free movement of workers, and freedom of movement for students was not provided for. Today, Community law confers far-reaching educational rights upon workers and their family members, and it entitles all Union citizens to move to other Member States to take up studies. Nonetheless, Community law on cross-border access to education, as it stands today, is still debated. This is particularly true for the category of Union citizens who move to other Member States for the sole purpose of studying and who fall outside the scope of the *Socrates/Erasmus* programme. On the one hand, it is claimed that these students still face too many obstacles, such as non-recognition of diplomas, insufficient language knowledge, lack of sufficient financial aid and conditions for residing in the host State.[2] On the other hand, it is argued that Community law does not give sufficient regard to the educational and financial interests of Member States. Some Member States 'import' more students than they 'export'. The

---

* University of Maastricht.

[1] For recent overviews, see eg G Gori, *Towards an EU Right to Education* (Kluwer Law International, 2001) Part II; A P van der Mei, *Free Movement of Persons within the European Community—Cross-Border Access to Public Benefits* (Hart Publishing, 2003) Ch 5.

[2] See the Commission's *Green Paper on Education, Training and Research: The Obstacles to Transnational Mobility*, Suppl Bull EU 5/96. For a discussion of this Green Paper, see M Verbruggen, 'The Commission's Green Paper "Education, Training and Research: The Obstacles to Transnational Mobility"' (1997) 1 *European Journal for Education Law and Policy* 41.

imbalances in student movements would constitute a significant burden on the resources of some Member States for which they should be compensated.[3]

The question arises where to go from here. Should future activities be focused on further promoting student mobility, or should emphasis be placed on the protection of the educational and financial interests of Member States who receive more students than they 'send' abroad? Or, ideally, is it possible to combine both efforts? Given the fact that some educational systems have a stronger magnetic effect on students than others, is it possible to increase student mobility while giving full respect to the educational interests of the Member States? In this chapter, an attempt will be made to answer such questions and to explore whether the current legal framework can be interpreted or altered so as to achieve a more satisfactory compromise between the goal of promoting student mobility and the need to protect national educational systems.

II FREE MOVEMENT OF STUDENTS VERSUS THE PROTECTION OF EDUCATIONAL SYSTEMS

To answer the above stated questions, it is useful to ignore for a moment concrete legal issues involved in cross-border access to education and to approach the potential conflict between promoting free movement and safeguarding national educational interests from a political-economic perspective. Theories on fiscal federalism in particular may be of help.[4]

One of the commonly cited advantages of federal or multilevel systems of government is that they allow for a decentralised supply of public benefits. Decentralisation enables federal entities to respond to the different preferences which citizens in the various States, or other local governmental entities, may have for public benefits. In every State, citizen-voters can make collective choices as to what public benefits will be made available, what their quality should be, how public benefit systems must be organised and how much taxes have to be paid in order to finance them. The advantages of decentralisation are particularly relevant for the organisation of education in a legal-political entity like the European Community where the financial means available for, and the views on how to organise, education differ so considerably.

---

[3]   Eg S O'Leary, *The Evolving Concept of Community Citizenship—From the Free Movement of Persons to Union Citizenship* (Kluwer Law International, 1996) p 171.

[4]   On theories on the economics of federalism (or fiscal federalism) see, eg D Hyman, *Public Finance—A Contemporary Application of Theory to Policy* (Thomson Learning, 1998) Ch 18; H Rosen, *Public Finance* (Irwin, 1985) Ch 19; J F Due and A F Friedländer, *Government Finance* (Irwin, 1977) pp 456 *et seq*; R Musgrave and P Musgrave, *Public Finance in Theory and Practice* (McGraw Hill, 1976); W Oates, *Fiscal Federalism* (Harcourt Brace Jovanovich, 1972).

Fiscal federalism theories start from the presumption that freedom of movement among local government entities is fully guaranteed. On the one hand, freedom of movement is positively valued. According to the so-called Tiebout hypothesis, the right to move elsewhere enables individuals 'to vote on their feet'.[5] Individuals who prefer public benefits such as public education of a comparatively high quality, and who are willing to pay the price in the form of comparatively high taxes, are able to move to a State where such a pattern has been selected. Others who are not willing to pay such a price may move to States where the quality of public education and taxes are lower.

On the other hand, the theories warn of the possible negative implications for the right to freedom of movement. Cross-border mobility may be a threat to the efficient supply of public benefits such as education. The social benefits of the States' investments in education may spill over to other States. Upon graduation, students may decide to work in other States and use their knowledge and skills in, and to the benefit of the economies of, other States. A full freedom of movement may even enable students to move to other States for the sole purpose of receiving education and then to leave the State once they have finished their studies. Such 'free-riding students' are fully taxable in the States of their studies neither before nor after their studies and the economies of the States concerned do not benefit from the investment made in educating these students. Fiscal federalism theories teach that public benefits can only be efficiently provided for at local level if the persons who make the collective choices are also the ones who finance and consume the benefits.[6] In the area of education, the group of consumers (the students) will often not coincide with the group of contributors (the taxpayers). In the case of free-riding students, the necessary coincidence of consumers and contributors may even be virtually absent.

Spill-over effects, or negative externalities, could possibly trigger a 'race to the bottom'. Consider the following model. State A is grouped together with several other States in federal entity X. State A has to make a decision as to the nature and quality of its educational system. If State A were to opt for high quality, and thus rather expensive, education, it would have to levy high taxes. If it were to do so, State A might attract students from other States seeking high quality education. The more 'free-riding' students who come from other States, the greater the pressure on the funding of the educational system. Should the net-inflow of non-contributing benefit recipients prove to be considerable, State A might have to choose either to decrease its investment in education or to increase its tax rates. If State A

---

[5]   C Tiebout, 'A Pure Theory of Local Expenditures' (1956) 64 *Journal of Political Economy* 416.

[6]   Ideally, there should be a 'triple identity' of 'voters', 'contributors' and 'consumers'. See J-C Scholsem, 'A Propos de la Circulation des Étudiants: Vers un Fédéralisme Financier Européen?' [1989] *Cahiers de Droit européen* 306, 309–10.

were to choose the latter option, taxpaying citizens might move to other States, leading to a reduction in tax revenues. In order to avoid such a situation, State A might decide in advance not to spend too much on education in the hope that 'free-riding' students from other States will move to State B. If State A did indeed choose to do so, it would indirectly increase the magnetic effect of the educational system of State B. This State would be faced with problems comparable to those which State A initially encountered and State B might decide to lower educational investment to reach a level lower than that of State C in the hope that free-riders would move to C. State C might respond similarly and try to shift the burden to State D. The fear of becoming an educational magnet could trigger competition between States lowering investment in education in the hope that other States will educate students. This competition may result in a downward movement, 'a race to the bottom', leading to a decrease in educational investment in the entire federal entity X.

Fiscal federalism theories teach us that when negative external effects occur, measures have to be taken to internalise these effects. The question needs to be addressed first, however, whether there is actually a need to take such measures within the European Community. The 'race to the bottom' hypothesis is based on a number of assumptions, some of which do not necessarily hold true in practice and in European practice in particular.

An initial assumption is that students are mobile and that they move to the States where the best, and often the most expensive education, is offered. European students, however, do not seem as mobile as free-riders in the above described model. Mobility is severely restricted by linguistic barriers, problems concerning the recognition of diplomas and the lack of sufficient student financial aid. Also, the quality of educational systems does not seem to be the main criterion which European students apply when choosing the State in which they study. Practice demonstrates that the main criterion European students apply is knowledge of the language of the State concerned or in which the courses are taught,[7] and this explains why the big language countries especially (the United Kingdom, France and, to a lesser extent, Belgium) are faced with a net import of students.[8]

---

[7]   See House of Lords Select Committee on European Communities, *27th Report on Student Mobility in the European Community* (1989), para 84 (Professor Teichler); J Gordon and J-P Jallade, 'Spontaneous Student Mobility in the European Union: A Statistical Survey' (1996) 31 *European Journal of Education* 133, 137.

[8]   In fact, it could be argued that the problems that the former countries are confronted with are not caused by student mobility but rather by 'student immobility'. In the United Kingdom, for instance, it has been recognised that the imbalance in students movements, and the resulting financial burden, is not only caused by the number of foreign students attending British universities but also, if not primarily, by the small number of British students studying at foreign universities. In principle, foreign students are 'more than welcome' in the United Kingdom. Financial and educational problems do not necessarily have to be dealt with by discouraging foreign students or asking for some kind of compensation. They could just as well be tackled by encouraging more British students to study abroad. Compare the discussion (on *Erasmus* students) in House of Lords Select Committee on

The second assumption of the above model of a race to the bottom is that Member States actually limit investment in education in order to avoid becoming educational magnets. This assumption neither seems to hold true. Decisions concerning the quality of and investment in education are not primarily, or at least not solely, made on the basis of student mobility figures. There are no indications that the United Kingdom, France or any other Member State have ever raised, or will raise, taxes or reduce educational investment in direct response to an influx of foreign students. Generally, Member States attach great importance to, and often take pride in, making available high quality education; and public schools and universities are important providers of employment, which play a significant economic role in the communities in which where they are established.[9]

A third assumption is that taxpayers might leave a State if, due to an expected increase in educational costs caused by an influx of foreign students, tax rates were actually raised. Statistics and scientific evidence to support this point do not seem to be available, but it is doubtful whether individuals or companies will leave the Member State in which they reside or are established when they have to pay more taxes in order to maintain the quality of education. For many taxpayers, high quality education, from which they themselves can also benefit, would seem to be one of those public benefits to which they are willing to contribute by paying taxes. The reverse might even be the case. Even if this were to lead to a higher tax-burden, companies might move to States with comparatively well-developed educational systems because they may need highly educated employees.

The significance of the above model for the European Community thus seems rather limited. European students are not as mobile as the Tiebout-hypothesis assumes and even if student mobility was to increase in future years, an educational race to the bottom is unlikely to occur. In principle, there seem to be no compelling reasons why one should not consider how student mobility could be further promoted. The next section will discuss several options. Nonetheless, the relevance of fiscal federalism theories cannot be dismissed altogether. Applied to the European Community, the above described model may be seen as a warning that one cannot wholly ignore the position of States which are 'net importers' of students while promoting student mobility. A mismatch between 'contributors' to and 'beneficiaries' of educational systems may cause funding or capacity problems for some States, which may occur or increase when initiatives

---

European Communities, *27th Report on Student Mobility in the European Community* (1989), paras 64–96; J Gordon and J-P Jallade, 'Spontaneous Student Mobility in the European Union: A Statistical Survey' (1996) 31 *European Journal of Education* 133.

[9] Compare P von Wilmowsky, 'Zugang zu den öffentlichen Leistungen anderer Mitgliedstaaten der EG' (1990) 50 *Zeitschrift für ausländisches und öffentliches Recht und Völkerrecht* 231, 265–66.

for promoting student mobility prove to be successful. In the subsequent section, therefore, we will offer some observations as to how the interests of these States could be safeguarded.

III OPTIONS FOR PROMOTING
FURTHER STUDENT MOBILITY

Union citizens who wish to study in other Member States outside the framework of the *Socrates/Erasmus* programme still face a number of obstacles. This Section explores how two of these obstacles could be lowered or eliminated. The aim, however, is modest. This Section merely addresses the question whether and, if so, how the current legal framework could possibly be interpreted or adjusted with a view to promoting student mobility. For this reason, no attempt will be made to explore how linguistic obstacles to such mobility can be combated. Being intrinsically linked with the substance of education, which the Community must respect,[10] the linguistic thresholds are preferably worked on by encouraging voluntary action by Member States within the current legal framework governing free movement of students. Indeed, this is what is happening in practice. Within the context of established programmes such as *Erasmus*, *Comenius* and *Grundtvig*, the Community seeks to increase the knowledge of languages in which foreign courses are taught. In addition, this section will not discuss the various issues involved in diploma recognition. At present, the main activities currently take place within the context of the so-called 'Bologna Process', which seeks to harmonise the structures of the national systems of higher education with a view to promoting the transparency of diplomas and free student mobility in the 'European Higher Education Area'.[11] To avoid the bureaucracy and slowness of 'Brussels',[12] however, the States participating in this process have decided to operate outside the Community's institutional framework. As a result, this Section is limited to the obstacles concerning lack of sufficient student financial aid and problems relating to students' right to reside in the host State.

A Student Financial Aid

Community law, as it stands now, confers upon Union citizens who wish to study in other Member States outside the framework of the *Socrates/Erasmus*

---

[10] Arts 149(1) and 150(1) EC.
[11] See further I Berggreen-Merkel, 'Towards a European Educational Area' (1999) 3 *European Journal for Education Law and Policy* 1.
[12] *Le Monde* (24/25 May 1997) p 7.

program only a limited right to student grants. In the host State, students are only entitled to equal treatment as regards grants in as far as these cover the cost of registration and tuition. As the Court of Justice held in *Lair* and *Brown,* grants given to students for maintenance are matters of educational and social policy falling within the competence of the Member States and, thus, outside the scope Community law and the non-discrimination principle.[13] In principle, the cost of maintenance must be borne by the students themselves or their parents and this may, for students from low-income families in particular, imply that they will be unable to study abroad. To make studying abroad a genuine opportunity for all European students, it is thus significant to explore whether Community law can be interpreted as to include or be altered as to confer upon students a right to claim maintenance grants.

In doing so, two options could be considered.[14] The first would be to offer students a right to maintenance grants in the host State. Recent caselaw provides some arguments in support of this option. The judgments in *Martínez Sala* and *Grzelczyk* demonstrate that the Court no longer adheres to the view, previously expressed in *Lair* and *Brown,* that social or educational benefits such as maintenance grants fall outside the scope of the non-discrimination principle just because they derive from policy areas falling within the Member States' domain. More specifically, from *Martínez Sala* it follows that the right to equal treatment in relation to 'social advantages',[15] encompassing, *inter alia,* maintenance grants,[16] is no longer reserved for workers covered by Article 39 EC but applicable to all Union citizens lawfully residing in the territory of another Member State.[17] In *Grzelczyk,* the Court went one step further by indicating that the mere exercise of free movement rights guaranteed by Community is sufficient to bring a person or situation within the scope of Community law, without there being a need to specifically consider whether the benefit applied for falls within that scope.[18] *Martínez Sala* and *Grzelczyk* strongly suggest that the scope of Union citizens' right to equal treatment in other Member States is, in principle,

---

[13] Case C–39/86 *Lair* [1988] ECR 3161, para 24; Case 197/87 *Brown* [1988] ECR 3205, para 25.

[14] A third option that could possibly be considered is whether the Community itself could offer free-movers maintenance grants. For instance, one could explore whether 'Action 2' of the *Socrates/Erasmus* programme, making available grants for students who spent part of their studies in the home State in another Member State, could be extended to 'free-movers'. Alternatively, a common student financial aid scheme taking the form of a loan scheme could be considered. Given the financial and administrative implications, however, it would seem that the chances of having such proposals adopted are quite small.

[15] Art 7(2) Reg 1612/68 on freedom of movement for workers within the Community, 1968 OJ L257/2.

[16] Case 39/86 *Lair* [1988] ECR 3161, paras 21–22.

[17] Case C–85/96 *Martínez Sala* [1998] ECR I–2691, para 57.

[18] Case C–184/99 *Grzelczyk* [2001] ECR I–6193, para 33.

unlimited, which for students indeed seems to imply that they now enjoy in the host State equality of treatment in relation to maintenance grants.[19]

The practical significance of this conclusion, however, is rather limited. It does not necessarily imply that students can now actually claim maintenance grants in the host State. It merely implies that they cannot be refused such grants for reason of their nationality. Arguably, however, national rules that make entitlement to maintenance grants conditional upon residence or habitual residence and, in principle, deny residence status to students who, during the year (or other fixed period) immediately preceding commencement of their studies, did not live on the national territory, are necessary for, and proportional to, the aim of maintaining the financial stability of student grants schemes. Students who do not meet this residence requirement are likely to be 'free-riders'. Neither they nor their parents are likely to have contributed to the financing of education by making tax payments prior to their studies and they are likely to leave the host State upon graduation. In light of the huge differences between the Member States' student financial aid schemes, recognition of a right to maintenance grants for such 'educational tourists' might jeopardise the schemes of the most generous States. Indeed, that was the central message of *Lair* and *Brown* and, as innovative as the judgments may have been, *Martínez Sala* and *Grzelczyk* do not imply that the Court has altered its view on this point.

Until their graduation, students should, in principle, still be seen as members of the State where they lived prior to studying and to which they will often return upon completion of their studies. It is in that State that students (or their parents) will have contributed to the financing of education and grant schemes; and it is that State which in many cases will benefit from the skills and knowledge students have acquired during their training. It would thus seem preferable to impose the burden of providing students with financial aid on this State. In other words, it makes most sense to promote

---

[19] To be sure, no certainty exists on this point. Art 3 Dir 93/96 on the right of residence for students, 1993 OJ L317/59 explicitly provides that students have no right to maintenance grants in the host State. Compare AG Geelhoed in Case C–413/01 *Ninni-Orasche* [2003] ECR I–0000. Arguably, however, this provision does not compel the conclusion that students cannot rely on Art 12 EC to claim equality of treatment in relation to maintenance grants. First, Art 12(1) EC is drafted in clear and unconditional terms not leaving any room, as the free movement provision in Art 18(1) EC does, for conditions or limitations to be imposed or exceptions to be applied. It is thus, at the least, questionable whether a provision of a directive can deprive Union citizens of a right directly following from Art 12(1) EC. Second, the suggested conclusion would imply that Member States are entitled to make a direct distinction among nationals and non-national students who have moved from abroad to study at their educational institutions. Such a conclusion, however, is fully at odds with the notion of Union citizenship, which 'is destined to be the fundamental status of nationals of the Member States, enabling those who find themselves in the same situation to enjoy the same treatment in law irrespective of nationality' (Case C–184/99 *Grzelczyk* [2001] ECR I–6193, paras 30–31). Finally, in order to safeguard the financing of student grant schemes nationality requirements are not indispensable. Requirements of habitual residence or domicile suffice. Nationality is not a common, and in principle even prohibited, criterion for levying taxes and it is hard to understand why they would be needed to maintain benefit schemes.

student mobility by exploring whether Community law can be construed as to entitle students to export maintenance grants.[20]

Recent caselaw leaves room for the suggestion that Community law is indeed heading towards recognition of such a right to export grants. First, from the rulings in *Di Leo*,[21] *Bernini*[22] and *Meeusen*,[23] it follows that, if Member States decide to award their own national students grants for studies in other (Member) States, they must offer the same grants under the same conditions to children of nationals of other Member States working on their territory. The three rulings mentioned all involved direct discrimination on grounds of nationality, and did not in principle oblige Member States to make grants exportable. Yet, for linguistic or cultural reasons, non-nationals are likely to be more interested in studying abroad, in their State of origin in particular, and it would thus seem that national rules limiting the portability of grants affect non-nationals more than nationals. In other words, in the absence of justification, such rules would seem to constitute prohibited indirect discrimination on grounds of nationality.[24] Second, in recent years the Court has increasingly recognised that, in the absence of compelling justification, Community law also objects to nationality-neutral rules that are likely to hamper freedom of movement. In particular, national rules denying rights or benefits to citizens because they have exercised their free movement rights are at odds with Community law.[25] Union citizens, regardless of their nationality or the State in which they habitually reside, could thus claim that rules or decisions of the authorities in the State of their residence denying them export of student grants constitute unlawful impediments of their right to move abroad for study purposes.

What, then, could possibly justify restrictions on the portability of maintenance grants? The answer that living costs in other Member States may be higher than at home is not persuasive. Nothing would seem to prevent a Member State from limiting the amount of grants up to the maximum offered to students studying on the national territory.[26] The argument that the proper planning and the infrastructure of educational systems would be affected is not convincing either. At a time when educational

---

[20] See further A P van der Mei, 'Freedom of Movement and Financial Aid for Students: Some Reflections on *Grzelczyk* and *Fahmi and Esmoris-Cerdeiro Pinedo Amoris*' (2001) 3 *European Journal of Social Security* 181.

[21] Case C–308/89 *di Leo* [1990] ECR I–4185.

[22] Case C–3/90 *Bernini* [1992] ECR I–1071, para 28.

[23] Case C–337/97 *Meeusen* [1999] ECR I–3289.

[24] Cf AG Alber in Case C–33/99 *Fahmi* [2001] ECR I–2415, para 79 Opinion.

[25] In Case C–224/98 *D'Hoop* [2002] ECR I–6191, for example, the Court held that 'it would be incompatible with the right to freedom of movement', if a Union citizen, in the Member State of which he is a national, were to receive treatment 'less favourable than he would enjoy if he had not exercised the free movement rights guaranteed by Community law' (paras 29–35). See also Case C–18/95 *Terhoeve* [1999] ECR 1999 I–345, para 37; Case C–28/00 *Kauer* [2002] ECR I–1343, para 44.

[26] Cf Case C–237/94 *O'Flynn* [1996] ECR I–2617, paras 28–29 and Case C–158/96 *Kohll* [1998] ECR I–1931, para 42.

funding is increasingly put under pressure and where classrooms and lecture rooms are increasingly overcrowded, it is hard to understand how a possible increase in the number of students going abroad could affect the quality of the educational systems of the Member States in question.

At first glance, a more compelling objection to the portability of grants involves the quality of the education for which a grant is awarded. In *Fahmi*, Advocate General Alber argued that student grants primarily aim to enable students to qualify for certain professions and that, for this reason, it would be legitimate only to finance studies that meet certain quality norms. More specifically, the Advocate General was of the view that students should only have the right to export grants when the diploma they receive upon completion of a study abroad entitles them, upon return to their State of origin, to be admitted to professions in that State.[27] In *D'Hoop,* in which the Court was asked whether Belgium could refuse entitlement to special unemployment benefits and programmes for young work-seekers meant to facilitate the transition from education to employment to a Belgian university graduate on the ground that she had completed her secondary education in another Member States, the Court seemed sympathetic to this argument. Although the Court denied that Belgium could refuse the benefits on the stated ground, it held that it is legitimate for national authorities to ensure that there is a real link between applicants for such allowances and programmes and the national geographical market.

Is there a 'real link' between student grants and national labour markets? Arguably, the answer should be in the negative. There indeed does seem to be such a real, direct, link between employment benefits and programmes and national labour markets where beneficiaries have already decided they wish to work in that market. Yet, in a Community where young European citizens can study in the Member State of their choice and, upon graduation, choose the State in which they wish to work, it is hard to see a real link between grants and a specific national labour market. Rather, in a Community where freedom of movement for both students and workers is guaranteed, it would seem that Member States (should) have no power to indirectly force students to come home after graduation by limiting the portability of grants or other forms of financial aid.[28]

---

[27] AG Alber in Case C–33/99 *Fahmi* [2001] ECR I–2415, paras 80–87 Opinion.

[28] It could be objected that Community law can or should not demand that Member States indirectly invest in the labour market of other Member States. The objection, however, is unpersuasive. First, Member States have agreed to promote the professional recognition of diplomas and in this context never made issue of the fact that such recognition may incite students educated at their educational systems to work, and to use their skills and knowledge, in other Member States. Second, the Advocate General's view that grants primarily aim to enable students to qualify for certain professions is contestable. Student grant schemes are not in first place instruments of labour market policy; rather, they are first and foremost instruments of educational policy developed to make education accessible for the financially less strong members of society.

To summarise, a right to maintenance grants could significantly contribute to student mobility. The burden of providing students with financial aid should not be imposed on the host State but, in the absence of compelling objections,[29] on the State where students resided prior to their studies by entitling each student to export maintenance grants from this State.

B Conditions for Exercising the Right to Reside

The second obstacle to mobility to be addressed here concerns the conditions that students have to fulfil for exercising their right to reside in the host State. According to Directive 93/96, students must have sufficient health insurance and they have to make it plausible that they will not become a burden on the host State's social assistance scheme.[30] In 1992, in *Raulin*, the Court accepted the legality of these two requirements, reasoning that, as a corollary of the right to non-discriminatory access to education, the right of residence is confined to what is necessary to allow the student to study in other Member States.[31] Consequently, the right may be limited to the duration of their studies and be made subject to conditions deriving from the legitimate interests of the host Member State 'such as the covering of maintenance cost and health insurance' to which the principle of non-discrimination was said not to apply.[32]

In light of recent caselaw, however, it is doubtful whether the reasoning followed in *Raulin* can still be adhered to. First, as stated before, in *Martínez Sala* and *Grzelczyk* the Court seems to have moved away from the proposition that the non-discrimination principle does not apply to certain benefits such as maintenance grants.[33] Secondly, as the *Grzelczyk* and *Baumbast* rulings show, it no longer suffices for Member States that wish

---

[29] Furthermore, it may be pointed out many Member States offer financial aid for students indirectly, in the form of family benefits payable to the parents and that, by virtue of Reg 1408/71 on the application of social security schemes to employed persons and their families moving within the Community (last consolidated version published at 1997 OJ L28/1), such benefits cannot be denied on the ground that children are living and studying in another Member State. If family benefits can be exported, why should student grants not be exportable? Consider the Dutch legislation. Until 1986 the Netherlands offered financial aid for students in the form of child allowances, which were payable also to parents whose children were living and studying abroad. In 1986, however, the right to child allowances was replaced by a right to student grants, which, in principle, were reserved for students attending Dutch schools and universities recognised by the Dutch Minister for Education. The main justifications offered for imposing this restriction were that that the Dutch Minister lacked powers to impose conditions regarding the quality of education in other Member States and that the number and variety of educational courses in the Netherlands were deemed sufficient. The first justification, as has been argued above, is unpersuasive and the second, being so plainly at odds with the notion of a free movement of students, is simply to be dismissed altogether.

[30] Dir 93/96 on the right of residence for students, 1993 OJ L317/59

[31] Case C–357/89 *Raulin* [1992] ECR I–1027, para 39.

[32] *Ibid.*

[33] See nn 17–19 above and accompanying text.

to impose limitations on the right of residence of the economically inactive to just refer to the text of and the conditions laid down in the 1990 residence directives.[34] In *Grzelczyk*, the Court concluded that the mere fact that a student is in need of social assistance, and thus no longer meets the financial means requirement, cannot constitute an automatic ground for withdrawing his residence permit or refusing to renew it.[35] Such measures, the Court held, can only be taken if a student or other Union citizen were to become an 'unreasonable' burden on public finances, reasoning that the 1990 residence directives embody a degree of solidarity between Union citizens.[36] In *Baumbast*, which involved a German national who was refused residence in the United Kingdom on the ground that he was insured for medical in Germany and not in the United Kingdom, the Court held that Member States when applying the health insurance and financial means requirements laid down in Directive 90/364 on the right of residence, must observe the general principles of EC law, including in particular the principle of proportionality.[37] Thus, *Grzelczyk* and *Baumbast* teach us that restrictions on the right to reside of students (and other economically inactive Union citizens) are only permitted when necessary for, and proportional to, the goal of safeguarding the host States' public finances.[38]

For students, this could have implications for, in particular, the financial means requirement.[39] As *Grzelczyk* indicates, the requirement is meant to avoid students becoming an 'unreasonable' burden on the public finances

---

[34] Besides Dir 93/96 on the right of residence for students, 1993 OJ L317/59, also: Dir 90/364 on the right of residence, 1990 OJ L180/26; Dir 90/365 on the right of residence for employees and self-employed persons who have ceased their occupational activity, 1990 OJ L180/28.

[35] Case C-184/99 *Grzelczyk* [2001] ECR I-6193, para 42.

[36] *Ibid*, para 44.

[37] Case C-413/99 *Baumbast* [2002] ECR I-7091, paras 89-93.

[38] A P van der Mei, 'Residence and the Evolving Concept of European Union Citizenship' (2003) 5 *European Journal of Migration and Law* 117.

[39] The argument does not apply to the health insurance requirement to be met by students. In light of the common practice in the Member States that the uninsured or the insufficiently insured are generally offered cover when medically necessary, it is in principle justified to require from students that they are sufficiently insured. The proportionality principle, however, could be relevant for the interpretation and application of the health insurance requirement. First, Dir 93/96 does not specify what type of insurance is required or where beneficiaries must be insured. From the preamble to Dir 93/96, it merely follows that beneficiaries must not become an unreasonable burden on the public finances of the host Member State. Consequently, one may safely assume that both private and public health insurance may suffice and that it, in principle, is not required that the insurer or sickness fund is based in the host State. Second, one could question whether students must, as Dir 93/96 states, actually be insured for 'all risks in the host State'. Taken literally, the requirement could be interpreted to mean that students must also be insured for dental care, physiotherapy, plastic surgery or other types of benefits that the host Member States may have excluded from their own health insurance legislation. The mere fact, however, that Member States have decided to exclude certain medical benefits and to demand from patients to pay, or to insure themselves additionally, for such benefits already suggests that no unreasonable financial burden is expected. In light of the duty to respect the proportionality principle, it could thus be argued that the health insurance requirement is satisfied when beneficiaries are insured for the same risks covered by the host State's legislation on public health insurance.

of the host State and is only enforceable in such cases. In principle, this would only be the case when students have a right to receive in that State tax-funded social assistance benefits or maintenance grants. As a rule, however, students have no such right in the host State. Admittedly, in *Grzelczyk* the Court accepted that students may have a right to social assistance and thus may become a burden on public finances. Yet this only seems to be the case in where students are temporarily in financial difficulties.[40] It is only in such cases or circumstances that Directive 93/96 embodies a financial solidarity among Union citizens, and it seems only then that the Court will not regard the burden of students to be 'unreasonable'. In other situations, however, students will have no right to claim maintenance grants or social assistance in the host State. The starting point must be that beneficiaries should be able to claim such benefits in one Member State only. They should have no right to 'double their income'; overlap of entitlement to benefits needs to be avoided.

For students, this implies that a choice must be made between the Member State where they study and the State where they resided prior to commencement of their studies. Recalling what has been said in previous sections of this contribution, it simply does not seem desirable to confer upon students a right to social assistance or maintenance grants in the host State. Students must be presumed to be free-riders moving for the sole purpose of receiving benefits financed by others. A right to claim tax-funded minimum subsistence benefits such as social assistance and maintenance grants should only exist in the State of habitual residence,[41] which, for the purposes of legislation governing such benefits, is not the host State but in principle the State where students lived prior to studying. It follows that students cannot become an 'unreasonable' burden on the public finances of the host State. Why, then, should they have to submit documentation about their financial resources to make it plausible that they will not become such an unreasonable burden? Abolition or invalidation of the financial means requirement is not likely to have many, if any, financial implications for the host State.[42] The opposite is even more likely to be true. The administrative costs of enforcing the requirement could be saved. *Raulin* still stands, but it

---

[40] See n 35 above, para 44.

[41] Cf A P van der Mei, 'Regulation 1408/71 and the Co-ordination of Special Non-Contributory Benefit Schemes' (2002) 27 *European Law Review* 551.

[42] Indeed, there are no signs that students have, or will, become a burden on the social assistance schemes of host States. In a report to the Parliament and Council on the implementation of the 1990 residence directives, the Commission stated that it had asked the Member States how many students had become a burden on their social assistance schemes since the implementation of the directives and what steps had been taken in response. None of the Member States provided any data. This may not come as a real surprise. As a rule, students will not be able to claim benefits because they may not be able to meet substantive criteria for benefit entitlement such as being obliged to look for and accept (full-time) work. Compare also AG Ruiz-Jarabo Colomer in Case C–424/98 *Commission v Italy* [2000] ECR I–4001, para 28 Opinion. Admittedly, the above does not necessarily imply that no students have obtained social assistance benefits, but the States' responses do strongly suggest that the issue does not have much practical relevance.

is submitted that the duty imposed on students to persuade immigration authorities that they will not become an unreasonable public burden constitutes an unnecessary impediment to their Community right to study in other Member States. The financial means requirement laid down in Directive 93/96 should be abolished.[43]

IV OPTIONS FOR PROTECTING THE EDUCATIONAL INTERESTS OF MEMBER STATES

As stated above, student mobility is unlikely to trigger an educational 'race to the bottom' within the Community. Arguments for promoting further student mobility are more persuasive than calls for compensating or protective measures for the Member States that are net importers of students. Nonetheless, the problems that these States may face cannot be wholly ignored. An increase in student mobility could increase the imbalances in student movement, and this may cause financial or capacity problems for Member States facing a net influx of students. How can the interests of the net importers of students possibly be protected?

A Reimbursement Mechanisms

In response to concerns about the imbalances in student movement and the unequal financial burdens imposed on some Member States, it has been suggested that student mobility could be better promoted by requiring Member States to pay the true economic cost of the education which their nationals and/or residents receive abroad.[44] Such reimbursement systems have been expected to produce the dual effect of encouraging governments to improve the quality of their educational courses as an element of educational 'competition', while guaranteeing the quality of national education by not subjecting it to an open-ended and undetermined influx of foreign students.[45]

---

[43] Though it was, in fact, retained by Council and Parliament in Dir 2004/38 on the right of citizens and their family members to move and reside freely within the territory of the Member States, 2004 OJ L158/77.

[44] S O'Leary, *The Evolving Concept of Community Citizenship—From the Free Movement of Persons to Union Citizenship* (Kluwer Law International, 1996) pp 189–90; R Kampf, 'La Directive 90/366/CEE relative au Droit de Séjour des Étudiants communautaires: Sa Transposition en France' [1992] *Revue du Marché Commune* 307, 317; J-C Scholsem, 'A Propos de la Circulation des Étudiants: Vers un Fédéralisme Financier Européen?' [1989] *Cahiers de Droit européen* 306, 318.

[45] S O'Leary, *The Evolving Concept of Community Citizenship—From the Free Movement of Persons to Union Citizenship* (Kluwer Law International, 1996) pp 189–90. In developing such a scheme, one might draw inspiration from reimbursement scheme comparable to the one established by Regs 1408/71 and 574/72 for cross-border healthcare rights. In the words of AG Slynn in Case 263/886 *Humbel* [1988] ECR 5365, 5380: 'The analogy with health care is striking since, although Community nationals by and large are entitled to medical care throughout the Community, that entitlement is underpinned by a complex system designed to determine which State should ultimately bear the cost of treatment. It is to my mind unfor-

Reimbursement schemes seem to be an appealing option. They take into consideration the fact that student movement within the Community is not in balance and they relieve the net importers of students of the unequal financial burden they bear by imposing this burden on the States where taxes have been paid by the students (or their parents) and where they may (or are likely) to return to upon graduation. Nonetheless, the feasibility and, arguably desirability, of reimbursement mechanisms scheme is questionable. The core problem is that such schemes compel States to repay the costs incurred by other Member States. States are required to invest in the educational systems of other States. Since students may move to States with more expensive educational systems, such reimbursement mechanisms would imply that the 'poorer' Member States are required to reimburse the 'richer' Member States. The educational expenses of the poorer States would increase, and it is likely that these States would prefer to invest in the development of their own educational systems.[46] In the alternative, one could consider setting up a fund at Community level out of which the 'net

tunate that no such system for education throughout the Community exists'. It must be pointed out, however, that precisely as regards patients who would move to other States for the sole purpose of obtaining medical care, Member States have always opposed a duty to reimburse. See further A P van der Mei, *Free Movement of Persons within the European Community—Cross-Border Access to Public Benefits* (Hart Publishing, 2003) Ch 5.

[46] The Nordic countries (Iceland, Norway, Sweden, Finland and Denmark) have been working on a repayment scheme but so far they have not been successful. In 1991 the 'Co-operation Programme for Higher Education in the Nordic Countries' was adopted in which the five States agreed to further promote student mobility and competition among educational institutions with a view to improving the quality of education. In 1994, an additional agreement on admission to higher education was signed in which Nordic students were not only granted several equal treatment rights, but in which the five States also indicated that the promotion of student mobility should be planned in gradual stages. Thus, on a temporary basis, quotas for Nordic students were envisaged and the Nordic States declared their intention to reach a mutual agreement on the settlement of the costs of education. More concretely, it was intended that the State of origin should bear the cost of the education which their 'free-moving students' who study outside *Nordplus*—the Nordic equivalent of the *Socrates/Erasmus* programme—receive in other Nordic countries. Even though the total cost involved did not seem exorbitant, it has appeared quite difficult to reach agreement on establishing a reimbursement scheme. It was intended that such a scheme would only be set up for a limited group of studies, but no agreement could be reached on the selection of these studies. In addition, States have been unable to agree on the possibility of student-sending countries limiting the number of students on behalf of whom they have to bear the educational costs. Partial reimbursement from a special Nordic fund has been considered as an alternative, but such a fund has not yet been set up. See further P Nyborg, 'International Student Mobility: The Nordic Experience' (1996) 31 *European Journal of Education* 193. When the Nordic States proved unable to reach agreement on such a scheme, then, in view of the much bigger differences in public expenditure on public education among the Community's Member States, one may seriously doubt whether a system in which the State of origin has to 'pay the educational bill' is viable. The possibility cannot even be excluded that a reimbursement system will act as a brake on mobility within the EU. The cost incurred by mobile students might encourage the 'poorer' Member States to 'keep their nationals at home': Baligant *et al*, 'Economic Analysis of Student Mobility on a European Scale' as quoted in P Nyborg, 'International Student Mobility: The Nordic Experience' (1996) 31 *European Journal of Education* 193, 202.

importing' States would be reimbursed. The chances of having such a fund approved by the Member States may be somewhat greater, but still seem to be minimal. In whatever way such a common reimbursement fund might be financed, it can probably only operate effectively if richer Member States were the net recipients and poorer States the net contributors. The latter, as one might expect and arguably should respect, would be unwilling to co-operate.

B Differential Tuition Policies

Another method for protecting the educational interests of the Member States, and the student net importing countries in particular, could consist of differential tuition policies, comparable to those applied by American States and State universities. Each of the American States requires from non-residents payment of additional tuition fees. The argument for doing so derives from fiscal federalism theories and runs as follows. Residents pay taxes to the State and thus contribute indirectly to the funding of public education. Since non-residents do not contribute equally, States require non-residents to pay their 'equal share' by charging them higher tuition fees. Differential tuition policies enable States to distribute the cost of operating and supporting educational institutions more evenly between resident and non-resident students.[47] This so-called cost-equalisation argument is not based on the contributions paid during the period of the studies. The economic status of resident and non-resident students is, during this period, more or less the same. The argument relates to the situation before and after the course of study. Prior to studying, non-resident students have not resided in the State, and they are more likely to leave after graduation. Neither they nor their parents have paid taxes to the State to the same degree as residents have; and more so than residents, non-residents are likely to use their education in other States. The higher tuition fees paid by non-residents compensate the States for the fact that they often do not receive the benefits of the investment they have made in educating non-residents.

In the United States, differential tuition fees have as such never been controversial. The US Supreme Court has accepted the constitutionality of differential tuition fees reasoning that 'a State has a legitimate interest in protecting and preserving the quality of its colleges and universities and the right of its bona fide residents to attend such institutions on a preferential tuition basis'.[48] Would the European Court of Justice approve of such a line of reasoning?

---

[47] Note, 'The Constitutionality of Nonresident Tuition' (1971) *Minnesota Law Review* 1139, 1147.

[48] *Vlandis v Kline*, 412 US 441 (1973) at 452.

To answer that question, it is first necessary to go back to the landmark judgment in *Gravier* in which the Court had to express its view on the legality of the Belgian *minerval*. This additional tuition fee was introduced for reasons comparable to those given by American States: foreign students had to compensate for the fact that their income was not taxable in Belgium. In *Gravier*, the Court did not address this 'taxpayer argument'; it simply concluded that the *minerval* constituted prohibited direct discrimination on grounds of nationality.[49] In his Opinion in *Gravier*, Advocate General Slynn thought there was 'force in the argument that it is not discriminatory to require those who do not contribute directly or indirectly to the common weal to make some contribution'.[50] In practice, such rules would primarily work to the detriment of nationals from other Member States and they may therefore constitute indirect discrimination on grounds of nationality. However, differential tuition fees could possibly escape the prohibition of discrimination where it can be demonstrated that they are necessary for, and proportional to, the legitimate financial and educational interests of the Member States. As regards Member States which are structurally faced with a net import of European students, and which set the non-resident tuition fees at such a rate as to cover the marginal cost of foreign students, it could indeed be argued that there is force in the 'taxpayers argument'. Whereas other alternatives, such as non-resident quotas, directly restrict or hinder admission to universities, differential tuition policies

---

[49] Case 293/83 *Gravier* [1985] ECR 293, para 36. The Court's silence on the 'taxpayer argument' has been understood to imply that the Court also rejected the *rationale* behind the *minerval* and that this, for practical reasons, would have been a correct decision for the Court. See, eg C Timmermans, Annotation of *Gravier* (in Dutch) (1986) *Sociaal-economische Wetgeving* 86. During their studies, foreign students pay indirect taxes and they or their parents may before or after their studies work and be taxed in the State concerned. Also, not all residents pay taxes, but they can nonetheless benefit fully from public education. Compare P von Wilmowsky, 'Zugang zu den öffentlichen Leistungen anderer Mitgliedstaaten der EG' (1990) 50 *Zeitschrift für ausländisches und öffentliches Recht und Völkerrecht* 231, 256. The relationship between the paying of taxes and the right to benefit from education funded out of the tax revenues would be too confusing to make a connection between the taxes paid and the rates for tuition. With respect, this interpretation of *Gravier* is not wholly persuasive. First, under Belgian legislation, Belgian (and Luxembourg) students did not have to pay the additional tuition fee. The law governing the *minerval* was partly based on nationality criteria and thus constituted direct discrimination on grounds of nationality. The question whether the Belgian rules could be justified was not, and did not have to be, addressed by the Court. Second, the above reading of the 'tax-payer-argument' does not seem based on a correct reproduction of the arguments for pursuing differential tuition policies. Neither the Belgian authorities (nor any of the American States) have ever claimed that the amount of tuition to be paid should be calculated on the basis of the taxes which have been, are or will be paid. In the logic behind differential tuition policies, there is no scope for non-resident students to prove that they have in the past paid 'more than enough' taxes. Such policies are not based on the principle of *juste retour*. As part of re-distributive policies, they are based rather on a notion of residence or membership. As a class, non-residents have not contributed to the funding of public education through the payment of taxes and, as a class, they cannot benefit from the lower tuition rate for residents.

[50] Opinion of AG Slynn in Case 293/83 *Gravier* [1985] ECR I–593, 604.

merely make admission more expensive. If States were to calculate non-resident tuition fees in such a way as to cover the total cost of education offered to non-resident students, student mobility would not impose additional pressure on their educational budget and they would possess the funds to cope with possible capacity problems. With non-residents completely paying their own way, Member States could spend whatever amount they wished to educate their own residents and accommodate non-residents at the same time.[51]

Nonetheless, differential tuition policies also have clear disadvantages. First, there exists the danger of selfish and excessive use. If States were to have the right to charge non-resident students higher tuition fees, they could set the fee at a rate which exceeds the marginal cost of the education offered to non-resident students. In theory, they could shift part of the burden of funding resident students onto non-resident students. Moreover, differential tuition policies would enable Member States to regulate or to control the admission of students from other Member States. Tuition fees for non-resident students could even be made so high that not a single student would consider studying in the Member State concerned. In other words, there is no guarantee that the power to charge higher tuition fees on non-resident students would not be excessively used or even abused. In the United States, no 'abuses' have been reported, but this does not mean that these could not occur in the European Community. Member States have no experience of differential tuition policies and, much more than the American States, they have always expressed concerns about the impact of student mobility on their systems of higher education. Differential tuition policies would seem to require some form of supervision as to how, when and to what extent the power to charge higher tuition fees to non-residents would be used. Who should be entrusted with that task? Given the judicial reluctance to second-guess economic choices, one may doubt whether courts in general, and the Court of Justice in particular, would be willing to perform that task.

Furthermore, differential tuition policies raise questions as to which students can be required to pay the additional tuition fee. What criterion should be applied? Nationality, as *Gravier* demonstrates, is a prohibited criterion. Current residence—the place or State where an individual effectively lives—is not an option either, since even free-riding students only moving for educational reasons and leaving upon graduation would meet this criterion whilst studying. Given the *rationale* behind differential tuition policies, the criterion of habitual residence—the place or the State where an individual's 'habitual centre of interests' is found[52]—would seem to constitute the most logical option. In the United States, application of this criterion has proved to be quite difficult. For tuition purposes, American States and

---

[51] Paraphrasing Note, 'The Constitutionality of Nonresident Tuition' (1971) *Minnesota Law Review* 1139, 1150–51.
[52] Cf Case C–90/97 *Swaddling* [1999] ECR I–1075, paras 29–30.

universities apply the criterion of bona fide residence or domicile, which has been defined as an individual's 'true, fixed and permanent home and place of habitation' and 'the place to which, whenever, he is absent, he has the intention of returning'.[53] This concept is quite difficult to apply in practice because the element distinguishing it from 'normal' residence involves the students' subjective intent, which is difficult to establish objectively. For practical reasons, American States therefore define bona fide residents as all students who prior to enrolment have not resided or been domiciled in the State for a minimum period of time (usually one year). Students who do not meet this criterion are, after one year, given the opportunity to rebut the presumption of non-residence.[54]

It is submitted that such a definition of bona fide or habitual residence would be incompatible with Community law. The problem is not so much that students who do not satisfy the requirement of one year of prior residence are presumed not to be habitual residents, but rather that they would only have the opportunity to rebut this presumption after one year. Applying the American definition to the European Community, would imply that workers, their family members, pensioners and other Union citizens moving for reasons other studying would, during the first year of their residence, all have to pay the additional tuition fee in order to gain admission to education. In the field of social assistance, the Court of Justice has condemned durational residence requirements;[55] and arguably it should do the same in the field of education. The *rationale* behind differential tuition fees does not apply to workers and the other categories just mentioned and there do not seem to be any sound reasons as to why these categories should have to wait for one year before being entitled to prove that they are not free-riding students but habitual residents.

The answer to the question whether students are free-riders or bona fide residents ultimately depends on their subjective intent and does not seem in any rational way related to the time at which students are given the opportunity to demonstrate their true intentions.[56] American-like definitions of

---

[53] *Vlandis v Kline*, 412 US 441 (1973) at 454.

[54] They can do so by submitting employment contracts, marriage certificates, evidence of registration as a voter of the State, registration of a car in the State, or any other means that they believe to be evidence of their 'domiciliary intent'.

[55] Case 249/83 *Hoeckx* [1985] ECR 982, paras 23–24; Case C–326/90 *Commission v Belgium* [1992] ECR I–5517, paras 2–3.

[56] The US Supreme Court has accepted States or university rules that only entitle students to rebut the presumption of non-residence after one year reasoning that States can establish 'reasonable criteria for in-state status as to make virtually certain that students who are not, in fact, bona fide residents of the State, but who have come there solely for the educational purposes, cannot take advantage of the in-state rates': *Vlandis v Kline*, 412 US 441 (1973) at 452–54. The Supreme Court, however, has never adequately explained why students have to wait for one year before they can provide evidence of being a bona fide residence. As I have argued elsewhere, this may come as no surprise simply because there do not seem to any sound reasons for this one year 'waiting-period': A P van der Mei, *Free Movement of Persons within the European Community—Cross-Border Access to Public Benefits* (Hart Publishing, 2003) section 8.4.

habitual residence would thus only seem to be compatible with Community law if students are given, upon registration, the opportunity to come up with proof that they have established the 'habitual centre of their interests' in the host State.

Furthermore, in light of the *rationale* behind differential tuition policies, it would seem that only those States that are confronted with a net import of students would be justified in imposing additional tuition fees on free-riding students. In the United States, however, all States impose, and are (according to the Supreme Court) indeed entitled to impose, non-resident tuition fees. However, such fees hamper freedom of movement for students and one could seriously question whether European Member States that may be regarded as net exporters can escape the prohibition of indirect discrimination on grounds of nationality and whether they ought to have the power to charge additional fees that seem in no way necessary to protect their educational systems. Logic would seem to require that only the net importers can possibly charge additional fees. Yet, how does one in practice determine whether a given Member State is a net importer or a net exporter? Should the possible power to impose additional fees be made conditional upon prior statistical proof of a net import of students?

Community law, as it stands at present, does not wholly exclude the possibility that, under certain conditions, differential tuition policies for resident students and free-riding students can pass judicial scrutiny. Yet, in practice, numerous questions are likely arise and one could question whether such policies would constitute an efficient and the most appropriate method for ensuring the financial and educational interests of the few Member States currently faced with a net influx of students.

C Quantitative Restrictions

A third option for protecting Member States' educational interests could be to allow Member States, and net importers of students in particular, to impose limits on the number of students they admit to their universities. At first glance, such quantitative restrictions do not seem to be desirable. They would seem to hamper student mobility far more than differential tuition policies do, and they may even be regarded as a *de facto* denial of the right to study in other Member States once the fixed number has been reached. Nonetheless, Community law does not necessarily object. The lawfulness of quotas would seem to depend on the criterion applied. Nationality criteria are prohibited, but the same does not seem to hold true for *numerus clausus* regulations limiting the number of student places on the basis of social need.

The question to be addressed here is whether Member States, with a view to protecting their educational interests, are permitted to adopt rules limiting the number of non-residents, that is, students who prior to the commencement of their studies resided in other Member States, who will be admitted to their universities. Such quantitative restrictions, albeit in exceptional circumstances, might escape the classification of a prohibited indirect discrimination on grounds of nationality where it can be proven that they are necessary for maintaining the quality and accessibility of educational systems. It does not seem wholly impossible that such evidence could be provided. A substantial influx of students from other Member States could have implications for the funding and infrastructure of educational systems. Such an influx could cause overcrowded lecture rooms, affect professor-student ratios or limit housing and other student-related facilities. States that decided to expand educational facilities might face problems of overcapacity if in subsequent years the number of enrolments was to drop. Such problems, which might affect the quality and/or funding of higher education, could be avoided if States were entitled to control and limit numbers of students.[57] Some form of preferential treatment of residents might be necessary for maintaining adequate educational systems.[58] It is submitted that Member States should be entitled to limit the number of non-residents that will be admitted to their education systems where they can prove that such measures are truly needed to guarantee a 'balanced educational system open to all',[59] or *de facto* force them to adopt measures which inflict upon their autonomy in the field of education.

V CONCLUSIONS

Lurking beneath many questions on cross-border access to education lies a potential conflict between, on the one hand, the goal to promote student mobility and, on the other hand, the need to protect national educational systems. The Community and Community law have so far not been able to reconcile these two interests in a wholly satisfactory manner. Students are still confronted with various obstacles and the burdens of student mobility are unequally divided among the Member States. In seeking a more satisfactory solution, it must be kept in mind that, given the Community's linguistic diversity, the conflict probably cannot be solved altogether. Also in future years, language is likely to be one of the criteria,

---

[57] Compare J Varat, 'State "Citizenship" and Interstate Equality' (1982) 48 *University of Chicago Law Review* 487, 553–54.

[58] For instance, many Dutch students have decided to study in Belgium. They were even encouraged to do so by the Dutch Minister of Education who allowed them to export student grants when they embarked on certain studies at Belgian universities for which *numerus clausus* regulations are applied in the Netherlands. As a result, in some Flemish faculties more than 50% of the students were Dutch. In such situations, would it not be desirable to allow Belgium or the Flemish community to impose certain limits on access of students from other Member States (including the Netherlands)?

[59] Cf Case C–158/96 *Kohll* [1998] ECR I–1931.

if not the main criterion, students apply when deciding where to study. For this reason, some Member States will probably remain more popular among students than other Member States. The quest for protective or compensating measures is, and will continue to be, expressed. It is submitted that that quest must be respected, by allowing Member States to impose quantitative restrictions on the number of non-residents to be admitted to their educational institutions when they can prove that such restrictions are necessary to guarantee a 'balanced educational system open to all'. Given that safeguard for the few net importers of students, there are no reasons as to why student mobility should not be further promoted. In combination with the activities currently undertaken in the context of the 'Bologna Process', recognition of a right to export student grants and abolition of the financial means requirement could facilitate student mobility and thus contribute to the 'European Higher Education Area'.

11

Inclusion and Exclusion of Persons and Benefits in the New Co-ordination Regulation

FRANS PENNINGS*

I INTRODUCTION

At the end of December 1998, the European Commission published a pro-posal[1] for a new co-ordination regulation that was meant to replace Regulation 1408/71.[2] The purpose of proposing a new regulation was twofold: to introduce a much shorter co-ordination instrument, and to modernise the existing co-ordination rules. The modernisation involved, in particular, the personal and material scope of Regulation 1408/71. Extension of both scopes was considered necessary as the present Regulation excludes considerable parts of the population and considerable parts of social security. During the process which followed the publication of the 1998 proposal, the Council and Parliament reached a consensus on a much more limited extension than that envisaged by the European Commission, which was eventually adopted as Regulation 883/2004 on the co-ordination of social security systems.[3] This chapter will study this reform process so as to clarify which categories of persons and benefits are still excluded from the co-ordination regime.

---

[*] Professor of International Social Security at Tilburg University and Utrecht University, the Netherlands.

[1] COM(1998) 779.

[2] Reg 1408/71 was published for the first time in 1971 OJ L149/2 and since then has been revised several times. A consolidated version of Reg 1408/71 and Reg 574/72 was published in 1997 OJ L28/1. For the website of the (non official, but most recent) consolidated version, see <http://europa.eu.int/eur-lex/en/consleg/pdf/1971/en_1971R1408_do_001.pdf>. On the Regulation, see F Pennings, *Introduction to European Social Security Law* 4th edn (Intersentia, 2003).

[3] 2004 OJ L200/1.

II THE REASONS FOR SIMPLIFICATION
AND MODERNISATION OF THE REGULATION AND
THE PROCEDURE WHICH WAS FOLLOWED

The objective of Regulation 1408/71 is to take away impediments in the area of social security in order to facilitate the free movement of workers and self-employed persons. The Regulation is based on Article 42 EC, which provides for both the obligation and the power to take measures which are 'necessary in the field of social security to provide freedom of movement for workers'. Apart from certain provisions in the field of non-discrimination,[4] Regulation 1408/71 is the only Community instrument that restricts the powers of the Member States to decide exclusively on main elements of their social security systems, including the latter's personal and territorial scope, and the distribution of the costs of benefits. It will not require much explanation to understand that Member States are aware of possible extra expenses for their country as a result of the Regulation and are therefore not very enthusiastic about extending its scope.

In comparison with the co-ordination instruments of other international organisations, such as the ILO,[5] Regulation 1408/71 has incomparably more impact: it is unique in that it contains rules binding all Member States. These rules have to be interpreted in the same way and, very importantly, interpretation problems are solved by the supranational Court of Justice, which gives binding judgments that are often very important for the development of social security co-ordination.

From a different perspective, one's assessment of Regulation 1408/71 can be more critical. In the course of time, the Regulation has been extended considerably by amending regulations. These amending regulations were often accepted only after long negotiations, sometimes taking even several years. Member States try to avoid and/or limit the costs resulting from changes to the Regulation; and for this reason, changes, if found necessary, often take the form of very complicated compromises—which often means new exceptions to the main rules. The result is usually difficult for migrant workers to understand. This may lead to uncertainty which can seriously infringe on the main objective of the Regulation: free movement of workers.

Moreover, there are gaps in the coverage of the present Regulation, such as the position of third country nationals, the non-working population and the exclusion of non-statutory social security. Although these gaps have been acknowledged for many years, there has been but very slow

---

[4] Such as Dir 79/7 on the progressive implementation of the principle of equal treatment for men and women in matters of social security, 1979 OJ L6/24.
[5] In particular: ILO Conventions Nos 48, 118 and 157.

progress in filling them. The 1998 Proposal for simplification and modernisation of the Regulation was a radical and comprehensive attempt to
extend the scope of the Regulation.[6] It was inspired by a series of conferences, addressing the problems with Regulation 1408/71, organised in all
Member States.[7]

It was a far from easy process to have a new regulation adopted. Article
42 EC requires unanimity of the Council in the decision making process. In
addition, the Council has to follow the co-decision procedure of Article 251
EC, which means that the European Parliament is involved. This made the
realisation of a new regulation problematic.

For a long time after the publication of the 1998 Proposal, little progress
was made and the fate of the Proposal did not look very favourable. In 2001,
however, an important development took place, since so-called 'parameters'
for the new regulation were worded. These were to serve as starting points,
based on general consensus, for drafting the new regulation.[8] After the
adoption of these parameters, progress was made. In several meetings of the
Council, the chapters of the Proposal were successively discussed. The
Council succeeded in reaching political agreement on the Proposal in
December 2003.[9] Meanwhile the European Parliament was involved via the
co-decision procedure. It adopted 47 amendments on the Proposal, of
which the Council agreed to 37.

The final text differs considerably from the 1998 Proposal. A provisional
version was published in January 2004,[10] and was finally adopted by
Council and Parliament in April 2004 as Regulation 883/2004.[11]

Regulation 883/2004 deserves, of course, extensive discussion and analysis, but that would require a book on its own. In this chapter, I will concentrate on the inclusion and exclusion of (new) categories of persons and
benefits, and their legal position. For this purpose, a comparison of
Regulation 883/2004 with the 1998 Proposal is important.

---

[6] COM(1998) 779. On the principles of a new co-ordination regulation, see E Eichenhofer,
'How to Simplify the Co-ordination of Social Security' (2000) 2 *European Journal of Social
Security* 231; M Sakslin, 'Social Security Co-ordination: Adapting to Change' (2000) 2
European Journal of Social Security 169; M Sakslin, 'Can the Principles of the Nordic
Conventions on Social Protection Contribute to the Modernisation and Simplification of
Regulation (EEC) No 1408/71?' in *25 Years of Regulation (EEC) No 1408/71 on Social
Security for Migrant Workers—A Conference Report* (Swedish National Social Insurance
Board and European Commission, 1997) p 197. On the 1998 Proposal, see F Pennings,
'The European Commission Proposal to Simplify Regulation 1408/71' (2001) 3 *European
Journal of Social Security* 45.
[7] The final report of the results of the discussions can be found in D Pieters (ed), *The Co-ordination of Social Security at Work* (Acco, 1999). For the conferences, preparatory materials
were published in P Schoukens (ed), *Prospects of Social Security Coordination* (Acco, 1997).
[8] Council Document 15045/01 (6 December 2001).
[9] 2549th Council Meeting (1–2 December 2003).
[10] The text was published as COM(2004) 44.
[11] 2004 OJ L200/1.

III THE PERSONAL SCOPE

A Extension of the Personal Scope to all Nationals

Regulation 1408/71 is limited to employed persons and self-employed persons. The 1998 Proposal was much broader in scope: it would have applied to all nationals of a Member State resident in the territory of a Member State who are or have been subject to the social security legislation of one or more Member States, as well as to the members of their families and to their survivors. This important and principal extension is maintained in Article 2(1) Regulation 883/2004: consequently, the right to free movement—in so far as social security is involved—is no longer limited to employed persons and self-employed persons. Although in the memorandum to the parameters,[12] some Member States made a reservation in respect of this extension, as they could not accept all of its potential consequences, the extension was accepted as part of the final version. Remarkable in this respect is that Recital 7 of the Preamble to Regulation 883/2004 reads that 'due to the major differences existing between national legislation in terms of the persons covered', it is preferable that the Regulation applies to nationals of a Member State. Recital 7 seems to consider the extension of the personal scope to all Community nationals as a form of harmonisation of the terms 'employed' and 'self-employed' persons.

However, the practical effect of this extension seems to be limited, given recent developments in EU law. From the main elements of co-ordination (non-discrimination; aggregation of periods of insurance, work or residence; payment of benefits; and determining the legislation applicable), for persons who are not an employed or self-employed person, the non-discrimination rule seems the most important. But for non-workers and non-self-employed persons who are members of a worker or self-employed person's family, the *Cabanis* judgment had already permitted them to invoke the non-discrimination rule contained in Article 3 Regulation 1408/71.[13] In fact, the Court of Justice ruled that members of the employed or self-employed person's family can invoke all the provisions of Regulation 1408/71 unless these specifically refer to employed or self-employed persons. In addition, for non-workers and non-self-employed persons who are not members of an employed or self-employed person's family, the interpretation of Article 18 EC by the Court is relevant. In the *Martínez Sala* judgment, the Court ruled that the claimant, a Community national, could invoke Articles 18 and 12 of the Treaty to have discrimination on nationality in a social security scheme removed.[14]

---

[12] Council Document 12296/01 (28 September 2001).
[13] Case 308/93 *Cabanis-Issarte* [1996] ECR I–2097.
[14] Case 85/96 *Martínez Sala* [1998] ECR I–2691.

Still, there can be situations in which these non-discrimination provisions do not have the same effect as the application of Regulation 1408/71 itself,[15] or when it is unclear whether Regulation 1408/71 is applicable.[16] For that reason, the extension of personal scope in Regulation 883/2004 is to be welcomed. Moreover, this extension may also be useful in cases where there is no discrimination *strictu sensu*, but when aggregation of periods and assimilation of facts abroad (as provided for under Articles 5 and 6 Regulation 883/2004) are necessary for an individual to qualify for benefits.[17] The extension of the personal scope to all Member State nationals therefore simplifies the co-ordination rules.

B (No) Extension to Third Country Nationals

The personal scope of Regulation 1408/71 has often been criticised for its limitation to nationals of one of the Member States. The European Commission proposed the extension of Regulation 1408/71 to third country nationals in 1997, but that proposal was not adopted.[18] The exclusion of third country nationals means, for instance, that if a Moroccan national works successively in Germany and the Netherlands, he cannot have his periods of employment completed in Germany aggregated to those fulfilled in the Netherlands. Such aggregation may be desirable for the person concerned if the periods completed in the Netherlands are insufficient to become entitled (for example) to unemployment benefit. For persons falling within the scope of Regulation 1408/71, aggregation enables them to satisfy the benefit conditions of the State where they have to claim benefit. It is not easy to justify this difference in treatment between EU nationals and non-EU nationals.

The 1998 Proposal made a new attempt to include third country nationals within the personal scope of the social security coordination system. This attempt was, however, effectively overruled by the judgment of the Court of Justice in *Khalil*,[19] from which it followed that Article 42 EC cannot be a legal basis for co-ordination rules covering third country nationals. In the light of that judgment, the Commission made a separate proposal, this time based on Article 63(4) EC, for a new regulation

---

[15] For instance, if a residence scheme of disability benefits does not take periods fulfilled abroad into account.

[16] Such as in the case of *Martínez Sala*, where it was unclear whether she was still covered by Reg 1408/71.

[17] See p 253 below for an example of such a situation.

[18] COM(1997) 561. On this topic, see Y Jorens and B Schulte (eds), *European Social Security Law and Third Country Nationals* (die Keure, 1998).

[19] Case 95/99 *Khalil* [2001] ECR I–7413.

extending the advantages of Regulation 1408/71 to third country nationals. This proposal was adopted and became Regulation 859/2003.[20]

Regulation 859/2003 provides that the provisions of Regulation 1408/71 shall apply also to persons who, solely because of their nationality, cannot invoke Regulation 1408/71. Article 63(4) EC, which concerns the Community's powers to adopt measures defining the rights and conditions under which nationals of third countries who are legally resident in a Member State may reside in other Member States, was accepted as a legal basis for this new Regulation. However, Article 63(4) EC allows certain Member States to be exempted from the instruments based upon it—an opportunity which Denmark made use of, though this perhaps explains why there was now sufficient 'consensus' on extending the co-ordination rules to third country nationals. Article 90(1) Regulation 883/2004 now states that Regulation 1408/71 shall remain in force and continue to have legal effect for the purposes of Regulation 859/2003, for as long as the latter instrument has not been repealed or modified.

There is, however, still an important difference between Regulation 1408/71 (and now Regulation 883/2004) on the one hand and Regulation 859/2003 on the other hand. This is the result of an addition to the text of Regulation 859/2003 during the negotiations, to the effect that this measure cannot be invoked in a wholly internal situation. This means that only in a situation concerning facts in at least two EU Member States (as with a Moroccan worker who subsequently works in both France and the United Kingdom) is Regulation 859/2003 applicable. The fact that the person concerned is originally from another State, not an EU State, is irrelevant. This limitation can also be found in the *Khalil* judgment, and earlier in the *Petit* judgment.[21] Still, its effect is different for third country nationals than for EU nationals such as Mr Petit, as the former are from a third country and therefore much more likely to be discriminated against on grounds of nationality than Union citizens. An example in which the non-discrimination rule would be useful for third country nationals can be found in the *Sürül* case,[22] where national law excluded foreigners from the national security system. In this particular case, Decision 3/80 of the EC-Turkey Association Council could successfully be invoked. This instrument contains a non-discrimination provision which can be invoked by Turkish nationals in an EU Member State. In the *Sürül* case, it was relied upon by Turkish nationals who were disqualified from German family allowance on the grounds that they did not have a permanent residence permit. This was considered a form of discrimination

---

[20] Reg 859/2003 extending the provisions of Reg 1408/71 and Reg 574/72 to nationals of third countries who are not already covered by those provisions solely on the ground of their nationality, 2003 OJ L124/1.

[21] Case 153/91 *Petit* [1992] ECR I–4973.

[22] Case 262/96 *Sürül* [1999] ECR I–2685.

on grounds of nationality. For third country nationals having a nationality other than Turkish, Decision 3/80 is not applicable, and Regulation 859/2003 does not have the same result. This is an unsatisfactory result. Moreover, the reservation that Regulation 1408/71 is not applicable in the strictly internal affairs of one Member State is not even necessary in respect of Regulation 859/2003, since the latter instrument is not based on Article 42 EC, but on Article 63(4) EC, so the *Petit* and *Khalil* judgments do not actually require this limitation. Consequently, the modernisation of the co-ordination rules is not yet complete.

IV THE MATERIAL SCOPE

A A Limitative or Enumerative Approach

Under the 1998 Proposal, the material scope of the co-ordination regime was no longer to be limited to specified risks. Article 2 of the Proposal provided that 'this Regulation shall apply to all social security legislation concerning the following, in particular.' This approach did not survive the discussions in the Council and is not reflected in the material scope as described in Article 3 Regulation 883/2004.

The material scope as defined in the 1998 Proposal has interesting implications: it takes account of the continuous stream of new types of benefits, for example, parental benefits, care insurance benefits and benefits in case of interruption of employment (for whatever reason). The fact that Article 42 EC requires measures 'in the field of social security' can be used as an argument for this broad approach.

However, an enumerative list has its own problems. Since the term 'social security' is not defined, the material scope envisaged in the 1998 Proposal could become very wide and the consequences would be hard, if not impossible, to oversee. What to do with housing benefits and study grants? And what about tax reductions?

The problems caused by the non-limitative enumeration would have been particularly serious, as the 1998 Proposal included the liability of employers. Under Regulation 1408/71, the liability of employers falls within the material scope of the Regulation only in so far as national law imposes an obligation for employers which is related to the contingencies falling under the Regulation. An example is the employer's obligation to continue to pay wages during sickness, which can be found in several systems, such as the German and the Dutch ones. In the 1998 Proposal, there was no longer any limitation to risks, and therefore employers' obligations with respect to, for instance, holiday payments and loyalty payments could have fallen within the scope of the new co-ordination regime as well.

Regulation 883/2004 does not follow the 1998 Proposal; its extension is limited to statutory pre-retirement and paternity benefits.[23] As the scope of the final version is limited to legislation, pre-retirement benefits governed by collective agreements (which is in fact the usual situation) are still beyond the scope of the Regulation (unless they are declared generally binding and the Member State concerned makes a declaration that the agreement is within the scope of the Regulation). In the Preamble to Regulation 883/2004, Recital 33 reads that, given the fact that statutory pre-retirement schemes exist in a very restricted number of Member States, the rule on the aggregation of periods should not be included. Apart from the lack of logic in this consideration (why not include the rule for the rare cases where it can be used?), it shows indeed that the extension of the material scope carried out under Regulation 883/2004 is very limited.

B Supplementary Social Security

The 1998 Proposal provided that agreements declared generally binding fall within the material scope of the coordination regime; a declaration from the Member State concerned that the scheme is within the material scope would no longer have been required. This extension did not reach the final version of Regulation 883/2004.

The approach of the 1998 Proposal was meant to terminate the exclusion of important parts of social security from the co-ordination rules. Supplementary social security provisions in collective agreements do not fall within the scope of Regulation 1408/71 and export of these benefits is therefore not required if the collective agreement limits payment to the national territory. Nor can periods fulfilled abroad be used to satisfy waiting periods in supplementary pension schemes. For posted workers, for instance, the problem arises that contributions levied on the basis of collective agreements for supplementary benefits in the State of employment may overlap with the benefits for which they remained insured in the State of residence.[24]

The effects of extending the co-ordination rules to collective agreements and other contractual schemes are, however, hard to oversee, since all kinds of provisions can be found in collective agreements. Holiday pay, study and training grants, sabbatical leave, loyalty stamps and bad-weather stamps are common examples of supplementary social security.

---

[23] Paternity benefits were added as a result of an amendment adopted by the European Parliament.

[24] Such double contributions were the subject of the judgment in Case 272/94 *Guiot* [1996] ECR I–1905, in which the Court considered levies in some cases inconsistent with the freedom to provide services. See M Houwerzijl and F Pennings, 'Double Charges in Case of Posting of Employees: the *Guiot* Judgment and its Effects on the Construction Sector' (1999) 1 *European Journal of Social Security* 91.

Sometimes collective agreements provide for supplements to statutory social security (increases to the benefit rates) or replace statutory protection which was withdrawn (privatisation). Some co-ordination rules are very well applicable to the advantages mentioned in collective agreements, such as the non-discrimination clause and the provision on export of benefits. In fact, non-discrimination rules are already applicable on collective agreements, such as Article 7(2) Regulation 1612/68.[25] Other co-ordination rules can lead to problems if they are applied to these advantages without restrictions. One example is a sabbatical leave provision which requires a waiting period of seven years of work for the same employer. An employer cannot be expected to allow an employee to aggregate the periods of work for other employers for the purpose of satisfying this condition, since this employer has to pay the full costs of the sabbatical. The same problem arises in the case of loyalty benefits. Problems arise also in the case of employees working in two countries. If the rules for determining the legislation applicable apply to these agreements as well, the employee concerned falls under one collective agreement only, insofar as its social security provisions are considered. The effects are hard to oversee and some of the effects are undesirable. Member States could prevent these problems by no longer extending collective agreements, but that would be an unattractive effect.

In the final version of Regulation 883/2004, the approach of Regulation 1408/71 is fully maintained, so there is no further extension to include supplementary social security. Although it is understandable that contractual schemes, even if extended or made obligatory by the public authorities, are not brought unconditionally within the scope of the Regulation, the progress made in extending the co-ordination rules to these types of benefit is disappointing. So far very little use has been made of the declarations,[26] even in cases when there are no obvious problems. It is preferable that Member are encouraged to issue in more cases declarations to include extended contractual schemes within the scope of Regulation 883/2004 and for this purpose they should have the burden of proof to explain why such a declaration cannot be given.

In the memorandum to the parameters, it is remarked that contractual schemes are by nature not suitable to be subject to the co-ordination rules applicable to statutory schemes. Other forms of co-ordination are sometimes more adequate, according to the memorandum.[27] The memorandum does not explain which other forms of co-ordination are meant, but cur-

---

[25] Reg 1612/68 on freedom of movement for workers within the Community, 1968 OJ L257/2.
[26] France has been the exception so far and has brought supplementary pensions and unemployment benefit schemes governed by collective agreements within the scope of Reg 1408/71.
[27] Council Document 12296/01 (28 September 2001) p 9.

rently these 'other forms of co-ordination', whatever they are, are not often used.[28] In any case, they leave many problems for migrant workers unsolved. As in the 1998 Proposal, the solution should not have been found in a mere simplification of the rules, as they lead to many new problems, but in making additional, specific rules for these types of schemes.

In the Preamble of Regulation 883/2004, Recital 6 reads that the close link between social security legislation and those contractual provisions which complement or replace such legislation and which have been the subject of a decision by the public authorities rendering them compulsory or extending their scope may call for similar protection with regard to the application of those provisions as that afforded by the new regulation; as a first step, the experience of Member States who have notified such schemes might be evaluated. This recital was inserted into the text after adoption of an amendment proposed by the European Parliament. To this text, the Council added the cautious last phrase that, first, appropriate national experiences have to be studied. The question is whether such an evaluation is really necessary. There are very few declarations, and the schemes concerned—which have national scope—seem to fit very well into the co-ordination system.

Still, the recital leaves more room than the text of the parameters, as now it is no longer argued that co-ordination of supplementary social security has to take place outside the Regulation.

C Social Assistance and Benefits for Victims of War

In both the 1998 Proposal and Regulation 883/2004, social assistance remains excluded from the material scope of the co-ordination regime. It is not explained why this is the case. Given the nature of social assistance, two co-ordination aspects are relevant to this type of benefit: non-discrimination and export. Aggregation of periods is not necessary, as social assistance has no requirements as to periods of insurance etc.

The non-discrimination rule applies already to social assistance, on the basis of the EC Treaty.[29] Export could, if this were considered undesirable, have been excluded on the basis of a specific rule in the new Regulation relating to social assistance, as is the case with special non-contributory benefits.

The 1998 Proposal no longer excluded benefits for victims of war or its consequences. As in the case of social assistance, only two co-ordination aspects are relevant to such benefits: non-discrimination and export. But here, the application of these aspects will be different: such benefits require room

---

[28] Perhaps the drafters had in mind Dir 98/49 on safeguarding the supplementary pension rights of employed and self-employed persons moving within the Community, 1998 OJ L209/46; this directive provides a very limited solution to the problems with the supplementary pensions.

[29] See Case 85/96 *Martínez Sala* [1998] ECR I–2691.

for the national authorities to discriminate, as benefits for the victims of war are meant to compensate for the consequences of war. The co-ordination rules should not lead to the obligation to pay these benefits also to the nationals of the former enemy or of neutral countries.[30] It is, however, hard to see any good arguments against export of this type of benefit. Exclusion of export may lead to infringements on the right to free movement, as appears from experiences with Regulation 1408/71: think of an elderly woman, entitled to this type of benefit, who wishes to join her daughter living in another Member State. The free movement of these persons is limited if export is not allowed and there are no good reasons for this from the point of view of co-ordination. This is even more true now that Regulation 883/2004 is meant to enable free movement of persons, instead of free movement of workers only.

D Non-Contributory Benefits

One of the problems with Regulation 1408/71, which attracted considerable political attention, concerns the so-called special non-contributory benefits. Regulation 1408/71 provides that these benefits, if listed in Annex IIa, do not have to be exported. In the past, Member States met but few problems if they wished to have special non-contributory benefits listed in this Annex. However, the Court's judgments in *Jauch*[31] and *Leclere*[32] meant that not all benefits listed in Annex IIa could stand the test. The Court required that these benefits have to be special, in that they are not granted to all residents, but only to those with insufficient means of their own. As this description still leaves much uncertainty on which benefits are allowed to be listed in the Annex and which are not, the 1998 Proposal attempted to give a sharper definition. It defined the benefits concerned as non-contributory cash benefits whose granting procedures are closely linked to a particular economic and social context and which are granted after means-testing or which are intended solely to afford specific protection for the disabled in so far as such benefits are mentioned in Annex I. This provision requires a means test, except in the case of benefits for the disabled. As a result, the non-means tested British mobility allowances (DLA and DWA) benefits, discussed in the *Snares* judgment,[33] can, being disability benefits, if they are also listed in the new Annex, still be restricted to the territory of the UK. However, a non-means-tested old-age benefit, for example, is no longer a special benefit.

---

[30] See the judgment in Case 207/78 *Even* [1979] ECR 2019, in which the Court ruled that Member States are free to award this special form of compensation based on solidarity with the victims of the war only to their own nationals.
[31] Case 215/99 *Jauch* [2000] ECR I–1901.
[32] Case 43/99 *Leclere* [2001] ECR I–4265.
[33] Case 20/96 *Snares* [1997] ECR I–895.

In the final version of Regulation 883/2004, the rules concerning special non-contributory benefits are found in Article 70. Article 70(2) defines special non-contributory cash benefits as benefits which:

(a) are intended to provide either:
   (i) supplementary, substitute or ancillary cover against the risks covered by the branches of social security referred to in Article 3(1), and which guarantee the persons concerned a minimum subsistence income having regard to the economic and social situation in the Member State concerned;

or
   (ii) solely specific protection for the disabled, closely linked to the said person's social environment in the Member State concerned,

and
(b) where the financing exclusively derives from compulsory taxation intended to cover general public expenditure and the conditions for providing and for calculating the benefits are not dependent on any contribution in respect of the beneficiary. However, benefits provided to supplement a contributory benefit shall not be considered to be contributory benefits for this reason alone,

and
(c) are listed in Annex X.

These benefits are payable in the State of residence only.

It follows that according to the final version of Regulation 883/2004, a means test is no longer required to make a benefit special. Instead, the Regulation requires that the benefit has to provide for a minimum subsistence income, which does not necessarily require a means test. The text excludes the benefits disputed in the *Leclere* judgment as these were not subsistence benefits, but were payable to all persons who gave birth to a child. However, the issue of the special non-contributory benefit is not unambiguous. If a benefit is considered a special non-contributory benefit, it means that it is no longer exportable and therefore persons are disqualified who are insured in the country concerned and then move to another Member State. Consequently, it *excludes* persons who leave the country. However, the approach that these benefits are payable in the country of residence also means that persons who move to a country with such benefits are *included* in the scheme. For instance, if a country has a scheme for the young handicapped, a person born and grown up in another country who goes after the age of 18 to the country with the disability scheme, has to be treated as if he had grown up in that country. This follows from the present Article 10a Regulation 1408/71. Article 70 Regulation 883/2004 does not have this assimilation rule, but the more general Article 5(2) of the new Regulation would still apply. This provides that where, under the legislation of the competent Member State, legal effects are attributed to the occurrence of certain facts or events, that Member State shall take account of like facts or events occurring in any Member State as though they had taken place in its own territory. This is an important assimilation rule.

Note that, in respect to this set of rules (Article 70 on special non-contributory benefits and Article 5(2) on the assimilation of facts), the extension of the personal scope of the Regulation to all Community nationals may be relevant in a situation such as the following. A person disabled from birth who moves to another Member State can now, in his own right, invoke Article 5(2) and apply for the benefit under the young disability benefit scheme. A non-discrimination clause would not have the same effect: if events which occurred outside the territory of the Member State would have been excluded, that would be a form of indirect discrimination on nationality (the same rule would apply to persons of the nationality of the State who were born abroad as well). In that case, there could be an objective justification for not taking foreign facts into account. Article 5(2) places claimants in a much stronger position.

The same set of rules also shows that the limitation placed by Regulation 859/2003 on the right of third country nationals to invoke the co-ordination regime if all the facts are limited to one Member State can have important effects: a person from Russia cannot invoke these rules if he is in a Member State and there is no relation with another Member State.

V THE RULES FOR DETERMINING THE LEGISLATION APPLICABLE

A General

The 1998 Proposal contained important reductions in the texts of Regulation 1408/71. This was an important improvement. Regulation 883/2004, however, still has 91 articles and is much less reduced in extent than the 1998 Proposal. Fortunately, the section concerning the rules for determining the applicable legislation in the final version is still shorter than that of Regulation 1408/71.

Article 11(1) Regulation 883/2004, like Article 13 Regulation 1408/71, provides for the exclusive effect of the rules for determining the legislation applicable. But Article 11(3) Regulation 883/2004 is a simplification compared to Article 13(2) Regulation 1408/71, since the former refers to employed and self-employed persons in one single phrase. In the text of Article 11(3) Regulation 883/2004, the phrase 'even if he resides in the territory of another Member State' (which can now be found in Article 13(2) Regulation 1408/71) is lacking. This phrase was the basis for the binding effect of the rules for determining the legislation applicable; we assume that the new Regulation does not depart from this caselaw and that the drafters wish the caselaw on this topic to remain applicable.

Article 11(2) Regulation 883/2004 provides that, for the purposes of this Title, persons enjoying cash benefits because of or as a consequence of their activity as an employed or self-employed person shall be considered to be pursuing the said activity. This shall not apply to invalidity, old-age or survivors' pensions or to pensions in respect of industrial accidents or occupational diseases or to sickness benefits in cash covering treatment for an unlimited period.

A person pursuing an activity as an employed or self-employed person in the territory of a Member State is subject to the legislation of that State (Article 11(3) Regulation 883/2004). Any person to whom the other subparagraphs of Article 11 (concerning civil servants and persons called up for military or civilian service etc) do not apply, shall be subject to the legislation of the Member State in whose territory he resides. This provision makes clear that, among other categories, persons are subject to the legislation of the State of residence.

The approach of Article 11(2) Regulation 883/2004 towards non-active persons is interesting and clearer than that of Regulation 1408/71. The new article provides that, as a main rule, the persons receiving benefit are considered as pursuing their activity, provided these benefits are related to their activities as an employed or self-employed person. Consequently, they remain covered by the legislation of the country where they last worked. An exception applies for recipients of the benefits listed in Article 11(2); they are subject to the legislation of the State of residence.

According to the present rules—Article 13(2)(f) Regulation 1408/71 and Article 10b Regulation 574/72—Member States can decide when a person who no longer resides in their territory is no longer insured by their system. This rule does not offer (explicit) limitations on the scope for excluding non-residents who are no longer in work from coverage; the Court of Justice accepted these rules in the *Kuusijärvi* judgment.[34] The Court's interpretation of Article 13(2)(f) Regulation 1408/71—in theory—does not preclude Member States also from applying it in the case of temporary interruptions of work, such as sickness or unemployment. During the negotiations over the amending regulation which inserted Article 13(2)(f) into Regulation 1408/71, it was proposed that, in the case of short interruptions to work, this Article should not be applicable. However, these negotiations were not successful. The final version of Regulation 883/2004 shows that more progress has now been made in this respect. It gives new criteria for determining situations in which a person no longer falls under the legislation of the former country of employment. This is, therefore, an improvement.

For some categories, however, Regulation 883/2004 may represent a deterioration in their legal position. At present, a Member State can provide, for instance, that persons remain covered by their legislation if they

---

[34] Case 275/96 *Kuusijärvi* [1998] ECR I–3443.

reside in another Member State and receive disability benefit. The new text no longer provides for this opportunity.

A special provision is made for a person receiving unemployment benefit according to Article 65 Regulation 883/2004; this concerns the situation in which he receives unemployment benefit according to the rules of the State of residence. He is subject to the legislation of the State of residence. This is an improvement. Suppose a person falls ill. Under the old rules, he has to claim sickness benefit in the country of work. Now he remains subject to the same legislation. This solves one of the problems highlighted in the operation of Regulation 1408/71.[35]

B Posting

Article 12 Regulation 883/2004 concerns posting, which was called in the 1998 Proposal 'the temporary pursuit of an activity in another Member State', but is now referred to simply as 'special rules'. Article 12(1) concerns the situation in which a person who pursues an activity as an employed person in a Member State on behalf of an employer which normally carries out its activities there and who is posted by that employer to the territory of another Member State to perform work on that employer's behalf. This person continues to be subject to the legislation of the first Member State, provided that the anticipated duration of that work does not exceed 24 months and that he is not sent to replace another person. This provision, which allows for posting during 24 months, is more generous than Regulation 1408/71 and even than the 1998 Proposal (which mention only 12 months).

Article 12(2) provides for the opportunity of posting as a self-employed person. This provision concerns a person normally pursuing an activity as a self-employed person in a Member State who goes to perform a similar activity in the territory of another Member State. Also here, posting is possible for a maximum period of 24 months. The new text requires 'similar activities', whereas Regulation 1408/71 merely required 'work', which could be of a different type from that which was performed before, and indeed, could also be work as an employed person (as emerged from the *Banks* judgment).[36] It is not clear whether, under Article 12(2) Regulation 883/2004, the term 'similar activity' requires that the work in the host State must be self-employed work, though that is not explicitly required.

Although the new provisions are more clearly drafted than the present ones, they leave several of the present questions concerning posting unanswered and

---

[35] See F Pennings, 'The European Commission Proposal to Simplify Regulation 1408/71' (2001) 3 *European Journal of Social Security* 57.
[36] Case 178/97 *Banks* [2000] ECR I–2005.

do not give specific criteria, such as for what is meant by 'normally pursues an activity' in Article 12(2). For such provisions, the caselaw developed under Regulation 1408/71 has kept its relevance.

VI CO-ORDINATION OF SICKNESS BENEFITS

In the 1998 Proposal, the European Commission proposed to give the members of families of frontier workers the possibility of obtaining benefits in kind according to their own choice, in the State of residence or the State of employment, just as in the case of frontier workers themselves. In particular, members of the family of a frontier worker who move from the State of employment to another State (whereas the frontier worker remains to work in the former State) may want to continue to make use of the healthcare of their country of origin, since they are often more familiar with the system. The frontier worker has the choice, and it is not easy to explain why his children and spouse have to go to the healthcare providers in the State of residence. The final version of Regulation 883/2004 follows the new approach but with certain restrictions. Member States are given the opportunity to limit the right of the members of the family to choose *if* they make use of Annex III. In that case, members of the family can apply for benefits in kind only if they become necessary during their stay in the competent State. The right to choose was added after an amendment adopted by the European Parliament, but the Council inserted the possibility of deviating from this rule by means of the Annex, in order to reach consensus among the Member States.

If the frontier worker terminates his activities as a frontier worker, he can claim benefit in the State of residence only. In Article 17 of the 1998 Proposal, the Commission had proposed to give the post-active frontier worker and his family members the right to choose between the system of the State of residence and the State of employment, if they have already made use of this freedom to choose before the retirement of the frontier worker. This Proposal would have answered criticism of the rules contained in Regulation 1408/71,[37] whereby, if a frontier worker already has a general practitioner or specialist in his country of employment (for instance, because he lived there previously), it is problematic if he has to visit another general practitioner or specialist after his retirement. Consequently, acceptance of this proposal would have been desirable. During the discussions in the Council, the Commission's proposed provision was deleted, but it was re-introduced as a result of an amendment adopted by the European Parliament. Article 28(2) Regulation 883/2004 provides that a pensioner who, during the last five years before he became entitled to an old-age pension or invalidity pension, worked at least two years as a frontier worker is

---

[37] See Y Jorens and B Schulte (eds), *European Social Security Law and Third Country Nationals* (die Keure, 1998), p 30.

entitled to benefits in kind in the Member State where he worked as a frontier worker. Here, the compromise was made possible in Council by providing that this is possible only if the Member State in which the person worked as a frontier worker and the Member State in which the competent institution responsible for the costs of the benefits in kind have agreed on this and are both listed in Annex V.

VII CO-ORDINATION OF UNEMPLOYMENT BENEFITS

A Determining the Applicable Unemployment Legislation

The 1998 Proposal contained a single rule on unemployed persons who, during their last employment, resided in a Member State other than the competent State. Such a person who resides in the territory other than the competent State, and who makes himself available to the employment services of the State of residence, would have received benefit from the competent State. The claimant would have had to be available to the employment services in the State of residence. This proposal was in line with the argument of the Court that the unemployed person has the best chances of finding work in his State of residence and would, therefore, have been consistent with the coordination system.[38]

An effect of the proposal is also that the problems related to the present rules which allow non-frontier workers who do not work in the competent State to choose between benefits in the State of employment and the State of residence are taken away.

Finally, the 1998 Proposal would have added a provision which is new compared to Regulation 1408/71. Article 50(2) of the Proposal provided that a person seeking work who satisfies the conditions of maintaining the right to benefit will receive unemployment benefits whose aim it is to facilitate access to work under the same conditions as its own nationals. The benefits meant here are not cash benefits, but (for instance) training opportunities. This provision concerned only those seeking work abroad.

This provision treated wholly unemployed, partially unemployed persons and persons unemployed because of unforeseen circumstances in the same way: they are entitled to receive unemployment benefit in (mostly) the State of employment. This was a real simplification compared to the present rules. The concept of frontier worker would have disappeared entirely. The 1998 Proposal would also have taken away a series of interpretation problems with Regulation 1408/71, such as what is meant by 'partially unemployed' or 'wholly unemployed'.[39] Also, the distinction between frontier worker,

---

[38] Consider, eg Case C–454/93 *Van Gestel* [1995] ECR I–1707.
[39] See the judgment in Case 444/98 *De Laat* [2001] ECR I–2229.

the non-frontier worker who returns to his State of residence and the so-called *Miethe* cases[40] (persons not considered frontier workers) would have disappeared as a result of the Commission's proposal.

Moreover, the 1998 Proposal would have solved the problem that the rules contained in Regulation 1408/71 constitute a form of indirect discrimination against frontier workers. Although the Court accepted an objective justification for these rules, in the *Miethe* judgment mentioned above, this does not take away from the fact that these rules are not really satisfactory. Another advantage of the Commission's proposal would have been that unemployment benefits are to be paid by the country which also received the insurance contributions, and this is a fair result.

The rules on unemployment benefits caused considerable problems for the Council and belonged to the last file which had to be discussed before political agreement was reached. The new approach contained in Regulation 883/2004 is much less simple than the 1998 Proposal, and largely follows the approach of Regulation 1408/71. Under the new regime, there is again a distinction between the person, not living in the competent State, who became partially unemployed or unemployed because of unforeseen circumstances (on the one hand) and a wholly unemployed person (on the other hand). According to Article 65(1), the partially and unforeseen unemployed person must be available for his employer or the employment services in the competent State. He is entitled to unemployment benefit from the competent State.

According to Article 65(2), the wholly unemployed person who does not live in the competent State while performing his last activities, and keeps living in or returns to that other Member State, has to be available to the employment services of the State of residence. A new rule is that, in addition, he may make himself available to the employment services in the Member State where he performed his last activities. If he is not a frontier worker and he does not return to the Member State of residence, he has to be available to the employment services of the State to whose legislation he was last subject. This person is entitled to unemployment benefit from the State of residence. Although these costs are for the Member State of residence, Article 65(6) now sets out reimbursement rules with the competent institution of the Member State to whose legislation the claimant was last subject. Consequently, this section of the coordination regime has hardly been modernised or simplified. Instead of giving wholly unemployed persons the right to benefit from the competent State, there is now a reimbursement rule. Meanwhile, as with sickness benefits, the concept of the frontier worker has returned once more to the text of Regulation 883/2004.

---

[40] Case 1/85 *Miethe* [1986] ECR 1837.

B Export of Benefit

In its 1998 Proposal, the Commission proposed extending the period during which a person can seek work from three months to six months. This proposal fits with the principle of free movement of persons which underlies the Treaty: unemployed persons, in particular, may wish to make use of freedom of movement since they have to seek work wherever it is available. The European Commission gave few arguments for its proposal: it did not make clear why the three-month period is too short, and it did not give any statistical data for the proposed extension. The Proposal was not followed and Article 64 Regulation 883/2004 provides that the maximum period for seeking work in another Member State while remaining in receipt of unemployment benefit is limited to three months. This period can be extended up to a maximum of six months by the competent State.

Under Regulation 1408/71, if a person is late in returning to his Member State of origin, and the three-month period abroad has not been extended, the claimant loses all remaining benefit rights. This is an unsatisfactory rule, as this can involve the loss of potentially long periods of benefit. A proposal made by the European Commission in 1980 to mitigate the present rules was never adopted.[41] According to the 1980 Proposal, unemployed persons would have retained their right to unemployment benefits in accordance with the national legislation of the competent State, provided that they returned to the territory of that State either within the three-month period laid down in Article 69 Regulation 1408/71, or after the expiry of this period but before the expiry of the period during which (under the legislation of the competent Member State) the worker may leave the national territory without thereby forfeiting his right to benefits.

In the final version of Regulation 883/2004, Article 64(2) provides that forfeiture of the right to benefit will not take place where the legislation of the competent Member State is more favourable. In other words, the new Regulation still allows forfeiture of benefit rights, but does not impose such forfeiture upon the Member States.[42]

VIII CONCLUSIONS

The Commission took the task of simplifying Regulation 1408/71 very seriously and reduced the extent of the text considerably in its 1998 Proposal. It did not restrict itself to simplifying the text: many politically sensitive proposals were made. The connection between the simplification and the

---

[41] COM(1980) 312; see also 1980 OJ L169/22.
[42] Under the Dutch rules, for instance, a right to benefit can be revived provided that no more than 6 months has elapsed between leaving the country and returning.

modernisation operations is not easy. Although some modernising rules would have made the coordination regime more simple (and vice versa), it also meant that they were very radical in the eyes of the Member States, for example, on the material scope of the new regulation, where it was also hard to foresee the effects of the Commission's proposals. The final result—now embodied in Regulation 883/2004, is much more modest in its modernising effect, and also far less simple than the 1998 Proposal.

Of course, this is not the end of the process, and the Commission can continue to investigate the possibilities for extending the scope of the coordination regime. The European Parliament in fact offered a good basis for this by stressing the relevance of the link between statutory and non-statutory social security. The adoption of Regulation 883/2004 should not bring the process of modernisation to a halt, as there are still pressing issues. For this purpose, it is necessary to analyse in more detail the problems which arise in particular areas, such as the exclusion of generally binding contractual schemes. New initiatives should contain a thorough analysis of the problems and of the effects of any proposed new text. Such an analysis was missing in the 1998 Proposal and this made it difficult to understand the full consequences of what the Commission envisaged.

One possibility would be to make an inventory of different types of non-statutory schemes, and the likely effects of the co-ordination rules on each of these types. For some types, there will not be any effect (such as a national scheme with centralised funds); whereas for other types, there may be more problems (such as a collective agreement applicable in the construction sector only). Subsequently, the Commission could elaborate special chapters to be added to Regulation 883/2004 for each of these types. For modernisation to be truly effective, there are probably *more* co-ordination rules needed in Regulation 883/2004 rather than *fewer*!

After all, simplification means a reduction in the number of problems, and this may sometimes require even more rules. And so, sometimes it is preferable to have more text, especially in the case of known problems under Regulation 1408/71 which are still unsolved under Regulation 883/2004. There is indeed a tension between simplification and modernisation.

12

Between a Rock and a Soft Place: Internal Market versus Open Co-ordination in EU Social Welfare Law

NICK BERNARD*

I INTRODUCTION

For a long time, the direct impact of EU law on national welfare systems has been very limited. Of course, regulations on social security for migrant workers have long required Member States to extend the umbrella of their welfare system to economically active nationals of other Member States residing on their territory. Regulation 1612/68, in particular Article 7(2) on non discrimination with respect to 'social advantages', as well as the Treaty provisions on free movement themselves have also been used by migrant workers and, more exceptionally, visitors to claim various benefits from a host Member State. None of this, however, fundamentally challenged the organisational principles of national welfare systems. While social welfare, like any other area of policy for that matter, never constituted a reserved domain entirely protected from incursion by EU law, the Court nonetheless seemed to implicitly acknowledge that it had to proceed with caution in this area.

While it might perhaps be excessive to state that the Court has now entirely thrown such caution to the wind, it has nonetheless developed a much more active stance and confronted more squarely the issue of how far internal market principles can interfere with the organisation of national welfare systems. While one would be hard-pressed to find an explicit overruling of the earlier, more guarded, caselaw, one may ask whether the current position adopted by the Court is in fact compatible with the principles it had established earlier.

* Queen Mary, University of London.

For its part, the Community legislator has always been limited by a refusal of Member States to countenance an amendment to the Treaties that would result in the establishment of a broad EU competence in the field of social welfare. The Lisbon agenda, however, radically altered the picture. If the strategic goal of the EU is 'to become the most competitive and dynamic knowledge-based economy in the world, capable of sustainable economic growth with more and better jobs and greater social cohesion' by 2010,[1] it could not afford to ignore the difficulties encountered by national welfare systems. Indeed, the Lisbon agenda explicitly places the modernisation of the European social model as one of three pillars of its strategy.[2] The Treaty of Nice provided a legal basis for action by the Community in the fields of social security, social protection and social exclusion.[3] However, the means of action at the disposal of the institutions in this field are severely constrained. Thus national social welfare law seems poised between increased juridification through the caselaw of the Court on the internal market and an EU social welfare policy based, if not exclusively on informal means, nonetheless on softer, non-binding instruments.

One could see this as an old story of triumphant, court-led and market-linked negative integration versus weak political processes of positive (social) integration, characterised by a double dominance of legal over political processes and of economic over social values. And, to some extent, it *is* that. Limited legislative competence is a reflection of weak political processes of integration linked to a fragile legitimacy. However, a discipline bias as lawyers may lead us to overstate the importance of binding law and court-led processes and correlatively under-estimate the significance of political processes based on softer instruments. Is the value system of EU social welfare law dominated, as a result of the Court's internal market caselaw, by economic concerns or do the softer processes of cooperation between the Member States provide for the development of a policy promoting social values? This chapter will first consider the evolving role of the Court and its impact on national welfare systems before considering the development of an EU social policy through the open method of coordination.

II SOCIAL WELFARE AND THE INTERNAL MARKET
IN THE CASELAW OF THE COURT

Internal market principles apply to economic activities. While the precise phrasing of the question will depend on the economic freedom at issue, the requirement of an economic activity is central to the notion of internal market.

---

[1]   Lisbon European Council, Presidency Conclusions (23–24 March 2000), para 5.
[2]   *Ibid.*
[3]   See Art 137(1)(c),(j) and (k), further discussed below.

Contemporary economists usually refer to notions of choice and scarcity to define their discipline. Earlier definitions tended to focus more narrowly on notions of production and exchange. Even this earlier and narrower approach to what economics is about is not premised on any particular mode of production or distribution of wealth. In particular, the presence or absence of market mechanisms is not central to the identification of what constitutes an economic activity. While economic theory might have things to say about the relative merits and appropriateness of particular modes of production, an activity does not cease to be 'economic' because it is carried out through public-style, taxation-based mechanisms rather than market-based ones.

If one sets aside recent cases of the Court concerning cross-border health-care provision, the caselaw of the Court on the scope of internal market law seems, by contrast, to be premised on the existence of market mechanisms. This is at its clearest in the *Gravier* and *Humbel* cases,[4] where the Court held that second and third level education provided in the context of the national education system and financed primarily through the taxation system rather than through tuition fees charged to the pupils or students did not constitute a service within the meaning of Article 59 EEC.[5] Remarkably, the Court found that this remained so even for those individuals who, as non-nationals, were denied the benefit of free education at the point of delivery and had to actually pay substantial tuition fees. According to the Court,

> [T]he nature of the activity is not affected by the fact that pupils or their parents must sometimes pay teaching or enrolment fees in order to make a certain contribution to the operating expenses of the system. *A fortiori, the mere fact that foreign pupils alone are required to pay a minerval can have no such effect.*[6]

Thus, in *Gravier* and *Humbel*, the Court looks broadly at the kind of economics at work in the situation. If the activity is generally governed by public economics principles, financed through taxation and more or less free at point of delivery, internal market principles do not apply. On the other hand, if the activity broadly follows private, market-based, principles, internal market discipline has to be followed.

Translating this simple idea to social welfare provision, however, is not without difficulties. Although generally immersed in a public sector economics environment, something that can be symbolised by the idea of a solidarity-based welfare system, national systems also rely on market or market-like mechanisms for delivery of welfare services.

---

[4] Case 293/83 *Gravier v City of Liège* [1985] ECR 593; Case 263/86 *Belgian State v Humbel* [1988] ECR 5365.
[5] Now Art 49 EC.
[6] Case 263/86 *Belgian State v Humbel* [1988] ECR 5365, para 19 (my emphasis).

A State and Market in Social Welfare Provision

In most, if not all, cases concerned with social welfare, the Court repeats in mantra-like fashion that

> Community law does not detract from the power of the Member States to organise their social security systems.[7]... [I]n the absence of harmonisation at Community level, it is therefore for the legislation of each Member State to determine, first, the conditions concerning the right or duty to be insured with a social security scheme.[8]

In broad terms, four main types of arrangements can be conceived:

1   Direct provision of welfare benefits (in cash or kind) by the State itself or an emanation thereof, and funded through the taxation system;
2   Provision of benefits, financed from public funds, but with a delivery system devolved to distinct, private or public, entities;
3   Welfare provision left entirely to market mechanisms with no state intervention other than as regulator;
4   Welfare provision left to market mechanisms, but with financial assistance provided directly by the State to individuals.

In the first two categories, the State is seen as being responsible for the provision of welfare services to its citizens. Either by providing such services directly (category 1) or by procuring for the delivery of these services by somebody else (category 2), the State 'is not seeking to engage in gainful activity but is fulfilling its duties towards its own population in the social, cultural and educational fields'.[9] The first situation is indistinguishable from *Humbel*. On the assumption that *Humbel* is still good law, viz. that an exchange/market mechanism is still essential to the qualification of an activity as 'economic', it would have to follow that type 1 arrangements do not fall within the scope of internal market rules. Type 2 arrangements are, as far as the individual is concerned, not fundamentally different. In so far as the entity delivering the benefits does so de facto on behalf of the State, we remain within a non-market paradigm and the *Humbel* logic should apply here too. On the other hand, as far as the relationship between the State and

---

[7]   See, *inter alia*, Case 238/82 *Duphar* [1984] ECR 523, para 16; Case C–70/95 *Sodemare* [1997] ECR I–3395, para 27; Case C–158/96 *Kohll* [1998] ECR I–1931, para 17; or Case C–157/99 *Smits and Peerbooms* [2001] ECR I–5473, para 44.
[8]   See Case C–157/99 *Smits and Peerbooms* [2001] ECR I–5473, para 45.
[9]   Case 263/86 *Belgian State v Humbel* [1988] ECR 5365, para 18. In *Humbel*, this phrase was applied to the provision of secondary education in the context of a national educational system. However, it would apply equally well here.

the entity delivering the service is concerned, this entity is delivering a service to the state so as to enable the latter to fulfil its duties towards its population. Looked at broadly, and independently of the precise legal mechanism chosen, the situation is, in essence, one of public procurement, which is subject to the discipline of the internal market, possibly in terms of the procurement directives if the conditions for the application of these directives are fulfilled and, in any event, of other internal market rules concerning, in particular, the free movement of goods and services.

In arrangements of type 3 and 4, the market is the primary engine for the satisfaction of welfare needs. The State only intervenes in a corrective manner to prevent/alleviate some market failures. In these situations, the relationship between service provider and individual recipient of welfare services is clearly of an economic nature and internal market rules should apply.

If Community law does not detract from the power of the Member States to organise their social security systems, the Court's reading of the applicability of the free movement provisions to national welfare systems should not lead to a change to the underlying key organising principles of these systems and, in particular, lead to the transformation of an essentially state-based system founded on solidarity into an essentially market-based system. To put it in the framework developed above, a type (1 or) 2 system should not be transformed into a type 4 (or 3) system.

In theory, what distinguishes a taxation-based system of type 1 or 2 from a market-based system of type 3 or 4 is the scope of individual choice. Under a taxation-based system, the individual may choose not to avail himself of the services and benefits under the scheme, but he has no choice as to whether or not to contribute. His choice is also constrained as to the range of services or suppliers. All this is decided by the State. On the other hand, under type 3 or 4 arrangements, the individual is in principle free to choose whatever services are available, constrained only by what the market will offer (and, of course, his resources).

While the distinction is relatively easy to maintain between type 1 and 3, it becomes blurred as between type 2 and 4. As regards the scope of choice as to services and suppliers, the State may, under arrangements of type 2, in fact leave a wide choice to the individual. Conversely, the conditions that may be attached to the granting of financial assistance under type 4 may considerably restrict the scope for choice for the individual. Starting from very different philosophies, one may end up with practical arrangements which are, in fact, quite similar, at least in their effects.

With regard to the issue of whether there is a choice or not to contribute, the distinction is also problematic. Few welfare benefits are funded directly and entirely out of the State budget. Central government resources constitute on average approximately only a third of social protection receipts in the EU, with the rest coming primarily from contributions from individuals and, where applicable, their employers.[10] In *Humbel*,[11] the Court considered that the contribution sometimes made by pupils and their parents to the cost of public secondary education in the form of teaching or enrolment fees did not suffice to bring such education within the realm of freedom to provide services. However, there is surely a distinction to be drawn between the token gesture that such fees represent in the overall budget of the education system and the much more substantial contributions made by individuals and firms to the functioning of the social security system. Thus, the question must be considered whether such contributions should be seen as taxation or analysed as payment for an insurance service.

If affiliation is compulsory, there is a strong case for viewing contributions as taxation. The fact that this 'taxation' is earmarked for a specific purpose and by-passes the general state budget to go directly into the coffers of social protection institutions does not per se deprive such contributions of their essentially fiscal nature. Then again, compulsory (private) insurance is not unknown, as is shown by the example of motor insurance. Perhaps a better guide, then, is whether individuals or firms have a choice of scheme or are by law tied to a specific one. Even then, Article 86 EC forces us to consider the possibility that social protection funds might be regarded as 'undertakings entrusted with the operation of services of general economic interest', which are subject to internal market rules to the extent that this does obstruct in law or in fact the performance of the particular tasks assigned to them. Ultimately, there is no simple single criterion that can be used to adequately distinguish a taxation-based, state-centered system from a market-based one. The mode of funding is, no doubt, a very important criterion but it cannot be conclusive in all cases and has to be allied to other criteria to determine whether the balance falls more on the public or private side. This is indeed the approach taken by the Court[12] and, in this respect, it seems a sound approach.

B Competition Cases

Together with the affirmation that Community law does not detract from the power of the Member States to organise their social security systems went a caselaw that originally seemed to preserve a substantial amount of national decision-making in the social welfare field unencumbered by Community law. In addition to the *Humbel* and *Gravier* cases, which, although not in the field of social protection, seemed readily transposable

---

[10] Eurostat, *European Social Statistics—Social Protection Expenditure and Receipts 1992–2001* (Office for Official Publications of the European Communities, 2004) pp 84 *et seq*. Even in Denmark, which has the highest proportion of social protection receipts coming out of central government contributions, the government share is under two-thirds.

[11] Case 263/86 *Belgian State v Humbel* [1988] ECR 5365, para 19.

[12] See, *inter alia*, Case C–67/96 *Albany* [1999] ECR I–5751.

to this field, the decision of the Court in *Poucet and Pistre*[13] could be taken as bearing witness to the caution of the Court in relation to social welfare.

Asked by the national court, rather bluntly and directly, 'whether an organization charged with managing a special social security scheme is to be regarded as an undertaking for the purposes of Articles [81] and [82] of the Treaty', the Court replied, in an equally terse and concise manner that:

18   Sickness funds, and the organizations involved in the management of the public social security system, fulfil an exclusively social function. That activity is based on the principle of national solidarity and is entirely non-profit-making. The benefits paid are statutory benefits bearing no relation to the amount of the contributions.

19   Accordingly, that activity is not an economic activity and, therefore, the organizations to which it is entrusted are not undertakings within the meaning of Articles [81] and [91] of the Treaty.

While, on close analysis, paragraph 18 contains quite a few elements and while, earlier in the judgment, the Court also looked in more detail at the characteristics of the funds concerned, the overall tone of the judgment and its brevity as well as the generality of the affirmation contained in paragraphs 18 and 19 might have been interpreted as a signal from the Court that genuine social security systems remained largely untouched by EU internal market law and that national courts need not err on the side of caution and refer over-zealously.

The judgment of the Court in *FFSA*,[14] however, sounded a warning bell against the risk of too hasty a conclusion of non-applicability of internal market rules. The case concerned a pension fund supplementing the basic and compulsory pension fund for self-employed farmers. While the rules relating to the functioning of the fund were, for the most part, enshrined in law, these rules were, in fact, largely similar to those one might find in a life assurance contract. Significantly, affiliation was optional and, while some rules reflected an idea of solidarity, these were of limited import in the overall scheme. It was not, or should not have been, too surprising then that the Court would find that the pension fund constituted an undertaking engaging in an economic activity.

The judgments of the Court in *Albany*, *Brentjens* and *Drijvende Bokken*,[15] confirmed that, far from assuming the prima facie non-economic character of the activities of entities entrusted with the management of social welfare funds unless manifestly otherwise, the Court would in fact

---

[13] Joined Cases C–159/91 and C–160/91 *Poucet and Pistre* [1993] ECR I–637.
[14] Case C–244/94 *FFSA* [1995] ECR I–4013.
[15] Case C–67/96 *Albany* [1999] ECR I–5751; Joined Cases C–155–57/97 *Brentjens* [1999] ECR I–6025; Case C–219/97 *Drijvende Bokken* [1999] ECR I–6121. All three judgments were handed down on the same day by the Court sitting in plenary. AG Jacobs delivered a very detailed common Opinion for all three cases.

scrutinise carefully the characteristics of these entities before coming to a conclusion as to the applicability of internal market rules. The Court does not treat any single feature as per se determinative but uses a range of criteria to weigh the public and private aspects of the schemes. The central question that the Court seems to seek to answer is: could a private actor conceivably offer a service broadly similar to that offered by the entity concerned?[16] Thus, in the context of pension funds, if a fund determines itself the level of contribution and benefits and functions on the basis of the principle of capitalisation, it is likely to be regarded as an undertaking for internal market purposes.[17] On the other hand, if redistributive features are prominent so that solidarity constitutes a central aspect of the scheme, it will remain outside the scope of internal market law.

While this approach seems in principle sensible, one may nevertheless question its compatibility with the idea that Member States remain free to organise their social security system as they like. The pension fund at issue in *Albany*[18] was typical of the kind of supplementary pension funds prevalent in the Netherlands. The Dutch pension system relies on a fairly basic state pension, ordinarily complemented by a supplementary pension. In most sectors of the economy, the social partners have concluded collective agreements setting up such supplementary pension funds and the Dutch Minister for Social Affairs has by decrees rendered affiliation to those funds compulsory for all persons belonging to the relevant sectors. Thus, while the basic legal framework contemplates other possibilities than compulsory affiliation to a sectoral fund, such as voluntary affiliation or conclusion of individual pension/life insurance contracts, in practice such compulsory affiliation is the de facto norm in virtually all sectors of economic significance.[19] By making affiliation compulsory in such sectors, the Netherlands have chosen to organise the second tier of their pension system on a non-market, non-competitive basis. Stating that what the sectoral funds offer could, save for a few features, be offered by private insurance companies and that, therefore, the funds could potentially be in competition with such companies is perilously close to taking that *quod est demonstrandum* as the starting point of the reasoning, *viz* that the supplementary pension funds sector constitutes a virtual market.

---

[16] Cf AG Jacobs in Case C–218/00 *Cisal di Battistello Venanzio* [2002] ECR I–691: 'The basic test is whether the entity in question is engaged in an activity which consists in offering goods or services on a given market and which could, at least in principle, be carried out by a private actor in order to make profits' (para 38 of the Opinion).

[17] Cf Joined Cases C–180–84/98 *Pavlov* [2000] ECR I–6451, para 114.

[18] As indeed the other two pension funds in *Brentjens* and *Drijvende Bokken*.

[19] According to figures submitted by the Dutch government in the trilogy of cases, 80% of the workforce in the Netherlands is compulsorily affiliated to a sectoral fund. Even in those sectors where no decree has been adopted by the Minister to make affiliation compulsory, and except for a limited number of small sectors of negligible economic significance, affiliation to a sectoral fund is also the de facto norm, as a result of either collective agreements or voluntary affiliation by all companies.

Admittedly, even if the funds are regarded as undertakings, this does not dispose of the question since compulsory affiliation may be construed as an exclusive right granted to an 'undertaking entrusted with the operation of a service of general economic interest,' which may be accepted as necessary for the 'performance, in law or in fact, of the particular tasks assigned to it' under Article 86(2) EC. However, approaching it in those terms means already seeing the fund as market actor, albeit one entrusted with a special task, and may give a distorted view of the role and function of the fund. It is, in this respect, very significant that both the Advocate General and the Court approached the issue of compulsory affiliation in a *Corbeau*[20] frame of mind: for them, the issue is that the solidarity-linked aspects of schemes such as that at stake in *Albany*, although not sufficient to lead to the conclusion that the fund is not an undertaking, nonetheless make them less competitive than private insurance schemes. In so far as the scheme will be attractive to the net beneficiaries of the solidarity aspects, the scheme will suffer from adverse selection problems, as low risk persons move to a private, more attractive insurance scheme. Therefore, compulsory affiliation is necessary to counter the adverse selection problem.

While, undoubtedly, solidarity/redistribution is a distinguishing feature of most public social security systems, it does not follow, however, that this is the only reason why an alternative to a market-based system might be preferred. There are various reasons, other than redistribution, why a Member State might encourage and favour the conclusion of collective agreements between the social partners to set up and administer schemes and to make those schemes compulsory to all in the relevant sectors. First and foremost, compulsory affiliation may be a means to ensure that all workers are covered by adequate pension arrangements, as individuals may underestimate their needs and/or employers may be tempted to conclude insufficient pension arrangements. Management of pension funds by the social partners may be considered as a more effective way for workers, through their representative organisations, to have greater control over their pensions.

It is true that such objectives could perhaps be achieved by other means which would leave greater room for a competitive market to emerge. This, however, would also be true of most social security schemes. Any standard, basic and universal social security system could be refashioned into a market-based one, coupled with fiscal transfers and state guarantees where appropriate to inject the elements of solidarity desired. The question is not whether a more market-friendly alternative could be conceived that would allow for the same social objectives to be satisfied but whether the existing system can be justified by the Member State's exercise of its competence in organising its social security system. If a Member State can, 'in the exercise of the powers it retains to organise its social security system' insist that

---

[20] Case C–320/91 *Corbeau* [1993] ECR I–2533.

social welfare services providers be non-profit-making,[21] then it is difficult to understand why such a Member State might not be able to insist that supplementary pensions be provided by funds created and administered by the social partners.

C Free Movement Cases

Free movement law has also recently seen a spate of cases concerning cross-border provision of social welfare services, and, more specifically, healthcare.[22] The trend started with *Kohll* and *Decker*,[23] in which the Court considered that it would constitute a breach of Articles 28 and 49 EC for a Member State to refuse to reimburse the cost of medical goods and of dental treatment obtained in another Member State, at the rate applicable under the social security sickness insurance scheme of the Member State making the payment. This finding was later extended to other forms of treatment including hospitalisation, whether in the context of a benefits in kind scheme or a reimbursement scheme, subject to the proviso, as regards hospital treatment, that the Member State may impose a requirement of prior authorisation, based on objective and impartial criteria known in advance.[24]

All these cases are based on the premise that an individual obtaining medical treatment in another Member State is a recipient of services, even when reimbursement is obtained for the treatment.[25] The Court even considers that hospital treatment financed directly by a sickness fund under contractual arrangements between the hospital and the fund is providing a service to the patient within the meaning of Article 49 EC. The Court relies, for this purpose, on its finding in *Bond van Adverteerders*[26] that remuneration need not come from the recipient of the service but may be provided by somebody else. While the latter affirmation is no doubt true, its application in *Bond van Adverteerders* was already rather dubious.[27] It is even

---

[21] See Case C–70/95 *Sodemare* [1997] ECR I–3395, para 32.

[22] See further the contribution of P Koutrakos in this collection.

[23] Case C–158/96 *Kohll* [1998] ECR I–1931; Case C–120/95 *Decker* [1998] ECR I–1831.

[24] See Case C–368/98 *Vanbraekel* [2001] ECR I–5363; Case C–157/99 *Smits and Peerbooms* [2001] ECR I–5473; Case C–385/99 *Müller-Fauré and Van Riet* [2003] ECR I–4509; Case C–56/01 *Inizan* [2003] ECR I–0000; Case C–8/02 *Leichtle* (Judgment of 18 March 2004).

[25] See, *inter alia*, Case C–157/99 *Smits and Peerbooms* [2001] ECR I–5473, para 53.

[26] Case 352/85 *Bond van Adverteerders* [1988] ECR 2085.

[27] In the case, the Court found that a television cable network operator was providing a service to broadcasters by re-transmitting their broadcast to the network's customers and that this service was paid for by these customers in the form of the subscription fees they pay to the network operator. This is tantamount to saying that the seller of the house pays for a service provided by the estate agent to the buyer. The fact that two parties have a mutual interest in a service being provided to one of them by a third party does not mean that the service is provided to both of them. I may have an interest, as an airline passenger, in air traffic control providing navigation services to the airline on whose plane I am a passenger. It does not mean that air traffic control is providing me with a service.

more questionable in this context. In effect, the fund is entering into a contract with a supplier so as be in a position to fulfil its obligations towards its members. The hospital may be providing a service to the fund in that situation. It does not follow from this that it is supplying a service to the patient. In effect, we are in what was described above as a type 2 situation: provision of benefits, financed from public funds, but with a delivery system devolved to distinct, private or public, entities. If one were to follow the Court's reasoning in *Bond van Adverteerders* and in *Smits and Peerbooms* to its logical conclusion, one would have to consider that all subcontractors, suppliers and everybody involved in the production chain of a product or service is ultimately providing goods or services to the end user. This surely cannot be right: buying South African grapes at my local supermarket does not make me the recipient of the transport service under which the grapes were brought from South Africa to Europe.

If one places oneself from the perspective of the Member State in which the service is provided, the finding in *Smits and Peerbooms* that an individual in this situation is a recipient of a service because he or she, not being insured under the host scheme's state, is required to pay for the service seems to fly directly in the face of *Humbel*.[28] It will be recalled that, in that case, the Court considered that, in order to determine whether public sector education was to be regarded as a service, one had to consider the ordinary situation of most pupils, and not the atypical situation of a pupil coming from another Member State. Moreover, if there is provision of a service in this situation, it would mean that the recipient falls within the personal and material scope of the Treaty and therefore benefits from the principle of non-discrimination on grounds of nationality enshrined in Article 12 EC. Thus, a public hospital would not be in a position to charge higher fees to visiting nationals of another Member State. Indeed, if treatment is provided free of charge and financed out of the public purse, requiring those who are not affiliated to the social security system of the host state to pay for treatment would constitute indirect discrimination on grounds of nationality.[29] Similarly, if the host state reimburses the cost of treatment, it would also be indirectly discriminatory not to reimburse nationals of other Member States not affiliated to the social security system.

One might be tempted to argue that those who are affiliated and those who are not affiliated are not in comparable situations. However, a similar argument could have been made in *Humbel* or *Gravier* with respect to those who contribute through taxation and those who do not.[30] Consistency would thus seem to require the Court to overrule these cases and hold that

---

[28] Case 263/86 *Belgian State v Humbel* [1988] ECR 5365.

[29] See Case C–411/98 *Ferlini* [2000] ECR I–8081, paras 52 *et seq.*

[30] See also Case 186/87 *Cowan* [1989] ECR 195, in which the Court rejected an argument by the French government that a criminal injuries compensation scheme was based on a logic of solidarity and could not be extended to visiting nationals of other Member States.

Member States can, after all, charge higher fees to non-resident non-nationals in relation to vocational training. Alternatively, it would have to be accepted that, for instance, any Community national could come to the UK and demand free treatment under the NHS on a par with UK residents.[31]

Even if cross-border medical treatment ultimately paid by the home state national security system is regarded as a service for the purposes of Article 49 EC, the characteristics of that social security system may nonetheless still be taken into account in order to justify a derogation from the freedom to provide and receive services. The competence of the Member States to organise their social security system must surely include the competence to decide how much should be spent on it. There are wide variations in social expenditure among Member States. For instance, Eurostat figures[32] indicate that, in 2001, Ireland spent a mere 14.6 per cent of its GDP on social protection expenditure whereas Sweden, France, Germany and Denmark spent more than twice as much. In the context of the free movement of goods, the Court accepted long ago in *Duphar* that Member States could take measures to 'promote the financial stability of their healthcare insurance system'.[33]

Since *Kohll*, however, the Court has narrowly circumscribed the scope of this derogation. Cost control per se is not a sufficient ground of derogation, as this would constitute an aim 'of a purely economic nature which cannot as such justify a restriction on the fundamental principle of freedom to provide services'.[34] Thus, it would seem that, in order to invoke a cost-related argument successfully, a Member State has either to show that there exists a credible threat to the financial equilibrium of its social expenditure system or use the cost argument in support of another, non-economic argument. Thus, the Court accepts that Member States may adopt policies designed to ensure that there is sufficient and permanent accessibility to a balanced range of high-quality hospital treatment in the State concerned. In that context, following a form of reasoning similar to its judgment in *Campus Oil*,[35] the Court accepts that Member States may impose restrictions on hospital treatment in another Member States so as to ensure to their own hospitals a sufficient level of demand and therefore financial viability.

From this, the Court draws two conclusions. First, a system of prior authorisation may be imposed by a Member State as a condition of reimbursement of the cost of hospital treatment received in another Member

---

[31] Cf the chapter by M Dougan and E Spaventa in this collection.

[32] Eurostat, *European Social Statistics—Social Protection Expenditure and Receipts 1992–2001* (Office for Official Publications of the European Communities, 2004) pp 12 *et seq.*

[33] Case 238/82 *Duphar* [1984] ECR 523, para 16.

[34] See Case C–385/99 *Müller-Fauré and Van Riet* [2003] ECR I–4509, para 92.

[35] Case 72/83 *Campus Oil* [1984] ECR 651. In that case, the Court upheld a requirement imposed by the Irish State on operators importing oil into Ireland to obtain a proportion of their supply from a refinery owned by the Irish State. The rule was justified on grounds of public security, in order to ensure that Ireland maintained a refining capacity, the rule being necessary in the light of the alleged intention of the operators to source their supplies from their own refineries in the UK.

State but may not, bar exceptional circumstances, be imposed in relation to other medical services. In relation to the former, national authorities must be in a position to plan the number of hospitals, their geographic distribution, the facilities which they provide and the services they offer to ensure that 'there is sufficient and permanent accessibility to a balanced range of high-quality hospital treatment in the State concerned' and 'prevent, as far as possible, any wastage of financial, technical and human resources'.[36] Non-hospital services, however, do not require such heavy investments and therefore planning. The costs are not on the same scale as hospital services, and a system of prior authorisation is not, in the eyes of the Court, necessary.

The second conclusion drawn by the Court is that, when assessing the need for hospital treatment in another Member State,

> ... national authorities are required to have regard to all the circumstances of each specific case and to take due account not only of the patient's medical condition at the time when authorisation is sought and, where appropriate, of the degree of pain or the nature of the patient's disability which might, for example, make it impossible or extremely difficult for him to carry out a professional activity, but also of his medical history.[37]

The Court specifically rejects the possibility of refusing an authorisation solely on the ground that waiting lists exist for the treatment at issue and that granting an authorisation in these circumstances would be allowing an individual to jump the queue. According to the Court, 'a waiting time which is too long or abnormal would be more likely to restrict access to balanced, high-quality hospital care'.[38] This is true, but beside the point. Community law does not at present require Member States to provide their citizens with access to 'balanced, high-quality hospital care'. It is for each Member State to decide what kind of social protection system it wants and how many resources to devote to it. It is perfectly appropriate for the Court to impose on Member States obligations of neutrality, objectivity and transparency in a system of prior authorisation for treatment in another Member State as well as procedural requirements to guarantee observance of such obligations.[39] It is, however, another matter to give guidelines as to the substantive criteria national authorities are to use. Should resources be directed towards providing a model with cosmetic surgery in another Member State, in priority to more cataract operations for the elderly, on the ground that the former needs the treatment to carry out his professional activity?

---

[36] See Case C–157/99 *Smits and Peerbooms* [2001] ECR I–5473, paras 76–80; Case C–385/99 *Müller-Fauré and Van Riet* [2003] ECR I–4509, paras 76–81.
[37] Case C–385/99 *Müller-Fauré and Van Riet* [2003] ECR I–4509, para 90.
[38] *Ibid*, para 92.
[39] The Court does indeed impose such requirements: see Case C–157/99 *Smits and Peerbooms* [2001] ECR I–5473, para 90.

Perhaps or perhaps not. However, the suggestion that this is a freedom to provide services issue fails to convince.

If the reasoning of the Court in recent cases on cross-border provision of healthcare fails to convince, from a pragmatic point of view, the probability that these cases will throw national healthcare systems into disarray is admitedly extremely low. We are unlikely to witness hordes of 'medical tourists' generating traffic jams at the Community internal borders in their quest to exercise their right to receive medical services in another Member State. The Court rarely considers in free movement cases the practical significance of the rights that it recognises. Remarkably, however, it notes in *Müller-Fauré* that 'linguistic barriers, geographic distance, the cost of staying abroad and lack of information about the kind of care provided' in other Member States and the fact 'care is generally provided near to the place where the patient resides, in a cultural environment which is familiar to him and which allows him to build up a relationship of trust with the doctor' all act as disincentives to seeking treatment in another Member State.[40]

From this perspective, arguments about the risk of destabilisation of national social welfare systems as a result of 'medical tourism' bear much resemblance to arguments about the danger of a 'race to the bottom' in regulatory standards through competitive deregulation between Member States: the argument is often asserted but rarely supported by actual empirical evidence establishing the real rather than hypothetical nature of the threat. The case of Austria is, in this respect, interesting. As a matter of domestic law, and even before the Court's recent series of judgments on cross-border healthcare, Austria has been reimbursing patients for medical treatment received abroad. The incentive for seeking medical treatment abroad is particularly strong, as Austria shares a border with Hungary where the cost of medical treatment is substantially lower. Despite these very favourable factors, the reimbursement of medical treatment abroad represents just 0.03 per cent of the Austrian social security budget.[41]

Nonetheless, and especially because few are likely to invoke their rights, the caselaw raises ethical issues from the perspective of equality. Precisely because of 'linguistic barriers, geographic distance, the cost of staying abroad and lack of information about the kind of care provided' in other Member States, it is not in general in La Courneuve, Finglas, Tower Hamlets or any other deprived area of a major European capital that one will find those most likely to exercise their right to receive medical services in another Member State. Thus, there is a high degree of likelihood that the net effect of the Court's caselaw will be to operate a (small) redistribution of resources within national social protection systems in favour of the middle classes.

---

[40] See paras 95–97 of the Judgment.
[41] European Commission, *Report on the Application of Internal Market Rules to Health Services*, SEC (2003) 900, at paras 33–34.

Besides, the argument about the probable limited economic impact of free movement rights on national social protection system is a two-edged sword. If the right to be reimbursed for medical treatment in another Member State is going to make, at best, no difference to the overwhelming majority of people, why bother? Why stretch Treaty articles to breaking point if this will have negligible impact?

D Follow-up and Policy Development

Following the *Kohll* and *Decker* cases, the Commission initiated a process of reflection on the implication of the Court's caselaw on national welfare systems and on EU policy as well as, more generally, on the issue of patient mobility in the EU. In that context, the High Level Committee on Health, which provides advice to the Commission on the development of the Community's health strategy, set up in 1999 a working group on the Internal Market and Health Services, which produced a report endorsed by the High Level Committee in December 2001.[42] In 2002, a high level process of reflection on patient mobility, involving health ministers and other key stakeholders was launched, on the initiative of the Commission and following endorsement by the Health Council in June 2002. As a result of this process, a Report was produced in December 2003[43] and the Commission further published in April 2004 a Communication on the follow-up to the process.[44] In terms of 'hard law', Article 23 of the Commission's proposed Directive on services in the internal market[45] would place the Court's caselaw on the assumption of costs for treatment in another Member State on a legislative basis.

The December 2001 High Level Committee Report provided a sound base to begin a reflection on patient mobility in the internal market. It attempted to place the issue in the wider context of the overall integration process, noting the existence of a right to health in the EU Charter of Fundamental Rights,[46] the importance of health as a fundamental part of the standard of living and quality of life referred to in Article 2 EC and acknowledging the division of powers between the EU and the Member States in this field. After reviewing the organisation of national health systems, it noted

---

[42] European Commission (Health and Consumer Protection DG), *The Internal Market and Health Services—Report of the High Level Committee on Health* (17 December 2001).

[43] European Commission (Health and Consumer Protection DG), *High Level Process of Reflection on Patient Mobility and Healthcare Developments in the European Union* (9 December 2003) Commission Document HLPR/2003/16.

[44] Commission, *Follow-Up on the High Level Reflection Process on Patient Mobility and Healthcare in the European Union*, COM(2004) 301.

[45] Commission, *Proposal for a Directive of the European Parliament and of the Council on Services in the Internal Market*, COM(2004) 2 Final.

[46] Art 35 Charter of Fundamental Rights of the European Union, 2000 OJ C364/1.

that 'health is not a typical market' and that 'Treaty rules governing free movement of goods and services can appear to be rather blunt tools which require careful handling'. According to the Committee, the search for equitable access to care and a secure local supply of services both militate against the movement of patients to other countries in large numbers and experiments in deregulation and the development of organisation solutions mimicking the competitive market have not proved entirely satisfactory.[47] As regards action to be taken, the Report insisted on the need not to rush, but to launch a process of discussion, reflection and exchange of views. The general gist of the recommendations in the Report was to promote convergence and coherence between Member States health systems through various initiatives designed to stimulate co-operation and the generation and exchange of knowledge between the Member States.[48] As regards internal market law as such, the Report recommended considering specifically the issues of outpatient care, specific pathologies, excessive waiting times and border areas.[49]

Unfortunately, the 'high level process of reflection' did not carry this reflection much further. Compared to the 2001 High Level Committee Report, the 2003 Report contains little new and makes no attempt to provide a roadmap for a clear strategy or vision of what the overall purpose of an EU policy on patient mobility might be and how it might relate to EU policies in the field of health and of the internal market. Nor was that task taken up in the subsequent Commission Communication. Yet, this issue cannot be taken as self-evident. As the High Committee noted, health is not a typical market and, moreover, there are major cultural and geographical disincentives to patient mobility, as acknowledged by the Court in *Müller-Fauré*. Identifying what contribution the internal market can make to health policy would seem a rather central task in any reflection on patient mobility. In the absence of such a reflection, it is questionable whether crystallising the caselaw of the Court in Article 23 of the proposed Directive on services in the internal market is wise.[50]

Be that as it may, an internal market in health services is likely to remain of limited significance. Linguistic, cultural and geographic considerations, as well as social and equity concerns, all limit the scope for development of an internal market in healthcare, at least at the front end.[51] While there is more room for the market to play a role in relation to pensions, the attachment of European States and of the EU itself to a European social model characterised

---

[47] See pp 7–8 of the Report.
[48] See pp 25–26 of the Report.
[49] At p 25 of the Report.
[50] See n 45 above.
[51] *Viz* at the level of the interface between the individual and welfare providers. There is more room, albeit still limited, for market mechanisms to play a role as between the relevant national authorities and ultimate providers of welfare services. Arguably, it would have been a more fruitful route for the Court to analyse the issue in those terms, ie as a public procurement issue, rather than by analysing it in terms of the provision of services to the individual.

by a high degree of solidarity limits the relevance of market mechanisms in the delivery of welfare services. Although its significance has no doubt increased, the internal market nonetheless is likely to remain a sideshow as far as social welfare is concerned.

III SOCIAL WELFARE AND THE LISBON AGENDA

Most commentators agree that the Lisbon European Council in Lisbon in March 2000 constituted a crucial point for the development of Community policy in the field of social welfare.[52] While it is possible to point to earlier initiatives and instruments, the significance of Lisbon lies in the adoption of a strategic vision, linking together economic, employment and social policy, the so-called 'Lisbon triangle' and the adoption of a method for the pursuit of this strategic vision, namely the 'open method of co-ordination' (OMC).

A The Rejection of 'Hard' Competences

From a purely theoretical perspective, one could make a case for a wholesale transfer of key competences in the social welfare field to the EU level as a consequence of the internal market and, at least as concerns Euro-zone countries, of monetary policy. As regards the latter, the argument would be that, in view of the limited potential labour mobility in the EU owing, in particular, to cultural and linguistic factors, financial transfers are the main tool available to soften asymmetric shocks. Transferring competence at the EU level for social welfare would allow for inter-regional financial transfers via the social welfare system. The internal market-based argument for a transfer of responsibility for social welfare from the Member States to the Union would be based on that old favourite: the equalisation of the conditions of competition and the prevention of 'social dumping'. The idea here would be to prevent Member States from lowering welfare standards so as to provide a competitive advantage to undertakings established on their territory. Equalising the conditions of competition in this context would not just be concerned with the overall level of social protection but also with how the cost of such social protection is distributed between undertakings and households, whether directly in the form of employer and employee contributions to social protection funds or indirectly through taxation. Addressing the equalisation of the conditions of competition seriously would therefore need to encompass not just either centralisation or harmonisation of social welfare regimes but also a substantial degree of harmonisation of (direct) taxation.

[52] See, eg M Ferrera, M Matsaganis and S Sacchi, 'European Briefing: Open Coordination against Poverty: the New EU "Social Inclusion Process"' (2002) 12 *Journal of European Social Policy* 227, 230 *et seq.*

Either argument would imply an unprecedented transfer of resources to the EU, which neither the governments of the Member States nor their population are at present ready to countenance, as the regular bitter discussions on the limited EU budget show. One may or may not agree with Majone's vision of the EU as a regulatory order in which economics/efficiency should be strictly separated from politics/redistribution.[53] However, it is difficult not to concur that large-scale redistributive policies at EU level present serious legitimation problems.[54] It is therefore not surprising that, although the competences of the Union in the field of social welfare were increased at Nice, these competences are mainly of the 'soft' type—and the Draft Constitution would not alter this.[55]

One can think of the distribution of these competences in terms of three concentric circles.

The inner circle is concerned with the co-ordination of social security systems for migrant workers. This was enshrined in the Treaty of Rome right from the start and, owing to its close link with the internal market, is an area where EU competence is least controversial. As a result, the Community is empowered under Article 42 EC to take measures in this field through the co-decision procedure. The Community has exercised this competence by adopting, and regularly amending, Regulation 1408/71.[56] Article 42 EC is quite clear that it is concerned about *co-ordination*, not harmonisation, of social security schemes, along the principles of aggregation of periods of insurance in different Member States and exportability of benefits within the EU.

Social security and social protection of workers under Article 137(1)(c) EC constitute the middle circle. While hard law, and in particular harmonisation measures, are not excluded, such measures can only be adopted through the consultation procedure and require unanimity in the Council.[57] This constitutes a derogation from the procedure normally applicable for measures adopted under Article 137 EC, *viz* co-decision. Remarkably, whereas it is contemplated that other measures subject to that derogatory

---

[53] See G Majone, 'Europe's "Democratic Deficit": the Question of Standards' (1998) 4 *European Law Journal* 5.

[54] *Ibid*, 13–14.

[55] Convention on the Future of Europe, *Draft Treaty Establishing a Constitution for Europe*, 2003 OJ C169/1. See now the final text of the Constitutional Treaty agreed by the Intergovernmental Conference meeting in Brussels (17–18 June 2004).

[56] Reg 1408/71 on the application of social security schemes to employed persons, self-employed persons and to members of their families moving within the Community (last consolidated version published at 1997 OJ L28/1; for a recent amendment introducing a European Health Insurance Card, see Reg 631/2004, 2004 OJ L100/1). See now: Reg 883/2004 on the coordination of social security systems, 2004 OJ L200/1 (partially repealing and replacing Reg 1408/71); discussed by F Pennings in his contribution to this collection.

[57] See Art 137(2) EC.

procedure[58] may be brought back into the fold of co-decision following a Council decision, social security and social protection of workers is the only field where this *passerelle* is not available.

Finally, social exclusion and the modernisation of social protection systems under Article 137(i) and (k) EC constitute the outer circle, in which only 'soft' measures designed to encourage cooperation between the Member States are allowed.[59]

B Modernising the European Social Model

Lisbon approaches social welfare from a different perspective. The primary responsibility of the Member States in the field of social welfare is recognised, thereby avoiding the difficult legitimation problem that would result from a transfer of competence to the EU. Institutional arrangements for the provision of social welfare will therefore vary from Member State to Member State. Behind that institutional diversity, however, there lies a core set of common values, encapsulated in the idea of a 'European Social Model'. In broad terms, the European Social Model has three main features:

— An employment policy based on a high level of productivity;
— A relatively high floor of employment rights and standards;
— A relatively generous safety net of social services and benefits based on compulsory schemes characterised by a high degree of solidarity.

The first two features are related, in the sense that the high floor of labour standards requires a correspondingly high level of productivity to make employment worthwhile for the employer. As Begg and Berghman put it, 'implicitly, therefore, the EU has "chosen" a higher productivity strategy by giving only the most productive workers access to the labour market'.[60]

These features of the European Social Model make it especially susceptible to the risk of a high level of unemployment, as low-skilled, low-productivity workers find themselves effectively excluded from the labour market. Unemployment affects the financial viability of the safety net, both on the income side (fewer contributions) and the expenditure side (unemployment benefits need to be paid). The problem is further compounded by demographic trends, which result in a smaller fraction of the population being in employment and therefore contributing to the financing of social welfare.

---

[58] *Viz* measures relating to termination of employment, collective labour law and conditions of employment for third country nationals under Art 137(1)(d),(f) and (g) EC respectively.
[59] See Art 137(2)(a) EC.
[60] I Begg and J Berghman, 'EU social (exclusion) policy revisited?' (2002) 12 *Journal of European Social Policy* 179, 182.

Thus, the Member States are faced by common challenges: how to increase participation in the labour market, so as to maintain a viable social welfare system, *and* maintain labour standards and the solidarity principles underlying their social welfare systems? Furthermore, not only are these challenges to national welfare systems common but they are also closely linked to economic and employment policy, which are subject to Treaty-based processes of co-ordination under Articles 99 and 128 EC. By bringing together economic, employment and welfare policy into an overall coherent approach, the Lisbon strategy thus aims at limiting the risk of choices being made by default primarily on an economic logic with a limited consideration of a more social perspective.

C Policy Learning and Convergence

It is possible to view the development of a Community social welfare policy through the OMC rather than on the basis of the Community method as a fall back position. Due to the impossibility for the EU to develop sufficient legitimacy to support a much stronger role, we have to use the OMC *'faute de mieux'*. This is no doubt true for some actors. The implicit distrust of the OMC expressed by the Commission in its Governance White Paper would suggest that it is likely to be among these.[61] Nonetheless, there are also positive reasons why the OMC might seem particularly appropriate in this area. First, the problems encountered by national welfare systems may be common, but it does not follow from this that a uniform solution is necessarily appropriate. While it may be useful to discuss, exchange experiences, and co-ordinate so as to avoid solutions that might pull in opposite directions, paths to solutions may nonetheless be different from one Member State to another. Secondly, to the extent that solutions to the problems are complex and require experimentation rather than the application of well-known remedies, more flexible, softer instruments allowing for local experimentation may again be preferable to more or less uniform rules.

While one can exaggerate the difference between binding and non-binding instruments,[62] it nevertheless remains the case that the open method is, among the various instruments and modes of decision-making developed in the EU, the one that best fits the idea of exchange of ideas, experimentation and adaptation to local circumstances.

There is, however, a fundamental ambiguity in the open method. At the Lisbon European Council,[63] the OMC was seen 'as the means of spreading

---

[61] Commission, *White Paper on European Governance*, COM(2001) 428 Final.

[62] After all, the very idea of a directive, if not necessarily institutional practice, was to allow for tailoring to the individual circumstances of a Member State.

[63] See n 1 above, para 37.

best practice and achieving greater convergence towards the main EU goals'. However, while not exactly polar opposites, there is some tension between the policy-learning and convergence dimensions. Lisbon highlighted four characteristic elements of the OMC:[64]

— fixing guidelines for the Union combined with specific timetables for achieving the goals which they set in the short, medium and long terms;
— establishing, where appropriate, quantitative and qualitative indicators and benchmarks against the best in the world and tailored to the needs of different Member States and sectors as a means of comparing best practice;
— translating these European guidelines into national and regional policies by setting specific targets and adopting measures, taking into account national and regional differences;
— periodic monitoring, evaluation and peer review organised as mutual learning processes.

The second and fourth elements are clearly oriented towards policy learning. However, the first and third are geared towards co-ordination and convergence. By emphasising some features and not others, one can therefore end up with different types of processes.

Cooperation in the social protection field consists of three distinct processes at various degrees of development in the areas of social exclusion, pensions and healthcare/care for the elderly respectively. The decision to apply the OMC to social exclusion was taken at Lisbon itself and it is the most established of the three processes. Broadly speaking, it follows the format developed for the European Employment Strategy with, however, important differences: there are no detailed guidelines nor recommendations to Member States in the OMC inclusion process and the cycle is two-yearly rather than annual. The decision to apply the OMC to pensions is more recent. The idea was canvassed at the Stockholm European Council in March 2001,[65] and confirmed by the Göteborg European Council in June 2001.[66] The first Joint Report of the Commission and Council was published in March 2003, based on national strategy reports submitted by the Member States in September 2002.[67] The pensions OMC is less developed, with common indicators to facilitate comparisons and mutual learning having yet to be worked out. The next reporting stage for the pensions OMC is 2006. Finally, it has not yet been agreed to apply the OMC to healthcare and

---

[64] *Ibid.*
[65] Para 32.
[66] See Presidency Conclusions, Göteborg European Council (15–16 June 2001), para 43.
[67] European Commission and Council of the European Union, *Joint report by the Commission and the Council an adequate and sustainable pensions*, 7165/03 ECOFIN 76, SOC 115 (10 March 2003).

care for the elderly, but a joint Commission/Council Report was adopted in March 2003[68] on the basis of responses to a questionnaire submitted to the Member States. While the Report envisaged that a 'process of mutual learning and co-operative exchange should be continued' on the basis of the issues identified in the Report, the precise form of that process was not agreed. In a Communication issued in April 2004,[69] however, the Commission has proposed to apply the OMC to healthcare and long-term care.

It is thus clear that the social protection processes are, at this stage at any rate, much less convergence oriented than the employment and economic co-ordination processes. The fact that the latter processes are Treaty-based and explicitly provide for the adoption of guidelines and, where necessary, recommendations strengthens the position of the EU institutions and gives the process a more 'top-down' feel. It may be that social protection processes will eventually move in that direction. It is, however, also notable that the Draft Constitution does not propose any Treaty change in this respect.[70]

D Actors, Processes and Values

A central aim of Lisbon, in agreeing a broad strategic goal 'to become the most competitive and dynamic knowledge-based economy in the world, capable of sustainable economic growth with more and better jobs and greater social cohesion' was to promote a more balanced approach to policy-making between the three points of the 'triangle': economic, employment and social protection policies. Thus, the Lisbon strategy was to lead to a strengthening of the weakest of these three points, *viz* social protection.

However, providing mechanisms for the linkage of these policies does not, in itself, guarantee that such re-balancing will occur.[71] The manner in which the policies are co-ordinated between themselves and the actors involved in the processes are of crucial importance.

---

[68] European Commission and Council of the European Union, *Joint report by the Commission and the Council on supporting national strategies for the future of health care and care for the elderly*, 7166/03 SOC 116, ECOFIN 77, SAN 41 (10 March 2003).

[69] Commission Communication, *Modernising social protection for the development of high-quality, accessible and sustainable health care and long-term care: support for the national strategies using the 'open method of coordination'*, COM(2004) 304.

[70] Convention on the Future of Europe, *Draft Treaty Establishing a Constitution for Europe*, 2003 OJ C169/1. See now the final text of the Constitutional Treaty agreed by the Intergovernmental Conference meeting in Brussels (17–18 June 2004).

[71] Cf I Begg and J Berghman's remarks that the agreement that the Spring European Council each year would discuss the interrelationship between economic, employment and social policy 'offers no guarantees': 'EU social (exclusion) policy revisited?' (2002) 12 *Journal of European Social Policy* 179, 191.

1 The Social Protection Committee

A significant element in this context is the role played by the Social Protection Committee (SPC). SPC was created by a Council decision of June 2000.[72] Its existence was given a direct Treaty basis in Article 144 EC following the Nice Treaty.[73] SPC is a comitology committee of the advisory type. It consists of two representatives for each Member State and two representatives of the Commission. It is modelled on the Employment Committee (EMCO) and the Economic Policy Committee (EPC).[74] In formal terms, its functions are, according to Art 144 EC:

— to monitor the social situation and the development of social protection policies in the Member States and the Community;
— to promote exchanges of information, experience and good practice between Member States and with the Commission;
— to prepare reports, formulate opinions or undertake other work within its fields of competence, at the request of either the Council or the Commission or on its own initiative.

In practice, SPC, together with the Commission Directorate General for Employment and Social Affairs, plays a substantial role in the formulation and development of EU policy pertaining to social protection. In that role, it has been instrumental in ensuring that co-ordination processes incorporate social values and in providing a counter-balance to economically oriented actors, such as EPC,[75] notably in the context of pensions.[76] It has often been critical of iniatives and documents which do not, in its eyes, sufficiently reflect social values and the social dimension of the Lisbon strategy.[77]

SPC is assisted by an Indicators' Sub-Group (ISG). ISG's function is to define and formulate common European indicators related to social protection to measure and evaluate progress towards the objectives agreed in the context of OMC processes. Given the centrality of comparison and benchmarking in the OMC, the development of appropriate indicators is a

---

[72] Council Dec 2000/436 setting up a Social Protection Committee, 2000 OJ L172/26.
[73] Political agreement was reached by the Council at its meeting on 1 and 2 June 2004 to re-establish the Committee following the Nice amendment.
[74] See Council Dec 2000/98 establishing the Employment Committee, 2000 OJ L29/21 and Council Dec 2000/604 on the composition and statutes of the Economic Policy Committee, 2000 OJ L257/28, amended by Council Dec 2003/475, 2000 OJ L158/55.
[75] See M Ferrera, M Matsaganis and S Sacchi, 'European Briefing: Open Coordination against Poverty: the New EU "Social Inclusion Process"' (2002) 12 *Journal of European Social Policy* 227, 232–33.
[76] See C Barbier, C de la Porte, R Peña Casas and P Pochet, 'European Briefing—Digest' (2001) 11 *Journal of European Social Policy* 363, 370–72.
[77] See, for instance, its Opinion of 26 February 2001 on the Commission's Communication 'Realising the European Union's Potential: Consolidating and Extending the Lisbon Strategy (Synthesis Report)', EU Council Document No 6455/01, esp para 4.

crucial, and often controversial, task. While ISG has been able to develop a number of indicators pertaining to social inclusion, development of agreed indicators relating to pensions, over which SPC works together with EPC, has proved more difficult.

2 *Economic versus Social Processes and Streamlining*

The development of co-ordination processes in the field of social protection has been, if not haphazard, nonetheless relatively ad hoc and fragmented as new mandates were given by various European Councils. As stated above, the field is characterised by distinct processes in social inclusion, pensions and healthcare at various degrees of development, structured on the basis of different timetables and using different tools. Moreover, unlike co-ordi-nation in the field of economic and employment policies, these processes do not have an explicit Treaty basis. Social protection, therefore, is in danger of remaining structurally the junior partner in the Lisbon triangle with its processes lost in the plethora of OMC processes initiated in various fields.

In May 2003, the Commission put forward a proposal to consolidate and streamline the various social protection processes into a single OMC process on social protection.[78] This follows on from the streamlining of the Treaty-based economic and employment co-ordination processes—*viz* Broad Economic Policy Guidelines (BEPGs) under Article 99 EC and Employment Guidelines under Article 128 EC—on the basis of a unified timetable and a three-yearly full review cycle.[79] The new consolidated social protection OMC would be structured along the same timetable to allow for better co-ordination and coherence between the three sides of the Lisbon triangle.

Streamlining and adopting a common timetable for economic, employ-ment and social protection processes would be in the spirit of Lisbon of a coherent strategy bringing together all three dimensions. The parallelism between the three processes could also increase the visibility and political salience of the weaker link and conceivably pave the way for a future Treaty/Constitution amendment to endow it with a Treaty basis.

On the other hand, streamlining is not without its risks. The merging of the current social protection processes into a single one could affect the visibility of the existing components and continuity with what has already been achieved. This is especially the case for the social inclusion process, which has a more established structure than the other strands. The European Anti-Poverty Network, a European NGO which has been espe-

---

[78] Commission Communication on '*Strengthening the social dimension of the Lisbon strategy*: *streamlining open coordination in the field of social protection*' (28 May 2003) available online (June 2004) at <http://europa.eu.int/comm/employment_social/news/2003/may/lisbonstratIP280503_en.pdf>.

[79] For full details, see Commission Communication, *Streamlining the Annual Economic and Employment Policy Co-ordination Cycles*, COM(2002) 487.

cially active in relation to social inclusion, has, in this respect expressed concerns about the possible disappearance of the National Action Plans on Inclusion ('NAPs/incl'), modelled on the National Action Plans of the European Employment Strategy, and their replacement by a 'watered down' reporting exercise.[80] Merging the processes could also present potential problems from the perspective of participation of all relevant actors, to the extent that the three strands imply contacts with different groups of actors. There is a danger here of a step back from the progress achieved in the field of social inclusion.[81]

In its opinion on the Communication,[82] SPC, while welcoming the principle of streamlining, nevertheless echoed these concerns about the risk of dilution of existing processes and their achievements. The Council endorsed SPC's Opinion at its meeting on 20 October 2003.[83]

IV CONCLUSION

Undoubtedly, the recent caselaw of the Court on the internal market constitutes a shift towards a market logic in welfare services. The picture that emerges from cases such as *Albany*, *Smits and Peerbooms* and *Müller-Fauré* is a different one from *Poucet and Pistre* and *Humbel*. Indeed, it is hard to see how *Humbel* can still constitute good law in the light of the cross-border healthcare services cases. However, the significance of the shift should not be exaggerated. Even though social welfare services may, in principle, be capable of falling within the ambit of internal market rules, the Court has nonetheless recognised that these rules may have to be kept in abeyance to allow social welfare schemes to fulfil their solidarity-based social functions. Secondly, as regards rights to cross-border healthcare specifically, these rights will only have a significant impact if they are actually used. Cultural, geographical and linguistic factors often combine to make the use of these rights unattractive to citizens.

If there is a threat to social welfare systems and the values they represent, this threat is likely to come from broader economic pressures than the application of internal market rules to welfare services. Pressures on public finance, in the context of Economic and Monetary Union but also, beyond

---

[80] See European Anti-Poverty Network, *Maintaining a visible European Social Inclusion Strategy—EAPN position on streamlining open coordination in the field of social protection* (EAPN, 4 July 2003).

[81] On progress in the second round of NAPs/Incl concerning participation of relevant actors, see Commission and Council, *Joint Report on Social Inclusion* (5 March 2004) Council Document 7101/04, section 8, at pp 109 *et seq.*

[82] Social Protection Committee, *Opinion on the Commission Communication 'Strengthening the social dimension of the Lisbon Strategy: streamlining open coordination in the field of social protection'*, (29 September 2003) Council Document No 12909/03.

[83] See Council Document 13538/03 REV 1, p 13.

it, of globalisation as well as that of an ageing population constitute a more significant problem for national welfare systems to tackle. The great merit of Lisbon was to put forward a vision in which social welfare concerns constitute an integral part of the economic, employment and social equation that has be solved. Beyond the broad vision, however, how exactly Lisbon is institutionalised in practice may or may not result in social welfare concerns being treated on an equal footing with economic and employment perspectives. If we are concerned about a risk of economic values dominating social ones, it is there rather than in the caselaw of the Court of Justice on the internal market that we should focus our attention.

Index